Transforming Literacy Curriculum Genres

Working With Teacher Researchers in Urban Classrooms

Transforming Literacy
Curriculum Genres

Working With Teacher Researchers
in Urban Classrooms

Edited by

Christine C. Pappas
University of Illinois–Chicago

Liliana Barro Zecker
DePaul University

2001

LAWRENCE ERLBAUM ASSOCIATES, PUBLISHERS
Mahwah, New Jersey   London

Lawrence Erlbaum Associates, Inc., Publishers
10 Industrial Avenue
Mahwah, NJ 07430

Cover design by Kathryn Houghtaling Lacey

Library of Congress Cataloging-in-Publication Data

Transforming literacy curriculum genres: working with
teacher researchers in urban classrooms / edited by Chris-
tine C. Pappas and Liliana Barro Zecker.
    p. cm.
Companion vol. To Teacher inquiries in literacy teach-
ing-learning. C2001.
    Includes bibliographical references and index.
    ISBN 0-8058-2401-4 (alk. paper)
    1. Language arts (Elementary)—Illinois—Chicago—
Case studies. 2. Education, Urban—Illinois—Chicago—
Case studies. 3. College-school cooperation—Illinois—
Chicago—Case studies.   I. Pappas, Christine C.
II. Zecker, Liliana Barro.   III. Teacher inquiries in literacy
teacher-learning.
    LB1576 .T755   2001
    372.6'09773'11—dc21   00-026730
                                  CIP

Printed in the United States of America
10 9 8 7 6 5 4 3 2 1

*Our collaborative school–university project
was a productive—and reproductive—one.
Thus, we dedicate this book to all of the children
in our inquiries and of our 11 "Project Babies."*

*Sarah Cohen—Abraham
Diane Escobar—Sophia
Linda Montes—Christian
Sonia Torres Pasewark—Sophia and Michaela Joy
Caitlyn Nichols—Alyssa and Zachary
Pamela Wolfer—Tori Jo and Haley Rose
Liliana Zecker—Camilla and Lucas*

Contents

Preface

This book consists of coauthored chapters written by university and teacher researchers concerning these thirteen urban-elementary teacher researchers' year-long inquiries on a variety of literacy topics. As part of a collaborative school–university action-research project, these teachers—all of who taught in two Chicago elementary schools during the year of their studies—attempted to transform their teaching practices to meet the needs of students who came from diverse ethnic and linguistic backgrounds. These teachers' inquiry efforts resulted in developing more collaborative styles of teaching.

Collaborative classroom interactions occur when teachers move away from teaching-as-transmission approaches, to ones in which they center more on student meanings, by sharing power and authority with their students. In doing so, the teacher researchers in the project challenged the deficit perspective that many urban personnel—and the society at large—still hold about the low-SES children who populate urban schools. Although each teacher posed and grappled with difficult questions in his or her inquiry, all of these questions reflected common concerns: How do I hear the voices of my students, and, at the same time have them hear my voice as a mediator of the culture at large? How do I include my students' local and culturally varied knowledge in literacy–learning transactions and also create ways for integrating my expertise?

The everyday interactions between teachers and students are realized by the social talk in the classroom. Thus, in our project, we analyzed classroom discourse to study and document the teacher-researchers' efforts to make changes in the locus of power in literacy teaching and learning. The coauthored chapters, therefore, reflect many classroom-discourse examples to illustrate the critical points for incidents of these teachers' inquiries. They show the successes *and* struggles involved in shedding teacher-controlled *IRE patterns* of talk—that is, the discourse structures of teacher Initiating, child Responding, and teacher Evaluating—to develop alternative, collaborative discourse. The book covers the *process* of urban teachers' journeys to create dialogically organized literacy instruction in particular literacy routines—called here, *curriculum genres*—that the teachers chose as sites of inquiry.

The book is organized in terms of these curriculum genres—inquiries in writing curriculum genres, reading-aloud curriculum genres, drama curriculum genres, and so forth. Teacher inquiries were conducted in various elementary grade levels—from kindergarten to the eighth grade. Three occurred in bilingual classrooms and one in a special education classroom. The first and last chapters, written by the editors, provide the background, and the theoretical and methodological underpinnings of the project.

Sharing power with students in collaborative-classroom interactions and discourse not only provides better literacy instruction—such practice has higher expectations for students, it engages students more fully, and it enables teachers to meet students' current understandings, and so forth—it also has a broader political significance. When teachers, at the local school site, assign new roles for urban students as valued informants and thinkers in collaborative discourse, they illustrate how to resist and challenge the historically entrenched coercive macrointeractions in the broader society.

We wish to acknowledge the support of grants from Spencer Foundation and the Center for Urban Educational Research and Development at the University of Illinois at Chicago for the research reported in this book, as well as its companion book about the project also published by Lawrence Erlbaum Associates—Pappas and Zecker (2000), *Teacher Inquiries in Literacy Teaching-Learning: Learning to Collaborate in Elementary Urban Classrooms*. The data presented, the statements made, and views expressed in both books are solely the responsibility of the authors.

Chapter 1

Urban Teacher Researchers' Struggles in Sharing Power With Their Students: Exploring Changes in Literacy Curriculum Genres

Christine C. Pappas
University of Illinois at Chicago

Liliana Barro Zecker
DePaul University

This book represents the major findings of a collaborative school–university action-research project. In the project 13 urban-elementary teacher researchers engaged in year-long classroom inquiries on various literacy topics, which university-researcher partners supported and helped to document. All of these teachers taught at two Chicago public schools during the course of this year of study. All made efforts to transform their literacy practices to better meet the needs of their students, who came from diverse ethnolinguistic backgrounds. These changes resulted in their taking on more collaborative styles of teaching, which enabled them to develop culturally and linguistically responsive pedagogy (Ladson-Billings, 1994).

This book consists of coauthored chapters written by the university researchers and individual teacher researchers who discuss and use classroom discourse to relate the ways by which these particular teachers examined their literacy practices. We argue that *collaborative teaching* occurs when teachers explicitly attempt to share power and authority with their students. Although the teachers, here, were largely successful in this enter-

1

prise, this effort was easier said than done. Thus, these chapters portray both the struggles and vulnerabilities in these teachers' accomplishments.

This introductory chapter provides the background and theoretical perspectives of the collaborative school–university project and of this book. It is organized into four major sections. The first briefly describes how the project evolved and its initial assumptions and goals. The second section covers the conceptual framework that informed all of the teacher inquiries, as well as the role that classroom discourse played in the project. The third section outlines the methodological features of the project and how the chapters in this book were created. Finally, the last section provides a short overview of the book, and foreshadows the important ideas to be covered in the last, summary chapter. An Appendix at the end of this chapter provides a key for the classroom-discourse transcriptions so that you will be able to understand the examples that are found in all of the inquiry chapters.

BACKGROUND OF THE COLLABORATIVE SCHOOL–UNIVERSITY PROJECT

The 1989 Chicago Illinois School Reform Act resulted in many changes in the Chicago Public Schools. For example, it mandated governance changes. A major feature was the formation of a local school council (LSC) at each school, charged with primary responsibility for setting the school's educational policy. A 5-year School Improvement Plan, which was developed by the principal at each school in consultation with teachers, the LSC, and the community, was an integral component of this reform initiative. This plan mapped out the school's strategies for improving student achievement and reaching other goals set out in the reform legislation.

The 13 teachers in this book taught in two elementary schools whose School Improvement Plans included the use of a whole-language curriculum and approaches. Various faculty at the University of Illinois at Chicago (UIC) became involved in some of these schools' activities, given the already ongoing formal connection between UIC and these two schools (as well as several other Chicago schools). Chris Pappas, who just joined the UIC faculty, was asked to work with teachers at the two schools that had specifically requested help with implementing whole-language ideas. After this inservice was completed, some individual teachers from each school contacted her to take up her invitation to work collaboratively in a more long-term basis as they attempted to change literacy teaching and learning in their classrooms.

From 1990 to 1993 a small group of teachers at each school met regularly (usually weekly) with Chris to discuss their inquiries about their efforts to enact more collaborative styles of teaching literacy. Chris also periodically observed in the classrooms, audiotaped interactions in various literacy activities or routines, and wrote up fieldnotes that she shared with the teachers to foster ongoing investigation and discussion. Finally, external research support from Spencer Research Foundation and the Center for Urban Educational Research and Development, University of Illinois at Chicago, made it possible to extend and document this school–university collaborative action research in a more systematic way so that its findings could be shared with a larger audience through this book (and its companion volume, Pappas & Zecker, 2000, *Teacher Inquiries in Literacy Teaching-Learning: Learning to Collaborate in Elementary Urban Classrooms*) and other papers and articles.

After this external funding was provided, other university researchers joined Chris in the project. Liliana Barro Zecker worked with the teacher researchers in the three bilingual classrooms, and also provided expertise for the project as a whole. Other university researchers who were graduate students at University of Illinois at Chicago (Diane Escobar, Shannon Hart, Linda Montes, Jane Liao, Caitlyn Nichols, Dian Ruben, and Hank Tabak) also became collaborators. They were the team members who worked closely with teacher researchers and are coauthors—with the particular teacher researchers—of the chapters of this book.

Initial Assumptions and Goals of the Teacher Researchers

The initial goals of the teachers during the early work with Chris involved their attempts to design more student-centered approaches to teach literacy. These teachers' efforts challenged the transmission-oriented instructional model that Freire (1970, 1972) criticized as the *banking concept of education*, where teachers seek to make deposits or fill students up with all of the essential points and right answers. It is this content that constitutes the authoritative, official discourse of the classroom (Nystrand, 1997). Such a method treats students as having no ideas or theories of their own—their heads are seen as empty vessels—and it frequently led to unchallenging, rote learning for students, especially those low-SES, ethnic, and linguistic "minority" children who populate urban schools (Bartolome, 1994; Cummins, 1994; Moll & Gonzalez, 1994). Too frequently, the asymmetrical power relations of society have been reproduced in the schools for these children (Allington, 1991; Anyon, 1983; Shepard, 1991). As a result, many urban teachers—and, unfortunately, the public at large—still still do not value or consider using student's existing knowledge bases when they structure literacy teaching–learning experiences. Instead, what has been pervasive is a pedagogy that reflects a "deficit view of subordinated students" (Bartolome, 1994) where rigid, teacher-directed classroom practices underestimate and constrain what these children can display intellectually (Moll, 1992).

Challenging such a deficit perspective by developing alternative curriculum and teaching practices, which recognize the active and constructive learner, is hard work. Some of the teachers of the project had many years of experience with the teaching-as-transmission model and felt that they had much to overcome. The newer teachers found it difficult to conceive of, because they had never observed or directly tried it personally. Thus, in many ways, these teachers' efforts were what Cochran-Smith (1991) termed "learning to teach against the grain."

Very early on, a major focus of these teachers' struggles centered around their questions about when and how to share power and authority with their students as they began to utilize a more collaborative style of teaching. Because these teachers considered their students as active meaning makers, they believed that they had to develop different forms and structures of social interaction in teacher–student and student–student classroom routines. The process of reconceptualizing the teaching relationship in terms of *social transaction* rather than in terms of transmission entails creating new roles as teachers (Wells & Chang-Wells, 1992). It involves teachers trying to figure out how to fashion instructional interactions so that they can share their expertise, but at the same time foster children's constructions of their own knowledge or expertise. Moreover, an integral aspect of these changes has to do with developing collaborative talk that would be culturally and linguistically responsive to urban students' understandings and discourse patterns. These were the problems or goals that the emerged for the teachers during the early years, and that they posed for themselves at the onset of the inquiries they undertook in the collaborative action-research project that is covered in this book.

CONCEPTUAL FRAMEWORK OF THE PROJECT AND BOOK

The conceptual framework of the project integrates two major areas of theory and research: *New Literacy* (Willinsky, 1990) ideas that reflect socioconstructivist views and are informed by sociocultural theory, and a sociosemiotic perspective on classroom discourse within which teachers attempted to include urban students' various voices in collaborative classroom talk. Theories underlying teacher research and collaborative school–university action research are also important in this project, but these are covered at the beginning of the methodology section.

New Literacy Ideas

In the transmission-oriented, or Freire's banking concept, of education, which is easily aligned with the deficit perspective, the cultural differences of students are considered as barriers to literacy acquisition. Diversity is seen as something to be reduced or displaced. In contrast, the teachers here had alternative views of their students' abilities. Diversity was recognized and fostered as a strength or an asset in learning. Their inquiries were attempts to change their literacy curricula so that they would reflect the aims of what Willinsky (1990) has called the New Literacy. Willinsky argued that the New Literacy perspective sees "*literacy as a social process with language that can from the beginning extend the students' range of meaning and connection*" (p. 8, emphasis in the original). This is a "socio-constructivist" perspective on literacy—it assumes that students (all humans) construct their own knowledge in various social contexts (including classrooms). It represents a fundamental shift from the idea that meaning resides *within* texts, to a sense of literacy as an active transformation of texts. In such a view, literacy is redefined by *building on* the diversity of students' ideas, and by valuing and incorporating students' local and culturally varied understandings into the curriculum.

New Literacy, then, has many implications for teaching. It means that reading and writing, and the curriculum in general, must be more connected to the lives of students by making them more personally meaningful. Central in this transformation is changing the power relationships in literacy activities in classrooms, for both teachers and students. In Willinsky's (1990) words:

> The New Literacy speaks directly to teachers reasserting control over the work that goes on in the class, even as it attempts to hand a greater part of the local of meaning over to the student. It represents a taking hold of the curriculum by the teacher at a fundamental level by challenging the meaning of literacy in the classroom as well as the nature of a teacher's work with the students. (p. 19)

New Literacy calls for teachers to have more autonomy of what happens in their classrooms. Moreover, it has teachers reevaluating the everyday instructional patterns of interaction that they have with their students. Thus, issues of power and authority are at the root of these changes (Oyler, 1996a, 1996b; Pappas, 1997a, 1999).

As indicated previously, the teacher researchers tried to enact New Literacy aims by centering more on students' meanings in literacy routines. They challenged the teaching–learning relationship of transmission and reception by attempting to establish collaborative interactions with their students. In doing so, individualistic conceptions of learning were also questioned by emphasizing that learning activities take place not *within* individuals, but in transactions *between* them (Wells & Chang-Wells, 1992). This perspective reflects a sociocultural theory consistent with Vygotskian ideas (Gee, 1996; Mercer, 1995; Moll, 1990, 1992; Newman, Griffin, & Cole, 1989; Vygotsky, 1962, 1978; Wells, 1994a; Wertsch, 1991). That is, there is a "recognition of the interdependence of individual and society, as each creates and is created by the other" (Wells & Chang-Wells, 1992, p. 29). From such a perspective, the teaching–learning relationship represents the coconstruction of meaning and knowledge where the teacher shares his or her expertise to guide and assist learners in the *zone of proximal development*—that is, where the teacher responds to learners' own intentions and understandings, but beyond their current levels of unaided performance—so that students are empowered to construct new knowledge and are able to manage tasks on their own.

New roles for the teacher are necessary in such interactions that support students' literacy understandings—teacher as responder, teacher as guide or facilitator, and so forth. Many of the teachers, however, questioned what that really meant in their day-to-day practices. Again, it seemed much easier said than done. In our project, the teacher–researchers' struggles of innovations regarding the shift of the locus of meaning of texts to students focused around the analysis of classroom discourse because it is the medium by which most teaching takes place, and in which students demonstrate much of what they have learned (Cazden, 1988). Classroom discourse provides a lens into what Edwards and Mercer (1987) termed the "common knowledge" in classrooms—"the ways in which knowledge ... is presented, received, shared, controlled, negotiation, understood and misunderstood by teachers and children in the classroom" (p. 1).

Creating Collaborative Classroom Discourse

So many of the processes of school teaching and learning are encoded in language. As Lemke (1985) expressed it, "classroom education, to a large degree, *is* talk: it is the social use of language to enact regular activity structures and to share systems of meaning among teachers and students" (p. 1). Thus, this is a social–semiotic perspective (Halliday, 1978, 1993; Halliday & Hasan, 1985; Lemke, 1990; Young, 1992) that focuses on how various educational routines, realized by their corresponding discourse patterns, are organized during a school day (Erickson & Schulz, 1977; Green & Dixon, 1994; Lindfors, 1999; Wells, 1993).

Classroom studies have indicated that most classroom talk is teacher talk. It is dominated by teacher questions, typically certain kind of questions called *psuedo questions* (Ramirez, 1988). These are test questions eliciting student recitation, or what Mehan (1979) called "known information questions"—ones for which the teacher already knows the answers. These questions are usually embedded in a characteristic *initiate-respond-evaluate* (IRE) talk structure that is controlled by the teacher (Cazden, 1986, 1988; Edwards & Mercer, 1987; Lemke, 1990; Nystrand, 1997; O'Connor & Michaels, 1993; Shuy, 1988; Sinclair & Coultard, 1975; Young, 1992). In this IRE pattern, the teacher *initiates* a sequence by calling a child to recite, then the nominated child *responds* to the initiation or question posed by the teacher, and finally the teacher *evaluates* what the child has said, and on and on. As Cazden (1988) stated, "IRE is the 'default' pattern—what happens unless deliberate action is taken to achieve some alternative" (p. 53). Because the teacher so tightly and rigidly structures the talk, the IRE pattern is frequently characterized as being a monologic script (Gutierrez, Rymes, & Larson, 1995; Nystrand, 1997). This mode of discourse is the essence of the traditional transmission-oriented instruction. It is especially pervasive in urban schools, allowing few opportunities for the consideration of students' different culturally and linguistically interactional styles (Cummins, 1994; Foster, 1992; McCollum, 1991).

What was central in the our project, then, was to study the ways in which the teacher researchers were attempting *alternatives* to these IRE patterns to realize New Literacy ideas. In contrast to monologic scripts, their efforts involved creating collaborative interactions and classroom discourse. They wanted to provide "spaces" for students' voices—they wanted to craft, with their students, *dialogic* literacy instruction and classroom discourse.

Undertaking Dialogically Structured Talk

Viewing discourse as dialogic is a perspective influenced by the work of Bakhtin (1986), who saw discourse as the continuous weaving of utterances where speakers take turns offering meanings or ideas, but more important, where these utterances are always anticipatory or are responsive to each other. This is multivoiced discourse that has continual tension or conflict because voice—which is Bakhtin's term for "speaking consciousness"—is always expressing, through its utterances, a point of view, or is enacting particular values while it takes account of the other voices being addressed, whether in speech or in writing (Cazden, 1992; Nystrand, 1997). As Bakhtin (1981) stated, "language is populated—overpopulated—with the intentions of others. Expropriating it, forcing it to submit to one's own intentions and accents, is a difficult and complicated process" (p. 294).

It is this "juxtaposition of relative perspectives and struggle of competing voices" (Nystrand, 1997, p. 8) that was the goal of the teacher researchers. They wanted to privilege both student and teacher voices by having both teacher and students be responsible for topics and elaborations. In this kind of discourse, there is an "equality of participation by teachers and students in the process of text creation" (Wells, 1993, p. 33). The teacher researchers wanted to encourage students' initiations of their own meanings and ideas; they wanted to find ways to ask students authentic questions (as opposed to pseudo questions) and to be able to work with students to elaborate and clarify each other's contributions in negotiated, jointly determined talk. Thus, such collaborative, dialogic discourse is quite different from the IRE monologic talk in many ways. Rather than having utterances be focused on accurate transmission of information, they can serve instead as "thinking devices" (Lotman, 1988). There can be a figuring-things-out atmosphere where teachers take seriously what students say, so as to explore and examine collaboratively what is not understood (Barnes, 1993; Barnes & Todd, 1995; Nystand, 1997).

Collaborative Discourse as Dialogue for Knowing and Knowledge Building

When talk is no longer seen as a vehicle for the one-way transmission of knowledge from teacher to student, "knowledge" itself is viewed quite differently. According to Nystrand (1997) discourse as dialogue becomes "a dynamic social and epistemic process of constructing and negotiating knowledge" (p. xiv). He claims that, in dialogically organized instruction, there is a transformation of understandings, and that knowledge emerges from the interaction of voices. Moreover, teacher or textbook authorities are no longer seen as the sole sources of valued knowledge, (which is so characteristic in IRE, monologically organized instruction), but instead, students' interpretations and personal experiences are also considered as valid. As Gutierrez, et al. (1995) argued, collaborative discourse makes possible "the joint construction of a new sociocultural terrain, creating spaces for shifts in what counts as knowledge and knowledge representation" (p. 445).

Indeed, Wells (1998) recently argued that our mistakes in education have been to place the emphasis on knowledge rather than on *knowing*. Too much attention has been given to memorizing facts and being able to reproduce information rather than to develop an understanding of information that can inform and guide action. He also made the case for classroom discourse that offers dialogic responsivity. Knowing or knowledge building occurs in a particular place and time in which participants attempt to solve a problem of some kind *in dialogue with others*.

Another aspect of this new view of knowledge was already mentioned earlier, namely, the idea that meanings are not considered within texts. That is, the notion of textual autonomy—that written texts are somehow instances of timeless, "decontextualized" language—is questioned (Cazden, 1992; Nystrand, 1986, 1997; Nystrand & Wiemelt, 1991). Texts always involve reinterpretation; there is no absolute meaning of a text (Olson, 1991).

Such a view of texts and knowledge means that what it means to be literate is different. Wells' (1990, p. 379) definition is, "To be literate is to have the disposition to engage appropriately with texts of different types in order to empower action, thinking, and feeling in the context in purposeful social activity."

To further explicate this characterization of literacy, Wells proposed and described several modes of engagement of text. He argues that one of them, the *epistemic mode of engagement*—where "meaning is treated as tentative, provisional, and open to alternative interpretations and revision" (Wells, 1990, p. 369)—fully exploits the potential of literacy because it empowers the thinking of those who use it. In this sense of engagement, *text* is extended to mean "any artifact that is constructed as a representation using a conventional symbol system" (Wells & Chang-Wells, 1992, p.

145), which can also include classroom discourse. Of course, children learn to interpret and contribute to oral texts in many ways in the various social contexts that have supported their spoken language development. However, in most of these settings, language accompanied action, and attention focused only partially on what was said (Halliday, 1978, 1996; Hasan, 1984, 1996; Pappas, Kiefer, & Levstik, 1999; Wells, 1986). Thus, according to Wells, children engaging in oral texts from an epistemic orientation—that is, in collaborative, dialogic classroom discourse—have opportunities to view the role of language differently. They are introduced to literate thinking because epistemic engagement of text fosters reflections on, and reformulations of, meanings, thereby making this primarily silent and covert mental ability explicit to them.

This epistemic engagement of text is consistent with the aims of New Literacy because it is a major way by which students' ranges of meaning and connection can be achieved. Moreover, epistemic engagements are similar to what Lindfors (1999) called *inquiry*. Inquiry consists of "language acts by which children bring others into their sense-making" (p. ix). Inquiry here is not just students asking questions, but it also includes their engaging others in many various expressive ways—their negotiating, agreeing, comparing, evaluating, generalizing, disagreeing, predicting, reflecting, and so forth. Thus, collaborative discourse promotes inquiry and epistemic engagements; it provides an arena for give and take. Such interactions between teacher and students "must configure (intermingle) or reconfigure the respective purposes of the conversants; [they] must *effect a transformation of shared knowledge*" (Nystrand, 1997, p. 17–18, emphasis in the original).

Curriculum Genres: The Sites of Teacher Inquiry

From a social–semiotic perspective, language is understood only as it relates to social structure—systems of *meanings* are related to a *social* system or culture (Halliday, 1978; Halliday & Hasan, 1985; Lemke, 1990; Young, 1992). Consequently, different social–semiotic relationships are seen to occur in the classroom through the shifts of the various teaching–learning activities that transpire during a school day. These recurring-interaction events or routines are usually marked by particular names (show-and-tell, reading-aloud, author's chair). The various routines are encoded in particular, clearly demarcated behavioral patterns, which have corresponding linguistic patterns that express particular types of meanings (Bloome & Bailey, 1992; Christie, 1987a, 1987b; Green, Kantor, & Rogers, 1991; Santa Barbara Classroom Discourse Group, 1992; Lindfors, 1999). Using a term suggested by Christie (1987a, 1989, 1993), Pappas (1990, 1991, 1997a, 1997b, 2000) has called these demarcated event and participant structures or routines *curriculum genres*.

Particular curriculum genres are particular activity structures—that is, each particular curriculum genre represents a socially recognizable sequence of actions that realized particular meanings or purposes for teachers and students in the overall classroom curriculum. Each curriculum genre has its own "structures of expectations" (Tannen, 1993) where classroom participants come to know how to interact and mean. They learn to treat each curriculum genre as a distinctive frame in which they share certain expectations about how to construct text or classroom discourse together (Lindfors, 1999).

Thus, a *curriculum genre,* as an action genre or as a distinctive frame of expectations, is analogous to Bakhtin's (1986) idea of *speech genre*:

> All of the diverse areas of human activity involve the use of language. Quite understandably, the nature and forms of this use are just as diverse as the areas of human activity. ... Language is realized in the form of individual concrete utterances (oral and written) by participants in the various areas of human activity. The utterances reflect the specific conditions and goals of each such area ... [T]hematic content, style, and compositional structure ... are inseparably linked to the *whole* of the utterance and are equally determined by the specific nature of the particular sphere of communication. Each separate utterance is individual, of course, but each sphere in which language is used develops its *relatively stable types* of these utterances. These we may call *speech genres*. (p. 60, emphasis in the original)

Because there are recurring situations in the culture in which people interact and enact social activities—what Bakhtin called the "areas of human activity" or "particular spheres of communication"—this contextual regularity gives rise to regularities in texts (Halliday, 1994; Halliday & Hasan, 1985; Hasan, 1995, 1996; Kress, 1993; Swales, 1990). In the classroom, these similar kinds, types, or classes of communicative events and texts are curriculum genres. That is, curriculum genres reflect patterns of textual and social regularity. Each curriculum genre represents "the ways of doing, ways of being, *and* ways of saying" (Hasan, 1995, p. 99).

In our project, each teacher researcher posed an inquiry that usually concerned a particular curriculum genre (although there were some inquiries that involved several curriculum genres or a complex curriculum genre [e.g., writing workshop], which consisted of several subcurriculum genres). That is, there were distinctive routines, particular times during the day, in which the teacher researchers decided to concentrate their inquiry efforts. These curriculum genres or sites of inquiry were sometimes ones that individual teacher researchers may have already included in their previous curricula, but were now being considered for modification. Or, sometimes teacher researchers created very new curriculum genres to achieve new goals in teaching and learning in their classrooms.

As we already indicated, the teachers all attempted to take on collaborative styles of teaching—trying to create dialogically organized instruction—within these curriculum genres. Individual children have unique personal characteristics, and in urban schools they come from a variety of cultural backgrounds. Such cultural and linguistic diversity means that children bring their own complex "ways with words" to classroom interactions (Heath, 1982, 1983; Lindfors, 1987; Michaels, 1981; Philips, 1972, 1983). The IRE talk structure, with its strict teacher-centered, turn-taking format, has shown to affect minority students' learning adversely because it does not provide many opportunities for negotiation or consideration of these children's styles of interaction or funds of knowledge (Au & Jordan, 1981; Foster, 1992; Heath, 1983; Losey, 1995; McCollum, 1991; Michaels, 1981; Moll, 1992; Philips, 1972, 1993).

However, these teachers also thought that any alternative to IRE patterns must incorporate the teacher mediation and scaffolding of literacy events that are necessary to benefit these ethnolinguistically diverse students (Delpit, 1988, 1992; Reyes, 1991, 1992). They felt that effective teacher–student collaboration is knowing when and how teachers should share their teacher expertise on a topic with students while also fostering students' own expertise; knowing when and how teachers should provide students guidance in learning some convention of language while also expecting and supporting students' approximations to these language conventions; knowing when and how teachers should ask questions to help students think more deeply about what they might be reading while also encouraging students to pose and answer their own questions about their reading.

Thus, the teachers, here, dealt with these kinds of questions as they attempted to craft collaborative interactions and discourse in the various curriculum genres. They were involved in asking why, to whom, how, and when it is appropriate to provide teacher guidance and mediation (Wells, 1998) to enact New Literacy ideas. They were trying to figure out how to transform curriculum genres so that *both* teacher and student voices were privileged in collaborative or dialogical interactions. There were efforts to craft power relationships with their students that were *power with,* not *power over* (Kreisberg, 1992). Thus, struggles to develop curriculum genres that accommodate for diversity in this complex way were the root of these teacher–researchers' changes. The objective of this book, then, is to tell the stories of these teacher–researchers' journeys. It reports on the *process* by which these urban teachers developed culturally and linguistically responsive literacy pedagogy.

METHODOLOGY OF THE PROJECT

The Rationales for Teacher Research and Collaborative School–University Action Research

Our project was a type of collaborative school–university action research partnership in which teacher research was a critical feature. Next, we briefly outline the important characteristics of teacher research and then cover some of the major features of school–university partnerships.

The Role and Importance of Teacher Research.   Most of traditional educational research has dichotomized theory and practice by emphasizing that researchers from the university (or research laboratories) produce the theoretical background for all and any educational innovation (Altricher, Posch, & Somekh, 1993). This is obviously a hierarchical, "outside–in" stance that sees knowledge for teaching as something that is generated at the university and then used in schools (Cochran-Smith & Lytle, 1993). The voices of teachers, their points of view, have been missing in traditional research because it has rarely addressed the questions of teachers. As a result, such research "strengthens the assumptions that practitioners do not produce knowledge, their personal knowledge is not useful" (Gitlin, 1990, p. 444).

Although the idea of teachers reflecting on their practice to create their own theories of teaching and learning can found as early as Dewey (1904) and Lewin (1948), the more current concept of teacher as researcher is more commonly traced to the idea of "action research" that was characterized in the work of Stenhouse (1985) and others (Elliot, 1985, 1991; Nixon, 1981). Cochran-Smith and Lytle (1990, 1993) defined *teacher research* as systematic, intentional inquiry by teachers. It is *systematic* because there are ordered ways of gathering and documenting information in some written form, as well as ongoing, ordered methods of recollecting, rethinking, and analyzing classroom events. Although teachers can always glean fresh insights through more spontaneous teaching–learning activities, teacher research is an *intentional,* planned enterprise. Finally, it is *inquiry* because it emanates from, or generates questions about, classroom events, and it involves reflection by teachers to make sense of their experiences.

Teacher inquiry represents cycles of action research in which four major components or activities are implicated (Pappas, Kiefer, & Levstik, 1999; Wells, 1994b): *observing* to make systematic notes on particular, relevant aspects of classroom life to determine what is really happening; *interpreting* these observations by reflecting on why things are or what factors might be responsible for them; *planning change* by creating hypotheses about how different actions might result in the improvement of unsatisfactory aspects of the current situation; and then *acting out* the planned change. The core of teacher inquiry is how a teacher's interpretative framework informs and is informed by these cycles of action research. By adopting the stance of reflectiveness, teacher researchers make the connections between theory and practice more explicit. Their theories are grounded by their practice and vice versa, and they are able to develop a more conscious understanding of the underlying basis of their actions.

Thus, in contrast to traditional educational research, Cochran-Smith and Lyle (1993) claimed that knowledge for teaching promoted by teacher research is "inside/outside." It is a distinctive way of knowing about teaching, one that privileges teachers as those who have the authority to know—"to construct Knowledge (with a capital K) about teaching, learning, and schooling" (p. 43). Here, then, there is no need to translate findings in the traditional educational research sense, because teacher research is steeped in praxis (Lather, 1986); it is critical reflection *on* practice (Noffke & Stevenson, 1995).

School–University Collaborations as Collaborative Action Research

School–university partnerships have been formed, in large degree, as a challenge to traditional educational research (see Pappas, 1997a, for a more detailed account of the major influences that contributed to the development and nature of school–university collaborations). In past decades, different questions have been posed in educational research that have led to these collaborative arrangements: Who owns knowledge in education? Who benefits from research? (Apple, 1993; Gitlin, et al., 1992; Ladwig, 1991; Noffke & Stevenson, 1995; Richardson, 1994a, 1994b).

Many of the current partnerships are considered as *collaborative action research* (CAR). A general aim of CAR is the modification and elaboration of teaching and learning. Although this research can take different forms (depending on the purpose of particular projects and the ways in which teachers and other school personnel are involved), Oya and Smulyan (1989) presented four major characteristics that CAR projects have in common. First, of course, CAR is *collaborative in nature.* It permits mutual understanding among teacher and university researchers, working together to set common goals, planning the details of the research, and so forth. Second, it *focuses on practice,* addressing the immediate problems, questions, and concerns defined by the participating teachers. Third, CAR enhances teachers' *professional development* by supporting or providing the impetus to improve and change classroom practice. Teachers gain both professional knowledge and acquire research skills for teacher inquiry. Finally, CAR stresses the need for *a project structure* that enables the above three elements to occur. Such a structure requires regular and open communication among participants, democratic project leadership, recurring cycles of the four activities of action research described previously, and positive relationships with the schools in which the project is conducted.

These four characteristics are reflected in our school–university project, as seen as the procedures of our project are outlined.

Teacher–Researcher Participants and School Contexts

Our school–university action research project involved collaboration with
a small group of elementary teachers from two Chicago schools (seven at
one school; six at the other). Most of teachers worked with Chris Pappas
before the 1994–1995 school year; a few heard about the project from
these colleagues and then joined it.

Both of the schools serve low-SES students, nearly all of whom qualify
for federally assisted meals. The support for the project from the princi-
pals at both schools—Fausto Lopez at Joseph Jungman Elementary
School and Peggy Iska, principal of Hans Christian Andersen Elementary
School until 1995, and Suzanne Dunaway, the current principal—was invaluable to the success of the project.

Jungman has mostly a Mexican and Mexican-American student population. In the past few years, a small number of African-American and other
non-Latino students also attended. It is very close to the University of Illinois at Chicago in the Pilsen area of the city. The community surrounding
the school consists of mostly Spanish-speaking families and businesses.
The school has a pre-K through sixth-grade program. Six teacher researchers taught at this school while they conducted their inquiries, three of
them in trailers, which have since been removed, next to the main school
on the edges of the parking lot.

Hans Christian Andersen (now renamed Hans Christian Andersen Acad-
emy) offers a pre-K through eighth-grade program. The community surrounding the school is diverse, and is showing early signs of gentrification.
Seven teacher researchers did their inquiries in this school. The school, lo-
cated farther from the University than Jungman, has a more diverse student population. The majority of the students are from families originally
from Mexico, Puerto Rica, and other Latin American countries. There is a
also substantial number of African-American students, as well as a small
minority of Anglo students (many of Polish or Eastern-European descent).

Procedures of the Project

The description of the major techniques and research activities is in the
next two parts. The first part covers methods used during the 1994–1995
school year, which was the major classroom data collection year—the one
in which the teacher researchers conducted their inquiries. The second
part goes over those activities of subsequent years, where project personnel were busy analyzing and writing up these data together for conference
presentations, journal articles, book chapters, this book—and for the
companion book that was noted in the beginning of this chapter. This latter part of this section specifically addresses the ways in which the chapters in this book were written.

Data Collection of Teacher–Researcher Inquires (the 1994–1995 School Year)

Teacher–Researcher Journals.   In our project, teachers determined and chose the area—the curriculum genre—in which they did their literacy inquiries. In the fall, they were given a form that asked what they would study that year. This form asked the major questions that they would be attempting to address in their inquiries, when they would be doing the inquiries, and in what initial ways the university partners might help or support their inquiries.

The teacher researchers were also encouraged to use their own private research journals. Because only some of the teachers had previously kept such journals, we shared with them the chapter of Altrichter, et al. (1993), "The Research Diary," which provides a rationale and useful suggestions for using one. Teachers sometimes spontaneously referred to entries they noted in their journals during our weekly school meetings. At our individual end-of-the year interviews with them, they more purposefully consulted these journals (as well as their fieldnotes—see next section) to talk to us about what stood out for them during the past year's research. The teachers also relied on these journals during the subsequent years, especially when they were writing up their own chapters for the companion volume, and when they were collaborating with the university researchers in writing the chapters in the present book.

Fieldnotes.   In our project, three two-member teams of university researchers—one at each of the two schools and one who worked in three bilingual classrooms at both schools—completed fieldnotes, which complemented the videotaping records (see next section). Data collection in terms of fieldnotes and videotaping was done weekly—that is, each team attempted to collect these data in each of the teacher–researchers' classrooms at least 1 day a week (although sometimes university researchers were there more than 1 day if the particular inquiry required it [also some of the teachers started the year with two inquiries, which meant more visits to their classroom]). For the most part, these fieldnotes were descriptive in nature and focused on the talk used in the classroom. They also included comments or questions of clarification addressed to the teacher researcher.

Chris Pappas, the director of the project, was in all of the 13 teachers' classrooms regularly to observe their inquiries. She could not manage in any practical way to write up in-depth fieldnotes, so she developed shortened versions of fieldnotes she called *Summary/Queries.* She provided a brief summary of what she observed, with perhaps a pertinent example or two of interaction, and then posed questions or provided other comments for the teacher to consider relative to his or her inquiry. If she thought of an article or book that might be helpful in addressing a particular problem or issue a particular teacher researcher seemed to be tackling, a note about her bringing the resource for the teacher researcher soon was also added. The teachers reported that both of these versions of fieldnotes were invaluable in their inquiries.

Of course, writing fieldnotes has been a mainstay in qualitative research, but what is different in collaborative studies, such as ours, is that these fieldnotes were shared with the teacher researchers in an ongoing way. That is, unlike noncollaborative ethnographies where the researcher "keeps" the fieldnotes and rarely ever discloses them with the "subjects(s)" of research, the purpose of observation, here, was to give feedback and support on what the teachers attempted to accomplish in their inquiries. Thus, our fieldnotes of these observations were given to the teachers as quickly as possible (usually a day or so later).

Videotaping.   As already indicated, videotaping in teacher-researchers' classrooms was done weekly because classroom discourse was the major means by which we documented the processes of the teachers' inquiries. The videotaping was done by the two-member teams, who worked with the same teachers the whole year. One person of the team operated the camera, and the other took the fieldnotes. The duration of the videotaping sessions varied according to the length of the curriculum genres in which the teachers had their inquiries—as short as 20 minutes or as long as an hour.

An edited version (usually 10–15 minutes long) of the footage of one or two teachers' classrooms was shared at weekly meetings at each school. Because we did not want university researchers to make all of the decisions about what should and should not be included in these edited videotapes, we developed a form that asked for the teachers' input. After each videotaping session in teachers' classrooms, teachers noted on this form the "good" parts and "vulnerable" parts that they thought would be important to include in the editing. Using that as a guide, with fieldnotes that were taken to complement the videotaping, university researchers selected several portions that they felt captured the focus of a teacher's inquiry to date.

Regular Weekly Meetings.   We had weekly meetings of the university and teacher researchers at each school (and had several meetings with all of the teachers), which were also videotaped. As indicated previously, edited classroom videotapes for one or two teachers were shared in an author's chair fashion. This usually occurred a week or so later after the raw videotaping data were collected. Also, we found it useful to provide a brief note, listing short descriptors of the edited segments, for everyone at the meeting so that we could all better follow what was shown. These edited videotapes enabled the teachers—in collaboration with others—to examine carefully the everyday routines of teaching–learning they chose to investigate. Frequently, ideas gained from the colleagues of the project helped the teacher researcher decide on his or her next course of action in the inquiry.

Individual Conversations and Interviews.   There were many incidental and informal conversations throughout the year, some of which were audiotaped, and some of which were captured as additions to fieldnotes if they had been recently related to something that had just happened in the classroom regarding a teacher's inquiry.

We (the respective university-research team and Chris Pappas) also had individual end-of-the-year interviews with the teachers about what stood out for them—both ups and downs—regarding their inquiries. The teacher researchers prepared in advance for these interviews by going through their journals and fieldnotes. These interviews provided a means to obtain the teachers' perspectives about what they believed were the critical points of their inquiries.

Analyzing, Interpreting, and Writing Up the Data (the Subsequent Years)

Because both teacher and university researchers in the project were caught up in the cycles of action research involved in particular teacher inquiries, initial analysis and interpretation of the data took place while the data were collected during the 1994–1995 school year. However, more systematic, concerted efforts regarding these research activities occurred subsequently. At the publication time of this book (and the companion volume), other papers based on the work of the project are planned for now and the future. However, the following two activities illustrate how the project addressed some of the major methodological issues in analysis and interpretation.

Identifying the Critical Incidents in the Teacher-Researchers' Inquiries.   A major goal of our analysis was to determine the critical points or incidents (Burgess, 1993; Patton, 1990) in the teacher inquiries. Even though an important aim of teacher research—and qualitative research in general—is to make the everyday experience strange so as to better understand it, when we realized the amount of data that was amassed in the previous year, we all felt overwhelmed. Thus, identifying critical incidents offered areas of transparency "on the otherwise opaque surface of regular uneventful social life" (Turner, 1957, p. 93). It also served other purposes. It helped in the routine process of reducing data in interpretative qualitative analysis. As Wolcott (1990) argued, "The major problem we face in qualitative inquiry is not to get data, but to get rid of it!" (p. 18). He suggested that we discover "those essences with sufficient context, yet not become mired trying to include everything that might be possibly be described" (p. 35). Revealing the critical incidents also provided us with a means of triangulation.

Although our identification of critical incidents was an ongoing activity, the major events occurred at the end of the year of the teacher inquiries and the beginning of the following year. As indicated earlier, we had end-of-the-year interviews with the teacher researchers about their inquiries. They planned in advance for this meeting, going over their journals and the fieldnotes they received from the university researchers over the course of the year, to indicate what stood out for them—that is, their perspectives of what they deemed to be the critical incidents of their inquiries. During the summer following these interviews, the university researchers went through a similar process. The university teams who worked with individual teacher researchers reviewed the fieldnotes of that study to create an overview of what the teams considered to be the critical points or incidents. This process also involved doing a macroanalysis from the videotapes that would realize these critical incidents and could offer illustrative examples for them. Each team also viewed the videotapes of the end-of-the-year interviews and created a another overview of a list of topics that the teacher researchers highlighted in their talk with us. In several meetings at the beginning of the next year (videotaped), these teams shared both sets of overviews with their respective teacher researchers.

Thus, triangulation was achieved in several ways—by using several data sources and by relying on the perspectives of both university and teacher researchers (Denzin, 1978; Patton, 1990). The process that we just described in our initial identification of critical incidents subsequent to the year of inquiry also showed how university researchers did double checking with the teacher researchers over interpretations that were made. It has been commonplace in qualitative research to share findings or interpretations with informants or participants as both a courtesy and as a means of validation or trustworthiness (Delamont, 1992; Glesne & Peshkin, 1992; Lincoln & Guba, 1985; Page, Samson, & Crockett, 1998; Wolcott, 1990). However, because it was a collaborative project such efforts of "member checking" were constant throughout the project. It was one of the ways to make problematic collaboration itself to deal with the inherent power relationships of collaborative school–university action research (Pappas, 1997a).

Writing Up Findings in Collaboration.   During that first year after the teacher-inquiry data collection, we began to write up our findings. Two major places of dissemination are this volume and the companion book, where teachers authored their own chapters. For this second book, teachers began to write their own stories of their inquiries, using their journals, fieldnotes, and the two overviews mentioned previously. As they did, they asked for particular transcriptions that they could use to illustrate the points they wanted to make in their chapters. They wrote several drafts, each time getting feedback from each other, as well as both the university-researcher team they worked with during their inquiries, and Chris Pappas. Each of these latter conversations were audiotaped. The present book began at the same time. The university researchers began to draft chapters—in collaboration—with the respective teacher researchers involved. The conversations with the teachers in this process were also audiotaped. Thus, in writing these chapters in both books, there were many more discussions about the analyses and interpretations of both university and teacher researchers because project personnel were involved in reflecting anew on the work of the teacher inquiries.

A real issue in writing up collaborative action research is how to represent the teacher researchers with whom university researchers worked. University researchers were not trying to do research *on* the teacher researchers, but rather were attempting to work *with* teacher researchers by centering on the important questions the teachers raised in their own teaching. So, now the time arrives to write up the findings in coauthored chapters, that is, to report the critical incidents of the inquiries that the teachers conducted in their classrooms and that the university researchers attempted to support and document. What should we do about the dilemma regarding the representation of teacher researchers in these chapters? How should we deal with the issue of authorial voice?

Of course, the problem question of authorial voice is very critical in all qualitative research (Wolcott, 1990). As Van Maanen (1988) stated it: "How social reality is conveyed through writing involves, among other things, authorial voice. The author's perspective exhibited through voice marks particular ethographic styles and genres. But, reader beware" (p. ix). The difficulties regarding authorial voice are exacerbated in collaborative projects such as ours.

It was a practice to use pseudonyms for the names of participants in educational research, and strong arguments were offered for the need to protect identity (e.g., see Delamont, 1984, 1992). However, many teacher researchers, seeking recognition for their contributions in the collaborative work they do with university researchers, no longer want anonymity. (See Shulman, 1990, for a useful discussion of this topic.) Any time a university researcher, who has a commitment to study and understand the perspective of an interacting individual, authors a text describing that individual, the sticky area of representation is evoked (Lincoln & Denzin, 1994). As Nepor and Barylske (1991) argued, representation is "not just a matter of epistemology or method, but a matter of power" (p. 806). When we (university researchers) represent others, there is always the potential to reduce them; that is, the relationships of power in this discourse favor the representers (the university researchers) over the represented (the teachers about whom we write).

In this book (and the companion volume), the teachers identified themselves (and their schools, but not their students, for whom pseudonyms are used). In the chapters, the university researchers took the lead in the drafting the texts that were coauthored with the teacher researchers. The teacher researchers had many ample opportunities for input and review because we wanted multivoiced, collaborative texts. However, because these texts focus on the teachers' experiences in their classrooms, the use of third person to refer to the teacher researchers is frequent, but such a practice seems to us to be a subtle way to inflate the power of university researchers in the ways mentioned previously.

Thus, in attempt to counterbalance the use of third person and to strengthen the voices of the teacher researchers in the chapters, we included sections in each chapter where the teachers "speak" from the first person. Creating these sections was done in several ways. In the development of the chapters, university researchers took the wordings of the teachers—from audio- and videotape transcriptions, from the drafts of their chapters in the other book, and so forth—and expressed them as "quasiquotes." That is, these segments are not totally direct quotes, but instead are close paraphrases of the teachers' utterances in various contexts. University researchers then got the teachers to review what and how their ideas were expressed. Sometimes, university researchers included just a little of this first-person narrative and then asked the teacher researchers to read the draft and elaborate on it. Discussions would then be held about this draft. The university researchers, then, listened to the tape of that conversation about that part of the chapter, and expanded that part. Sometimes the teacher researchers, as they read a draft, prepared their own sections to answer the queries of the university researchers. At other times, the university researchers wrote a regular section of the paper that included some interpretations they came up with, and asked for the teacher researchers to respond. These clarifications or explanations from the teacher researchers—from an audiotape of the discussion or the teachers' own written responses—would again be included by the university researchers at this part of the chapter. For each chapter, there were many drafts, discussions, revisions, and on and on.

Next, we use an example from chapter 2 to illustrate this process. In this case, we use one of the last draft versions of the text written by university researchers, Jane Liao and Dian Ruben, and teacher researcher, Pam Wolfer, who did her inquiry on writing in her first-grade classroom. We focus on a part of the Conclusions section at the end of the chapter. In this part, successes about how Pam's inquiry to create a writing workshop for first graders—who began the year with limited writing skills and little confidence in themselves as writers, but at the end became confident writers who were experts on the books they wrote—were covered. Subsequently, the university researchers offered some limitations or drawbacks of Pam's study. In the draft they pointed out that most of the texts her students wrote were stories or personal narratives and that these first-grade students might have sometimes marginalized other students in the texts they wrote. Underneath, the university researchers listed—in brackets—several questions for her to respond to. Table 1.1 below shows the early draft.

Pam was given this draft to read and was ready to answer the questions that were posed to her at the subsequent discussion. Table 1.2 presents the revision that included her wordings from the audiotape of the discussion. When Pam got to this part of the chapter, she said, "Oh, I have a lot to say here." She was quite articulate about what she felt about these questions. The university researchers, then, listened to the tape and used the major points Pam made by adding wordings of her talk to the chapter in the next revision—see Table 1.2 for Pam's first-person explanation.

TABLE 1.1

Excerpt from a Draft From Chapter 2: "Creating the Writing Workshop in First Grade: How to Teach Literacy 'Skills' and Help Children 'Come to Voice'" (Liao, J., Ruben, D., & Wolfer, P.)

However, because students had total control of their topics in writing, they did not all attempt a range of genres (Chapman, 1994). That is, they tended to write personal narratives or stories, so that opportunities to write reports or informational texts, for example, were lacking (Christie, 1987; Martin, 1985). Thus, how to foster the development of genres in more breadth and depth is an ongoing concern for Pam. More recently, advocates of the writing-process approach have been experimenting with genre studies (Calkins, 1991, 1994), where the whole class works on writing particular genres at different times of the year. Thus, not always following individual students' inclinations on topic or style, and not just letting genres emerge (Chapman, 1994) are both being considered.

Moreover, as Lensmire (1994) argued, children are not always so innocent in the intentions and content of their texts when they have complete power over what they write. Through their writing, some of his third graders marginalized other students and accomplished other political ends. This occurred at the first-grade level in Pam's classroom when children sometimes erased certain students' names from their texts to show their displeasure about how various social relationships were acted out. Thus, who was included or excluded in their texts was frequently part of larger issue of "who gets to play" (Paley, 1992). It was deep in the unofficial peer-governed school world that Pam did not bring up for critical examination (Dyson, 1996). Consequently, as Lensmire proposed, there is a need to have a critical revision of the writing workshop that avoids merely a romantic or expressionistic view about the texts that children create. Teachers like Pam need to think about how they might intervene and fashion the curriculum so as not to be blind to these facets of teaching.

[Pam, what do you think of these "critical" responses of the writing workshop in general and how they reflect yours? Is this an accurate account? What are your feelings about what we said here?]

TABLE 1.2

Pam Wolfer's First-Person Response to the Draft in Table 1 that is now Included in Chapter 2: "Creating the Writing Workshop in First Grade: How to Teach Literacy 'Skills' and Help Children 'Come to Voice'" (Liao, J., Ruben, D., & Wolfer, P.)

Pam: I think it is important to point out that although children did face their classmates' hard questions about their writing, I really tried to promote author appreciation. I got this from Rassel [see Chapter 4]—the idea that you are always saying positive things first and having respect for the author. Although sharetime was student directed, I taught them this in the very beginning. I'd say: "That's their books and it means to them what your books mean to you. Don't ever say you don't like that. You say, 'I like this.' If you don't like it, don't tell the author. You can ask questions, 'I don't understand this' or 'I think you have to say more because I don't understand it.'" So author appreciation was really important. You clap, three people say what they liked, and then you ask questions. That's why they could take the questions because of all of the positive things before it. So even though it is hard to face questions as a writer, it was also easier for these reasons. The questions become a positive thing, a helpful thing. That's why they were so eager to share their writing.

It is true that most of the texts children wrote were personal narratives or stories. I had so many reluctant and very emergent writers in the beginning, I just couldn't figure out how to get them to do research and write informational texts. However, I had most of these kids next year in second grade, and we did many more genres. For example, they read books on animals and they all wrote their own papers on them. In first grade, I didn't know how to do it. In second grade they also frequently wrote class newspapers that they typed themselves, which included many kinds of genres. I was able to do it better in second grade. Maybe in first grade I was also just figuring out the system.

Sometimes I obviously didn't know that there was this issue of including or not including particular kids' names in their texts. But sometimes I was aware of it, but it wasn't always negative because it brought up social issues among the children into the open. Someone might say, "How come I'm not in here?" "Because you weren't nice to me this morning." Sometimes these little things would help them actually solve them themselves. Someone would say then, "I'm sorry," and then the writer would say, "Oh okay, I'll put you in there if you are sorry." Of course, there were other times when they weren't so little, but hurtful, and I had to intervene. Most of the time, though, it got resolved easily, but I guess this is something to think more about.

Subsequently, Pam had another opportunity to review and evaluate this part (as well as others) of the subsequent revision of the chapter. She and other teacher and university researchers, even as the chapters were sent out to the publisher, had another opportunity to further examine and make any relevant changes.

The adding of first-person sections in texts written by university and teacher researchers in this collaborative action research project is certainly not the whole answer. We offer one possibility. To return to the Bakhtinian framework offered earlier in the chapter, it was an attempt to include the point of view and voice—the *speaking consciousness* of both university and teacher researchers in the dialogue in collaborative action research. However, it is clear that much more work will be required on the problem of power and method in the production of academic discourse (Ladwig & Gore, 1994; Pappas, 1997a).

A BRIEF OVERVIEW OF THE REST OF THE BOOK

Except for the last, summary chapter, the rest of the book is organized in terms of curriculum genres. Part I covers teacher inquiries in writing curriculum genres, Part II is about studies done in the reading-aloud curriculum genres, Part III is about drama curriculum genres, and Part IV covers four inquiries on miscellaneous curriculum genres. In this last section, one chapter is about the pretend-reading curriculum genre and another is about literature-discussion groups curriculum genres. The other two chapters present teacher researchers' inquiries that encompass several curriculum genres.

A brief introduction to the relevant chapters precedes each part. The chapters in each part are ordered according to increasing grade level. We tried not to replicate the information in this introductory chapter in the other chapters, so it is important that this present chapter be read before reading the other ones. It is also important to take note of the transcription key in the appendix on this and the next page so you can easily decipher the classroom-discourse excerpts in the chapters.

The last chapter in the book briefly summarizes the important themes in all of the chapters. We argue that the kind of collaborative, dialogic instruction and discourse created in literacy curriculum-genre inquiries fostered important learning in these classrooms. In addition, we claim and discuss that there are critical political implications when urban teacher researchers develop collaborative discourse.

APPENDIX: CONVENTIONS OF TRANSCRIPTION FOR CLASSROOM DISCOURSE EXAMPLES

Unit:	Usually corresponds to an independent clause with all dependent clauses related to it (complex clause or T-unit). Sometimes includes another independent clause if there is no drop of tone and is added without any pausing. Units here are punctuated as sentences.
Turn:	Includes all of a speaker's utterances or units.

Key for Speakers:	First name is listed for teacher researcher. C, C1, C2, and so forth are noted for individual children (with "m" or "f" to refer to the gender of a child): C is used if a child's voice cannot be identified; Cs followed by a number are used to identify particular children in particular sections of the transcript (so that C1 or C2, etc., is not necessarily the same child throughout the whole transcript). Cs (or SCs) represents many or some children speaking simultaneously.
——	False starts or abandoned language replaced by new language structures.
...	Small or short pause within unit.
... ...	Longer pause within unit.
....	Breaking off of a speaker's turn due to the next speaker's turn.
< >	Uncertain words.
(...)	One word that is inaudible or impossible to transcribe.
(... ...)	Longer stretches of language that are inaudible and impossible to transcribe.
Italic:	Emphasis.
# #	Overlapping language spoken by two or more speakers at a time.
CAPS	Actual reading of a book.
{ }	Teacher's miscue or modification of a text read.
[ ]	Identifies what is being referred to or gestured and other nonverbal contextual information.
....	Part of a transcript has been omitted.

REFERENCES

Allington, R. L. (1991). Children who find learning to read difficult: School response to diversity. In E. F. Heibert (Ed.), *Literacy for a diverse society: Perspectives, practices, and policies* (pp. 237–252). New York: Teachers College Press.

Altrichter, H., Posch, O., & Somekh, B. (1993). *Teachers investigate their work: An introduction to the methods of action research.* New York: Routledge.

Anyon, J. (1983). Social class and the hidden curriculum of work. In H. Giroux & D. Purpel (Eds.), *The hidden curriculum and moral education* (pp. 143–167). New York: Routledge.

Apple, M. (1993). *Official knowledge: Democratic education in a conservative age.* New York: Routledge.

Au, K. H., & Jordan, C. (1981). Teaching reading to Hawaiian children: Analysis of culturally appropriate instructional event. *Anthropology and Education Quarterly, 11,* 91–115.

Bakhtin, M. M. (1981). *The dialogic imagination: Four essays by M. M. Bakhtin.* M. Holquist (Ed.), M. Holquist & C. Emerson (Trans.). Austin: University of Texas Press.

Bakhtin, M. M. (1986). *Speech genres and other late essays*. C. Emerson & M. Holquist (Eds.), & V. W. McGee (Trans.). Austin: Austin University Press.

Barnes, D. (1993). Supporting exploratory talk for learning. In K. M. Pierce & C. J. Gilles (Eds.), *Cycles of meaning: Exploring the potential of talk in learning communities* (pp. 17–34). Portsmouth, NH: Heinemann.

Barnes, D., & Todd, F. (1995). *Communication and learning revisited: Making meaning through talk*. Portsmouth, NH: Boynton/Cook.

Bartolome, L. I. (1994). Beyond the methods fetish: Toward a humanizing pedagogy. *Harvard Educational Review, 64,* 173–194.

Bloome, D., & Bailey, F. (1992). Studying language and literacy through events, particularity, and intertextuality. In R. Beach, J. L. Green, M. L. Kamil, & T. Shanahan (Eds.), *Multidisciplinary perspectives on literacy research* (pp. 181–210). Urbana, IL: National Conference on Research in English.

Burgess, R. G. (1993). Event analysis and the study of headship. In M. Schratz (Ed.). *Qualitative voices in educational research* (pp. 23–39). London: Falmer Press.

Calkins, L. M. (1991). *Living between the lines*. Portsmouth, NH: Heinemann.

Calkins, L. M. (1994). *The art of teaching writing*. Portsmouth, NH: Heinemann.

Cazden, C. B. (1986). Classroom discourse. In M. C. Wittrock (Ed.), *Handbook of research on teaching* (3rd ed., pp. 432–463). New York: Macmillan.

Cazden, C. B. (1988). *Classroom discourse: The language of teaching and learning*. Portsmouth, NH: Heinemann.

Cazden, C. B. (1992). *Whole language plus: Essays on literacy in the United States and New Zealand*. New York: Teachers College Press.

Chapman, M. L. (1994). The emergence of genres: Some findings from an examination of first-grade writing. *Written Communication, 11,* 348–380.

Christie, F. (1987a). The morning news genre: Using a functional grammar to illuminate educational issues. *Australian Review of Applied Linguistics, 10,* 182–198.

Christie, F. (1987b). Learning to mean in writing. In N. Stewart-Dore (Ed.), *Writing and reading to learn* (pp. 21–34). Rozelle, Australia: Primary English Teaching Association.

Christie, F. (1989). Language development in education. In R. Hasan & J. R. Martin (Eds.), *Language development: Learning language, learning culture* (pp. 152–198). Norwood, NJ: Ablex.

Christie, F. (1993). Curriculum genres: Planning of effective teaching. In B. Cope and M. Kalantzis (Eds.), *The powers of literacy: A genre approach to teaching writing* (pp. 154–178). Pittsburgh, PA: University of Pittsburgh Press.

Cochran-Smith, M. (1991). Learning to teach against the grain. *Harvard Educational Review, 61,* 279–310.

Cochran-Smith, M., & Lytle, S. L. (1990). Research on teaching and teacher research: The issues that divide. *Educational Researcher, 19,* 2–11.

Cochran-Smith, M., & Lytle, S. L. (1993). *Inside/outside: Teacher research and knowledge*. New York: Teachers College Press.

Cummins, J. (1994). From coercive to collaborative relations of power in the teaching of literacy. In B. M. Ferdman, R.-M. Weber, & A. G. Ramierz (Eds.), *Literacy across languages and cultures* (pp. 295–331). Albany: State University of New York Press.

Delamont, S. (1984). The old girl network: Recollections on the fieldwork at St. Luke's. In R. G. Burgess (Ed.), *The research process in educational settings: Ten case studies* (pp. 15–38). London: Falmer Press.

Delamont, S. (1992). *Fieldwork in educational settings: Methods, pitfalls and perspectives.* London: Falmer Press.

Delpit, L. D. (1988). The silenced dialogue: Power and pedagogy in educating other people's children. *Harvard Educational Review, 58,* 379–385

Delpit, L. D. (1992). Acquisition of literate discourse: Bowing before the master? *Theory into Practice, 31,* 296–302.

Denzin, N. K. (1978). *The research act: A theoretical introduction to sociological methods.* New York: McGraw-Hill.

Dewey, J. (1904). *The relation of theory to practice in education: The third NSSE yearbook* (Pt. 1). Chicago: University of Chicago Press.

Dyson, A. H. (1996). Cultural constellations and childhood identities: On Greek gods, cartoon heroes, and the social lives of school children. *Harvard Educational Review, 66,* 471–524.

Edwards, D., & Mercer, N. (1987). *Common knowledge: The development of understanding in the classroom.* London: Routledge.

Elliot, J. (1985). Facilitating action research on teaching: Some dilemmas. In R. Burgess (Ed.), *Field methods in the study of education* (pp. 235–262). London: Falmer Press.

Elliot, J. (1991). *Action research for educational change.* Milton Keynes, England: Open University Press.

Erickson, F., & Schultz, J. (1977). When is a context? Some issues and methods in the analysis of social competence. *The Quarterly Newsletter of the Institute for Comparative Human Development, 1,* 5–12.

Foster, M. (1992). Sociolinguistics and the African-American Community: Implications for literacy. *Theory into Practice, 32,* 303–311.

Freire, P. (1970). *Pedagogy of the oppressed.* New York: Seabury.

Freire, P. (1972). *Cultural action for freedom.* Harmondsworth, England: Penguin Books.

Gee, J. P. (1996). *Social linguistics and literacies: Ideology in discourses.* London: Taylor & Francis.

Glesne, C., & Peshkin, A. (1992). *Becoming qualitative researchers: An introducion.* White Plains, NY: Longman.

Gitlin, A. D. (1990). Educative research, voice, and school change. *Harvard Educational Review, 60,* 443–466.

Gitlin, A., Bringhurst, K., Burns, M., Cooley, V., Myers, B., Price, K., Russell, R., & Tiess, P. (1992). *Teachers' voices for school change: An introduction to educative research.* New York: Teachers College Press.

Green. J. L., & Dixon, C. N. (1994). Talking into being: Discursive and social practices in classrooms. *Linguistics and Education, 5,* 231–239.

Green, J. L., Kantor, R. M., & Rogers T. (1991). Exploring the complexity of language and learning in classroom contexts. In L. Idol & B. F. Jones (Eds.), *Educational values and cognitive instruction: Implications for reform* (pp. 333–364). Hillsdale, NJ: Lawrence Erlbaum Associates.

Gutierrez, K., Rymes, B., & Larson, J. (1995). Script, counterscript, and underlife in the classroom: James Brown versus *Brown v. Board of Education. Harvard Educational Review, 65,* 445–471.

Halliday, M. A. K. (1978). *Language as social semiotic: The social interpretation of language and meaning.* London: Edward Arnold.

Halliday, M. A. K. (1993). Towards a language-based theory of learning. *Linguistics and Education, 5,* 93–126.

Halliday, M. A. K. (1994). "So you say 'pass' … thank you three muchly." In A. D. Grimshaw (Ed.), *What's going on here? Complementary studies of professional talk (Vol. 2 of the multiple analysis project). Vol. XLIII in Advances in Discourse Processes* (pp. 175–229). Norwood, NJ: Ablex.

Halliday, M. A. K. (1996). Literacy and linguistics: A functional perspective. In R. Hasan & G. Williams (Eds.), *Literacy in society* (pp. 339–376). London: Addison-Wesley Longman.

Halliday, M. A. K., & Hasan, R. (1985). *Language, context, and text: Aspects of language in a social-semiotic perspective.* Victoria, Australia: Deakin University Press.

Hasan, R. (1984). The nursery tale as a genre. *Nottingham Linguistic Circular, 13,* 71–102.

Hasan, R. (1995). The conception of context in texts. In P. H. Fries & M. Gregory (Eds.), *Discourse in society: Systemic functional perspectives (Meaning and choice in language: Studies for Michael Halliday). Vol. L in Advances in Discourse Processes* (pp. 183–283). Norwood, NJ: Ablex.

Hasan, R. (1996). *Ways of saying: Ways of meaning.* In C. Cloran, D. Butt, & G. Williams (Eds.), London: Cassell.

Heath, S. B. (1982). What no bedtime story means: Narrative skills at home and school. *Language in Society, 11,* 49–76.

Heath, S. B. (1983). *Ways with words.* Cambridge, England: Cambridge University Press.

Kreisberg, S. (1992). *Transforming power: Domination, empowerment, and education.* Albany: State University of New York Press.

Kress, G. (1993). Genre as social process. In B. Cope & M. Kalantzis (Eds.), *The powers of literacy: A genre approach to teaching writing* (pp. 22–37). Pittsburgh, PA: University of Pittsburgh Press.

Ladson-Billings, G. (1994). *The dreamkeepers: Successful teachers of African-American children.* San Francisco: Jossey-Bass.

Ladwig, J. C. (1991). Is collaborative research exploitative? *Educational Theory, 41,* 111–120.

Ladwig, J. C., & Gore, J. M. (1994). Extending power and specifying method with the discourse of activist research. In A. Gitlin (Ed.), *Power and method: Political activism and educational research* (pp. 227–238). New York: Routledge.

Lather, P. (1986). Research as praxis. *Harvard Educational Review, 56,* 257–277.

Lemke, J. L. (1985). *Using language in the classroom.* Victoria, Australia: Deakin University Press.

Lemke, J. L. (1990). *Talking science: Language, learning, and values.* Norwood, NJ: Ablex.

Lensmire, T. J. (1994). *When children write: Critical re-visions of the writing workshop.* New York: Teachers College Press.

Lewin, K. (1948). *Resolving social conflicts.* New York: Harper & Row.

Lincoln, Y. S., & Denzin, N. K. (1994). The fifth moment. In N. K. Denzin & Y. S. (Eds.), *The handbook of qualitative research* (pp. 575–586). Thousands Oaks, CA: Sage.

Lincoln, Y. S., & Guba, E. (1985). *Naturalistic inquiry.* Englewood Cliffs, NJ: Prentice Hill.

Lindfors, J. W. (1987). *Children's language and learning*. Englewood Cliffs, NJ: Prentice Hall.

Lindfors, J. W. (1999). *Children's inquiry: Using language to make sense of the world*. New York: Teachers College Press.

Losey, K. M. (1995). Mexican American students and classroom interaction: An overview and critique. *Review of Educational Research, 65*, 283–318.

Lotman, Y. M. (1988). Text within a text. *Soviet Psychology, 26*, 32–51.

Martin, J. R. (1985). *Factual writing: Exploring and challenging social reality*. Victoria, Australia: Deakin University Press.

McCollum, P. (1991). Cross-cultural perspectives on classroom discourse and literacy. In E. H. Heibert (Ed.), *Literacy for a diverse society: Perspectives, practices and policies* (pp. 108–121). New York: Teachers College Press.

Mehan, H. (1979). *Learning lessons*. Cambridge, MA: Harvard University Press.

Mercer, N. (1995). *The guided construction of knowledge: Talk amongst teachers and learners*. Clevedon, England: Multilingual Matters.

Michaels, S. (1981). "Sharing time": Children's narrative styles and differential access to literacy. *Language in Society, 10*, 423–442.

Moll, L. C. (Ed.). (1990). *Vygotsky and education: Instructional implications and applications of sociohistorical psychology*. Cambridge, England: Cambridge University Press.

Moll, L. C. (1992). Literacy research in community and classrooms: A sociocultural approach. In R. Beach, J. L. Green, M. L. Kamil, & T. Shanahan (Eds.), *Multidisciplinary perspectives on literacy research* (pp. 211–244). Urbana, IL: National Conference on Research in English.

Moll, L. C., & Gonzalez, N. (1994). Lessons from research with language-minority children. *JRB: A Journal of Literacy, 26*, 439–456.

Nepor, J., & Barylske, J. (1991). Narrative discourse and teacher knowledge. *American Educational Research Journal, 28*, 805–823.

Newman, D. P., Griffin, P., & Cole, M. (1989). *The construction zone: Working for cognitive change in school*. Cambridge, England: Cambridge University Press.

Nixon, J. (Ed.). (1981). *A teacher's guide to action research*. London: Grant McIntyre.

Noffke, S. E., & Stevenson, R. B. (Eds.). (1995). *Educational action research: Becoming practically critical*. New York: Teachers College Press.

Nystrand, M. (1986). *The structure of written communication: Studies in reciprocity between writers and readers*. Orlando, FL: Academic Press.

Nystrand. M. (1997). *Opening dialogue: Understanding the dynamics of language and learning in the English classroom*. New York: Teachers College Press.

Nystrand, M., & Wiemelt, J. (1991). When is a text explicit? Formalist and dialogical conceptions. *Text, 11*, 25–41.

O'Connor, M. C., & Michaels, S. (1993). Aligning academic task and participation status through revoicing: Analysis of a classroom discourse strategy. *Anthropology and Education Quarterly, 24*, 318–335.

Olson, D. (1991). Children's understanding of interpretation and the autonomy of written texts. *Text, 11*, 3–23.

Oya, S. N., & Smulyan, L. (1989). *Collaborative action research: A developmental approach*. London: Falmer Press.

Oyler, C. (1996a). *Making room for students in an urban first grade: Sharing teacher authority in room 104*. New York: Teachers College Press.

Oyler, C. (1996b). Sharing authority: Student initiations during teacher-led read-alouds of information books. *Teaching and Teacher Education, 12,* 149–160.

Page, R. N., Samson, Y. J., & Crockett, M. D. (1998). Reporting ethnography to informants. *Harvard Educational Review, 68,* 299–334.

Paley, V. G. (1992). *You can't say you can't play.* Cambridge: Harvard University Press.

Pappas, C. C. (1990, July). *The reading-aloud curriculum genre: Exploring text and teacher variation.* Paper presented at the 17th International Systemic Congress, Stirling, Scotland.

Pappas, C. C. (1991, April). *The reading-aloud curriculum genre: Book genre and teacher variation.* Paper presented at the annual meeting of the American Educational Research Association, Chicago, IL.

Pappas, C. C. (1997a). Making 'collaboration' problematic in collaborative school-university research: Studying with urban teacher researchers to transform literacy curriculum genres. In J. Flood, S. B. Heath, & D. Lapp (Eds.), *A handbook for literacy educators: Research on teaching the communicative and visual arts* (pp 213–229). New York: Macmillan.

Pappas, C. C. (1997b). Reading instruction in an integrated perspective: Collaborative interaction in classroom curriculum genres. In S. Stahl & D. A. Hayes (Eds.), *Instructional models in reading* (pp. 283–330). Mahwah, NJ: Lawrence Erlbaum Associates.

Pappas, C. C. (1999). Becoming literate in the borderlands. In A. Goncu (Ed.), *Children's engagement in the world: Sociocultural perspectives* (pp. 228–260). Cambridge: Cambridge University Press.

Pappas, C. C. (in press). *Learning written genres: A social-semiotic perspective.* Cresskill, NJ: Hampton Press.

Pappas, C. C., Kiefer, B. Z., & Levstik, L. S. (1999). *An integrated language perspective in the elementary school: An action approach.* New York: Longman.

Pappas, C. C., & Zecker, L. B. (2000). *Teacher inquiries in literacy teaching-learning: Learning to collaborate in elementary urban classrooms.* Mahwah, NJ: Lawrence Erlbaum Associates.

Patton, M. Q. (1990). *Qualitative evaluation and research methods.* Newbury Park, CA: Sage.

Philips, S. U. (1972). Participant structures and communicative competence: Warm Springs children in community and classroom. In C. B. Cazden, V. P. John, & D. Hymes (Eds.), *Functions of language in the classroom* (pp. 370–394). New York: Teachers College Press.

Philips, S. U. (1983). *The invisible culture: Communication in the classroom and community on the Warm Springs Indian Reservation.* New York: Longman.

Ramirez, A. (1988). Analyzing speech acts. In J. L. Green & J. O. Harker (Eds.), *Multiple perspective analyses of classroom discourse* (pp. 135–163). Norwood, NJ: Ablex.

Reyes, M. de la Luz. (1991). A process approach to literacy instruction for Spanish-speaking students: In search of a best fit. In E. F. Hiebert (Ed.), *Literacy for a diverse society: Perspectives, practices, and policies* (pp. 157–171). New York: Teachers College Press.

Reyes, M. de la Luz. (1992). Challenging the venerable assumptions: Literacy instruction for linguistically different students. *Harvard Educational Review, 62,* 427–446.

Richardson, V. (1994a). Conducting research on practice. *Educational Researcher,* *23,* 5–10.

Richardson, V. (1994b). *Teacher change and the staff development process: A case in reading instruction.* New York: Teachers College Press.

Santa Barbara Classroom Discourse Group [Dixon, C., de la Cruz, E., Green, J., Lin, L., & Brandts, L.]. (1992). Do you see what we see? The referential and intertextual nature of classroom life. *Journal of Classroom Interaction, 27,* 29–36.

Shepard, L. A. (1991). Negative policies for deal with diversity: When does assessment and diagnosis turn into sorting and segregation. In E. F. Hiebert (Ed.), *Literacy for a diverse society: Perspectives, practices, and policies* (pp. 279–298). New York: Teachers College Press.

Shulman, J. H. (1990). Now you see them, now you don't: Anonymity versus visibility in case studies of teachers. *Educational Researcher, 19,* 11–15.

Shuy, R. (1988). Identifying dimensions of classroom language. In J. L. Green & J. O. Harker (Eds.), *Multiple perspective analyses of classroom discourse* (pp. 115–134). Norwood, NJ: Ablex.

Sinclair, J. M., & Coulthard, R. M. (1975). *Towards an analysis of discourse.* London: Oxford University Press.

Stenhouse, L. (1985). *Research as a basis for teaching.* London: Heinemann.

Swales, J. M. (1990). *Genre analysis: English in academic and research settings.* Cambridge: MIT Press.

Tannen, D. (1993). What's in a frame? Surface evidence for underlying expectations. In D. Tannen (Ed.), *Framing in discourse* (pp. 14–56). New York: Oxford University Press.

Turner, V. W. (1957). *Schism and continuity in an African society: A study of Ndembu village life.* Manchester, England: Manchester University Press.

Van Maanen, J. (1988). *Tales of the field: On writing ethnography.* Chicago: University of Chicago Press.

Vygotsky, L. S. (1962). *Thought and language.* Cambridge, MA: MIT Press.

Vygotsky, L. S. (1978). *Mind in society: The development of higher psychological processes.* Cambridge, England: Cambridge University Press

Wells, G. (1986). *The meaning makers: Children learning language and using language to learn.* Portsmouth, NH: Heinemann.

Wells, G. (1990). Talk about text: Where literacy is learned and taught. *Curriculum Inquiry, 20,* 369–405.

Wells, G. (1993). Reevaluating the IRF sequence: A proposal for the articulation of theories of activity and discourse for the analysis of teaching and learning in the classroom. *Linguistics and Education, 5,* 1–37.

Wells, G. (1994a). The complimentary contributions of Halliday and Vygotsky to a "language-based theory of learning." *Linguistics and Education, 6,* 41–90.

Wells, G. (1994b). *Changing schools from within: Creating communities of inquiry.* Portsmouth, NH: Heinemann.

Wells, G. (1998). Some questions about direct instruction: Why? To whom? How? And when? *Language Arts, 76,* 27–35.

Wells, G., & Chang-Wells, G. L. (1992). *Constructing knowledge together: Classrooms as centers of inquiry and literacy.* Portsmouth, NH: Heinemann.

Wertsch, J. V. (1991). *Voices of the mind: A sociocultural approach to mediated action.* Cambridge, MA: Harvard University Press.

Willinsky, J. (1990). *The New Literacy: Redefining reading and writing in the schools*. New York: Routledge.

Wolcott, H. F. (1990). *Writing up qualitative research*. Newbury Park, CA: Sage.

Young, R. (1992). *Critical theory and classroom talk*. Clevedon, England: Multilingual Matters.

Part I

Writing Curriculum Genres

Three of the teacher researcher's inquiries primarily focused on writing.

In chapter 2, university researchers, Jane Liao and Dian Ruben, collaborated with teacher researcher, Pamela Wolfer, to describe Pam's venture to create contexts in which her first graders' would "come to voice" in writing, but would also learn "skills." Many of her emergent-literacy learners had great doubts about their abilities to become authors at the beginning of the year. After some troublesome first starts, Pam created her own version of a daily writing-workshop curriculum genre. One of the longest classroom activities to be investigated by our project, it consisted by three subcurriculum genres—teacher-led minilessons; a block of time in which students did their writing and when Pam had one-on-one conferences; and student-led sharetimes. There were ongoing difficulties along with the successes. In the chapter, the authors attempt to outline both as they illustrate how Pam enacted the various activities of this complex curriculum genre.

In chapter 3, the focus is on the writing in a second-grade bilingual classroom taught by teacher–researcher Sarah Cohen. The impetus of Sarah's inquiry began early in the year. In explaining the purpose of the writing conferences she would be having with them, she had referred to her students as authors. One of them responded, "Pero, nosotros no somos autores!" (But, we are not authors!). In the chapter, Liliana Barro Zecker, Caitlyn Nichols, and Linda Montes worked together with Sarah to give an account of Sarah's journey to change her students' views about themselves as writers. An important emphasis in Sarah's plans was to have children think and talk about the meanings of their texts. In this process, however, she struggled with the "right measure" of explanation in author's chair and minilesson sessions—especially how and in what ways she should be explicit in fostering revision.

The final chapter in this section centers on writing in the eighth grade. Like Pam, teacher–researcher Michael Rassel is concerned with voice.

Here, the inquiry involves exploring how he could foster his students' voice in their informational research reports. Dian Ruben, Jane Liao, and Michael collaborate to describe his efforts in various writing workshop activities or subcurriculum genres—minilessons, individual teacher–student conferences, and whole-class sharing. All were used by Michael to encourage these eighth graders (many of whom are second-language learners) to write reports that were not plagiarized versions of the resources they used for their research, but instead were texts that "sounded like them."

All three chapters, then, cover similar, but yet different, dimensions of writing. All of the three teacher researchers attempted to create contexts in which students' own meanings were paramount. At the same time, all had high expectations for their students' writing. They tried strategies that enabled students to see ways that they could make their texts more effective and more coherent. In doing so, all of the students—the first and second graders, as well as the older eighth graders—also became more confident authors.

Chapter 2

Creating a Writing Workshop in First Grade: How to Teach Literacy "Skills" *and* Help Children "Come to Voice"

Jane Liao

Dian Ruben

Pamela Wolfer

Bakhtin (1981) argued that life and consciousness are filled with a living language that is populated by the words of others:

> The word in language is half someone else's. It becomes "one's own" only when the speaker populates it with his [sic] own intention, his [sic] own accent, when he [sic] appropriates the word, adapting it for his [sic] own semantic and expressive intention. ... Language is not a neutral medium that passes freely and easily into the private property of the speaker's intentions. ... Expropriating it, forcing it to one's own intentions and accents, is a difficult and complicated process. (pp. 293–294)

The introduction chapter of the book provides the theoretical and methodological background for the larger collaborative school–university action-research project and this chapter about Pam's inquiry on writing. See also the last chapter, which further discusses the implications of Pam's inquiry—as well as those of the other teacher researchers.

Bakhtin used the notion of *voice*, a "speaking consciousness," to emphasize that language reflects a point of view. Voice always enacts particular social values by addressing—or being in dialogue with—other voices (Burbules, 1993; Cazden, 1992; Nystrand, 1986, 1987; Nystrand & Wiemelt, 1991; Wertsch, 1991). Helping children, many of whom had very limited literacy understandings and were unsure about their abilities to be writers, "come to voice" in writing was an important goal of Pam's inquiry. However, she also wanted her 28 first-grade students to learn literacy skills. This chapter documents the major facets of Pam's two aims in her study.

Pam: A major question of mine was: "How do you make it okay in school to experiment with your choices and speak your thoughts?" I wanted to figure out how to teach writing so that the children would enjoy it, to allow students to bring their personal experiences into our classroom. I wanted their writing to become "theirs," where they would be able to share personal feelings that would not only educate me but also others in the room. But, my students this year seemed immature developmentally so I also felt that I needed to see how I could incorporate skills into whatever I came up with.

Pam's early trials to teach writing in this way tended to not be very successful. It was only when she began to implement her own version of a process-approach writing workshop (Calkins, 1986, 1994; Graves, 1983) that she began to find ways to accomplish the goals of her inquiry. We focused mainly on this latter venture because it occurred during most of the year.

Finding a way to support and scaffold individual voices while making room for many voices is a challenge (Gallas, 1994; Gutierrez, Rymes, & Larson, 1995). As Dyson (1989) noted, although young children may understand the many social functions that writing might serve in a general way, children may not necessarily understand or appreciate specifically how print might mediate between them and other people. Thus, creating this awareness and developing ways to wield the symbolic tools for writing texts (Dyson, 1993) represented a major challenge for Pam's first-grade emergent learners because they were so unsure about becoming writers.

Pam began with ideas from Fisher (1991) and saw the structure of this curriculum genre as a useful vehicle with which she might scaffold her students' voices in writing, and at the same time address their attempts to encode texts to be shared with others in the classroom community. In this context, children are learning to "mean" in writing (Christie, 1987). Thus, throughout her inquiry, an authentic concern for audience (Rowe, 1989) and for discovering ways to promote the teaching and learning of writing in a collaborative manner were paramount. Certain values were assigned in the writing process that developed, within which children's identities as writers were created (MacGillivray, 1994).

The structure of Pam's 1-hour workshop consisted of three major sub-curriculum genres—*minilessons*, the students' actual *writing period*, where Pam also met with individual students in conferences, and *sharetime*, an author's chair experience where children offered their texts for review and discussion. In the first section, we cover minilessons and sharetime. The next section focuses on the nature of Pam's conference interactions with students about their writing. Children were left alone, to draw and write their books for most of the period while she met individually with others. During this time, they socialized and borrowed materials from each other, shared ideas for stories and texts, and reread their texts to their peers. The third section focuses on these latter experiences, illustrating some of the ways children collaborated in reading their published books.

CREATING A WRITING WORKSHOP FOR FIRST GRADERS

Despite Pam's misgivings about the maturity of her students, she constructed a writing workshop that allowed for a great deal of student autonomy, requiring them to be responsible for doing work independent of continuous, direct, teacher supervision. Also, students wrote about their own ideas and experiences instead of using teacher-generated topics. Instruction about phonics skills and writing mechanics and conventions was conducted primarily during Pam's one-to-one conferences with the children, although she sometimes did whole-class minilessons on these issues. The minilessons were teacher directed, and although she was a participant in sharetime, it was mostly a student-directed routine.

Minilessons

Pam's whole-class minilessons usually began each workshop. Although Pam had high expectations for her students, she introduced the different experiences comprising the writing process very gradually, upping the ante slowly. When children moved beyond just drawing pictures and were all finally producing some approximation of connected discourse, Pam began (from January through April) to go over concepts of the writing process—prewriting (or brainstorming as Pam called it with the children), writing drafts, conferencing, revising, editing, publishing, and sharing written work. She frequently used children's literature or students' writing to clarify or explain these ideas.

Keeping on a Main Topic

Example 1 illustrates one of Pam's content minilessons, in which she tried to explain the importance of the concept of a main topic or theme in their texts. She began the minilesson by quickly reading aloud a book; then she had children find the main idea(s) of the story. She connected this idea of theme or main topic with the use of a type of brainstorming activity—webbing. She hoped that children might create a web before they began writing or drawing their books, thereby helping them to produce texts that would be more coherent.

Example 1

1	Pam:	During writing workshop, when I come around to conference and to talk about your stories, I've been noticing that a *lot* of us need to learn to stay on the same topic. That means to write about the same idea or to write about just one thing or give us lots of information to revolve our story about one idea. Instead of talking about "I went to the store, I went to the park, I went to my friend's house," I want you to take just one of those ideas and write *all* about it.

....

2	Pam:	Maybe, [you would pick] "I went to the park" and talk about everything you did at the park and what you saw at the park. I'm going to read a story here. We'll talk more about our own writing in a minute. But I'm going to read a story and I want you to think about the *one thing* that this story is all about. Okay? I want you to think and tell me what the *main idea* or *what the main topic* that this story is written about.

....

		[Pam quickly reads the book and there is a short discussion where she encourages students to come up with the main topic or theme of the book. Children offer quite appropriate ideas, and Pam accepts most of them.]
3	Pam:	[R]ight now I want to talk about how to write a story all about one idea. And I want to show you a way that can help you. A lot of us——a lot of us write stories about going to the park. Very many of us write stories about going to the park. So we're going to show you a way to write a story all about the park … and ways to help you think of lots of ideas about the park. I'm going to write the word "park" in the middle of my page. #[writing on paper on an easel]#
4	Cs:	#[Read off the letters P A R K as Pam writes them.]#
5	Pam:	And I'm going to circle it. This is a getting ready page. It's a brainstorming page where we think of all of our ideas before we start writing our book. We want to write a story all about the park. I write the word "park" on the paper. Who can tell me something about the park that might go into a story about a park? Clarissa.
6	Clari.:	Play.
7	Pam:	[writing the word] Okay, you play in the park. [then looks at Ronnie to let her know she can have a turn to speak]
8	Ronnie:	You can walk your dog.
9	Pam:	You can walk your dog in the park.
10	Lena:	You can ride your bike in the park.
11	Pam:	[writing] You can ride your bike. Karen?

12	Karen:	Rub your cat.
13	Pam:	Okay, you can bring your cat to the park. [writes]
14	Cf:	And pet it.
15	Pam:	And pet your cat there.
16	Julissa:	(...) and you can play with the swings.
17	Pam:	Okay there are swings you can play on. [writes]
....		[This discussion continues. Children mention playing their radios, slides, roller skates, ice skating, bringing a ball and a bat, playing basketball, baseball, walkie talkies, and playground wheel. Several children have their hands raised and seem very eager to add their comments. Pam comments that now she will call on those who haven't said anything yet. Most of the children put their hands down. Pam calls on Ana.]
18	Ana:	You can eat.
19	Pam:	Oh, that's a good one. You can eat, you can have a picnic. You can have a picnic. [pointing in a circular motion at the brainstormed ideas written on the paper] All of these things we listed on our paper have to do with the park. So, if we talk about any of these things that have to do with the park, then we will be talking about just the park. Should we talk about going to the store here?
20	Cs:	No.
21	Pam:	So that won't be in our story. That might be a separate story. {Videotape, 03/14/95}

This minilesson was designed to guide children to stay on the same topic. Pam first helped them to identify the main topic of a book she quickly read to them, and then she and the students created a web together about the park topic. Although this was a teacher-directed routine, it was collaborative because she scaffolded students' own contributions about the park to promote the concept she wanted to illustrate. Students' ideas encompassed a range of activities or "things that have to do with the park." Pam accepted all of these possibilities, sometimes extending them as she wrote them down around the "park" web center. At the end she contrasted these things at the park with going to the store, again reinforcing the concept that each individual text should revolve around one main topic.

Pam had another minilesson using a web, this time engaging and guiding Alberto to construct one. He had a written a version of a *bed-to-bed* text (Fletcher, 1993), listing all of the places he went—to school, to the park, to home in a day from rising to bedtime—and Pam asked him to pick one of these places on which to focus (which ended up being the topic, park, again). Pam never really insisted that children make webs, but she continued to direct their attention to the idea of a main topic in their texts when she conferenced with them. (However, see next section for a discussion where Pam and Ana worked on a web.) The previous minilesson and her others were always based on Pam's ongoing assessments of her children's writing.

Sharetime

Although the entire class gathered at the rug during sharetime and the students were all under Pam's watchful eye, each author who shared was given almost full responsibility for conducting the proceedings while he or she was in the author's chair. Initially, children signed up on a sharetime list, but when Pam noted that the same children signed up and that some of them did not really have anything substantial to share, she began to select who would participate. However, beyond choosing the writers who would share or directing misbehaving children on where or how to sit quietly, Pam did not lead the sharetime. She joined the children on the rug as a member of the audience.

Consequently, children's voices dominated sharetime; these interactions were primarily between the authors and their classmates. This was made possible, however, by the way Pam had set up rules for this subgenre curriculum genre: Two or three authors read their work. After a text (or partial draft) was completely read, the illustrations were shown. Children raised their hands if they wanted to comment or ask questions about an author's work, and the writer could select three of them for responses. Applause followed after this third exchange. Pam did join in by commenting about a particular author's writing, but this was usually to highlight or further extend the meanings that the children had brought up.

Alan's Spider Story

Both author and audience benefited from these sharetimes, which can be seen in Alan's sharing of his story, *I See a Spider,* during two separate sharetimes. Pam asked him to read his rough draft version in March and then had him share the published version of his book in April. Each time, Alan's story entertained his classmates and also initiated discussions about various content issues. Example 2A provides an excerpt of the initial sharetime.

Example 2A

1	Alan:	*I SEE A SPIDER.* I SEEN A SPIDER. HIS NAME IS JOHN.
2	Cs:	[giggling]
3	Cm:	What's so funny?

4	Cf:	A spider named John.
5	Alan:	I SEEN A SPIDER. HE WAS JOHN.

....

6	Alan:	JOHN IS MY PET. JOHN AND ME PLAY HIDE AND GO SEEK.
7	Cs:	[giggles from several children]
8	Alan:	I FEED JOHN WITH FLIES.
9	Cs:	[laughter from audience]
10	Cm:	Spiders don't like flies!
11	Alan:	They——they suck flies. So that's why I give him flies. I BOUGHT JOHN. THE END.
....		[Alan shows the pictures he drew to accompany the story. There is some consternation on the part of the other children about how tiny his pictures are. Alan defends them by saying that the picture seems small to them because "It was too far." Pam brings them back to the sharetime structure by asking Alan if he is ready for questions. The first question is asked by Manuel.]
12	Manuel:	Was your spider a daddy longlegs?
13	Alan:	Huh?
14	Manuel:	Was your spider a daddy longlegs?
15	Alberto:	What?
16	Alan:	[shakes his head negatively]
17	Pam:	What kind of spider was it then, Alan?
18	Alberto:	[interrupting] Alan, let me see up the pictures, *si*?
19	Pam:	*Shhh!* Alberto! Let Alan think of the question! Alan, what kind of spider was John?
20	Cf:	A nice (...).
21	Alan:	A nice spider!
22	Pam:	A nice spider. Do you know what type of spider he was though?
23	Alan:	[nods, but does not answer]
24	Cs:	[a group in front trying to clarify the question for Alan] Color! What kind? Kind!
25	Pam:	What kind? What type of spider was he?
26	Alberto:	[whispering to Alan] Tarantula? (...) a tarantula spider.
27	Alan:	[to Pam and class] A tarantula spider. {Video, 03/23/95}

Children were amused about several aspects of Alan's story—that he named the spider John, that they played hide-and-go-seek, and that Alan fed him flies. Alan usually had very small, precise illustrations, about which the children complained, mostly here because they were so interested and delighted in John and the events about him.

In line 12, Manuel, asked about what kind of spider John was, "Was it a daddy long-legs?" When Alan nodded negatively, Pam followed up on the question (in line 17). Alberto interrupted to ask to see the pictures again, but Pam insisted that Alan needed time to think about the question. In line 20, someone offered "nice" as a possibility, which Pam accepted, but still further challenged Alan to consider the *type* of spider it was. Other children in the front near him chimed in to encourage him to respond, and then Alberto whispered a possibility to him, "tarantula." Alan then accepted that idea by responding that it was indeed a tarantula spider.

In April, Alan's rereading of his story, now published, led to new questions about some of its events. Example 2B began after Alan read and showed the pictures of his book, and chose Victor for comments.

Example 2B

1	Alan:	Victor.
2	Victor:	Why did you catch John?
3	Alan:	I didn't catch him!
....		
4	Alan:	I bought John. I didn't grab him. If I grab him then he'll be bad to me ....
....		
5	Cm:	How you bought John?
6	Alan:	I went to the store——the <department> store, and I bought John.
7	Cm:	With what money?
8	Alan:	I had money. [opens his book looking for a picture] I just forgot to make [draw] the money.
		{Videotape, 04/11/95}

In this second sharetime, students wanted to know how Alan obtained the spider, and Alan responded that he bought John, further explaining that if he grabbed him, he might hurt ("be bad to") him. Further questions centered about how he bought the spider, and in line 8, Alan, in looking at his illustrations again, states that he forgot to include the money in his pictures.

Thus, in both occasions of sharetime, Alan gained useful feedback to make his text better, but, in getting help from other readers and writers in the classroom community about a particular text, he and his classmates all learned what was involved in crafting texts that were interesting and had important information included in them.

Considering Story Content, Not Just Pictures. Examples 2A and 2B clearly illustrate successful sharetimes. However, this does not mean that they always worked so smoothly. For example, earlier Pam had great difficulties in getting students to address the content of the students' texts when they wanted mostly to attend to their pictures. In January, as a preface to Clarissa's sharing her story about playing Power Rangers with her brother, Pam urged students, "Remember, think about the *story* and what questions you can ask about the *story*." {Videotape, 01/24/95} However, after Clarissa read her text, children were still adamant about asking questions about the pictures, which Pam stopped by interjecting questions of her own, "How many were you playing with, Clarissa? ... You were playing with six people? ... You're going to add on and draw it tomorrow?" {Videotape, 01/24/95} Thus, Pam tried to tell them that they should be concerned with the message of their writing *first,* then focus on illustrations.

In this same sharetime, right after Clarissa shared, Leon read a work in progress, also a story about Power Rangers. Again, children persisted in concentrating on Leon's pictures—namely, that the lead character in Leon's story was missing from a drawing of the "command center."

Example 3

1	Cm:	Why he ain't there?
2	Leon:	He's inside.
3	Pam:	Ah, for some of us who don't know what the command center is, are you going to tell us #a little about it in your story?#
4	Cs:	#I know! I know!#
5	Pam:	Excuse me, some people might not know.
6	Cs:	I do!
7	Pam:	Okay, thank you, Leon. {Videotape, 01/24/95}

Once again, Pam stressed the need to address the message aspects of a text by showing how questions about the drawings could be further developed into questions about the content of the story. When she was interrupted by many students stating that they knew what a command center was, she tried to reestablish the rationale for why Leon needed to include it in line 5. Unfortunately, her point seemed to be lost on many of the children. They continued to assert their knowledge about the setting of Leon's story even though he did not include these details because they were so familiar with the popular TV show from which Leon took his characters and settings.

Consequently, the journey in creating the sharetimes depicted in Examples 2A and 2B was sometimes an arduous one, fraught with rocky patches to overcome. Nevertheless, these sharetime opportunities emphasized the importance of the meanings of children's texts and how they needed to be expressed for an audience (MacGillivray, 1994). Despite the fact that many students' encoding efforts were quite still meager, they developed capabilities to write with confidence and voice. Alan, for example, who was extremely prolific and imaginative in the topics about which he wrote, had lots of trouble in recalling the accurate shapes of the letters he needed to spell his wordings. The sharetimes also modeled how they might help each other during the actual writing time when Pam was busy conferencing with individual authors.

Pam: I really had trouble in getting them to pay more attention to the content of their texts in sharetime. What I think finally seem to make a difference was when I began to stress the "what, when, where, how, and why" questions of their writing. I did that in a couple of minilessons. They did use these ideas first by focusing on the pictures, but then after a couple of weeks I started getting really good questions and comments on the content.

There was another change of extra motivation in them regarding writing around April or so. This was when I changed the structure of the whole writing workshop time by putting the sharetime right after the minilessons. This was accidental in the beginning, that is, it had no theoretical rationale at the time. I was just trying to deal with practical issues—maybe kids were being taken out to have their hearing checked or doing make-ups on the Iowas [standardized tests]. I don't remember exactly as to the exact reason. I switched it because I wanted to make sure it got done every day. It was so really important to them because I might have promised they could share on some day and they would miss it because they were out of the room then. I felt that if they missed the writing part of the workshop it wasn't that as bad for them. Thus, the rationale came after the fact when I noticed how it came out better. The rationale started out to be that having the sharetime after the minilesson made it that they knew what to do now. They were "all there" and more focused. They were more motivated in the writing part of the workshop then. "This guy just got his book published and that was really cool, so now I want to get mine done and published to share, too." It was more etched in their minds for that writing session instead of writing until the next day.

PAM'S CONFERENCES WITH EMERGENT WRITERS: LEARNING HOW TO SCAFFOLD "VOICE" AND "SKILLS"

Sandwiched between teacher-directed minilessons and student-led sharetimes was children's actual writing time, during which Pam conducted her

one-on-one conferences (except when she switched the time for sharetime
—see previous). As already indicated, it was only when Pam began to set up
the writing workshop and had opportunities to have individual interactions
with children about their own writing that her initial goals in her inquiry began to reach fruition. To show this contrast, we have included excerpts—Examples 4A and 4B—from Pam's work with Julissa.

Conferencing with Julissa

In January, Pam had began a Community thematic unit and both sets of
Julissa's writings had to do with neighborhood. In Example 4A, Pam wrote
a story-starter assignment on the board. Two sentences on the board and
children were to copy them and then complete them with their own ideas:

My neighborhood is special because ——————.

My neighborhood is fun because ——————.

Before the onset of Example 4A, Julissa had already written her version
of the first sentence starter when Pam came by. When Julissa was unable to
read the word "neighborhood" in her sentence, Pam and Julissa went back
and forth from the between-the-board sentence and Julissa's sentence at
her desk. They returned to Julissa's desk as Example 4A began:

Example 4A

1	Pam:	What word doesn't belong?
2	Julissa:	[Points to the word "neighborhood."]
3	Pam:	[rereading what Julissa had written.] I LOVE THE MY NEIGH-BORHOOD IS SPECIAL. Do you want to write this? What word doesn't belong?
4	Julissa:	[Points to "is."]
5	Pam:	What word doesn't belong? I LOVE THE MY NEIGHBORHOOD IS SPECIAL. Does that make sense?
6	Julissa:	[Points to the word "neighborhood."]
7	Pam:	I LOVE THE MY NEIGHBORHOOD IS SPECIAL. What word doesn't belong? Does "love" belong?
8	Julissa:	[Shakes her head "no."]
9	Pam:	I LOVE THE MY NEIGHBORHOOD IS SPECIAL. How about the word "my"?
....		[Other children interrupt with questions and then Pam returns to working with Julissa.]

10	Pam:	How about the word "my"? I LOVE THE MY NEIGHBORHOOD IS SPECIAL.
11	Julissa:	[Continues to point to "neighborhood."]
12	Pam:	That stays. [referring to "neighborhood," which she underlines] That is a whole word.
		{Fieldnotes, 01/17/95}

At the end of the session (not included here) Pam erased both "is special" and "my" from Julissa's writing, telling her that they "don't belong." When she left her chair next to Julissa's desk, Pam told Jane how frustrating the interaction was, and when she left, Julissa looked up and said, "I don't know how to do this."

Thus, although Pam was well meaning in her attempts to link her students' communities and real-life experiences with reading and writing activities in the classroom, the rigid boundaries of the sentence-starter assignment resulted in hindering both a student's expression of her experience and a teacher's openness to value of what the student did know.

Pam's interactions during the conferences with children during the writing workshop setting were radically different. Late in February, students were getting accustomed to the routines of this curriculum genre. Pam gave them a great deal more autonomy in the topics they could write about, and they wrote and began their stories and texts with their own sentences. Some of the students' anxieties about writing persisted, and Julissa was one of those who frequently insisted that she could not read or spell. However, Pam encouraged them to use invented spelling to express their ideas during the drafting process. Example 4B shows another Pam–Julissa interaction, but this time Pam is very supportive of Julissa's efforts.

Example 4B

1	Pam:	What is the main thing the story is about?
2	Julissa:	My dad told me to buy food. [reading from her text] I BOUGHT VEGETABLES AND COOKIES. I BUY SOME FLOWERS. I BUY SOME MILK. I SAW GENNA AT THE STORE. I SAW RONNIE. I SAW ALBERTO. I SAW ELENNA.
3	Pam:	OK and so that's the end. I loved the beginning.
....		[At Pam's request, Julissa rereads the first part about the grocery shopping.]
4	Pam:	Who did you buy the flowers for?
5	Julissa:	For my mother.
6	Pam:	Could you tell us that maybe on this page? On the next page? Could you tell us that?

7	Julissa:	[nods slightly]
8	Pam:	Yeah? Do you think we could add a page here and you can write who you bought the flowers for? And what would you say? How would you write it?
....		[With Pam's help, Julissa orally creates: "We bought flowers for our mother." Pam begins to help Julissa figure out how to spell this addition to her text. Julissa has written "We" and is beginning to tackle "bought."]
9	Pam:	How do you spell "bought" here? Okay, now you're writing the word "bought," right? [pointing to Julissa's already spelled version of the word in her text] This is the word "bought." I want you to write that word right here [referring to her new sentence]. That's how you spelled "bought" before. That's how you're going to spell "bought" now. Can you write that down?
10	Julissa:	[writes down the word, using her previous spelling]
11	Pam:	Unhuh. Okay, let's read it. [pointing to the two words written so far, and then to the next space]
12	Julissa:	WE BOUGHT ... ... flowers.
13	Pam:	Okay. Where did you write "flowers" before?
14	Julissa:	[Points to the word in her text.]
15	Pam:	Okay. If you wrote it like that before, it's going to be spelled and——you're going to use the same letters you used there.
16	Julissa:	[Adds "flowers" to her sentence: "We boutt Flrs. ... "]
		{Videotape, 03/22/95}

When Pam addressed the message or content of her text, Julissa was quite able to answer Pam's question about it and then to reread it. After Pam favorably responded to the first part of her story and had Julissa reread it once more, Pam tried to challenge Julissa to revise it by writing more about the person the flowers were for (lines 7 & 9). Pam's question, "Can you tell us that?", emphasizes the audience dimension of writing (MacGillivray, 1994; Rowe, 1989), which resulted in Julissa creating a new sentence to add to her text, "We bought flowers for our mother." During the rest of the conference, Pam showed Julissa that she could easily accomplish this revision because she already wrote reasonable invented-spelling approximations for "bought" and "flowers" in her preceding text. With Pam's help, Julissa learned how to apply this new strategy to extend the meaning of her text.

In this example, Julissa looked competent and confident. This was *her* text, and Pam was supportive of her efforts. Julissa was quite able to read her writing this time and was also willing to revise it, with Pam's help. In this case, in contrast to the story-starter experience in Example 4A, both Julissa and Pam thought Julissa's writing made sense.

Conferencing with Jon, Karen, and Ana

Pam's conferences with children focused primarily on developing the content or meanings of their writing by eliciting more details about their topics. If children were hesitant to start writing, she reminded them that the first part of the process of writing would be for them to try to sound out their words themselves. She told them that after they had done so, she would meet with them to help them—that is, during the revising or editing of their writing. During this part of the workshop structure, Pam indicated over and over that they could write without her presence. In addition, in her talk with them during conferences, she showed that she valued the message over the mechanics of their writing.

Pam's conference with Jon illustrates how she set the expectation that children can give voice to their experiences in writing. Here she scaffolded Jon's telling of his story, but again did not offer him guidance about spelling.

Example 5

1	Jon:	I'm almost done with this one.
2	Pam:	Okay. Do you have the story written down in this book?
3	Jon:	I'm not——I did the pictures but I'm (... ...) I'm gonna write this.
4	Pam:	Okay. So, what do you need me here for? What——What's....
5	Jon:	To write. [looking at Pam]
6	Pam:	To write. What do you——what are we supposed to do first? We're supposed to sound ... ... (waits for Jon to finish his sentence)
7	Jon:	Sound the letters out.
8	Pam:	Sound them out first and get one story. Do you want to tell me ... a little about what it's going to be and then you're going to sound them out on your own, right?
9	Jon:	Yeah. [softly]
10	Pam:	And then we're going to meet again. [with a tone of reassurance]
11	Jon:	Yep. [softly with a very slight nod]
12	Pam:	Why don't you tell me about——your own words——tell me what the story is going to be about?
13	Jon:	Okay. My brother (...) to his cousins' house because (...).
14	Pam:	Okay. And what else happened? Does anything else happen when you're following him?
15	Jon:	No.

16	Pam:	No?
17	Jon:	He already know.
18	Pam:	Oh, he knew you were following. Um … … What's your cousin's name?
19	Jon:	Mario.
20	Pam:	Mario? So anything else you can tell me? What else can you tell me?
....		[Jon tells Pam that he and his brother went to see his cousin's baby. Pam asks more questions that help Jon expand and elaborate on the oral text he will be writing.]
21	Pam:	You just told me a wonderful story. And what would be a good title that would explain, that would kind of sum that up?
22	Jon:	(looks up) "I" (...)——"I followed my brother."
23	Pam:	(...) "I followed my brother." [leaning very close to Jon to hear him]
24	Jon:	(...) "I went to my cousin's house."
25	Pam:	"I followed my brother" and "I went to my cousin's house." Those are two choices, right?
26	Jon:	Yeah.
27	Pam:	Okay, can you think of another choice?
28	Jon:	[shakes his head no]
29	Pam:	Which do you like better? "I followed my brother" or "I went to my cousin's house"? Which title do you like better?
30	Jon:	"I followed my brother."
31	Pam:	Okay, then I think that will be an okay title.
32	Jon:	I already wrote it. [smiling slightly and looking down at his book]
33	Pam:	Oh! I didn't know you already wrote it. So you already had the title.
34	Jon:	Yeah. [nodding]
35	Pam:	Are you ready to tell that whole story in words now?
36	Jon:	Yeah I'm <ready>.
37	Pam:	Next time we meet I'll be happy to read it. {Videotape, 02/23/95}

Jon had finished his illustrations for his book, but had not written words as yet. Jon seemed to want Pam to help on the encoding at first, but she reiterated the "rule" that "you're going to sound them out on your own … and then we're going to meet again." She spent her conference time helping him orally construct his text about following his brother to a cousin's house to see his new baby. Through Pam's questions for details and elaborations, Jon crafted a coherent recount of that experience. Afterwards, beginning on line 21, she got him to come up with a title to sum it up, which apparently he had already written (line 32). At the end, both Pam and Jon agreed that he was now "ready to tell that whole story in words now," and Pam promised that she would be happy to read it the next time they met.

Pam did address writing conventions in conferences, but she balanced that with her supporting the expression of children's voice. Moreover, how this balance was realized in conferences was very individualized based on her evaluation of a child's needs. Pam kept extensive assessment notes regarding children's writing during her conferences and her weekly review of their writing folders.

Typically, with students who were finished with a draft of their books, Pam had them reread what they wrote and monitored it to see if the sentences made sense. If anything was to be added to the text, Pam might or might not remain to assist the child with sounding out the words and forming sentences (see again Example 4B as an occasion where she did help). For Karen, Pam did not make any reference with spelling concerns, but showed her how to go over her text to revise or edit.

Example 6

1 Pam: [Pam takes notes as she leans close to Karen to listen to her reading.]

2 Karen: [rereading a page that says, "We plat togat tob" (We play together today)] (... ...).

3 Pam: I don't understand this. Are those words that you're saying?

4 Karen: (... ...). [Apparently, she is reading, "We *got* together today." See next.]

5 Pam: Okay, why don't you change it?

6 Karen: [erases "plat" and replaces it with "got"]

7 Pam: Okay.

8 Karen: [starts reading another part of her text: "I wnt the to zoo"] (... ...).

9 Pam: Let's see. Is this the right place to put "the"?

10 Karen: [Silently reads and edits to read: "I wnt to the zoo"]

....

11 Pam: Do you think, Karen, we're ready to publish this book? Do you think that you can go over it? Read it over and do exactly as you're doing, adding words, changing.

12 Karen: [nods "yes"]

13   Pam: Wonderful. We call that revising and editing. You're doing a won-
                 derful job.
             {Fieldnotes, videotape, 02/23/95}

Here Pam showed Karen how to apply the revising and editing processes on the first part of her text, but then left her to complete the task. Spelling was not a concern in this conference.

For another student, Ana, Pam assisted in the sounding out of words, but it was embedded within another concern. This conference occurred the same day of the webbing minilesson discussed in Example 1. Ana was one of the five children who raised their hands to say that they would try to use the web for writing. Before Pam had joined her at her desk, Ana already began to write on a blank book (folded sheets of paper stapled together). She wrote "The park," which was the topic Pam used to demonstrate web-bing, and wrote her name, "by Ana," but had not written anything else. Getting Ana to use a separate sheet of paper for prewriting planning, Pam tried to have Ana visualize what she did at the park. First, Ana put a list of the friends on her web and then Pam asked about other parts of Ana's park experiences to add to that web. When they got to the part where Ana con-sidered what she and her friends might do at the park, Pam helped her by exaggerating or stretching the words Ana wanted to write so Ana could hear the sounds and put down letters for them—first "picnic," then "sand-wich." Pam continued to ask Ana other things she might eat at the picnic and Ana added names of foods. Ana often indicated that she wanted more help with spelling, but Pam responded that she did not need to be overly concerned with the spelling at this time. "We can always change the spell-ing later. This is just the list." {Videotape, 03/14/95}

Ana's web became quite complex—after the picnic and food, she told of the activities (e.g., freeze tag) that she and her friends would be engaged in. Then Pam helped Ana put numbers on the things that were included on the web to indicate the order in which these would be written down in her actual drafting. "First you're going to tell us who you go with. Then you're going to tell us all about what you eat and do on your picnic. ..." Here, be-cause Pam's goal of the conference was to help Ana organize her written work by creating a web, and because Ana needed assistance on sounding out words to complete that task, Pam assisted her in doing so. Pam did not insist on conventional spellings, but encouraged Ana to use her current knowledge of letter–sound relationships to spell the words she needed.

Summary

Through these one-to-one conferences (and the other writing workshop experiences) Julissa, Jon, Karen, Ana, and the other students, who at the beginning of the year were reluctant writers, became confident in developing the symbolic tools "to mean" in writing. Pam's ways of interacting in these conferences enabled her to balance teaching the skills *and* helping children come to voice.

Pam: I think that I was successful in my conferences with children because I took notes on them and other aspects of their writing, but this was hard for me—how to document. I really tried to make myself see everybody every week. Sometimes a kid might be absent when I had visited his or her table for conferences, but I'd look at the end of the week and say to myself, "Who do I want to get to first next week?" Also, I looked at their folders weekly. If I saw someone who had three pieces in there, but never finished any of them, then those were the people I'd make sure I saw, first off, next time during the writing and conferencing period. But that was a goal of mine, to get to everybody—even if that everybody was sometimes 30 kids with children coming and going in and out of the class, and even though my conference might be only a few minutes long. I always reviewed my documentation to see where I thought kids were and had that in mind when I conferenced with them, even though I also always attempted to address the present issues they were grappling with in their writing.

STUDENT COLLABORATION: BECOMING READERS OF THEIR WRITING

That children relied on themselves and each other was necessitated by Pam's one-to-one conferencing. Although there was a "no traveling (from your desk)" rule, this was only loosely enforced because children independently went to pick up more paper, use the stapler, sharpen their pencils, copy names from the desk labels of classmates they were including in their texts, and so forth.

However, student collaboration during this part of the writing workshop was not altogether happenstance. It was Pam's view that other writers could and should help each other. She arranged students' desks (usually 4–5) together to form a table, and she encouraged them to call on these friends in the many and various aspects of writing—in choosing their topics, in helping with spelling, in coming up with ideas during drafting, and in revising their texts. As Pam explained, "You have 4 or 5 people at your table to ask about sounds or to share crayons with. ... [If you don't know words], ask the people at your table." {Fieldnotes, videotape, 02/23/95}

Thus, the social dimensions that so many argue are inherent in young children's writing (e.g., Dyson, 1989, 1993; Gallas, 1994; Himley, 1991; MacGillivray, 1994; Rowe, 1989; Schultz, 1997) were especially apparent in these peer-collaborative exchanges. Pam wanted children to converse with each other and to see each others as sources of information that could inspire and support both the message and medium aspects of their writing. This does not mean that the task of creating a classroom context that made this kind of collaboration possible was done easily. She had to continually scaffold her expectations for these young writers. For example, she reminded students about their new roles as authors during her one-to-one conferences, and during her brief daily roving visits with each group of students, before she began these conferences. In addition, there were many whole-class debriefing sessions about the ways children could help each other, as well as discussions about how they had to whisper to keep the noise level down so they could hear each other, and so forth.

As more and more children's books were published—which consisted of Pam's typing their texts on the computer, using conventional spelling and punctuation, and assembling them as books that the children illustrated—writing time also included time for reading. The young writers more often sought to read and reread each other's books, sometimes wandering over to the table in the back of the room that displayed the published books. They would then frequently find the child author of the particular book they selected or asked another classmate for assistance in reading the book. Our last two examples illustrate the collaborative nature of these interactions.

Coming to Voice in Reading, Too

In the beginning of first example, Leon was about to read a book he had written, *The Rainbow,* to a group of his friends. However, as he began to read it, he realized that some of the pages were out of order. As he sorted out this book problem, Ana decided to read another book written by Leon called *Halloween.*

Example 7A

1	Leon:	[Busy rearranging his *The Rainbow* book pages.]
2	Ana:	I'll read first. I'll read first. *HALLOWEEN* BY LEON [LAST NAME]. [turns the page] ILLUSTRATED BY LEON [LAST NAME]. [turns the page] HALLOWEEN. IT WAS ... <THE> BEST DAY. I——I GET A LOT OF CANDY. MY SISTER SHE WAS A PUMPKIN HEAD. [hesitating briefly after enunciating each word, turning frequently to Leon]
3	Leon:	[Smiles back at Ana and picks up the microphone on the table so it is closer to her.]
4	Manuel and Cf1:	[move closer to see the pictures of the book]
5	Ana:	I GOT——I GOT TO EAT ALL MY ... [pointing to the word in the book] CANDY. [now pointing to each word as she reads] MY

		SISTER GOT THE MOST CANDY. HALLOWEEN MY SISTER WAS A PUMPKIN HEAD AND I WAS um....
6	Leon:	BATMAN.
7	Ana:	BATMAN. IT WAS THE BEST DAY IN MY LIFE. [turns page] HALLOWEEN. IT WAS THE BEST DAY. THIS IS THE END. {Videotape, 05/10/95}

Ana was almost an independent reader of this book written by Leon, needing his assistance only on "Batman." Thus, as children began to publish more and more books, they had many more opportunities to be readers—to be successful readers because they had so many to help. An author like Leon is always excited to help another enjoy his book. Moreover, when Leon finally began reading *The Rainbow* and it became clear that Leon still needed help in reading his own book, another classmate was usually available and eager to support his efforts.

Example 7B

1	Ana:	[to Leon] Read it! Read it!
2	Leon:	*THE RAINBOW.* BY LEON [LAST NAME].
3	Ana:	Read it louder.
4	Manuel:	[stands behind Leon who is seated, looking over Leon's shoulder]
5	Ana:	[pointing to the words in the book] *THE RAINBOW.*
....		[Leon seems initially to resent Ana's help, and as he tries to get the book more under his physical control, pages get loose from the binding again. They sort out the book again and how to get going on the reading. Ana once more begins by reading the title page, with Leon quietly "shadow" reading after her. Then Ana relinquishes control to Leon by turning the page, pointing to the first word, and waiting for Leon to read.]
6	Leon:	[pausing briefly before uttering each word] MY ... MOM ...
7	Ana:	WAS ...
8	Leon:	WAS IN THE HOUSE.
....		[They briefly exchange glances at each other and turn the page together.]
9	Ana:	[pointing to the word, almost whispering] SHE ...
10	Leon:	SHE ...
11	Ana:	#LOOKED OUT THE WINDOW.#
12	Leon:	#LOOKED OUT THE WINDOW.#

....		[They both turn the page and point at each word.]
13	Leon:	[begins to read this new page on his own] ME AND MY MOM SAW A RAINBOW.
14	Ana:	[turns the page]
15	Leon:	THE RAINBOW ... DIS ... A ... PPEAR.
16	Ana:	Now the pictures.
17	Leon:	[holds up the illustrations, turning the pages one by one]
18	Ana:	The end. [briefly applauds]
		{Videotape, 05/10/95}

Although Leon seemed a little peeved over Ana's initial efforts to help him, it was clear for the rest of the reading that he appreciated her help. Students were very patient with each other in reading their classmates' books. They seemed to know exactly how much assistance individual readers needed and even the very emergent readers felt confidence due to this collaboration. Thus, collaborating to promote the coming to voice in writing inherently fostered children's coming to voice in reading.

Pam: I wasn't really aware that they were doing so much reading of their own published texts during writing workshop until it happened. That is, it was more of a student initiative; I didn't really explicitly focus on this reading activity then or do anything special to get it going. I did encourage them to read their books during Sustained Silent Reading. They were in the library, where they stayed for that purpose—for us to read, along with the other books that were there. I guess they felt that it would be okay to read these books during writing time, too.

And I was happy that they read their own books. Kids seem to learn sight words easier. As writers they used words that were part of their oral vocabulary and as they read the books, they learned some really difficult words, ones that are rarely found in most first grade readers, for example. Even when they might have problems in figuring out some words, it was easier for them to get them because they had used their own language, they wrote as they spoke. And because their classmates knew their language too, they were able to be great helpers in this reading. They could help each other many more times than I could possibly have been able to.

CONCLUSIONS

Pam was successful in orchestrating a writing-workshop curriculum genre in her classroom that promoted her inquiry goals—to help her students learn skills, but more important, to write with voice. Had instruction centered solely around skill mastery, students who had limited abilities of this kind would have never been able to show their writing talents. For example, Alan would have appeared to be a child who was behind most of his classmates in even knowing how to shape letters. Yet, he was the author of books that provoked some of the richer and more interesting sharetimes, and his books were among his classmates' favorites for reading. Alan, Julissa, Karen, Jon, Leon, Ana, and the rest of their classmates learned these skills as they attended to sound–symbol relations as tools to craft meaningful texts (Dahl, 1993).

Pam made many structural changes in the various subcomponents of the writing workshop based on her careful monitoring of her students' ongoing understandings and challenges. She balanced explicit structures and information about written language for them, with flexible ways of interacting with students to best scaffold both the message and medium aspects of her students' emergent writing. Students of all ability levels were seen as experts about their own books. They had authority over the content of their texts; they also highly valued them, often choosing to reread their classmates' books in the classroom library. Students' writing—and reading—abilities developed through this process, and by the end of the year, all students were confident, motivated writers, always eager to share their texts despite having to face classmates' questions at sharetime.

New Questions and Reflections

However, because students had total control of their topics in writing, they did not all attempt a range of genres (Chapman, 1994). That is, they tended to write personal narratives or stories, so that opportunities to write reports or informational texts, for example, were lacking (Christie, 1987; Martin, 1985). Thus, how to foster the development of genres in more breadth and depth is an ongoing concern for Pam. More recently, advocates of the writing–process approach have been experimenting with *genre studies* (Calkins, 1991, 1994; Lensmire, 1994), where the whole class works on writing particular genres at different times of the year. Thus, not always following individual students' inclinations on topic or style, and not just letting genres emerge (Chapman, 1994) are both being considered.

Moreover, as Lensmire (1994) argued, children are not always so innocent in the intentions and content of their texts when they have complete power over what they write. Through their writing, some of his third graders marginalized other students and accomplished other political ends. This occurred at the first-grade level in Pam's classroom when children sometimes erased certain students' names from their texts to show their displeasure about how various social relationships were acted out. Thus, who was included or excluded in their texts was frequently part of larger issue of "who gets to play" (Paley, 1992). It was deep in the unofficial peer-governed school world that Pam did not bring up for critical examination (Dyson, 1996). Consequently, as Lensmire proposed, there is a need to have a critical revision of the writing workshop that avoids merely a romantic or expressionistic view about the texts that children create. Teachers like Pam need to think about how they might intervene and fashion the curriculum so as not to be blind to these facets of teaching.

Pam: I think it is important to point out that although children did face their classmates' hard questions about their writing, I really tried to promote author appreciation. I got this from Rassel (chapter 4, this volume)—the idea that you are always saying positive things first and having respect for the author. Although sharetime was student directed, I taught them this in the very beginning. I'd say: "That's their books and it means to them what your books mean to you. Don't ever say you don't like that. You say 'I like this.' If you don't like it, don't tell the author. You can ask questions, 'I don't understand this' or 'I think you have to say more because I don't understand it.'" So, author appreciation was really important. You clap, three people say what they liked, and then you ask questions. That's why they could take the questions, because of all of the positive things before it. So even though it is hard to face questions as a writer, it was also easier for these reasons. The questions become a positive thing, a helpful thing. That's why they were so eager to share their writing.

It is true that most of the texts children wrote were personal narratives or stories. I had so many reluctant and very emergent writers in the beginning, I just couldn't figure out how to get them to do research and write informational texts. However, I had most of these kids next year in second grade, and we did many more genres. For example, they read books on animals and they all wrote their own paper on them. In first grade, I didn't know how to do it. In second grade they also frequently wrote class newspapers that they typed themselves, which included many kinds of genres. I was able to do it better in second grade. Maybe in first grade I was also just figuring out the system.

Sometimes I obviously didn't know that there was this issue of including or not including particular kids' names in their texts. But sometimes I was aware of it, but it wasn't always negative because it brought up social issues among the children into the open. Someone might say, "How come I'm not in here?" "Because you weren't nice to me this morning." Sometimes these little things would help them actually solve them themselves. Someone would say then, "I'm sorry," and then the writer would say, "Oh okay, I'll put you in there if you are sorry." Of course, there were other times when they weren't so little, but hurtful, and I had to intervene. Most of the time, though, it got resolved easily, but I guess this is something to think more about.

In summary, although Pam's students were extremely reluctant writers at the beginning of the school year, she managed to create a context in which students could be both autonomous and collaborative. Her ways of interacting with students—finding how to balance the teaching of skills with fostering joyful experiences of writing—provided the learning needs of students of various academic abilities. They all learned to write with voice.

REFERENCES

Bakhtin, M. M. (1981). *The dialogic imagination: Four essays by M. M. Bakhtin.* M. Holquist (Ed.), M. Holquist & C. Emerson (Trans.). Austin: University of Texas Press.

Burbules, N. C. (1993). *Dialogue in teaching: Theory and practice.* New York: Teachers College Press.

Calkins, L. M. (1986). *The art of teaching writing.* Portsmouth, NH: Heinemann.

Calkins, L. M. (1991). *Living between the lines.* Portsmouth, NH: Heinemann.

Calkins, L. M. (1994). *The art of teaching writing.* Portsmouth, NH: Heinemann.

Cazden, C. B. (1992). *Whole language plus: Essays on literacy in the United States and New Zealand.* New York: Teachers College Press.

Chapman, M. L. (1994). The emergence of genres: Some findings from an examination of first-grade writing. *Written Communication, 11,* 348–380.

Christie, F. (1987). Learning to mean in writing. In N. Stewart-Dore (Ed.), *Writing and reading to learn* (pp. 21–34). Rozelle, Australia: Primary English Teaching Association.

Dahl, K. (1993). Children's spontaneous utterances during reading and writing instruction in whole language first grade classrooms. *JRB: A Journal of Literacy, 25,* 279–294.

Dyson, A. H. (1989). *Multiple worlds of child writers: Friends learning to write.* New York: Teachers College Press.

Dyson, A. H. (1993). *Social worlds of children learning to write in an urban primary school.* New York: Teachers College Press.

Dyson, A. H. (1996). Cultural constellations and childhood identities: On Greek gods, cartoon heroes, and the social lives of schoolchildren. *Harvard Educational Review, 66,* 471–524.

Fisher, B. (1991). *Joyful learning: A whole language kindergarten.* Portsmouth, NH: Heinemann.

Fletcher, R. (1993). *What a writer needs.* Portsmouth, NH: Heinemann.

Gallas, K. (1994). *The languages of learning. How children talk, write, dance, draw, and sing their understanding of the world.* New York: Teachers College Press.

Graves, D. (1983). *Writing: Teachers and children at work.* Portsmouth, NJ: Heinemann.

Gutierrez, K., Rymes, B., & Larson, J. (1995). Script, counterscript, and underlife in the classroom: James Brown versus *Brown v. Board of Education. Harvard Educational Review, 65,* 445–471.

Himley, M. (1991). *Shared territory: Understanding children's writing as works.* New York: Oxford University Press.

Lensmire, T. J. (1994). *When children write: Critical re-visions of the writing workshop.* New York: Teachers College Press.

MacGillivray, L. (1994). Tacit shared understandings of a first-grade writing community. *JRB: A Journal of Literacy, 26,* 245–266.

Martin, J. R. (1985). *Factual writing: Exploring and challenging social reality.* Victoria, Australia: Deakin University Press.

Nystrand, M. (1986). *The structure of written communication: Studies in reciprocity between writers and readers.* Orlando, FL: Academic Press.

Nystrand, M. (1987). The role of context in written communication. In R. Horowitz & S. J. Samuels (Eds.), *Comprehending oral and written language* (pp. 197–213). San Diego, CA: Academic Press.

Nystrand, M., & Wiemelt, J. (1991). When is a text explicit? Formalist and dialogical conceptions. *Text, 11,* 25–41.

Paley, V. G. (1992). *You can't say you can't play.* Cambridge, MA: Harvard University Press.

Rowe, D. R. (1989). Author/audience interaction in the preschool: The role of social interaction in literacy learning. *Journal of Reading Behavior, 21,* 311–349.

Schultz, K. (1997). "Do you want to be in my story?": Collaborative writing in an urban elementary classroom. *JLR: Journal of Literacy Research, 29,* 253–287.

Wertsch, J. V. (1991). *Voices of the mind: A sociocultural approach to mediated action.* Cambridge, MA: Harvard University Press.

Chapter 3

"Pero, Nosotros No Somos Autores!": Using Explanations to Scaffold Authorship in Latino Second Graders

Liliana Barro Zecker

Caitlyn Nichols

Linda Montes

Sarah Cohen

Sarah: I was new in this position teaching second grade in Spanish. I previously taught in a second-grade bilingual setting in Mexico, but there I taught only in English. I was very surprised at the beginning of the year when I realized that my second-grade students did not see themselves as writers. But, even when uncertain about many things, I wanted my students to become writers, to experience the satisfaction of authorship. I became aware of

---

The introduction chapter of this book provides the theoretical and methodological background for the larger collaborative school–university action-research project and this chapter about Sarah's inquiry on writing. See also the last chapter, which further discusses the implications of Sarah's inquiry—as well as those of the other teacher reseachers.

their feelings about writing when, as I asked them to write something during the first week of school, one of the girls answered that she "did not write." The finality of her statement impressed me because it seemed as if she did not see herself as a writer nor did she feel she could become one. I knew that most of my students had not been encouraged to write for meaning during first grade. Their experiences at school had been limited to worksheets that emphasized phonics. As I presented them with writing activities, they approached them with hesitation, as if I was asking them something well beyond their capabilities. Once, as I referred to them as authors while explaining the purpose of writing conferences, one of my students responded, "Pero, nosotros no somos autores!" (But, we are not authors!), summarizing what I felt was their generalized feeling of lack of competence in writing. As a result of these interchanges about writing and its "do-ability" with my students, I decided to concentrate my inquiry on the area of writing.

CHALLENGES IN SCAFFOLDING LITERACY

This chapter discusses Sarah's efforts to foster and support her second-grade, Latina and Latino students as they learned to see themselves as writers. Sociocultural theory explained learning processes by comparing them to an apprenticeship in which more experienced members of the social group "hand over" their expertise to a novice learner, scaffolding the learner's progress into a more advanced level of performance or understanding (Bruner, 1983; Vygotsky, 1978). However, the exact form that this handing over takes, or should take, is still puzzling to educators (Bruner, 1983, Edwards & Mercer, 1987). How much of the expertise is to be shared, and when, and how? What are the best ways to build on the learners' zones of proximal development (Vygotsky, 1978) to help them construct new knowledge? More importantly, in what ways should teachers build common knowledge with their students? Making the tacit explicit and finding the right balance between giving direct explanation and letting the learner progress through discovery are not easy (Edwards & Mercer, 1987).

This dilemma is especially salient in the area of literacy learning because it encompasses highly covert and internalized ways of thinking (Wells, 1990; Wells & Chang-Wells, 1992). Although there are many possible ways for readers and writers to relate to texts, Wells and Chang-Wells argue that it is the *epistemic* type of engagements with texts—that is, the kind where readers and writers reformulate ideas as result of their interactions with texts—that foster truly literate thinking. Moreover, in recent years, a more constructivist, collaborative approach to the teaching of reading and writing has been emphasized; an approach that is more inclusive of students' interests and knowledge bases (Hiebert, 1994; Willinsky, 1990). Thus, teachers like Sarah face many challenges as they attempt to provide more meaningful and fine-tuned instruction in literacy.

This endeavor is even more difficult because young readers and writers are also trying to figure out the complex conventions of written language as a code or medium of communication. Dyson (1985, 1993) compared the writing system to a kaleidoscope, a multifaceted instrument composed of mutually influencing parts that are constantly realigning. Writers, novice and experienced, need to learn how to orchestrate the perceptual, symbolic, discursive, and functional intricacies that make written communication possible. Young writers' products often show that they concentrate on one or more of these aspects of written language at the expense of the others (Ferreiro & Teberosky, 1982; Sulzby, 1985; Zecker, 1996). Teachers trying to scaffold early development in writing often face a dilemma as they attempt to provide students with balanced instruction that emphasizes meaningful communication, but also teaches them about mechanics and spelling (Atwell, 1991; Calkins, 1994; Labbo, Hoffman, & Roser, 1995; McIntyre, 1995a, 1995b; Sudol & Sudol, 1991, 1995).

Sarah's inquiry involved this latter dimension as she struggled to find the right balance between focusing on both the medium and the message of written language (Pappas, Kiefer, & Levstik, 1999), and between the process and the product of writing. However, this chapter more specifically addresses the ways in which she tried to make explicit—through explanation—many of the not-so-obvious whats, whys, and hows of conquering written language and authorship. It discusses Sarah's efforts to explain possible strategies for revision, and also the functions and characteristics of different genres. All areas, as described next, posed considerable challenges for her.

INVITATIONS TO WRITING: PROVIDING EXPLANATIONS OF PURPOSE

Sarah: I wanted my students to engage in writing on a daily basis and, soon after school started, I decided to introduce the idea of journals to them. I had found journals to be an effective way to communicate with students when I taught sixth grade. I explained to my students that journals would be a place for them to tell about themselves, about their lives, their feelings, and anything else they wanted to communicate to me. I said I would respond to their writing, but was initially overwhelmed by their need for immediate feedback. My second graders wanted my immediate reaction and had to learn to wait for me to be able to respond to all of them. This proved to cause some difficulty in communication because, if they waited too long, they could not always read to me their emergent spelling patterns, and I could not always decipher them. We worked out a routine in which they would do some reading while they waited for me to respond, at least orally, to most of them. My students embraced journal writing and soon it became one of their favorite activities. They never seemed to lose interest in it, rather they grew more eager. They seemed empowered by the opportunity to talk about themselves and what was important to them.

As mentioned before, in the beginning of the school year, most of the children in Sarah's class did not write or see themselves as authors. In her efforts to support her students' progress as writers, Sarah provided many contexts for writing. Within this framework, her explanations regarding the functions and different uses of written language were especially salient. She took time on an almost daily basis to articulate for her students the rationale and goals of their writing engagements. For example, when Felipe, a new student, joined the class 2 weeks after school started, Sarah showed him a classmate's journal and explained the purpose of journal writing, "El journal es donde ponemos nuestros pesamientos, lo que hicimos durante el día, el fin de semana, cómo te sientes, cómo es tu familia. Puedes hacer dibujos sobre lo que escribiste." (The journal is where we put our thoughts, what we did during the day, on the weekend, how you feel, what your family is like. You can make drawings about what you have written.) {Fieldnotes, 10/03/94}

Approximately 4 weeks after introducing journals, Sarah wanted to provide other contexts for writing, and thus presented the *libros de cuentos* (story books) to the class to encourage them to write stories that they could eventually publish. A few weeks later, Sarah presented yet another writing activity, the reader logs, where children wrote about the books they were reading. If the book was a story, they were to tell what it was about and what happened; if it was an informational book, they were to tell what they learned. Thus, Sarah always included specific explanations when she introduced new ways of communicating through writing.

EXPLANATIONS AND REVISION

Sarah also set up individual writing conferences. She had conferences at the back table; she summoned students one at a time to address editing strategies for punctuation and spelling in their texts. She also had shorter conferences as she roved around the classroom to give feedback on the content of individual authors' texts. At these times, she encouraged students to provide more details, to develop ideas further, to continue with a theme, and so forth. These were, for the most part, very quiet interactions in which students' remarks were practically inaudible to anyone except Sarah. However, Example 1 illustrates the ways she talked to them during these roving exchanges.

Example 1

....   [Sarah talks to Mario as she reads his story at his desk while the rest of the group works quietly. She seems confused about some of the characters' actions.]

1	Sarah:	¿Puedes decirnos mas sobre estos hombres? {Can you tell us more about these men?}
....		[Laura has just read her story to Sarah. Laura's responses were inaudible but she briefly answered all of Sarah's questions.]
2	Sarah:	¿Iban a salir? {Were they going to go out?}
3	Laura:	(... ...).
4	Sarah:	¿Juntos? {Together?}
5	Laura:	(... ...).
6	Sarah:	¿Iban a comprar cosas? {Were the going to buy some things?}
7	Laura:	(... ...).
8	Sarah:	¿Sabes lo que iban a comprar? {Do you know what they were going to buy?}
....		[Julio has read his story. Again, Julio's responses were inaudible as Sarah talked to him.]
9	Sarah:	¿Y qué le pasó al perro? {And what happened to the dog?}
10	Julio:	(... ...).
11	Sarah:	¿No encontró ningún amigo o familia? {Didn't he find any friend or relative?}
12	Julio:	(... ...).
13	Sarah:	¿Así terminó el cuento? {Is that how the story ended?}
14	Julio:	(... ...). {Fieldnotes, 10/19/94}

Sarah used these roving miniconferences to help her students make their texts more complete or clear by providing them with ideas to foster revision. In fact, revision was an important issue for Sarah. It also caused many dilemmas for her regarding how to provide the right measure of explanation to help students understand the rationale and means for revising their texts.

Struggling to Find the "Right Measure" of Explanation

Sarah: I often struggled with the right measure of explanation. They often seemed to understand when we were talking about these issues, but then they had trouble applying these ideas or ways of writing that I was explaining to them. I think many of these were just too metalinguistic, they required so much focus on language and, at this age, they are still trying to figure out some of the more basic aspects of language. I also knew that sometimes no measure of explanation would do. But I thought it was important for them to hear these ideas and to participate in these discussions. Just discussing

*these ideas was enriching for them. It was as if they could do the revisions at
the oral-language level, perhaps at that stage that was all we could afford. I
got them used to thinking about writing, even if it did not show up in their
products.*

Sarah's explanations and the discussions in which they were embedded
illustrate how difficult it can be to realize the notion of learning as apprenticeship. Tuning into students' zones of proximal development to provide
the right amount of assistance at the right time is a complex, multifaceted
phenomenon. However, students engaged in Sarah's explicit discussions
and participated enthusiastically, demonstrating that they were seriously
considering the issues at hand.

This was particularly evident as Sarah discussed with them the use of audience feedback for revision purposes, which she introduced early in the school
year. During author–chair (Graves & Hansen, 1982; Tompkins, 1998) sharing sessions, a student would read her or his piece to the class and the rest of
the group would pose questions to consider. In the course of these discussions, Sarah highlighted the purpose of audience feedback repeatedly:

> Vamos a dar nuestros comentarios, sugerencias, preguntas, ummm,
> comentamos como siempre y vamos a platicar en grupo después, cómo se
> pueden usar esos comentarios para cambiar el cuento, para desarrollar el
> cuento.... Lo que pasa es que muchas veces escribimos un cuento y ya
> pensamos que ya está terminado, pero a veces le faltan detalles en alguans
> partes, o se podría desarrollar mucho mas.

> We are going to give our comments suggestions, questions, ummm, we com-
> ment like always and we are going to talk as a group, how those comments can
> be used to change the story, to develop the story. ... What happens is that, of-
> ten, we write a story and we think that it is already finished, but sometimes it
> is missing details in some parts, or it could be developed much more.
> {Fieldnotes, 11/02/94}

Yet, despite these ongoing sessions to encourage and model revision,
students' subsequent final products more often than not did not include
the changes that Sarah tried to model for them.

Lorena's Attempts to Revise

An author's chair session around Lorena's text provides an good example of
these interactions, with the disappointing effects regarding revision.
Lorena read a story about Julia, a girl who liked to draw, color, and make
books. Julia had a friend who also liked to engage in drawing, coloring, and
book making. After finishing her reading in front of the group, Lorena was
in charge of selecting the students who raised their hands to provide her
with some feedback. Lorena answered their questions promptly, using short
utterances and not elaborating on details. Below are the questions that chil-

dren had brought up and that Sarah had written on the board as the conference took place. We include here only the English translation.

- What was the girl's name?
- Why did she like to make pictures, books, and stories?
- Why did she like to color them?
- Why did the books have pictures?
- Did her friend like to color too?
- Did her friend help her to make the stories?
- Did she go out?

Sarah expanded the last question into, "Did she like to do other things besides making books, like going out?"—which she added to the list. Sarah explained how Lorena could use this feedback to revise her story. Moreover, she modeled some possible changes that Lorena could consider based on this feedback.

=====

Example 2

1	Sarah:	Estas preguntas pueden ayudar, okay? Te preguntaron, "¿Por qué le gustaron los cuentos a la niña?" y "¿Por qué le gustaban los dibujos?" Eso es una cosa que no está en el cuento. Podrías poner estos detalles en tu cuento. Parece que la gente que lea tu cuento le gustaría saber mas sobre la niña. ¿Me entiendes, Lorena?
2	Lorena:	Sí, entiendo.
3	Sarah:	Y si pones esos detalles, sería mas completo. ¿Entiendes? También te preguntaron, "¿Por qué los coloreó, los cuentos y los libros?" Y si lo hacía sola o con su amiga. Si su amiga la ayudaba. Okay? Parece que tus compañeros, Lorena, están diciendo que quieren saber mas; podrías darnos un ejemplo. Podrías darnos una escena entre la niña y su amiga haciéndolo … lo que hacían. ¿Entiendes? Eso es diferente que decir, "A la niña le gustaban los dibujos." Podrías decirnos, umm, "Una niña, Julia, y su amiga un día estaban haciendo unos dibujos. Julia hacía eso y … después dijo su amiga, '¿Por qué no ponemos el color rosa en el conejo en el cuento?'"
4	Cm1:	(... ...).
5	Sarah:	Uh, huh. Puedes darnos una perspectiva sobre cómo se portan las niñas. ¿Entiendes?
6	Lorena:	[Nods.]
7	Sarah:	Hay otras cosas que podrías decir sobre la niña. ¿Cómo es su vida? A parte de que le gustaba hacer dibujos y cuentos, podrías

decirnos si va a la escuela, si sale, cómo es su familia, cosas así.
¿Verdad? Okay? Entonces, si tu crees que te gustaría hacer el
cuento mas grande, cambiar un poquito, contesta algunas
preguntas que te hicieron tus compañeros. Okay? Esas
preguntas, Lorena. [pointing to the board]

Translation

1	Sarah:	These questions can help, okay? They ask you, "Why did the girl like stories?" and "Why did she like the pictures?" That is something that is not in the story. You could put those details in the story. It seems as if the people that read your story would like to know more about the girl. Do you understand me?
2	Lorena:	Yes, I understand.
3	Sarah:	And if you put those details, it would be more complete, do you understand? They also asked you, "Why did she color the stories and the books?" And if she did it alone or with her friend. If her friend helped her, okay? It seems that your classmates, Lorena, are saying that they want to know more; you could give us an example. You could give us a scene between the girl and her friend doing that … what they did. Do you understand? That is different than saying, "The girl liked pictures." You could tell us, umm, "A girl, Julia, and her friend, one day were drawing pictures. Julia was doing that and … then her friend said, 'Why don't we color the bunny in the story pink?'"
4	Cm1:	(… …).
5	Sarah:	Uh, huh. You can give us a perspective about how the girls behave. Do you understand?
6	Lorena:	[Nods.]
7	Sarah:	There are other things that you can say about the girl. What's her life like? Besides liking to make drawings and stories, you could tell us if she goes to school, if she goes out, what her family is like, things like that, right? Okay? Then, if you think that you would like to make the story bigger, change a little, answer some of the questions that your classmates asked you, okay? Those questions, Lorena. [pointing to the board]
		{Fieldnotes, 11/02/94}

Sarah used the questions asked by Lorena's classmates to provide her with
specific examples of how to incorporate more information into her story.
She answered the questions specifically and then orally revised Lorena's
story to model for her an example of a possible new final product. Then,
students went to their desks. After a few minutes, Sarah saw that Lorena
had started a new piece that was unrelated to the story that was just discussed during the whole-class session. When Sarah reminded her to use

the audience suggestions to revise her story, Lorena's response was to copy the questions from the board.

Sarah: It is possible that Lorena was copying the questions so that she would have them later to revise her story, but my conversation with her did not indicate that this was her intention. Even with all my explicit explanations about what to do and my oral composition of a part for Lorena to add to her story, Lorena never changed her story in writing. Looking back, I think that during these times, I did all the talking; collaborating with them as I tried to model these changes was difficult. I ended up taking over and it was hard to decide how much to say or how much was too much. It is possible that while my students understood what I meant by adding details and clarifying, talking about possible changes and giving the information as it was requested by the audience "on the spot" was sufficient for them. I wish I had spent more time showing them how to actually introduce changes in their writing, modifying a real written product so that they could see how to do it.

Summary

Despite Sarah's repeated efforts to help the students revise their work, the richness of their conference discussions seldom translated in concrete changes in their written texts. Young writers often interpret teacher's talk about different aspects of writing in idiosyncratic ways; for them the connections between the teacher's example and their own work are less evident (McCarthey, 1994.) Sarah's students seemed to focus on just one aspect of her talk—namely, the talk that summarized their classmates' feedback on their texts—and to misinterpret the goal of the discussion as it applied to their own writing, that is, as a means for revision.

Thus, although Sarah's explanations and her attempts to scaffold in detail by making the implicit explicit, some of her students never realized revision in their final products, even when they were able to participate in oral revision discussions as authors. This, however, is not unusual behavior for young children. Revising frequently consists of their talking about their texts and a mismatch between what is talked about and what gets written down is not atypical (Calkins, 1994, Pappas, et al., 1999). Beginning writers need time to incorporate flexible revising strategies in their repertoires, and for Sarah's students, talking the talk of revision seemed to be all they could perform at this stage of their development (Calkins, 1994).

EXPLAINING GENRE: EFFORTS TO DISTINGUISH FICTION AND NONFICTION

Throughout the school year, Sarah attempted to provide explicit explanations for her students about the characteristics of writing various genres. As previously described in the area of revision, using the right measure of explanation was a challenge. As the year progressed, the students began to participate more actively in minilesson discussions (Atwell, 1987; Calkins, 1986, 1994), during which Sarah made the not-so-obvious aspects of writing more explicit to them. They posed their hypotheses and Sarah contingently responded to their initiations by sustaining and extending these emerging understandings (Wells & Chang-Wells, 1992), often using their work to illustrate the points she wanted to emphasize. This can be seen in Example 3, in which Sarah used a text produced by Felipe to explain the not-so-simple differences between fiction and nonfiction writing.

Example 3

	....	[Sarah is standing in front of the class, addressing the students while holding Felipe's piece.]
1	Sarah:	Felipe no está haciendo exactamente un cuento.
2	Cm1:	(... ...).
3	Sarah:	Está escribiendo algo——algo que no es ficción. Es sobre la ciudad de Chicago.
4	Cm2:	¿Cómo?
5	Sarah:	¿Mande? ¿Cómo? Dice cómo es Chicago … es lo que está escribiendo. Eso no es un cuento; no es ficción.
6	Cm2:	Yo no quiero hacer eso.
	....	[Sarah is interrupted by students telling her what they are writing about. There is lots of overlapping talk.]
7	Sarah:	Ummm, lo que estoy diciendo es que no tiene que ser un cuento. Si quieren hacer——escribir otra cosa, otro tipo de cosa, cómo son los animales, las plantas … otra cosa que no es——que no sea ficción. Kara, tú pronto vas a Puerto Rico. Podrías escribir cómo es Puerto Rico. Hacer no exactamente un cuento sino una descripción, como hemos estado haciendo descripciones sobre monstruos, sobre tu persona, sobre tu casa. Podrías hacer otro tipo de descripción sobre otra cosa, animales, o lugares, lo que sea.…
	....	[Children talk about the stories they have written.]
8	Sarah:	¿Mario? ¿Entienden la diferencia entre ficción.…
9	Cm2:	[completing Sarah's sentence] Y cuentos?
10	Sarah:	Cuentos y cosas que no son cuentos, que no son ficción. ¿Qué entiendes Vicente?
11	Vicente:	Que no debo hacer cosas de ficción.
12	Sarah:	No, no … no que no debes sino que——no que no tienes que hacer cosas de ficción. Puedes hacer cosas de ficción pero también puedes si quieres hacer cosas que no son ficción. ¿Qué es ficción, Alma? ¿Qué es ficción, Raúl? ¿Franco?

13	Franco:	Como de eso de … de brujas
14	Sarah:	Okay, brujas sí, si escribes sobre brujas generalmente … generalmente es ficción. ¿Por qué? [addressing the class]
15	Cm3:	Porque es mentira….
16	Sarah:	Mentira … o también se puede decir que no exactamente es mentira sino que no es real. ¿Okay? Una cosa que….
….		[There is an interruption as a child yells at Mario and Sarah needs to spend some time asking them to quiet down. Then she goes back to her discussion.]
17	Sarah:	Franco, una cosa que escribes sobre algo que no es real es, es como ficción. ¿Entiendes?
18	Franco:	¿Como básquetbol?
19	Sarah:	¿Mande?
20	Franco:	¿Como básquetbol?
21	Sarah:	¿Como básquetbol? Bueno, puedes hacer un cuento de ficción sobre básquetbol pero….
22	Cs:	(… …).
23	Sarah:	Un cuento, por ejemplo, de ficción es como diciendo cosas que no——que realmente no han pasado. Okay? Inventado, una historia.
24	Cs:	(… …).
25	Cm1:	(…) cuento de básquetbol (…).
26	Sarah:	¡Claro! Un cuento sobre cualquier cosa, de básquetbol, de pescados, todas esas cosas son reales. Solamante cuando hacen cuentos, usan esas cosas para inventar una historia. ¿Entiendes, Vicente?
27	Vicente:	Sí.
28	Sarah:	¿Bien? ¿Sí? ¿Pablo?
29	Pablo:	¿Cómo un pescado que juega básquetbol?
30	Sarah:	¿Cómo qué?
31	Pablo:	¿Un pescado que juega básquetbol?
32	Sarah:	Bueno, eso sería como muy, muy irreal, como fantasía. Ficción no tiene que ser fantasía. Ficción puede ser un niño jugando básquetbol, o un hombre, o una mujer jugando básquebol. Ficción no tiene que ser fantasía, Pablo. Okay? Solamante la diferencia entre ficción y fantasía es que——si no es ficción, tiene que haber pasado … haber pasado en la vida. Ummm, por ejemplo, una descripción sobre la vida de Michael Jordan es una historia sobre su vida, es real. Okay? Pero si tú quieres escribir un cuento sobre….
33	Cm1:	¿Michael Jordan?

34 Sarah: Sobre tu ... siendo una estrella de basquetbol, no sería real. ...

35 Cs: (... ...).

36 Sarah: Sería algo que estás creando en tu imaginación.

37 Pablo: (...) pero (...) puede ser real.

38 Sarah: Puede ser en el futuro. [turning to Franco] Franco, me molesta que estés haciendo ruido! [returning to the class] Puede ser real en el futuro pero ahorita no es real. Okay? Es algo que estás imaginando, Pablo, para escribir como un cuento. Okay? ¿Felipe?

39 Felipe: Maestra, lo que escribí, ¿qué es? [pointing to his text, which Sarah is holding up]

40 Sarah: ¿Esto? Lo que estás escribiendo, algo sobre Chicago, de cómo es Chicago en tus ojos, verdad? ¿Es algo real o irreal?

41 Cs: Algo ... real.

42 Sarah: Real? Sí ... es algo muy real ... estás haciendo como un librito explicando cómo es la ciudad. ...

43 Felipe: Como (...).

44 Sarah: No estás inventando una ciudad. ¿Verdad? Entonces es real, no es ficción. ¿De acuerdo? [to the entire class] ¿Otras preguntas? ...

Translation

.... [Sarah is standing in front of the class, addressing the students while holding Felipe's piece.]

1 Sarah: Felipe is not writing a story exactly.

2 Cm1: (... ...).

3 Sarah: He is writing something——something that is not fiction. It's about the city of Chicago.

4 Cm2: What?

5 Sarah: Pardon? What? He tells what Chicago is like ... that's what he is writing. That's not a story. It's not fiction.

6 Cm2: I don't want to do that.

.... [Sarah is interrupted by students telling her what they are writing about. There is lots of overlapping talk.]

7 Sarah: Ummm, what I'm saying is that it does not need to be a story. If you want to do——write something else, other type of thing, what are animals like, plants ... something else that is not——might not be fiction. Kara, you are going to Puerto Rico soon. You could write about what Puerto Rico is like. Write not exactly a story but a description, like we have been writing descriptions about monsters, about yourself, about your house.

		You could write a description about something else, animals, or other places, whatever....
....		[Children talk about the stories they have written.]
8	Sarah:	Mario? Do you understand the difference between fiction....
9	Cm2:	[completing Sarah's sentence] And stories?
10	Sarah:	Stories and things that are not stories, that are not fiction? What did you understand, Vicente?
11	Vicente:	That I should not write fiction things.
12	Sarah:	No, no ... it's not that you shouldn't——it's not that you shouldn't do fictional things. You can do fiction things but also, if you want, you can do things that are not fiction. What's fiction, Alma? What's fiction, Raúl? Franco?
13	Franco:	Like that about ... about witches.
14	Sarah:	Okay, witches yes, if you write about witches, in general ... in general it's fiction. Why? [addressing the class]
15	Cm3:	Because it's a lie....
16	Sarah:	A lie ... or we can also say that it's is not exactly a lie but it is not real, okay? Something that....
....		[There is an interruption as a child yells at Mario and Sarah needs to spend some time asking them to quiet down. Then she goes back to her discussion.]
17	Sarah:	Franco, something that you write about something that is not real, it's like fiction. Do you understand?
18	Franco:	Like basketball?
19	Sarah:	Pardon?
20	Franco:	Like basketball?
21	Sarah:	Like basketball? Well, you can make a fiction story, you can write a....
22	Cs:	(... ...).
23	Sarah:	A fiction story, for example, it's like saying things that——that have not really happened, okay? Making up, a story.
24	Cs:	(... ...).
25	Cm:	(...) basketball stories (...).
26	Sarah:	Right! A story about anything, about basketball, about fish, all those are real things. It's only that when you write stories, you use those things to make up a story. Do you understand what I am saying, Vicente?
27	Vicente:	Yes.
28	Sarah:	Good. Yes? Pablo?
29	Pablo:	Like a fish that plays basketball?

30	Sarah:	Like what?
31	Pablo:	A fish that plays basketball?
32	Sarah:	Well, that would be like very, very unreal, like fantasy. Fiction does not have to be fantasy. Fiction can be a boy playing basketball, or a man, or a woman playing basketball. Fiction does not have to be fantasy, Pablo, okay? It's only that the difference between fiction and fantasy is that——if it's not fiction, it has to have happened——have happened in real life. Ummm, for example, a description on Michael Jordan's life is a *story* about his life, it's real, okay? But if you want to write a story about....
33	Cm1:	Michael Jordan?
34	Sarah:	About you ... being a basketball star, that wouldn't be real....
35	Cs:	(... ...).
36	Sarah:	It would be something that you are creating in your imagination.
37	Pablo:	(...) but (...) it can be real.
38	Sarah:	It can be in the future. [turning to Franco] Franco, it bothers me that you are making noise! [returning to the class] It can be real in the future but now it is not real, okay? It is something that you are imagining, Pablo, to write as a story, okay? Felipe?
39	Felipe:	Teacher, that, what I wrote, what is it? [pointing to his text that Sarah is holding up]
40	Sarah:	This? What you are writing, something about Chicago, about what Chicago is like in your eyes, true? Is it something real or unreal?
41	Cs:	Something ... real.
42	Sarah:	Real? Yes ... it's something very real ... you're making like a flyer explaining what the city is like....
43	Felipe:	Like (...).
44	Sarah:	You are not making up a city, true? The——it's real, it's not fiction. All right? [to the entire class] Other questions? ... {Fieldnotes, 06/02/95}

The discussion in Example 3 was typical and illustrates how Sarah would contingently respond to children's initiations to extend their emerging understandings (Wells, 1993; Wells & Chang-Wells, 1992). She used Felipe's text about Chicago (lines 3 & 5) and other students' ideas about the topics of basketball, Michael Jordan, and witches to be explicit about the distinction between fictional and nonfictional writing. She built on their prior work on descriptions and provided other possible informational topics, such as Puerto Rico, for Kara (line 7). In her responses, Sarah pro-

vided additional information that clarified some of the children's understandings, as when she told them about the difference between fantasy and
realistic fiction (line 32) or when she explained that writing about witches
is generally considered a work of fiction (line 14). Students eagerly participated, asking questions and venturing possible answers and comments,
even when, as illustrated by Felipe's remark near the end of the excerpt
(line 39), they were not fully sure how Sarah's explanation applied to their
own writing.

However, because they are not scripted, collaborative classroom discussions can be complex and different from what teachers might have antici-
pated. When Sarah responded to Pablo's comment about a fish playing
basketball (line 31), she moved into an apparent unplanned discussion
about the fiction–fantasy distinction. Her explanation became somewhat
tangled when she talked about what could happen in *real life,* and what is
very, very unreal (line 32). Then it got even more convoluted by her use of
the word "story" to describe both nonfiction and fiction—"a description
on Michael's life is a *story* about his life, it's real. ... But if you want to write
a *story* about ... you being a basketball star, that wouldn't be real" (lines
32 & 34).

Nonetheless, this dialogue was coconstructed as Sarah and the children
jointly made explicit a set of very implicit ideas that writers often apply as
they compose different kinds of texts. Sarah was able to build on the students' understandings, however partial they were, to extend their comprehension and to help them consider new aspects of the fiction–nonfiction
differentiation. That is, Sarah was able to enact literacy instruction that
was explicit or direct, but at the same time she was immersed in the context of students' own work.

TRANSFORMATION INTO OWNING AUTHORSHIP

In the middle of February, Sarah took a maternity leave. She came back 12
weeks later, 6 weeks before the end of the school year. Because the teacher
substituting for Sarah indicated that she was not going to include the
same kinds of writing activities in the curriculum, Sarah had set the story
books children had written aside. To her surprise, even though her students had not written in their journals and storybooks during her absence,
they were delighted at the opportunity to look at the books again when Sarah returned and handed them out. They were very excited to be reunited
with their old work. Sarah asked the students to take a look at their old
work, to change or add anything they wanted. Students reread parts of
their work to neighbors and often changed spellings or added missing
words, an indication that they were now able to introduce some changes in
their writing by putting into practice some of Sarah's earlier modeling. After Sarah's return, the class began to have extended reading and writing
times. Sarah encouraged them to work together in different ways.

Sarah: They had always been very social; they loved working together. Some groups got more done than others, but I could see how they thrived. Their collaboration often took different forms. Some children wrote a piece together, although one of them once commented to me that "writing with another person was really hard." Many took advantage of the opportunity to work together to solve mechanical aspects of writing, spelling in particular. Some of them were better spellers and the children were aware of their different levels of expertise in this area. Some took the roles of editors; others liked to become the illustrators of someone else's pieces. I am not sure they worked together as well as I had envisioned in terms of the kind of feedback that they were able to provide to each other, or in the ways that they understood what to do with it, but the most amazing thing was to witness their growth as writers. That same student who had announced her inability to write so categorically at the beginning of the school year was now composing stories with others and explaining what and how to do it to less skilled students. These children were still struggling with many aspects of learning how to write, but they had become authors. I wished I had been able to have them for another year to accompany them in their growth, but I feel they left having had very positive experiences that would stay with them.

In the following weeks until the end of the school year, Sarah continued to struggle to find the right measure of explanation and the most adequate balance between process and product. As they roved around the classroom talking to each other and looking for someone to read their texts to, these second graders showed no hesitation about their ability to write to communicate their ideas. Although frequently still puzzled by many of aspects of written language that they were trying to master, they were now empowered writers, capable of reflecting on their own work and the work of others.

As a teacher researcher, Sarah also attained new insights into literacy instruction that were rooted in her own practice. She learned to accommodate theoretical principles to the reality of her students' developmental levels. She learned to adjust to their needs for immediate feedback and how to best scaffold their writing efforts. She managed to foster collaborative classroom discourse that facilitated growth in literacy learning and made explicit some of the very implicit aspects of literate thinking—for example, that texts can be seen as provisional and have potential for revision (Wells & Chang-Wells, 1992)—even when not all of the discussions immediately translated in changes in her students' written products. She accomplished her goal of helping her students discover the authors within themselves.

REFERENCES

Atwell, N. (1987). *In the middle: Writing, reading, and learning with adolescents.* Portsmouth, NH: Boynton/Cook.

Atwell, N. (1991). *Side by side: Essays on teaching to learn.* Portsmouth, NH: Heinemann.

Bruner, J. (1983). *Child's talk.* London: Oxford University Press.

Calkins, L. M. (1986). *The art of teaching writing.* Portsmouth, NH: Heinemann.

Calkins, L. M. (1994). *The art of teaching writing.* Portsmouth, NH: Heinemann.

Dyson, A. H. (1985). Individual differences in emergent writing. In M. Farr (Ed.), *Advances in writing research: Vol 1. Children's early writing development* (pp. 59–126). Norwood, NJ: Ablex.

Dyson, A. H. (1993). *Social worlds of children learning to write in an urban primary school.* New York: Teachers College Press.

Edwards, D., & Mercer, N. (1987). *Common knowledge.* New York: Routledge.

Ferreiro, E., & Teberosky, A. (1982). *Literacy before schooling.* Exeter, NH: Heinemann.

Graves, D., & Hansen, J. (1982). The author's chair. *Language Arts, 60,* 1176–1183.

Hiebert, E. H. (Ed.). (1991). *Literacy for a diverse society: Perspectives, practices, and policies.* New York: Teachers College Press.

Labbo, L., Hoffman, J., & Roser, N. (1995). Ways to unintentionally make writing more difficult. *Language Arts, 72,* 164–170.

McCarthey, S. (1994). Students' understandings of metaphors in teachers' talk about writing. *Language Arts, 71,* 598–605.

McIntyre, E. (1995a). The struggle of developmentally appropriate literacy instruction, *Journal of Research in Childhood Education, 9,* 145–156.

McIntyre, E. (1995b). Teaching and learning writing skills in a low-SES urban primary classroom. *Journal of Reading Behavior, 27,* 213–242.

Pappas, C. C., Kiefer, B. Z., & Levstik, L. S. (1999). *An integrated language perspective in the elementary school: An action approach.* New York: Longman.

Sudol, D., & Sudol, P. (1991). Another story: Putting Graves, Calkins, and Atwell into practice and perspective. *Language Arts, 68,* 292–300.

Sudol, D., & Sudol, P. (1995). Yet another story: Writers workshop revisited. *Language Arts, 72,* 171–178.

Sulzby, E. (1985). Kindergarteners as writers and readers. In M. Farr (Ed.), *Advances in writing research: Vol. 1. Children's early writing development* (pp. 127–200). Norwood, NJ: Ablex.

Tompkins, G. E. (1998). *50 literacy strategies: Step-by-step.* Upper Saddle River, NJ: Merrill.

Vygotsky, L. (1978). *Mind in society: The development of higher psychological processes.* Cambridge, England: Cambridge University Press.

Wells, G. (1990). Talk about text: Where literacy is learned and taught. *Curriculum Inquiry, 20,* 369–405.

Wells, G. (1993). Reevaluating the IRF sequence: A proposal for the articulation of theories of activity and discourse of the analysis of teaching and learning in the classroom. *Linguistics and Education, 5,* 1–37.

Wells, G., & Chang-Wells, G. L. (1992). *Constructing knowldege together: Classrooms as centers of inquiry and literacy.* Portsmouth, NH: Heinemann.

Willinsky, J. (1990). *The New Literacy: Redefining reading and writing in the schools.* New York: Routledge.

Zecker, L. B. (1996). Early development in written language: Children's emergent knowledge of genre specific characteristics. *Reading and Writing, 8,* 5–25.

Chapter 4

"Does That Sound Like You?" Exploring Ways to Foster Eighth-Grade Students' Voice in Their Written Research Reports

Dian Ruben

Jane Liao

Michael Rassel

"Voice" has become an important theoretical and pedagogical concern in language and literacy development. *Voice* is Bakhtin's (1981) notion for the "speaking personality," the "speaking consciousness." In this view, utterance or text exists only by being produced by a voice, a certain point of view that enacts particular social values by addressing—or being in dialogue with—other voices (Cazden, 1992; Nystrand, 1986, 1987; Nystrand & Wiemelt, 1991; Wertsch, 1991; Wiemelt, 1994). Moreover, because language is fundamentally *dialogic* in that we use and create language by speaking with others, any instance of use is entwined with other previous uses and voices. Thus, there is *conflict* in this process: "[Language] is pop-

---

The introduction chapter of this book provides the theoretical and methodological background for the larger collaborative school–university action-research project and this chapter about Michael's inquiry on research writing. See also the last chapter, which further discusses the implications of Michael's inquiry—as well as those of the other teacher researchers.

ulated—overpopulated—with the intentions of others. Expropriating it, forcing it to submit to one's own intentions and accents, is a difficult and complicated process" (Bakhtin, 1981, p. 294).

This finding, keeping, and expressing writer voice is especially difficult for upper-grade students when their writing involves research (Fletcher, 1993). Yet, despite the fact that most schooling requires that students do writing to learn, little research has addressed the complex enterprise of how students learn to write about a specific topic for an extended period of time (Many, Fyfe, Lewis, & Mitchell, 1996; Tierney, Soter, O'Flahavan, & McGinley, 1989). Moreover, research writing does not just impart information, it also conveys something about the writer, yet studies that focus on the construction of discoursal writer identities in producing this type of text have also been sparse (Ivanic, 1994).

This chapter focuses on Michael Rassel's inquiry on his eighth-graders' writing to learn about self-selected topics (mostly social studies and science topics). It is similar to Many et al.'s (1996) recent qualitative study of the self-directed reading, writing–research process of Scottish 11- and 12-year-old students. The findings of this latter work indicated that students held one of three task conceptions or impressions of their research investigations of World War II topics. Students' views influenced the different ways that they emphasized and approached subtasks (i.e., planning, searching, finding, recording, reviewing, and presenting). Students had the "research-as-accumulating-information" impression that focused on finding and recording interesting information, but were rarely concerned with any advance planning or subsequent searching for relevant texts. Other students, who had the "research-as-transferring-information" impression, thought that research was primarily searching for and then transferring relevant information and material into their booklets. Believing that they were expected to take information from a book and present it in their own words, they planned a purposeful search for texts relevant to their topics, using a variety of strategies to record information (e.g., "sentence-by-sentence reworking" or "read-remember-write"). Students having the "research-as-transforming-information" approach had three major foci in their work: recursive, ongoing planning (with frequent use of planning webs); constant reviewing to assure that they covered the information on the topic; and considering the needs of a perceived audience.

This audience dimension, or a writer's awareness of readers' needs, has been characterized as a major facet of metadiscourse (Cheng & Steffensen, 1996) and is clearly related to the development of voice. This factor and many other factors may also contribute to the writing of effective research reports: having prior experiences in the range of sub-tasks of research (e.g., planning, finding, searching, recording, reviewing, presenting, etc.) (Many et al., 1996); having opportunities to read and write informational texts at all grade levels (Christie, 1987; Daniels, 1990; Martin, 1985, 1990; Newkirk, 1989); being able to choose topics that are meaningful and relevant to students' lives (Macrorie, 1988; Wallace, 1966); and so forth.

As the Bakhtin ideas suggest, writing and learning to write are conceived as social acts (Dyson, 1996; Nystrand, 1986, 1987; Sperling, 1994). This perspective has influenced many classroom writing practices (e.g., the use of teacher–student conferences, and peer sharing), many of which were evident in the approach Michael implemented. Thus, although he conducted various teacher-directed minilessons on the various facets of the process, his writing workshop (Calkins, 1994) consisted of many conversations of a give-and-take nature between writers and their readers, all of which we attempt to illustrate in this chapter.

MICHAEL'S INQUIRY: THE ISSUE OF VOICE

Michael: I teach writing at the 6th–8th grade levels at Andersen. Most of the time I collaborate with particular teachers to implement writing workshops in their classrooms. I have been trying to teach writing from a "process" approach for several years now, each year learning new strategies and insights to implement ideas from the "gurus" (e.g., Atwell, 1987; Calkins, 1986; Graves, 1983) of this perspective into my urban context. My major goal has been to help urban, frequently ESL, students at Andersen to become confident, life-long writers.

During the year of my inquiry, eighth graders were given an ultimatum: to participate in graduation exercises at our school, they had to successfully produce research reports. I had experience in teaching informational, research writing when I taught in self-contained fourth- and fifth-grade classrooms at the school, but I had never taught this type of writing when the stakes were so high for students, many of whom, as I found out, had little experience in learning to research and write about a specific topic across an extended period of time.

I worked with one particular class of eighth graders with 28 students (most were Latina or Latino with a small number of African Americans and first-year Polish immigrants). I came into their classroom, collaborating with their teacher, Rebecca Gipson, to implement a daily 45-minute writing workshop. Two major questions of my inquiry were: How do I facilitate their voice in the informational texts they were to produce? How do I help them learn about the process of writing research reports?

Voice, then, was an overriding theme throughout Michael's inquiry, and he developed many strategies to foster students' voices in their informational reports. We organized the findings into three sections: First, we cover some of the major approaches Michael employed to deal with voice during the early parts of the research writing process. Second, because voice was also a common feature addressed by Michael during his content conferences with students about their initial, completed drafts, we provide two case studies to illustrate the nature of these interactions. Third, although not all students' final research reports were free from problems of voice, we examined the metaawareness of voice they acquired.

STRATEGIES FOR FOSTERING VOICE DURING THE EARLY RESEARCH PROCESS

Michael tried various ways to foster voice in his students' writing during the entire research-writing process. He had students choose their own topics and create their own questions about these topics; he implemented minilessons to show students how to paraphrase or record information from books and other resource materials; he drew on ideas from Macrorie's (1988) *The I-Search Paper* book by having students write about their personal rationales for their chosen topics; he found ways to have both brief roving and in-depth content conferences to talk to them about voice, and so forth. Here we focus on three early interrelated facets of the investigation process—brainstorming questions, lessons on paraphrasing and notetaking, and informal conferences during writing workshop.

Creating 10 Questions about the Research Topic

An early important way that Michael fostered voice was to have students brainstorm questions on what they wanted to find out about their topics. He felt that creating their own questions "sort of forced them to think about what they were really interested in" {End-of- year interview, 07/12/95}. He hoped that these student-generated questions would guide them to write about their topics in their *own* words.

In an early minilesson about brainstorming questions, Michael began by sharing with the class a conversation he had with a student about coming up with 10 questions.

Example 1

1   Michael: This student decided that he wanted to do his piece on outer space and I said, "Well, that's too much, could we narrow it down?" And then he said, "Well, I think I want to do it on stars." And I said, "Okay, now ... let's talk about stars." So then he started to make a list of his questions of what he wanted to find out about stars. He wrote things on there like, "What's the biggest star?" He said, "I want to find out what they're made of."

So you know that list of questions that everybody in here should have? Let me tell you this, if you haven't made a list of things that you want to find out about your topic, then you're not going to have such a good time and maybe you need to pick another topic.

{Videotape, 02/26/95}

Michael first used information from the ongoing conferences he was having with students to explain how to narrow down a topic like outer space to a more manageable topic like stars, and then gave possible questions that a particular student began to pose about this new topic. Then he emphasized that if they could not generate 10 questions, they might not have the right topic.

Later that same class period, Michael had many conversations with individual students regarding the status of their questions, as illustrated next.

Example 2

1	Michael:	How does it relate to the questions you wrote out … about what you want to find out about?
2	Maribel:	I didn't make any questions.…
3	Michael:	You have to make a list of questions about what you want to find out about. Okay, look … maybe what you're doing is okay, maybe you want to do a little reading first, skim your sources.…
4	Maribel:	Um huh.…
5	Michael:	Maybe that will give you some ideas for what it is you want to find out that you don't already know.
6	Maribel:	Um huh.…
7	Michael:	Until you start brainstorming like she did [he reaches for a paper of a nearby student], questions about what you want to find out about that person.…
8	Maribel:	After we find the answer, we have to like write it down, right? On the paper.…
9	Michael:	[shows the sheet to Maribel] One of the things she wants to know about this lady, Harriet Tubman … she wants to know "Did she learn how to read?" Okay, so now at the top of her note cards, she's putting things like "Education." Get it? So now as she goes through her sources, every time she sees something about reading or how she learned how to read, or if she learned to read, she'll jot it down. {Videotape, 02/26/95}

Apparently Maribel was already reading some resources when he met with her, so in the beginning Michael asked her how it was related to her questions. However, although he acknowledged that she might skim first to produce the questions, he again used another student's questions about Harriet Tubman to stress their utility in guiding the research process.

In fact, when students went on a field trip to a large public library in the city to find resources for their inquiries, he did not let them on the bus unless they showed him their questions. Michael has a theater background (his undergraduate degree is from the Goodman School of Drama at DePaul University) and he frequently had a dramatic flair when he encouraged his students to take on this and other facets of the research process: "Do it! Do it! [clapping his hands as he speaks] ... that's gonna be the thing that makes you want to write this stuff. When you find out!" {Videotape, 02/23/95}. Thus, for Michael, creating 10 questions about what students really wanted to know about their chosen topics was one of the initial necessary conditions for promoting voice.

Lessons in Paraphrasing and Notetaking

Another way that Michael fostered voice was through explicit instruction in paraphrasing in various minilessons. One of his early ones started like this:

Example 3

1   Michael: I know some writers like to copy their notes verbatim. They like to copy right out of the book onto note paper, and then do their paraphrasing as they're drafting. I wouldn't do that, I wouldn't do that! If you'll just paraphrase as you're taking notes, you won't have to worry about plagiarizing when you draft——when you actually write the piece. Do you understand?
{Fieldnotes, videotape, 02/23/95}

Although Michael gave students the message that writers frequently might take down quotes from various authors and then paraphrase the content into their own words, he was afraid for his students to go down that path. He was worried that they would not be able to do the paraphrasing *during* drafting, and that plagiarizing would be rampant.

In another minilesson he used excerpts of text on the overhead projector and asked students to read them and write down the ideas in their own words, "How could you say this without copying word for word?" On the first attempt, students were fairly successful in paraphrasing the text, but when he offered a longer, more complex passage to paraphrase, students had difficulties. In Example 4, a student shares what he's written, but Michael challenges him, saying that he had changed only two words.

Example 4

1   Michael: That's not paraphrasing, all you did was change two words.
2   Cs: #(... ...).#

3   Darrell: #Why can't you change it around?#

4   Michael: Wait, he's got a really good question. Say it again. [to Darrell]

5   Darrell: What if you had changed it around? It's not exactly like they got it. You just switch around the ideas?

6   Michael: It's because it's not your voice. You want it to be your voice. You want people——you want people who read your paper to say, "This really sounds like Darrell. He really knows a lot about this particular subject. He didn't just copy this out of a book. He really knows this, because it sounds like him." It's as if Darrell ... while I'm reading this ... it's as if Darrell is standing there telling me about the Komodo dragon....

[Fieldnotes, videotape, 02/26/95}

Darrell asked a question that must underlie many students' reasons for using close renditions of an author's wordings—"if you switch around the ideas, isn't that paraphrasing, doesn't that take care of the problem of plagiarizing?" Although he credited Darrell with a good question, Michael once again emphasized the importance of Darrell's voice—that readers of his text will recognize that he knew a lot about his topic of the Komodo dragon and because his writing "sounds like him."

Michael struggled throughout his inquiry to create minilessons that would help students to learn to paraphrase "with voice." He even developed several versions of a *three-step paraphrasing process*. An early one was where students would "read a chunk, turn over the page, put it in your own voice." Another strategy he tried was to have students jot down only key words or ideas while reading, put away the reference materials, and then compose sentences based on the key words or ideas. This approach even ended up depicted on posters all over the room.

It is clear that these lessons helped many of the students not to plagiarize or copy down verbatim wordings from resource materials in their own texts. However, most of Michael's strategies represented the "read-remember-write" process described by Many et al. and mentioned already, and thus might have led some students to adopt a view of research as mostly transferring information. (We examine this idea again in the last section of the chapter.) In retrospect Michael had his own perspective on these lessons.

Michael: In doing research writing myself, I've come to realize that when you paraphrase, so many things happen simultaneously. I had these posters put around the room; I thought this three-step process was going to do it. All they had to do was read a chunk, turn over the page, and put it in their own voice—Rassel's sure-fire-lock-step method of putting things into your own words. Well, what the heck does that mean? Only until I had to do it as part of my master's graduate work did I become aware of how many things are going on—I'm not sure what I do when writing research. I think you guys might have given me too much credit here.

Roving Content Conferences During Drafting

During the drafting process, Michael used ideas from Macrorie's (1988) *The I-Search Paper* book to assist students' writing with authentic voice. For example, he suggested that they consider writing an introduction to the paper that would explain personal reasons for why they had chosen their specific topics. This strategy helped many get going on their drafting and to begin their reports in an authentic voice. Next, Michael talks with a special education student who was stuck in beginning her draft.

Example 5

1	Michael:	Okay, here's some ideas. Think about these. Why did you choose it [the topic]? What was it that you hoped to find out before you began your research? Talk about the questions you had….
2	Maribel:	Okay….
3	Michael:	Uh … of all the things that you found out, what were the things that you wrote most about? Like what was most interesting to you? You can talk about….
4	Maribel:	(…) … look at it. [holds up sheet]
5	Michael:	Well, it doesn't have to be a book … #I mean … #
6	Maribel:	#<No, but it's too long.>#
7	Michael:	You're just giving the reader——you're setting the stage for the body. You're saying to the reader, "Here's what I was interested in. Here's what I wanted to find out. Here are some of the places that I went to find out." You know, talk about your trip to the library maybe, talk about a #conversation you had#….
8	Maribel:	#All that! Won't it be boring?#
9	Michael:	No——well, we can revise it later if you think it is, okay? Talk about any conversation you might have had … at home with somebody. Did you ever have a family member that was in one [a hurricane]?
10	Maribel:	No.
11	Michael:	What——Why did you choose this? What is it that was….
12	Maribel:	Because it was interesting. I wrote that.
13	Michael:	But what is it that was interesting to you?
14	Maribel:	It was because——I would hear about it and I always like … uh … and I always wondered what it was doing.

15	Michael:	So maybe you want to do an insert in the introduction about where you would hear about it. Where did you hear about it?
16	Maribel:	On the news.
17	Michael:	Okay, so you'd watch the local news. What would be some of the things that you would actually see on the television set that really sparked your interest?
18	Maribel:	All the things ... that fly around.
19	Michael:	So the big giant white thing [uses his hands to symbolize a big round cloud] ... so maybe you could say, "I always wondered what that big giant white thing on the TV screen that the weatherman would show ... when one was happening someplace else." How did you feel inside when he was talking about it on the news? Did you ever say to yourself, "God, I'm glad it's not here!"?
20	Maribel:	Yes.
21	Michael:	So maybe you want to put that in the introduction too. Things like that.
		{Videotape, 03/23/95}

Initially, Maribel was worried that relating a personal account of why she chose to investigate the topic of hurricanes would be too boring or too long. However, as Michael began to talk more to her about the underlying reasons for her wanting to find out about this topic in the first place, she reported that she was intrigued about hurricanes' effects depicted on TV—"all the things that fly around." Thus, in this exchange Michael showed Maribel that she did indeed possess some personal thoughts and knowledge about hurricanes and that what she had to say could be of interest to her readers. He felt these introductions often helped students like Maribel get started, and helped others to continue writing the rest of the paper—although not in a narrative style—in their own voice.

Other informal conferences directly addressed the voice issue as students wrote their first drafts, as illustrated in Michael's interactions with Leon. Here Michael just listened to Leon reading what he wrote so far on his research about George Washington.

Example 6

1	Michael:	Okay, hold on. Some of it still doesn't sound like you. Like, you're not the type of guy that would say, "married into the Fairfax family, prominent and influential Virginians." You would never say "prominent."
2	Leon:	Nawh, I'd say, "Virginians," but I wouldn't say "prominent."

3	Michael:	What do you think they mean by "prominent"?
4	Leon:	"Prominent" ... a well-respected family.
5	Michael:	Very good! That sounds like you! That sounds like you!
6	Leon:	Yeah, but instead of putting it real long, I just thought I would put "prominent" instead of putting "a well respected family." You know....
7	Michael:	#Prominent ... (...)#
8	Leon:	#Putting it down in short terms....#
9	Michael:	"Prominent" sounds too much like something this guy wrote [pointing to reference page]. Do you understand what I'm saying?
10	Leon:	Yeah.
11	Michael:	I think it sounds more like you when you say, "He married into this Fairfax family. They were very well respected." [clapping his hands with each word] <Zap!> That's it!
12	Leon:	[nodding his head in agreement] It sounds better too!
13	Michael:	It sounds better! Exactly! It sounds much better, because it sounds like you.

{Videotape, 03/08/95}

Although Leon clearly understood the meaning of the word "prominent" and could restate it in his own words, he admitted that he wouldn't "say *it*," the word used by the author of the reference text. However, once he heard how Michael inserted in his text his own definition of the phrase, "well respected," Leon agreed that it did sound more like his own voice.

Certainly voice is more than using individual vocabulary, but Michael's focus on particular wordings that students lifted verbatim from resource books provided him with fruitful places to question students regarding voice. Also, unlike Leon who knew the meaning of a word he had used, many students had no understanding of the words they included in their texts. Thus, these often became occasions for Michael to help them better understand the books they had read. Moreover, through his continual insistence that they use their own words, he scaffolded ways for them to hear their voices on paper. These miniconferences, then, enabled students to experience varying levels of success in discovering their own writer identities.

CONFERENCES FOR SCAFFOLDING—TWO CASE STUDIES

Michael had in-depth content conferences with students after they had completed their first drafts. Here, we present his work with Maribel and Leon, to illustrate the nature of these conferences and again show how the issue of voice was examined in these discussions.

Conferencing with Maribel

Maribel placed her draft sheets on the table. Her paper had already been reviewed by the classroom teacher (Ms. Gipson), who provided written comments about Maribel's text. Michael also read the paper and took notes to use in his talk with Maribel. Example 7 shows the beginning of the conference and their discussion of the introduction of her paper.

Example 7

1 Michael:	Why don't you tell me what's happened to it since you turned it in? Tell me what you noticed about Ms. Gipson's comments and what you've done to it and what you're trying to do.
2 Maribel:	Um … we put different words in.…
3 Michael:	Okay.…
4 Maribel:	We put like what kinds of damage do they cause and all that. And then we changed it … a little bit.
5 Michael:	Um hum.…
6 Maribel:	A lot.…
7 Michael:	What are some of the things that you changed a lot?
8 Maribel:	We changed——like … I repeated my question right here. [pointing to a section of her text]
9 Michael:	Okay, you said you repeated the question. You mean you repeated.…
10 Maribel:	A question.…
11 Michael:	Oh, like some of the information got said too many times?
12 Maribel:	#No.…#
13 Michael:	#Or just the question?#
14 Maribel:	Yeah——like I asked myself "How do they form?" and I said it again over here so I put a different thing in.
15 Michael:	You put a different question in?
16 Maribel:	Yeah.
17 Michael:	A different inquiry. What was the different one you put in there?
18 Maribel:	[looking down at the paper, she uses a pencil to find her place] Uh, it was … "How they get their names?"
19 Michael:	Okay.…
20 Maribel:	And "When is hurricane season?"
21 Michael:	Okay.
22 Maribel:	And "What is the definition of hurricane?"

23 Michael:	Okay. Oh, I see what you're saying. You had "How they are formed?" up here and then you restated it here ... two times in the introduction....
24 Maribel:	Yeah, yeah.
25 Michael:	So basically in the introduction, you're——what are you trying to tell your readers? What are you trying to do?
26 Maribel:	I'll tell 'em what they're gonna be hearing ... what they're gonna be reading.
27 Michael:	Okay.
28 Maribel:	And ... I think, what they're——what I want them to learn.
29 Michael:	What you want them to learn? Also what you wanted to find out before you started?
30 Maribel:	Yep. {Fieldnotes, videotape, 04/25/95}

This example illustrates the introduction she began in Example 5. It is apparent that Maribel already thought about her paper and Ms. Gipson's comments, as well as possible revisions she planned. She was clearly in charge of this part of her paper, knowing exactly what, "they're gonna be hearing ... what they're going to be reading ... what I want them to learn."

In the next part of the conference, they began to consider a margin comment—"Is this important?"—that Ms. Gipson made on her paper. Michael asked Maribel to read the passage in question and then they had more conversation in which he provided suggestions for improvement.

Example 8

1 Maribel:	[reading] WHEN YOU STEP OUTSIDE, YOU WILL SEE THAT THERE ARE A LOT OF DARK CLOUDS SURROUNDING YOU. IF YOU WATCH THE CLOUDS, THEY SEEM TO MOVE AROUND YOU IN A DARK CIRCLE.
2 Michael:	Where does that mean you're standing in relation to the hurricane itself? If you're standing here [puts his finger on the desk to indicate spot where one would be standing and uses his other hand to make circular motion] ... and the dark clouds are surrounding you ... you're standing in the ... ? Probably in the ... #eye of it.#
3 Maribel:	#Eye of the# hurricane.
4 Michael:	Of the hurricane. Is that what you were trying to say there? I mean is that what you're trying to——are you trying to tell the reader that as it passes over the area [uses his hands to show movement] that the eye also might pass over?

5 Maribel:	[nods her head in agreement]
6 Michael:	Do you talk about the eye of the hurricane anywhere else in the piece?
....	[Maribel locates and reads the portion where she has described the general size of the eye of a hurricane.]
7 Michael:	Okay ... maybe——this is just an idea——maybe if you were to move that sentence about "If you were to walk outside and see the clouds surrounding you." If you were to move that to where you're talking about the eye, maybe she'd realize why that's kind of important.
8 Maribel:	Oh ... so I move that part over here?
9 Michael:	I would. That's a suggestion. I mean ... I'm not telling you to do that. I'm saying, maybe that would make her understand why that part is important. You know, I grew up in Florida and a lot of people get very seriously hurt because they don't know that the hurricane has an eye. Especially if they've come from——you know ... a lot of people move to Florida when they retire, and they move from other parts of the United States where there are no hurricanes. And they come down there, and they don't know a lot about them like you do. And one will hit and then the eye will be passing over and there's a calmness, and they'll go outside and start taking their cars out and they'll start taking their things out there [motions with his hands]. And then ... the eye eventually [shows movement from one point to another with both hands, like a box]....
10 Maribel:	Comes back....
11 Michael:	And then the thing hits again. [brings hands together] That's how a lot of people get seriously hurt and have damaged caused to their automobiles. They just don't know about it. So I would say that that's a pretty important part of your ...
12 Maribel:	Research paper.
13 Michael:	People should know about that.
14 Maribel:	Yeah. [nodding her head in agreement] {Videotape, 04/25/95}

Here Michael followed up on the part that Ms. Gipson had a question about. Although the part she read in the beginning was related to the eye of the hurricane, Maribel had not connected these ideas to the ones that are found later in the paper. Thus, through Michael's artful scaffolding, Maribel found a way to solve this dilemma. In this exchange, Michael not only helped her with the organization of her text, he also prompted her to express implicit knowledge that she may not have realized she possessed. In her final draft, she added the following to her text as a result of this conference:

Then the wind dies down and the rain stops. The air begins to be very hot and still. The eye of the hurricane starts passing over. The eye of the hurricane may take an hour or more to pass. Then the hurricane comes back. The wind and the rain come back harder than ever.

Conferencing with Leon

In his conference with Leon, Michael again focused on the issue of using his own words instead of wholesale lifting of wordings from resource books. Michael often addressed individual words and phrases and showed Leon how to revise them to eliminate plagiarism and to make the text sound more like him. Throughout he had Leon read a part of his paper, then he questioned him about what it meant.

Example 9

1	Leon:	[reading] ALTHOUGH GEORGE WASHINGTON HAD VERY LITTLE OR NO FORMAL SCHOOLING, HIS ...
2	Michael:	What does that mean?
3	Leon:	What? "Had very little or no formal schooling?"
4	Michael:	Yeah.
5	Leon:	He had like, a little bit of schooling or he never went to school*...
6	Michael:	So you could put ... "George Washington had a little bit of schooling." So like if we were going to take this sentence——do you have a sheet of paper?
7	Leon:	[gets paper]
8	Michael:	If we were going to take this sentence and we were just going to write down key ideas, what would they be? What would be the key words or phrases? You could put "little bit of schooling," right?
9	Leon:	Yeah.
10	Michael:	Put it down. You said "little bit of schooling."
11	Leon:	[writes]
12	Michael:	What else did you say ... about the second part?
13	Leon:	AND HE READ WIDELY IN GEOGRAPHY.
14	Michael:	What could you put? You don't have to put all that, "he read widely in geography." What could you put?
15	Leon:	"Read widely in geography."
16	Michael:	Do you have to put "widely"?
17	Leon:	[shakes his head "no"]

18	Michael:	Just put key words … or key phrases. What could you put?
19	Leon:	Read geography.
20	Michael:	Yeah, read geography.
21	Leon:	[writes]
22	Michael:	What's geography about?
23	Leon:	Finding places.
24	Michael:	Put that——now, maybe between here and here [pointing to Leon's list] you could put something about the notebooks.
25	Leon:	Yeah.
26	Michael:	What could you put?
27	Leon:	[seemingly thinking out loud] Early notebooks.
28	Michael:	Think about how we know he read about finding places. How do historians know that?
29	Leon:	Cause he kept a lot of things in his notebooks.
30	Michael:	Good, that sounds great. He kept a lot of things in his notebook.
31	Leon:	[writes more notes]
32	Michael:	About what?
33	Leon:	About geography.
34	Michael:	Okay, so put "about" and then draw an arrow to "geography." There we go. Okay, now——[turning over the original sheet from which Leon was copying his key words and phrases] now, you have some notes there, right?
35	Leon:	Uhhuh.
36	Michael:	Write a couple sentences about his education. Make sure you make it complete sentences. Put it in your voice. This [referring to the key words and phrases list] is your voice, not——this sounds like you.
37	Leon:	[writes "George Washington had very little schooling, but he kept notes in his notebook about geography."]
38	Michael:	Read it.
….		[Leon reads what he's written.]
39	Michael:	Now that sounds like you. See? See how you took that information and you've internalized it and now you're going to teach somebody else in your voice. That's what research is. That's really what research papers are all about, isn't it?
40	Leon:	[nods his head in understanding and agreement]
41	Michael:	So now what you need to do is … so that you don't——don't think that you have to go through every single sentence in here. Just get the key words from each page and write them down.

42	Leon:	Just get the key words from each page and write them down.
43	Michael:	Right, just take the key words. For example, you could draft another sentence here if you wanted to about how this shows that he did know how to read because he read books about....
44	Leon:	Geography.
45	Michael:	Right, because how else could he put those notes in his notebooks?
46	Leon:	Right.
47	Michael:	So I know you can do this....
		{Fieldnotes, videotape, 05/09/95}

Michael helped Leon revise his paper so it "sounded like him." Using a separate paper Leon wrote down key words for those places that did not sound like him; Michael showed Leon in a very concrete way how he can go over his paper to revise it so it is more in his own voice. The sentences that clearly came from the reference book were revised and connected to information that Leon wrote about Washington's notebooks. It was clear that this procedure of finding key words and then using them to create sentences in his own voice resulted in a much shorter text. Thus, at the end of the conference (not included here), Michael told Leon not to worry about how long his paper would be after using this key-word-list strategy. "I'm sure that Ms. Gipson and I would rather have 3 to 5 pages of this where you tell us everything that you understood about what you read than have 10 pages of something that doesn't sound like you." And again, Michael reiterated that he was more interested in Leon understanding the literature he read, and that Leon would be demonstrating that knowledge by using his own voice.

METAAWARENESS OF VOICE

After many students had almost finished their final drafts, Michael had some whole-class sharing times wherein students read their writing to each other. These turned out to be great discussions, in which the distinction of "it doesn't" or "it does sound like you" began to be transformed into a developing appreciation of a more "sophisticated voice" in the process of writing to learn. In the following example, Jasmine already read her report.

Example 10

1	Michael:	Good. Reactions? What do you think? Does it sound like Jasmine?

2	Miguel:	No, it sounds like plagiarism.
3	Michael:	What should she do to make it sound like her?
4	Jasper:	She uses big words.
5	Carmen:	It's sophisticated writing.
6	Michael:	Is it possible to slip into a sophisticated voice because you're trying to teach something or to impress the teacher? You don't use words that you use everyday.
....		[Michael gives an example of a colloquial word and what might be used instead in written expression. Then Fernando reads his piece on cheetahs.]
7	Tania:	It doesn't sound like him.
8	Michael:	Well he didn't plagiarize. I read his piece and I could tell from the misspellings.
9	Jose:	I never heard him say "nonaggressive" or "approach."
10	Michael:	What does "aggressive" mean?
11	Fernando:	[does not have time to think and respond]
12	Maritza:	Being charged up.
13	Alberto:	[responding to "nonagressive"] Happy ... not harmful.
14	Michael:	[to Fernando, who has not come up with an acceptable response] You might want to change that.
....		[Darrell reads and Michael asks about the word "remarkable," which he is able to explain. All of the students believe that the writing is in Darrell's voice.]
15	Michael:	You must think he talks more sophisticated? I like his piece because you can see the thing just sitting there.
....		[Michael calls on Maribel to read about hurricanes. He comments, "I'm going to Florida, and I need to know." Maribel reads her text. Darrell thinks that she has copied from a book, but Maritza defends Maribel's writing.]
16	Michael:	Do you think writing changes——if you keep on writing, will it change the way you talk?
17	Francisco:	Yeah, you'll start to speak the stuff you write.
18	Alberto:	But we don't talk intellectual to each other.
19	Michael:	Do you try to sound more sophisticated when you write, not plagiarize, but your own voice? Tell me this, do you think she knows something about hurricanes?
20	Candida:	Yeah, she knows what "twirling" means.
21	Michael:	And "moisture"....
22	Maritza:	I visited Mexico in 1989 (... ...).
23	Michael:	Wow, that's interesting. It's in conversational voice and at the same time it's teaching.

24   Francisco: That's good, I know she didn't plagiarize.

25   Michael: If you know what a word means, you can keep it. Everybody go
                  through and find a part that doesn't sound like your sophisti-
                  cated voice but somebody else's voice ... make it better.
                  {Fieldnotes, 05/16/95}

Students debated about whether particular authors sounded or did not sound like themselves. When Jaspar said that Jasmine used "big words" (line 4), Carmen argued instead that, "it's sophisticated writing" (line 5). That idea of sophisticated writing got expanded and elaborated on through the rest of the discussion. It was taken up again by Michael in reference to Darrell's text on Komodo dragons, which all of students felt was in his voice. Subsequently, in line 16, Michael got students to consider another facet of sophisticated writing: "If you keep on writing, will it change the way you talk?" Francisco thought it would, but Alberto countered that "we don't talk intellectual to each other." In line 19 Michael tried to expand on both of these responses by suggesting that it was possible to sound more sophisticated in your voice when you write without plagiarizing. In line 25, he asked them to review their texts and to revise the parts that "[don't] sound like your sophisticated voice but somebody else's voice," which is similar to the advice that Fletcher (1993) offered in weeding out parts that sounded stiff or awkwardly formal in research writing. However, it is clear that writing with voice in this community became a much more complex phenomenon. A metaawareness of voice was created among the students.

REVISIONS, REFLECTIONS, AND AFTERTHOUGHTS

Throughout the research writing process, Michael helped students "stalk their inner voices" (Fletcher, 1993). Almost all of the students wrote successful research reports. Moreover, students reported at the end of the project that this was the first time that they ever had a teacher really teach them how to go about the *doing* of research writing. However, throughout these achievements, Michael had difficulties figuring out the best ways to promote his students' voice in writing this informational genre. For example, to help students avoid plagiarizing or just copying down verbatim from resource texts that they used for their papers, he tried various paraphrasing minilessons and other strategies in his interactions with students. Although he decided later that some of these were too simplistic, they did seem to interrupt the wholesale copying, to begin to get students to think more about what they read, and to help them express ideas in their own voice.

We also think that some of these strategies may have fostered students behaviors of merely transferring information from the books they read, which is a conception that many of students in Many et al.'s study had. In that study students did research on a self-selected topic about World War II and recorded the results in booklets. It is not clear whether these students then actually wrote up expository papers based on their findings like the students in Michael's study did. However, a major factor that seemed to be contributing to those Scottish students who held the conception of research-as-transferring-information was the difficulty of the resource materials they read for their research. This might have been an important influence here for Michael's students, many of whom were ESL learners, because he did not address reading strategies in any explicit way.

Michael: When I taught in a contained classroom, I did minilessons on strategies for reading informational and other texts that my students were using in their research that they might have found difficult. I didn't do that here. The writing wasn't connected enough to reading in this way, which might be why I might have pushed them into this conception that research is transferring information. However, I do think that some of the things I stress around voice made them have to deal with vocabulary that they didn't understand. I have had a similar experience just recently when I had to write a paper in a graduate course that deals with Dewey's work. I would read his stuff and then I would put the book away and think, "What in the heck does this mean?" And I would try to put down key words and then try to write it up in my own words. So, although I didn't cover explicitly reading strategies, my key word technique and other things I suggested to the students might have helped some of them to adopt new approaches to tackle difficult texts.

I was constantly struggling with how I should see my ESL students' efforts. Should I accept their close paraphrases as developmental approximations in learning English? How should I nudge them beyond this technique? But I've been thinking more about considering the reading side of the research process more explicitly. It might also be interesting to study kids' conceptions—maybe through interviews—about what they think the research process is in the first place, so I could understand where individual kids are in the beginning of the process so I can better scaffold them.

According to McGinley and Tierney (1989), a topic for investigation is "analogous to a landscape about which knowledge is best acquired by 'transversing' it from a variety of perspectives" (p. 250). In this kind of self-directed reading and writing, students can explore multiple ways of viewing and thinking about topics of inquiry. Such a stance is similar to what Wells (1990) termed the epistemic mode of engagement—where "meaning is treated as tentative, provisional, and open to alternative interpretations and revision" (p. 369)—and which he argued fully exploit the potential of literacy because it empowers the thinking of those who use it. In Many, et al.'s study, only the students who conceived of research-as-transforming-information seemed to consider multiple perspectives or to be concerned with audience. We do not know if having this impression is a developmental issue, but it is clear that Michael was fostering this epistemic mode in many of his interactions with his students, and he was also constantly getting them to pay attention to audience by always bringing up voice.

There were still parts of some of the students' final reports that were not completely free of plagiarizing or rearranged text. However, because of Michael's consistent emphasis and talk about finding strategies to promote voice, students developed a metaawareness of it. At the end of the project, they could talk about, and distinguish between, simple notions of the it-does-or-does-not-sound-like-you concept and an appreciation of their own and classmates' evolving sophisticated voice in the process of writing to learn. Thus, a possible future inquiry might be to consider this facet of writer identity (Ivanic, 1994) in writing informational texts, along with addressing students' reading strategies (as they are connected to the research writing process), and exploring more explicitly students' own views of the research process.

REFERENCES

Atwell, N. (1987). *In the middle: Writing, reading, and learning with adolescents.* Portsmouth, NH: Boynton/Cook.

Bakhtin, M. M. (1981). *The dialogic imagination: Four essays by M. M. Bakhtin.* M. Holquist (Ed.), & M. Holquist & C. Emerson (Trans.). Austin: University of Texas Press.

Calkins, L. M. (1986). *The art of teaching writing.* Portsmouth, NH: Heinemann.

Calkins, L. M. (1994). *The art of teaching writing.* Portsmouth, NH: Heinemann.

Cazden, C. B. (1992). *Whole language plus: Essays in the United States and New Zealand.* New York: Teachers College Press.

Cheng, X., & Steffensen, M. S. (1996). Metadiscourse: A technique for improving student writing. *Research in the Teaching of English, 30,* 149–181.

Christie, F. (1987). Learning to mean in writing. In N. Stewart-Dore (Ed.), *Writing and reading to learn* (pp. 21–34). Rozelle, Australia: Primary English Teaching Association.

Daniels, H. A. (1990). Young writers and readers reach out: Developing a sense of audience. In T. Shanahan (Ed.), *Reading and writing together: New Perspectives for the classroom* (pp. 99–129). Norwood, MA: Christopher-Gordon.

Dyson, A. H. (1996). Cultural constellations and childhood identities: On Greek gods, cartoon heroes, and the social lives of schoolchildren. *Harvard Educational Review, 66,* 471–524.

Fletcher, R. (1993). *What a writer needs.* Portsmouth, NH: Heinemann.

Graves, D. (1983). *Writing: Teachers and children at work.* Portsmouth, NJ: Heinemann.

Ivanic, R. (1994). I is for interpersonal: Discoursal construction of writer identities and the teaching of writing. *Linguistics and Education, 6,* 3–15.

Macrorie, K. (1988). *The I-search paper.* Portsmouth, NH: Boynton/Cook.

Many, J. E., Fyfe, R., Lewis, G., & Mitchell, E. (1996). Traversing the topical land-scape: Exploring students' self-directed reading-writing-research processes. *Reading Research Quarterly, 31,* 12–35.

Martin, J. R. (1985). *Factual writing: Exploring and challenging social reality.* Victoria, Australia: Deakin University Press.

Martin, J. R. (1990). Literacy in science: Learning to handle text as technology. In F. Christie (Ed.), *Literacy for a changing world* (pp. 79–117). Victoria, Australia: Australian Council for Educational Research.

McGinley, W., & Tierney, R. (1989). Traversing the topical landscape: Reading and writing as ways of knowing. *Written Communication, 6,* 243–269.

Newkirk, T. (1989). *More than stories: The range of children's writings.* Portsmouth, NH: Heinemann.

Nystrand, M. (1986). *The structure of written communication: Studies in reciprocity between writers and readers.* Orlando, FL: Academic Press.

Nystrand, M. (1987). The role of context in written communication. In R. Horowitz & S. J. Samuels (Eds.), *Comprehending oral and written language* (pp. 197–213). San Diego, CA: Academic Press.

Nystrand, M., & Wiemelt, J. (1991). When is a text explicit? Formalist and dialogical conceptions. *Text, 11,* 25–41.

Sperling, M. (1994). Constructing the perspective of teacher-as- reader: A framework for studying response to student writing. *Research in the Teaching of English, 28,* 175–203.

Tierney, R. J., Soter, A., O'Flahavan, J. F., & McGinley, W. (1989). The effects of reading and writing upon thinking critically. *Reading Research Quarterly, 24,* 134–173.

Wallace, D. L. (1996). From intentions to text. Articulating initial intentions for writing. *Research in the Teaching of English, 30,* 182–219.

Wells, G. (1990). Talk about text: Where literacy is learned and taught. *Curriculum Inquiry, 20,* 369–405.

Wertsch, J. V. (1991). *Voices of the mind: A sociocultural approach to mediated action.* Cambridge, MA: Harvard University Press.

Wiemelt, J. (1994). Texts, and shared understandings: Accounting for language interaction in student writing. *Linguistics and Education, 6,* 373–410.

Part II

Reading-Aloud
Curriculum Genres

Four teacher researchers had inquiries that focused primarily on reading-aloud routines in which they read children's literature to their students.

In chapter 5, Chris Pappas, Shannon Hart, and Diane Escobar collaborate with teacher–researcher, Anne Barry, to tell of Anne's inquiry regarding reading ABC books to her first graders. Anne always read books from a range of text genres in her read-alouds, but rarely read ABC books. Thus, this year she added this type of books because she was interested in finding out whether they would foster her students' phonemic awareness. Her students learned this and much more—namely, content knowledge on many topics or domains because of the many "informational" ABC books she used. The sessions were filled with many child-initiated intertextual responses in which students juxtaposed ideas from the book being read with ideas from other books, TV shows, songs, personal stories, and so forth. For several years, Anne worked hard to develop collaborative read-alouds and was used to handling student initiations. She was also experienced in decifering children's emergent invented spellings in their written texts. However, it was quite a different matter altogether to understand, appreciate, and evaluate their initiations as phonemic approximations while they were hurled at her in the oral read-aloud setting. Thus, this chapter tells of these difficulties, as well as of the successful strategies she developed in this curriculum genre.

Chapter 6 centers around two teacher researchers' inquiries—those of Hawa Jones and Dorothy O'Malley, who taught second and third grade, respectively. University researchers Chris Pappas, Shannon Hart, and Diane Escobar worked with these two teachers to relay their attempts to develop collaborative reading-aloud experiences for their students. Before this year of inquiry, both Hawa and Dorothy conducted teacher-controlled read-alouds where they asked all of the questions and dominated the talk. However, because Hawa wanted to help her students to become critical readers, and Dorothy was interested in understanding her students' understandings of a corpus of multicultural children's books that she had collected during the preceding summer, both were required to rethink the manner in which they orchestrated these sessions. The chapter describes the difficulties and successes of these teachers' efforts to manage the two interrelated dimensions of sharing teacher authority to create more collaborative interactions: the *process* aspect (who gets to do what, when, where, and how) and the *content* aspect (what counts as knowledge and who is validated as a knower).

Chapter 7, the last one in this section, covers Sonia Torres Pasewark's inquiry in her bilingual, third-grade classroom. Liliana Barro Zecker, Caitlyn Nichols, and Linda Montes worked with Sonia to explain what happened when Sonia tried to use the reading-aloud routine to bridge her students' learning of English. This was Sonia's first year of teaching, and her students had very limited English-language abilities. Many were frightened of the task of learning this second language, and Sonia was still figuring out many facets of beginning teaching as she attempted to read books in English to these Spanish-speaking students. The chapter gives an account of how Sonia dealt with issues of translation and code switching, how she reexamined the kinds of questions she asked her students, and how she tried to address various social issues in the books she read to them.

All three chapters describe and discuss what is involved in developing collaborative reading-aloud routines in which both student voice and teacher expertise are integrated. There has been recent research that has examined teachers' styles of conducting book-sharing sessions. None of these studies, however, studied this topic when the teachers purposefully attempted to transform their approaches to allow for students' meanings, and for teachers to create ways to contingently respond to them. These chapters, then, contribute new information to this area of work.

Chapter 5

Fostering First-Graders' Phonemic Awareness and Much More: Using ABC Books in the Reading-Aloud Curriculum Genre

Christine C. Pappas

Shannon Hart

Diane Escobar

Anne Barry

It has been argued that important hypotheses or understandings about literacy are facilitated in young children through book-reading experiences with adults (Holdaway, 1979; Morrow, 1988; Pappas, 1993; Sulzby & Teale, 1991; Wells, 1985, 1986). How the parent or teacher asks questions or directs the child's attention to aspects of the books being shared is a major

---

The introduction chapter of this book provides the theoretical and methodological background for the larger collaborative school–university action-research project and this chapter about Anne's inquiry on ABC books. See also the last chapter, which further discusses the implications of Anne's inquiry—as well as those of the other teacher researchers.

way by which emergent and beginning readers construct their early ideas about both the language and the conventions of books (Cochran-Smith, 1984; Heath, 1982; Ninio & Bruner, 1978; Panofsky, 1994; Snow, 1983; Wells, 1986; Yaden, Smolkin, & Conlon, 1989).

Recent research has examined the ways in which teachers conduct reading-aloud sessions and indicates that teachers vary in the style in which they orchestrate this sharing of books, which influences the kinds of literacy understandings that children construct (Dickinson & Keebler, 1989; Dickinson & Smith, 1994; Green, Harker, & Golden, 1986; Martinez & Teale, 1993; Teale & Martinez, 1996). However, what was also characteristic in most of these studies is that much of the classroom interaction—regardless of teacher style—has been one of control, with teachers initiating most of the talk. They also ask most of the questions, primarily *psuedoquestions* (Ramirez, 1988), ones to which teachers already know the answers. That is, there is little research on more collaborative or less teacher-controlled interactional styles in the reading-aloud curriculum genre (Oyler, 1996a).

Just a few years ago, Anne's style in reading-aloud was one of teacher domination. However, she worked for several years to make her reading-aloud curriculum genre more collaborative by encouraging her students' spontaneous questions and comments as she read to them, and learned ways for her follow-up on these student initiations to further extend their literacy development. (See Oyler, 1996a, 1996b, and Pappas & Barry, 1997, for research on Anne's earlier years of change in conducting reading-aloud routines.)

> *Anne: I have frequently noted that I would always have one or two children who still hadn"t developed stable understandings of letter–sound relationships, even at the end of first grade. Since my reading-aloud sessions have been the core of my literacy program during my latest several years of change, I wondered if my reading of alphabet books would help my students create more of a phonemic awareness. I read a range of genres of children's literature during my reading-alouds, but I haven't read that many ABC books. I want the three circles of reading—the three cueing systems: grapho-phonemic, semantic, and syntactic—to work more smoothly for kids. I thought that if I would read ABC books more frequently and could assess and study my students' initiations when I read this kind of book, I would be able to facilitate their phonics knowledge without using drill and skill types of instruction that I felt were boring and didn't connect well to real literacy and comprehension reading.*

Phonological or phonemic awareness is usually defined as the conscious attention of phonemes or units of sound that are normally unconsciously used in spoken words and has been positively related to children's learning the letter–sound relationships of printed words (Adams, 1990;

McGuinness, McGuinness, & Donohue, 1995; Richgels, Poremba, & McGee, 1996; Stahl & Murray, 1994). Thus, students' initiations—*children's* contributions of questions and comments to the book-sharing events to Anne's reading of ABC books—became a major focus during this year of inquiry. They revealed the developing phonemic knowledge of her 18 students. They were mostly Mexican-American children, many of whom were learning English as a second language, two African-American students, one Anglo student, and one first-generation middle-Eastern child. They also reflected much more than their learning their ABCs. As Anne began to discover more about the complex nature and variety of ABC books that comprised this genre, and began to share them with her students, children's contributions showed the kinds of content information about a range of topics that these books cover. It is difficult to separate these two kinds of understandings—phonemic awareness and content knowledge—reflected in children's responses to these books because they were often observed in the same reading-aloud sessions; nonetheless, we organized the two following sections so that each emphasizes one of these foci. In addition, although there was great success in children's learning in the use of ABC books, there were also challenges that Anne had to meet throughout, so illustration and discussion of these issues are included in both sections.

FOSTERING PHONEMIC AWARENESS THROUGH READING ABC BOOKS

An early pattern in students' initiations to the ABC books that Anne read was their making connections of the alphabet letters to sounds or letters of their names. What was also interesting was how Anne contingently responded to these efforts (Wells, 1986; Wells & Chang-Wells, 1992). These can be seen in Example 1, which occurred early in the year when Anne read the classic ABC book, *Alligators All Around: An Alphabet,* by Sendak (1962). When Anne read, she stood so that all of the children, who sat on their chairs (moved from their regular tables) are near and around her, could see the book. Here, we provide excerpts from the book, starting with Anne's reading of "K."

Example 1

1	Anne:	K KEEPING KANGAROOS
2	C:	Karen.
3	C1:	Kangaroo. My favorite animal.
4	C:	Casey.
5	Anne:	What about "Casey"? (... ...).

....

6	Anne:	N NEVER NAPPING
7	C1:	No.
8	Anne:	If you put "N" and "O" together it makes "no."
9	Cs:	And "Y" "E" "S" is "yes"!

....

10	Anne:	P PUSHING PEOPLE
11	C:	Peter Pan.
12	C:	Pinocchio.
13	C:	Peanut butter.
14	C:	Popeye.
15	C:	Penguin.
16	C:	Bat.
17	Anne:	"Pat," "bat," "bat" is a "B" word.

....

18	Anne:	Q QUITE QUARRELSOME
19	C:	Queatiful.
20	Anne:	[smiling] Queatiful.
21	C1:	Queen.
22	C:	King Kong. "King" starts with "K."
23	Anne:	"Quiet" is a "Q" word....

....

24	Anne:	RIDING REINDEER
25	C:	Robin Hood!
26	Reyn:	Reynaldo. "R" is for me.
27	C:	Riding on a bus!
28	Peron:	Peter Pan.
29	Anne:	Does "P," "Pa" [emphasizing the "P" sound] Peter Pan start with "R"?
30	Cs:	#No.#
31	Peron:	#[Shrugs his head side to side]#
32	Anne:	Peron, I think you're thinking of your name.
33	C:	Rice-a-roni.
34	Cs:	Ricky Lay. [referring to a large gorilla-like stuffed animal in the classroom that children frequently lean on when they read in the classroom]
35	Anne:	What comes after "R"? S SHOCKINGLY SPOILED

....

36	Anne:	Y....
37	Cs:	Yak, yak, yak.
38	Anne:	In our alphabet book, it is YACKETY-YACKING.
39	Cs.	Yak, yak, yak.
40	Anne:	The book says "yackety-yacking."
41	C:	Hawaii.
42	Anne:	You hear "Y" in the middle. Say the word "Ha-wa-ii." There is a "Y" sound in the middle of "Hawaii." Oh, this is interesting.
43	C1:	Yes.
44	C:	Why.
45	Anne:	The question word.
46	C:	Wife.
47	C:	White.
48	C:	Wire.
49	Anne:	No, that would be "yire." You are getting "Y" and "W" mixed up. We'll have to do something with this. {Fieldnotes, 10/05/94}

Several times students offer names of the children in the class for the letters of the book—for example, in lines 2 and 26 for "K" and "R," respectively. Sometimes they also gave approximations, for instance, when a child said "Casey" (line 4) for the same sound that "K" of "KEEPING KANGAROOS" represented. Much of Anne's response to this particular effort was inaudible (line 5), but we can see how she approached Peron's "Peter Pan" for the "R" letter (line 28). She got him to rethink that contribution by reinforcing the "P" "sound" in line 29, but also gave him credit for his approximation in line 32, telling him that he probably thought of it because there is an "R" in his name (although not at the beginning). Thus, because Anne found ways to show her students she valued risk taking in their initiations, they felt comfortable to continue to do so. As a result, she gave many more opportunities to provide more correct information about letter–sound relationships.

Other kinds of child initiations in this example reflect what they already knew about letter–sound relationships, all of which reflect their developing phonemic awareness (e.g., the "Peter Pan," "Pinocchio," "peanut butter," "Popeye," "penguin" contributions for the "P" letter and the wonderful "queatiful" and "queen" for the "Q" letter). Anne was very excited about the "Hawaii"" initiation for "Y" that they heard in the middle of that word (line 41), as well as the other words children subsequently offered—"why," "wife," "white," "wire"—which did not start with a "Y" but did show students' phonemic knowledge because children used what has been called the letter–name strategy. That is, they used the *name* of the letter (the name of "Y" is "wye") in presenting their approximations (Temple, Nathan, Temple, & Burris, 1993). Thus, students' developing ideas about letter–sound relationships observed in this and other ABC book sessions provided useful assessment information for Anne that she could follow-up on in other instructional contexts.

This example also showed certain vulnerabilities on Anne's part in responding to some of these approximations. Anne had quite a lot of experience deciphering invented spellings in her students' writing and being able to glean useful information about what they reveal regarding her students' phonemic awareness and phonics knowledge. In the writing context, there is the advantage of a visual representation as well as time to respond. However, it is quite a different matter to figure out how best to reply to or follow-up on children's ideas to build new understandings when they are throwing complex approximations at you one after another.

Quite soon, students moved beyond just relating the first letters of their names to letters or "sounds" found in the ABC books. This was apparent, for example, in Anne's reading of *The Monster Book of ABC Sounds* (Snow, 1991). In this rhyming book the text is at the top and then lower on the page the spelling out of an alphabet letter "sound" occurs, usually in a large dialogue bubble said by a creature depicted in the illustration—for example, a rat says "Aaaaah!" for "A," a monster says "Boo!" for "B," and so forth. The monsters and sometimes eerie sounds of the book, therefore, fit well with the mood of the Halloween season. Example 2 shows how students found "O's" in the middle of their names—both first and last. It also illustrates how such excitement emerged as a management issue for Anne and how she dealt with it.

Example 2

1	Anne:	What comes after "N"? O.
2	Cs:	O!
3	Anne:	Because——you have an "O" in your name, don't you? [pointing to a boy as she speaks to him] Your last name, Oscar, and....
4	Cs:	(...).
5	Cm1:	<And I got an "O"> (...).
6	Anne:	Well, he's (... ...) last name.
7	Cm2:	I got me an "O." I got me an "O." In mine. [He moves forward in his seat so Anne can hear him.]
8	Anne:	In the middle.
....		[Lots of children are talking at once and to each other. Anne starts trying to get them back as a group and to be quiet.]

9	Anne:	Ahh, one. I am going to count.
10	Cf1:	I got "O" in my last name. I got "O."
11	Anne:	Two.
12	Cm3	I got "O" in my last name too.
13	Anne:	I don't want to get to three. Let's hurry. Julissa?
14	Julissa:	"O" stands for O———[Oscar's last name]
15	Anne:	My, you were finding "O"s all over. The middle parts of your names.
16	Cs:	[Many speak out again.]
17	Anne:	[raising my hand as a motion to stop their talk] Wait. We are going to go to "O." HE FLIES UPSIDE DOWN AND DOES OTHER BRAVE TRICKS. [Points at print on the bottom of the page] OOOOOOH!
18	Cs:	Ooooooh.
19	Cm4:	Ooooom.
20	Anne:	Ooooooh.
21	Cm4:	Ooooooh.
22	Anne:	Okay? Ooooooh.
		{Fieldnotes, videotape, 10/26/94}

Although students already began to hook up connections with letters (sounds) in the books with places other than the first letter of their first names, we think that this might have been Anne's first explicit suggestion of this possibility. When Anne pointed out in line 2 that Oscar had an "O" in his last name as well (in this case, the first letter of his last name, which she never said, but Julissa did later in line 14), there is an avalanche of student initiations in which various children exclaimed about the presence of the "O"s in their names, most of them in the middle, which Anne confirmed twice (lines 8 & 15).

Because students' excitement led to a crescendo of voices where no ideas could be heard, Anne began in line 9 to employ her one-two-three procedure (see also lines 11 & 13), developed with her students to help them come together as group and to get some semblance of order. This technique enabled Anne to signal to her students that she expected them to get ready to attend to her. Then, after she allowed Julissa's remark and her comment, she returned to reading the book (line 17) when students appeared to begin to all want to speak again, which was another strategy Anne utilized to get back on track when read-alouds became too interactive.

In line 18, children repeated in chorus the "ooooooh" sound of the book. In line 19, C4, perhaps thinking that the string of "O"s might end with a non-"H," offered a different rendition that ends with an "M." However, Anne gave him feedback that such a possibility would not really represent the sound (lines 20 & 22). Subsequently, Anne also thought that he might have been merely engaging in word play, because the children did that a lot.

Thus, Example 2 showed children's further development regarding how to map letter–sound relationships to their names. Moreover, this particular book might have been especially conducive to examining these new possibilities for learning. At the same time, the format and textual features of the book had the potential to pose challenges for Anne in how to orchestrate and deal with the exuberance of students' contributions.

Developing More Sophisticated Letter–Sound Knowledge

As the months went by, children developed more and more sophisticated phonemic knowledge as responses to the various books Anne read to them. Their more complex understandings were due in part to the fact that Anne shared more challenging books with them. One such book was *Q is for Duck: An Alphabet Guessing Game* (Elting & Folsom, 1980). In this book there was no simple "A is for A———" format set forth, but instead, to provide appropriate responses, students had to link a letter and its sounds (e.g., "Q") with certain semantic-domain possibilities invoked by an animal—in this case "duck"—to come up with, "Because a Duck Quacks." As a result, the book provided many opportunities for students to offer many predictions in this guessing game, which reflected their growing phonemic resources. Example 3 shows some of our favorite responses.

Example 3

1	Anne:	G IS FOR HORSE. WHY?
2	Peron:	Run.
3	Anne:	That's how horses go [nodding in affirmation]. Perhaps gallop.
4	C1:	They graduate.
5	Anne:	Where do they go? [laughing]
6	C2:	To the farm school.

....

7	Anne:	L IS FOR FROG. WHY?
8	C1:	Lick.
9	C2:	Lily ponds.
10	C3:	Because they *love* flies.
11	C4:	They have a *long* tongue.

....

12	Anne:	N IS FOR CAT. WHY?
13	C:	Scratch.
14	C:	They eat rats.
15	C:	They have nails.
16	Karen:	They *nip* milk.
17	Anne:	Let's get the "N" words.
18	C:	Maybe his name is Nicky?

....

19	Anne:	P IS FOR CHICK. WHY?
20	C:	They *pop* out of their egg.
21	Peron:	[Makes gesture of pecking with his fingers.]
22	Anne:	[Nods with affirmation.]
		{Fieldnotes, 01/30/95}

Many of these are creative and playful ideas—for example, the idea that horses might graduate, or that a cat might nip milk. This example, however, also showed two other important features of Anne's responses to the children. On one hand, although students felt that they could brainstorm ideas to the various puzzles posed (e.g., students "scratch" and "they eat rats" for N IS FOR CAT) Anne, at the same time, raised the ante by expecting them to come up with more appropriate responses—"Let's get the "N" words." On the other hand, for certain students like Peron, a student who was very quiet and was frequently absent from school, she went out of her way to acknowledge any level of response. For example, in line 2 when Peron offered "run," which does not start with a "G," Anne affirmed it with both her gestures and her words, and then built on it by suggesting "gallop," a synonym for "run." At the end of the excerpt, Peron's mere *gesture* of pecking in line 21 is acceptable to Anne. Thus, in these interactive reading-aloud sessions, Anne was able to meet individual needs and also a range of levels of student initiations.

Anne read several books every reading-aloud session, usually books of different genres. Thus, as she began to read more and more ABC books, reading at least one each day, we began to see students' increased phonemic knowledge in their comments when she read non-ABC books. A very remarkable instance of this occurred in her reading of *What is Christmas?* (Hall, 1991). Anne chose to read this book to her students because all of them celebrated this holiday and because there were physical-format features of the book that they might want to use in the illustrated books they were writing. Here she is at the last page of the book, pointing to the words of the text as she reads.

Example 4

1	Anne:	Look what happens to the print in the book. All of a sudden it gets really big. "I KNOW!" SAID LITTLE MOUSE. Casey?
2	Casey:	Why did they put a "k" if it doesn't sound?
3	Anne:	Why did they put a "k" and it didn't sound? Really good question. There are some words in English——in English ... Oscar?
4	Oscar:	(... ...).
5	Anne:	Right. Just like some words in Spanish don't sound..
6	Cm1:	Like "H." Like "H" in Spanish doesn't sound.
7	Anne:	Doesn't sound?
8	Cm1:	Doesn't sound.
9	Anne:	So you see that there are some words in English that don't——some letters in the beginning that don't sound. You"re absolutely right.
10	James:	But you still have to put them.
11	Anne:	But you still have to put it down when you spell it. Yep. So you still have to *know* it (pointing to the "know" word in the book).
12	Cm2:	Words that start with "N"?
....		[There is a distraction by one of the students that Anne quickly deals with.]
13	Cm2:	Words that start with "N." First you have to put "K" [pointing to the book and then making the letter in the air]. Then an "N," then an "O," then a "W."
14	Anne:	Then an "N," then an "O," and then a "W." Yep.

{Fieldnotes, videotape, 12/07/94}

As already indicated, Anne wanted students to notice how the print was used in the book, when Casey, an African-American student who was still a very emergent reader in many ways, surprised Anne with his question about the word "know": "Why did they put a "k" if it doesn't sound?" In line 3 Anne lauded Casey's question and then began to answer it, but she was interrupted by Oscar, one of the bilingual Latino boys. His comment was inaudible but Anne's gloss in line 5 enabled us to know that he tried to explain to Anne, with her limited knowledge of Spanish, that this was the case in Spanish as well. Then C1 gave a particular example—"Like "H" in Spanish doesn't sound." Subsequently, after Anne confirmed that there are some beginning letters in some words in English (and Spanish) that don't sound, James, another bilingual student, pointed out that, "you still have to put them." Afterwards, another student followed up by reiterating how it applies to "know," which Anne confirmed.

Another nontypical ABC book that Anne shared with the students was Aylesworth's (1992) *The Old Black Fly.* This is a rhyming book with a repetitive refrain that tells of the havoc caused by an old black fly: "He ate on the crust of Apple pie. He bothered the Baby and made her cry. Shoo fly! Shoo fly! Shoooo." Here the "A" of "apple" and "B" of "baby" are capitalized, bold, and in different colors (red and blue in this case, respectively) to identify the letter of focus.

This book, with its exuberant and explosive illustrations (by Stephen Gammell), invoked many and varied responses from the children—from pointing out that "chips and chocolate rhyme" on the page that has the fly dive-bombing through huge chocolate chip cookies that read, "He coughed on the Cookies with the chocolate bits"; to a long discussion regarding who might have said the "shoo fly" refrain. Example 5 shows what happened during the reading of the "L" page.

Example 5

1	Anne:	HE LIT ON THE LIST FOR THE GROCERY STORE. SHOO FLY! SHOO FLY! SHOOO.
2	Oscar:	Paper! [standing and pointing at the book——there is a grocery list in cursive writing in upper right-hand corner of the page]
3	Anne:	What's that paper for?
4	C1:	School?
5	Anne:	School, huh?
6	C2:	For the grocery.
7	Anne:	[rereading part of the text] HE LIT ON THE LIST FOR THE GROCERY STORE.
8	C1:	What does it say on the paper?
9	Anne:	Would you like me to read the list. See this is what mom does. You can help her——you can write lists in your journals. We write lists for all different reasons. Mom needed a grocery story list. I'll read it. CHOCOLATE, EGGS, APPLES, OLIVE OIL, HONEY, MILK, SALAMI, JELLY....
10	C3:	What are noodles? ["noodles" is the last word on the list that Anne had not finished reading]
11	C1:	A kind of soup.
12	Anne:	Like soup? Do you get noodles in your soup?
13	C2:	Sometimes they"re green.
14	Anne:	Sometimes noodles are green. Absolutely right! [turning to show the "M" and "N" page]
15	C:	And yellow.
16	C3:	Instead of mostaccioli, it's "mostanoodles"!!

17   Anne: I like that! You got both things in the word. I like that! I"m so
                  glad you asked about noodles because ... [skipping the "M"
                  page and reading] HE NIBBLED ON #NOODLES# IN THE
                  CLASSEROLE....

18   Cs: #NOODLES#
                  {Fieldnotes, videotape, 02/01/95}

Oscar's initiation regarding the "paper" in the illustration led them to an
examination of this grocery list. This was February and many children were
reading from print, but probably because it was in cursive writing, they
wanted Anne to read it (line 8). This gave Anne a wonderful opportunity to
suggest that they could write lists in their journals, which were called
at-home journals, that Anne gave to students so they had materials to use
at home and that they brought back to school everyday to share with Anne
and other classmates. In line 10 a child, apparently able to read the last
word on the list that Anne had not as yet read, asked about "noodles." Another child answered the query—"A kind of soup"—which illustrates the
kind of *cross discussion* between peers without teacher mediation
(Cazden, 1988; Lemke, 1990) that was frequent in the classroom discourse. That is, not all of the talk by students was directly addressed to
Anne. Then Anne accepted the latter student response in a way that led
children to offer more ideas about noodles.
     Note also Anne's "absolutely right!" in line 16. She frequently said this
or "you're right" to her students' responses, but it is important to emphasize its role in the collaborative talk that these read-alouds represent. The
same evaluative wordings can often occur in teacher-dominated initi-
ate-response-evaluation (IRE) sequences (Cazden, 1988), but these function by telling the child that he or she has the right answer that the teacher
is looking for. That is not the case here because "absolutely right!" was
Anne's response to the child's initiation; it was her acceptance of the
child's claim of expertise. In other words, in teacher-dominated IRE talk
the ownership of knowledge is reserved to the teacher—the student is just
to parrot or reproduce according to the teacher's agenda—whereas in collaborative talk, students' ownership of knowledge is acknowledged and appreciated by Anne and other classmates.
     Anne also showed her appreciation of C3's "mostanoodles" in line 16,
which is quite a sophisticated feat of phonemic knowledge because the student transformed the name of a type of noodles—"mostaccioli"—to one that
will include "both things," namely the both letters "M" and "N," depicted on
the next page that Anne turned to. Then Anne skipped the "M" page to cele-
brate this rich discussion about noodles by reading the "N" page.
     In summary, students' responses to ABC books showed that more com-
plex and sophisticated phonemic awareness emerged throughout the year.

Early initiations showed their attempts to connect alphabet information in the books to the first sounds representing the first letters of their names and also to the first letter of the names of animals, objects, or topics that these books evoked for them (e.g., "Popeye," "peanut butter," "queen"; that "'L' is for frog" because frogs *love* flies or have a *long* tongue; and so forth). Subsequently, their contributions consisted of responses to sounds represented by noninitial letters of words and other complex constructions ("mostanoodles"), and they began to show their increased phonemic knowledge in comments during the reading of non-ABC books, even remarking on similarities or differences regarding the letter–sound relationships found in English and Spanish.

Although Anne developed a range of supportive strategies to sustain and extend student initiations during reading-alouds over the years and was adept in understanding students' phonological knowledge through deciphering their invented spellings in writing, she was at times baffled by how to accurately read the phonemic approximations expressed in her students' comments so that she could provide the appropriate contingent responses to them. Nevertheless, she managed to address many levels of student initiations in ways that showed students that she valued their risk-taking efforts in providing approximations. In addition, she developed procedures to cope with the sometimes very high-spirited manner of her students' responses.

Anne: I think that children developed much more sophisticated levels of phonemic awareness than I had originally thought they would. I guess that I thought that children would do overt sounding out in reading as a result of my reading the ABC books and I was sort of surprised that that didn't happen. But that did come out in their writing. I really hadn't thought it out enough in the beginning when I was asking my early questions. I didn't know enough to say that, "Oh yeah, they're going to get it because they are going to write a lot." So, it's not as important to sound out a word in the old traditional ways of thinking because of how it comes out in writing. I think kids don't sound out words in reading unless they have been taught that. It is not a natural thing, but sounding out is natural in their own writing. They showed much more knowledge of letter–sound relationships in their initiations to the ABC books, much more than mere sounding out.

Having a too much level of exuberance from the kids, a level where no one is profiting from my reading is one of the bumps of the inquiry. Again, too, I had used some books that had certain physical features to them (the sticker book and the refrigerator book, which are not books illustrated previously) that fostered more excitement. I was curious about what would really happen here. I'm not afraid to do that, but maybe my fault is going too far sometimes, probably because I know that so many other times when I let it go, great responses have emerged and chaos did not occur. Anyhow, maybe unlike other teachers, I am willing to risk this sort of unruly exuberance that makes management difficulties for me. To me, it's worth it.

ABC BOOKS ALSO FOSTER THE LEARNING
OF CONTENT KNOWLEDGE

Chaney (1993) argued that, although traditional practice has relegated the use of alphabet books to the emergent and beginning literacy levels, they should be considered for all ages and abilities and for a range of curricular purposes. As Anne explored the genre to use in her inquiry, she realized that many of these ABC books supplied considerable more than information about language (Smolkin & Yaden, 1992).

One of the children's favorite ABC books was *Pop-Up Animal Alphabet Book* (Cerf, 1994), frequently read at reading-aloud time, mostly at the children's request. Anne read many pop-up or "flap" books, as the children called them, and often had children come up to the front of their classmates and take turns to manipulate the tabs of the books, which is noted in the next example. She continued to do so even though university researchers suggested that this practice frequently seemed to cause unnecessary disruptions of the reading-aloud session.

Anne: Many of the children in my class have not been read to at home. I have found that these pop-up books are so inviting to children. They provide ways for them to physically act on them, to manipulate them that hooks some of the very reluctant readers to books. So, even though I agreed with Chris and Shannon and Diane that they were disruptive during the read-alouds sometimes, I feel that I will take that drawback if it entices a child to books and reading.

I also had two very immature students this year who sometimes tested my patience in that they had to learn how to behave or interact during read-alouds. The university researchers also wondered why I did not ask them not join the group if they couldn't act responsibly, especially because I do have them take short time outs at other times during the day when they had trouble coping in routines. However, I just couldn't do it. The reading-aloud sessions are the core of my literacy program so everyone just has to be part of the community, even though some students do have trouble following our rules sometimes. I will put up with the disruptions and slowly the children learn how to behave and be part of the group.

Student Initiations as Intertextual Links

The first reading of this pop-up book was in October, and even though children were excited to take their turns to pull a tab or lift a flap, this time it was done smoothly with few disruptions. Example 6 begins with students offering initiations for the upcoming "R" letter.

Example 6

1	C:	Radio.
2	C:	Rake.
3	Anne:	R's FOR THE RHINO, WHOSE TEMPER IS SHORT.
4	C:	What is "temper"?
5	Anne:	(... ...) [Gives a short definition that is inaudible.]
6	C:	People use horns for medicine.
7	Anne:	[Nods in affirmation.]
8	C:	He can go 30 mph.

....

9	Anne:	V'S FOR VARYING HARE, SOMETIMES WHITE, SOMETIMES BROWN.
10	C:	[Goes up to the book——which shows a white hare in snow——and pulls the tab——which now reveals a brown hare in green grass.]
11	C1:	It's like a picture.
12	C2:	It changes its hair.
13	C3:	White is for snow, brown is for spring.
14	Anne:	[Nods in confirmation.] W? WOLVES, WHO FORM PACKS TO HUNT GAME.
15	Cs:	Ooooooooooo.
16	C1:	Like a ghost, like a witch.
17	C2:	Wolves eat people and lions and leopards. I saw it on a program.
18	C3:	A dog looks like a wolf. {Fieldnotes, 10/12/94}

In line 4, a child asked about "temper," for which Anne provided an explanation (which was inaudible). Children offered other information about the rhino in lines 6 and 8, namely, that horns are used for medicine and that a rhino can go 30 mph.

Students also included extra information regarding the varying hare and wolves. For the varying hare, C2 noted that as another child moved the tab in the book "it changes its hair," and C3 followed up by remarking that this change was connected to different seasons—"White is for snow, brown is for spring." In lines 15 to 18, students produced a sound that wolves make, which led C1 to make a connection to ghosts and witches (which were topics of books being read during this month of Halloween), as well as to other information about wolves—that is, what they eat and what they look like.

Many of these student initiations represented the kinds of intertextual links in the classroom discourse that children made during the reading-aloud sessions (Bloome & Bailey, 1992; Bloome & Egan-Robertson, 1993; Lemke 1985). That is, they juxtaposed or tied content from other texts—other ABC books about animal topics or the many information books she also read aloud, songs, movies, TV shows, personal stories from their home and communities, and so forth—to the text being read.

Although there were many instances of such intertextual links in the examples in the previous section, they were even more prevalent when Anne read this "informational" type of ABC books. Frequently, children made connections to similar content found in many of the informational books that Anne also read a lot to her students. This is shown in the next example, which is another reading of the *Pop-up Animal Alphabet Book* a few months later. Here, Anne is about to read the "M is for Mongoose, best snake-fighter born" page. The illustration depicts a mongoose next to a large black-and-yellow snake (which, when the flap is lifted, is now in the mouth of the mongoose). There is no mention in the book of the type of snake it is, but Casey is sure it is a cobra.

Example 7

1	Casey:	That's the king of all of the snakes. That's——that's a cobra.
2	Anne:	That's a cobra. You know about the cobra?
3	Casey:	It's the strongest of all the snakes.
4	Anne:	The cobra is the——how did you know that? Did you read that in a book?
5	Casey:	Yes. In this book. [getting out of his chair and pointing to books on the side of the room]
6	Anne:	Oh. Maybe you can find it.
....		[Casey has gone to look for the book; most of the children turn in their chairs to watch what he is doing.]
7	Anne:	Okay. While he's looking——oh see how you can find lots of good things in books? He knew that and we didn't——I didn't know that. Did you know that?
8	C1:	(... ...).
9	Anne:	They have a flap on the side? Why? You know what I don't know. Maybe the snake book will help us.
10	Cf2:	(...) snakes.
11	Casey:	I found it.

12	Anne:	Okay. You can bring it over. Yes, in the *Zoo* book.
....		[There is a long pause as Casey looks for the cobra in the book. Children are very quiet. Casey finds the page and holds the book up over his head for classmates to see.]
13	Anne:	[Looking at videocamera operator.] See, he knew exactly. [addressing Casey] Come over here to the middle so everyone can see, sweetheart. Oh I am so proud of you. You did——want me to read it? Would you like to read a little bit about it?
....		[Casey gives the book to Anne and sits down.]
14	Anne:	[holding the book open in front of her, pointing to the picture of the cobra] Look, here's the cobra. [C1] was just talking about the big flaps at the sides. Right here. [pointing to the picture again] That's what he was talking about. The flaps.

{Fieldnotes, videotape, 02/22/95}

Children regularly took two books home to read, or "to practice," as Anne and the children called it. Although Casey would not have been able to read this book that he found on the shelf conventionally, someone in his family could have read the book to him or he might have also read it during their free reading time when students chose what they wanted to read—books, posters, wall stories, group-composed texts, and so forth—on their own or with peers. Thus, although the pop-up book did not mention the kind of snake, Casey and another child knew about cobras—they had flaps—and Casey knew exactly where to find the book to substantiate his claim. This was a case in which the children taught Anne, and she was explicit about this fact (lines 7 & 9).

It was typical for Anne to allow children who knew that there was a book that had relevant information to the topic in the book being read to leave the group to find that book during Anne's reading-aloud sessions. Although other teachers might treat such student actions as unwelcomed diversions or tangents, Anne loved it when they made these intertextual links, and was always amazed that her students knew exactly where the book was housed (even though there were tons of books in the room in different book cases, racks, and tables in different places in the room). Her obvious delight was probably why students continued to be so eager to do it.

Sharing *A for Antarctica*

The last example is from another informational ABC book, *A for Antarctica* (Chester, 1995), that Anne read in April. This book had many interesting photographs that evoked many student initiations, which also ended up as challenges for Anne in keeping some semblance of order. Example 8 provides only a flavor of what this very long, high-spirited session was like.

Example 8

1	Anne:	B. BOAT. EXPEDITIONERS OFTEN RIDE FROM SHIP TO SHORE IN INFLATABLE BOATS.
2	C1:	It doesn't look like a boat.
3	Anne:	It doesn't look like a boat, does it?
4	C2:	There's a penguin jumped on there and is cruising.
5	Anne:	There *is* a penguin on the boat.
6	C3:	Look at the guys' legs. [referring to the illustration on the bottom of the page that has two legs with boots sticking out of the snow]
7	Anne:	BALLOON. BALLOONS ARE USED BY METEOROLOGISTS TO STUDY THE WEATHER. When you listen to the weather man, he's——he's a meteorologist. That's his name.
8	C:	BOOTS [reading the text].
9	Anne:	WARM BOOTS MUST BE WORN AT ALL TIMES.
10	C1:	What's he doing with that?
11	Anne:	What do you think? I don't know.
12	C2:	Maybe he's fallen down.
13	Anne:	Let's have hands.
14	C3:	He's looking down in the ice.
15	Anne:	He's looking down in the ice.
16	C4:	Maybe he's sleeping in the snow.
17	Anne:	[laughing] Maybe he's sleeping in the snow.
18	C5:	Maybe he drowned.
19	Anne:	Maybe he drowned in the snow.
20	C6:	Maybe he fell down.
21	Anne:	Maybe he fell down.
22	C7:	Maybe (... ...) because he wouldn't (... ...) and he put him in the snow.
23	Anne:	Maybe the penguin put him in the snow?
24	C8:	Maybe he went for a swim.
25	Anne:	Maybe he went for a swim. One more.
26	C9:	Maybe he slipped.
27	Anne:	Maybe he slipped. [turning the page.]
....		
28	Anne:	C. CREVASSE. GIANT CRACKS FORM IN THE ICE WHEN GLACIERS TWIST AND TURN. DEEP CREVASSES ARE ICY BLUE COLOR. [sweeping her finger along the crevasse in the illustration]

29	C1:	#Can you....#
30	Anne:	#COMPASS# [pointing to the compass in the illustration]. Do you have a question? [having her hand out to silence children and addressing C1]
31	C1:	Can you——can you cross from there to over there?
32	Anne:	Let's look at the picture. You need to do something special. [holding up the book to show the picture]
33	Cs:	#(.........).# [Many children talk at once.]
34	C2:	#(.........)# crossing bridge.
35	Anne:	Let's have hands because I can't hear everybody. It looks like you can cross a crevasse but you would have to have a crossing bridge of some kind. That looks like a ladder.
36	C3:	That has to be real big.
37	Anne:	Yes.
38	C3:	Because you could fall down.
39	Anne:	Yes. Couldn't it be dangerous?
40	Cs:	Yes. [Many are nodding in affirmation.]
41	Anne:	Absolutely.
42	C4:	You have to walk carefully (.........).
....		[More discussion as children bring up the fact that some people cannot look down or they would fall. Then when many are speaking at the same time, Anne asks for "hands up" again and calls on C5.]
43	C5:	(.........).
44	Anne:	That's....
45	C5:	That's a real book.
46	Anne:	What kind of book?
47	Cs:	Nonfiction.
48	Anne:	Nonfiction.
49	C6:	It's a real live book.
50	Anne:	Is it a real live book?
51	C7:	It has real pictures.
52	Anne:	It's photographs, isn't it?
		{Fieldnotes, videotape, 04/12/95}

This is a long example even though we only touched on the interactions around "B" and "C" information, because the reading-aloud on this book was also very long. We have included it to illustrate four major points. First, many might argue that this particular book was too advanced for first graders, and this might be a valid claim in some sense because Anne chose to use it later in the school year. It is clear from the classroom discourse, however, that children did not find this book boring. We think that the photographs of the book helped the children understand the content of the text, because many of their initiations and responses seemed to be picture related, that is, because Anne gave them spaces to respond to the book from their perspective, they found ways to make it meaningful for them.

Second, the kinds of ideas children offered were interesting. Most of them were sort of inquiry acts (Lindfors, 1999) or problem-solving predictions. It is common to talk about predictions in the reading of stories, usually having children hypothesize or suggest what the story might be about, the actions characters are likely to take next, or how the story is going to end, and so forth. We saw predictions in earlier examples, especially as responses to the *Q is for Duck* book because the whole format of the text was to promote possibilities or to approach the book as a guessing game. However, predictions occur in the reading of information books (Pappas & Barry, 1997), as well as the informational ABC books like the *A for Antarctica*. Many of the predictions for the boots-sticking-in-the-snow photograph (lines 10–27), for example, reflected students' ideas of what could have happened to the "man" whose boots are seen. Almost everyone had a proposal (and this was even a longer section that has been edited because of space constraints), many of which beginning with a "maybe" to signal the tentativeness of what that picture might represent. Later, children were intrigued by how a crevasse could be crossed (line 31) and again scrutinized the photographs for possible solutions. A long discussion ensued about the use of a ladder and how dangerous it might be to cross (again edited for space reasons).

Third, the example illustrates Anne's role in responding to students' predictions and questions. Regarding the boots, Anne accepted their suggestions by repeating each offering, and in the crevasse section there was a joint enterprise initiated by children, but with Anne joining in to figure out the crossing-the-crevasse puzzle. Because so many were so eager to contribute, Anne frequently had to resort to using the hands up procedure several times (e.g., lines 13 & 35) to orchestrate these interactions.

Finally, at the end of the example, a child brought up the genre of this ABC book—it was a "real" (line 45) or "real live" book (line 49) that had "real" pictures (line 51). So many teachers have to give explicit instruction about fiction versus nonfiction distinctions, but here children's awareness of genre just emerged on its own because Anne had read so many types of ABC books, as well as many genres of books in general. Thus, unlike many first-grade teachers who concentrate mostly on the use of stories as the basis of their literacy instruction (Pappas, 1991, 1993), Anne encouraged her students to read and write a range of genres, and students developed these genre understandings as part of their response to these books.

Anne: I agree that it was the pictures that were so very salient for the children in the Antarctica *book. I don't normally handle predictions the way I did here. Usually they just emerge. Although the predictions did start here by a child initiation, I don't usually have them offer them one at a time in a successive manner, but I guess I just wanted to know what they would come up with. I am always curious that I go almost to the end, sometimes making, then, managerial problems for myself.*

But it is because I am real open and go a long time is why the intertextual links like Casey's all of the student initiations occur so much. I guess I have a high level of tolerance. The more you have experience in having interactive, collaborative interactions, the better you are at it. I have noticed that I have developed strategies that I draw on to deal with the bumps. And, of course, the amount of time for reading aloud is always growing because they also can tolerate it more. They learn so much from read-alouds—besides the fact that they have more opportunities for making intertextual links—they just listen better, they get more sophisticated about everything because they learn about all the different genres, they get excited about the books so that they can't wait to read them on their own. All of that and more is all tied to the read-alouds. You never know what they are going to say—that's the scariest part, but also the great excitement for me.

NOW I KNOW MY ABC'S ... AND ...

The reading of ABC books fostered many literacy understandings in Anne's students. Such success did not develop without struggle on Anne's part. Sometimes Anne missed the student phonemic approximations hurled at her in these reading-aloud sessions, thereby making it necessary for her to develop new skills for understanding students' phonological knowledge in this setting. Moreover, because many of the ABC books created much exuberance on the part of the students' responses, Anne was frequently challenged with fashioning various approaches to coordinate the collaborative interactions of these sessions.

Nevertheless, the reading of ABC books did certainly promote her students' phonemic awareness, which became more complex and sophisticated throughout the year. Because Anne worked hard at creating a collaborative reading-aloud genre, students were given many spaces to make sense of the complexities of letter–sound correspondences. They were given many opportunities to articulate their own oral dialects and to map them to the letter–sound knowledge afforded by the ABC books. Thus, the use of ABC books can provide a holistic way for urban children who have varied dialect phonology that is frequently very different from that of the teacher (Goodman, 1993), to learn phonics successfully. Here they learned to use phonics in the process of responding to ABC books, along with their use of phonics in the other reading and writing experiences that Anne created for them.

As Anne found out, the genre of ABC books is huge and varied, and as a result, children learned much more than their ABCs. They learned the content information on a range of topics that these books cover. Students' intertextual comments were rich, as they connected ideas and meanings on these content topics in ABC books with those found in other texts of different genres that Anne read to them, as well as the ones students learned at home from TV shows, movies, and so forth.

REFERENCES

Adams, M. J. (1990). *Beginning to read: Thinking and learning about print.* Cambridge, MA: MIT Press.
Aylesworth, J. (1992). *Old black fly.* New York: Henry Holt.
Bloome, D., & Bailey, F. (1992). Studying language and literacy through events, particularity, and intertextuality. In R. Beach, J. L. Green, M. L. Kamil, & T. Shanahan (Eds.), *Multidisciplinary perspectives on literacy research* (pp. 181–210). Urbana, IL: National Conference on Research in English.
Bloome, D., & Egan-Robertson, A. (1993). The social construction of intertextuality in classroom reading and writing lessons. *Reading Research Quarterly, 28,* 305–333.
Cazden, C. B. (1988). *Classroom discourse: The language of teaching and learning.* Portsmouth, NH: Heinemann.
Cerf, C. B. (1994). *Pop-up animal alphabet book.* New York: Random House.
Chaney, J. H. (1993). Alphabet books: Resources for learning. *The Reading Teacher, 47,* 96–104.
Chester, J. (1995). *A for Antarctica.* Berkeley, CA: Triangle Press.
Cochran-Smith, M. (1984). *The making of a reader.* Norwood, NJ: Ablex.
Dickinson, D. K., & Keebler, R. (1989). Variations in preschool teachers' storybook reading styles. *Discourse Processes, 12,* 353–376.
Dickinson, D. K., & Smith, M. A. (1994). Long-term effects of preschool teachers' book readings on low-income children's vocabulary and story comprehension. *Reading Research Quarterly, 29,* 104–122.
Elting, M., & Folsom, M (1980). *Q is for duck: An alphabet guessing game.* New York: Clarion.
Goodman, K. (1993). *Phonics phacts.* Portsmouth, NH: Heinemannn.
Green, J. L., Harker, J., & Golden, J. (1986). Lesson construction: Differing views. In G. W. Noblitt & W. T. Pink (Eds.), *Schooling in the social context: Qualitative studies* (pp. 46–77). Norwood, NJ: Ablex.
Hall, S. T. (1991). *What is Christmas?* Racine, WI: Western.
Heath, S. B. (1982). What no bedtime story means: Narrative skills at home and school. *Language in Society, 11,* 49–76.
Holdaway, D. (1979). *The foundations of literacy.* Auckland, New Zealand: Ashton Scholastic.
Lemke, J. L. (1985). Ideology, intertextuality, and the notion of register. In J. D. Benson & W. S. Greaves (Eds.), *Systemic perspectives on discourse: Selected theoretical papers from the 9th international systemic workshop, Vol. 1* (pp. 275–294). Norwood, NJ: Ablex.
Lemke, J. L. (1990). *Talking science: Language, learning, and values.* Norwood, NJ: Ablex.
Lindfors, J. W. (1999). *Children's inquiry: Using language to make sense of the world.* New York: Teachers College Press

Martinez, M., & Teale, W. (1993). Teacher storybook reading style: A comparison of six teachers. *Research in the Teaching of English, 27,* 175–199.

McGuinness, D., & McGuinness, C., & Donahue, J. (1995). Phonological training and the alphabet principle: Evidence for reciprocal causality. *Reading Research Quarterly, 30,* 830–852.

Morrow, L. M. (1988). Young children's responses to one-to-one story readings in school settings. *Reading Research Quarterly, 23,* 89–107.

Ninio, A., & Bruner, J. (1978). The achievement and antecedents of labeling. *Journal of Child Language, 5,* 1–15.

Oyler, C. (1996a). Sharing authority: Student initiations during teacher-led read-alouds of information books. *Teaching and Teacher Education, 12,* 149–160.

Oyler, C. (1996b). *Making room for students in an urban first grade: Sharing authority in room 104.* New York: Teachers College Press.

Panofsky, C. P. (1994). Developing the representational functions of language: The role-child book-reading activity. In V. John-Steiner, C. P. Panofsky, & L. W. Smith (Eds.), *Sociocultural approaches to language and literacy: An interactionist perspective* (pp. 223–264). Cambridge, England: Cambridge University Press.

Pappas, C. C. (1991). Fostering full access to literacy by including information books. *Language Arts, 68,* 449–462.

Pappas, C. C. (1993). Is narrative primary? Some insights from kindergarteners' pretend readings of stories and information books. *JRB: A Journal of Literacy, 25,* 97–129.

Pappas, C. C., & Barry, A. (1997). Scaffolding urban students' initiations: Transactions in reading information books in the reading-aloud curriculum genre. In N. J. Karolides (Ed.), *Reader response in the elementary classroom: Quest and discovery* (pp. 215– 236). Mahwah, NJ: Lawrence Erlbaum Associates.

Ramirez, A. (1988). Analyzing speech acts. In J. L. Green & J. O. Harker (Eds.), *Multiple perspective analyses of classroom discourse* (pp. 135–163). Norwood, NJ: Ablex.

Richgels, D. J., Poremba, K. J., & McGee, L. M. (1996). Kindergarteners talk about print: Phonemic awareness in meaningful contexts. *The Reading Teacher, 49,* 632–642.

Sendak, M. (1962). *Alligators all around: An alphabet.* New York: Harper & Row.

Smolkin, L. B., & Yaden, D. B. (1992). O is for mouse: First encounters with the alphabet book. *Language Arts, 69,* 432–441.

Snow, A. (1991). *The monster book of ABC sounds.* New York: Penguin Books.

Snow, C. E. (1983). Literacy and language: Relationships during the preschool years. *Harvard Educational Review, 53,* 165–189.

Stahl, S., & Murray, B. (1994). Defining phonological awareness and its relationship to early reading. *Journal of Educational Psychology, 86,* 221–234.

Sulzby, E., & Teale, W. H. (1991). Emergent literacy. In R. Barr, M. L. Kamil, P. Mosenthal, & P. D. Pearson (Eds.), *Handbook of reading research* (Vol 1, pp. 727–757). White Plains, NY: Longman.

Teale, W. H., & Martinez M. G. (1996). Reading aloud to young children: Teachers' reading styles and kindergartners' text comprehension. In C. Pontecorvo, M. Orsolini, B. Burge, & L. Resnick (Eds.), *Children's early text construction* (pp. 321–344). Mahwah, NJ: Lawrence Erlbaum Associates.

Temple, C., Nathan, R., Temple, F., & Burris N. A. (1993). *The beginnings of writing.* Boston: Allyn and Bacon.

Wells, G. (1985). Preschool literacy-related activities and success in school. In D. R. Olson, N. Torrance, & A. Hildyard (Eds.), *Literacy, language, and learning: The nature and consequences of reading and writing* (pp. 229–255). Cambridge, England: Cambridge University Press.

Wells, G. (1986). *The meaning makers: Children learning language and using language to learn.* Portsmouth, NH: Heinemann.

Wells, G., & Chang-Wells, G. L. (1992). *Constructing knowledge together: Classrooms as centers of inquiry and literacy.* Portsmouth, NH: Heinemann.

Yaden, D. B., Jr., Smolkin, L. B., & Conlon, A. (1989). Preschoolers' questions about pictures, print conventions, and story text during reading aloud at home. *Reading Research Quarterly, 24,* 188–214.

Chapter 6

Two Teachers' Efforts to Transform the Reading-Aloud Curriculum Genre for Collaboration: Examining Shifts of Process and Content Dimensions of Sharing Authority

Christine C. Pappas

Shannon Hart

Diane Escobar

Hawa Jones

Dorothy A. O'Malley

The introduction chapter of this book provides the theoretical and methodological background for the larger collaborative school–university action-research project and this chapter about Hawa's and Dorothy's inquiries on the reading-aloud curriculum genre. See also the last chapter, which further discusses the implications of Hawa's and Dorothy's inquiries—as well as those of the other teacher researchers.

This chapter focuses on two teachers' inquiries on the reading-aloud curriculum genre. Research has indicated that children's literacy understandings are facilitated through such book-reading experiences. Besides being exposed to what typical written language sounds like (Smith, 1985), how teachers ask questions—or otherwise direct students' attention to aspects of the books being shared—is one of the major ways that young readers begin to construct their ideas about the interpretations and conventions of books (Cochran-Smith, 1984; Dickinson & Keebler, 1989; Dickinson & Smith, 1994; Martinez & Teale, 1993; Morrow, 1988; Wells, 1986).

Recent research has indicated that teachers vary in the *style* in which they conduct these reading-aloud sessions (Dickinson & Keebler, 1989; Dickinson & Smith, 1994; Green, Harker, & Golden, 1986; Martinez & Teale, 1993; Teale & Martinez, 1996). For example, Teale and Martinez (1996) showed that each of the six kindergarten teachers in their study, who all read the same four books (chosen by the researchers), had a distinctive style that emphasized different aspects of the books in discussion. For instance, one teacher treated stories as cohesive entities composed of interrelated elements, and had students work systematically on textually explicit story information; another teacher focused more on the words in a book and emphasized children predicting upcoming words in text; yet another teacher's strategies involved eliciting ideas from the students, but much of the talk was concerned with unimportant information; and so forth. Thus, the talk, and the ways in which teachers direct and facilitate it, is a significant matter. The realized sign, or a teacher-reader's representation of a text in the discourse of reading-aloud sessions (Golden, 1990), affects how children might make sense of books in the reading- aloud events themselves. According to Elster (1995), this may even contribute to how young, emergent readers subsequently reenact books that were read aloud to them.

However, most of these studies about teacher style also show that the classroom interaction led by the teachers is mostly one of control, with teachers initiating most of the talk and asking all of the questions. That is, the examples provided in these studies show teachers working on explicit textual information, or reinforcing the story recall of their students, using mostly *psuedo-questions,* ones for which they already know the answers (Cazden, 1988; Ramirez, 1988). In a study conducted by Dickinson and Smith (1994), only some of the 25 preschool teachers (who chose the book they read, but who were videotaped only once) seemed to allow for spontaneous utterances of students. However, the nature of these student responses is not always easily understood from the examples provided by Dickinson and Smith. These student initiations were not always clear from the coding definitions that were used in the study, either. Thus, although there might be different styles to accomplish in orchestrating read-alouds, and there might be some teachers who allow for student initiations; a teacher-dominated discourse structure prevails in most of the classrooms in which book reading was investigated. Little has been documented wherein teachers have purposely encouraged *students*' contributions to the book- sharing events—that is, children's own questions or comments during reading-aloud sessions were used. This, however, is the focus of this chapter.

The teacher-dominated initiate-response-evaluate (IRE) format (Cazden, 1988), or what Gutierrez, Rymes, & Larson (1995) also call the teacher's controlling monologic script, realized traditional transmission-oriented instructional models and reflected dominant cultural values. It has not been conducive to collaborative construction of new meanings among classroom participants, nor has it afforded "the joint construction of a new sociocultural terrain, creating spaces for shifts in what counts as knowledge and knowledge representation" (Gutierrez, et al., 1995, p. 445). Developing strategies that both foster the love of reading and support students' growth as readers, in reading-aloud sessions, is no easy matter (Scharer, 1992). Moreover, making sure that children's contributions and interpretations of books are also privileged in this enterprise is frequently a struggle, as is seen here in Hawa's and Dorothy's inquiries.

Hawa: Before, I had just wanted my second graders merely to listen as I read-aloud and then answer my yes–no questions when I was finished. They would all sit at their desks, while I also sat at my desk. They seemed so bored and listless. I had taught fourth grade for 4 years, and this was my first year teaching second grade, which I was finding quite a challenge. My major goal in my inquiry was to foster my students' critical responses to the books I read aloud—good children's literature that I was just learning was available at this grade level. I also felt that I had to do something to get many of my still-emergent readers more interested in reading. I had hoped that by choosing and planning ahead of time the books I read aloud, and by changing how I read aloud them, I might accomplish these objectives.

Dorothy: The summer before my inquiry I collected a range of multicultural books. And, although I had usually felt more comfortable in dominating the discussions about books I read to students, this year I really wanted to understand my students' responses or their expressions about these books. Also, I found that my some of my third-grade students did not feel that proud of their Mexican heritage, so I also wanted to use a lot of books with Latino themes, topics, and characters. But, more than that, I wanted to use books that depicted other cultures, too. I wanted them to understand that each culture has its own traditions, and that they could see how their own cultural traditions might be different from these other ones. I had hoped that in seeing these differences, they might better appreciate their own. Before this year I had mostly English-dominant students, most of whom were born in the United States. But this year I also had more bilingual students, many of whom were born in Mexico and of course had Spanish as their native language. I had observed that, as they talked among themselves and to me, these students seemed to feel inferior, felt somehow that the monolingual English-speaking students in the class were smarter. I wanted to see if the use of these multicultural books might change that somehow.

Thus, both teachers had important reasons to examine and change their typical ways of conducting their reading-aloud routine or curriculum genre so as to encourage more student participation in the discussions about the books they read to them. Many of the teachers in our project group did inquiries around the reading-aloud routines during the preceding year, attempting to make them more interactive by fostering student initiations and responses. However, Hawa was new to the group and Dorothy had been a member in the earlier years, but not during the more recent years. Thus, both were "fresh" to the challenge of attempting to transform the reading-aloud curriculum genre to facilitate more collaborative talk (Wells & Chang-Wells, 1992). Therefore, their efforts in their reading-aloud inquiries illustrate both the difficulties and the successes involved in this process.

EFFORTS TO "HEAR" STUDENT VOICES: EMERGING ISSUES OF MANAGING PROCESS AND CONTENT DIMENSIONS OF TEACHER AUTHORITY

Questions about to who gets to learn and what is learned are connected to the power that lies in the relationships constructed in classrooms (Cummins, 1994; Gutierrez et al., 1995; Kreisberg, 1992; Oyler, 1996a, 1996b; Wells, 1994; Willinsky, 1990). Collaborative talk occurs when the traditional ways of teacher authority and control are altered and interrupted on both the interwoven dimensions of *process* (who gets to do what, where, when, and how) and of *content* (what counts as knowledge or who is validated as a knower) (Oyler, 1996a, 1996b; Peters, 1966). For collaborative talk to be possible, teachers have to make different choices in their interactions with their students, especially with regard to *tenor* (the kind of relationship they want to have with their students) and *mode* (the kind of role they want language to be assigned in the event) (Halliday & Hasan, 1985). They have to create opportunities where their students' voices are heard and the content of their input is valued (Bartolome, 1994; Wells, 1994, 1998; Young, 1992).

Thus, Hawa and Dorothy had to develop different supporting and intellectual teaching acts (Kilbourn, 1991). For example, motivated by wanting to give value to their students' ideas about the books they read to them (a content aspect), Hawa and Dorothy began to communicate more explicitly to their students that they (students) could interrupt their reading with student comments and questions (a process issue). The teachers also purposefully attempted to provide "spaces" in the classroom talk for their ideas. This was usually accomplished by obvious teacher pause in the discourse to allow for student initiations (again, mostly a process concern). Quite soon, student initiations increased (content), which led to process difficulties now that many students were offering comments and questions at the same time. Chaotic or unmanageable interactions sometimes occurred. Thus, Hawa and Dorothy needed to come up with various ways to manage these simultaneous student responses because neither were willing to give up their efforts to create more collaborative interactions. Although they considered the suggestions of other teacher- and university-researcher colleagues, each had to figure out how to resolve the problem for herself. Next, we illustrate some of the ways these new difficulties in sharing power manifested themselves, and the strategies they tried out to deal with them.

Encouraging and Managing Student Initiations

Hawa and her 28 students (all Latina or Latino students, except for an African American and one Anglo child) moved from their desks and had their reading-aloud sessions in the carpeted reading corner in the back corner of the room. She began by being very explicit in asking for their comments—see Example 1A:

Example 1A: Hawa's Inquiry

Hawa:	[after reading a page of *The Princess and the Pea* (Stevenson, 1992)] Look at this page. Do you have any questions?
....	
Hawa:	[addressing a few boys sitting on the floor near her] I want to hear from you today.
....	
Hawa:	[as a response to a child initiation, "He's rich."] How can you tell? I want to hear what everybody is saying. Let's not mumble, jumble all the time. {Fieldnotes, 10/17/94}
Hawa:	[in eliciting predictions for the book, *Mufaro's Beautiful Daughters* (Steptoe, 1987)] I want to hear from you. Take a guess. Risk free. There is no right answer.
....	
Hawa:	[as students are trying to figure out the illustrations to determine which daughter was which] I want to hear from those in the back. {Fieldnotes, Videotape, 10/24/94}

As noted in the excerpts, Hawa was quite specific in telling her students that she both expected and valued their initiations and responses to the books. Another important facet of her inquiry, which can be seen in her remarks here, was promoting equity of participation—namely, she wanted *all* children to be involved (more is discussed about this issue in the final section of the chapter).

Dorothy initially began with whole-class reading-aloud sessions that were followed by small-group rereading and discussions. In other words, in the beginning of the year, her inquiry was not limited to this reading-aloud curriculum genre because she was frequently attempting to foster her students' understandings of the multicultural books by giving them opportunities to discuss the books among themselves. Thus, sometimes we were videotaping and taking fieldnotes on the read-aloud sessions, and sometimes we were doing this observation during the small-group extension activities (discussions, acting out of a book, or pantomime experiences, etc.). But in those early whole-class read-alouds, Dorothy also communicated to her third-grade students that she wanted their initiations. For example, she began reading *On the Pampas* (Brusca, 1991) as follows:

Example 1B: Dorothy's Inquiry

1   Dorothy: Yesterday we read *On the Pampas*. Today I want to read it again. If a word or a question occurs to you, just bring it up. Just sit back and enjoy the book.
{Fieldnotes, 10/19/94}

Thus, Dorothy, like Hawa, told her students that it was okay to interrupt her reading to bring up their responses. Moreover, through her "just sit back and enjoy the book" comment and others, she tried to let them know that the talk about the book should be a pleasurable experience, not one that she would evaluate like in the typical teacher-dominated IRE structure. She also used more subtle ways to elicit student initiations by periodically pausing and looking at students and having longer wait times as she read.

As already indicated, as children began to offer initiations—many at one time—Hawa and Dorothy had to develop strategies to handle them. Chris brought up this difficulty in one of our early weekly meeting—see Example 2.

Example 2: Weekly Meeting

1   Chris: In looking at——in being in people's classrooms there are certain things that have come up that I thought would be interesting to talk about. There is a real dilemma ... of when you are trying to have kids have opportunities to initiate on their own. To give them spaces, you know, to talk. ... It's the process that I want to talk about. How then do you manage it? For example,

> Hawa kept saying to the kids, 'when you're at the tables you can talk but when you are at the [reading-aloud] group you all have to put your hands up.' But you don't really follow that. It's a natural part of getting the kids to initiate. So you don't want to cut that, but there's the problem of when there are more than one kid talking. ... [W]hat's some of the best ways that we can handle that? ... This one thing is part of a process part of sharing power. Instead of you always deciding when you're going to interrupt or respond to a book, you let the kids do it. But at the same time it could get like chaos. ... And you all seem to be inconsistent about it. You seem to be not sure about what you're doing and I just thought we ought to talk about it.

....

2   Anne: You don't know what they're going to say or how many are going to say it.

....

3   Sarah: Sometimes, for me, it seems more important to try and get some system going because (.. ...).
{Videotape, 10/19/94}

So, Chris posed the dilemma that she thought that Hawa and Dorothy seemed to be having regarding handling the procedures, or this process dimension of sharing power. Anne reiterated the problem—"you don't know what they're going to say or how many are going to say it." Sarah suggested that it would be important to "to get some system going."

Hawa decided to try a quick nominating system. That is, she told students that when they noticed that more than one person was trying to talk, to put their hands up. Then she pointed to an individual person with his or her hand up, numbering each one, after which students would take their turns to talk. This was fairly successful for Hawa throughout the year (although she did include other ways to help students better participate with each other, e.g., reminding them that someone had the floor, or having students better define their physical spaces so they could be more alert when others had comments to share).

Hawa: Using the nominating system was effective, but it also was a struggle. In fact, it is still a problem for me with the other students I have had taught subsequently. In some ways, it is not natural to wait to talk about a topic. They want to just get it out. But you can't have 28 students saying what's on their minds at the same time.

Dorothy also tried out this nominating by numbering strategy, but it didn't work for her. A major strategy she used successfully was to encourage her students to direct their questions or comments to each other. That is, she promoted and sanctioned cross discussion (Cazden, 1988; Lemke, 1990) where students talked to each other without teacher mediation.

> *Dorothy: I think was the most important part was to make more comments such as, "Why don't go on more on that?" I also think that my allowing for changes in the physical structure of the read-aloud helped that. In the beginning I decided where students sat to have them better listen. But then, I let students have more choice where they sat, which I think promoted their talking more to each other.*

Learning How to Respond to the Content of Students' Initiations

Once Hawa and Dorothy developed several techniques to manage the rush of student initiations, another difficulty emerged: What should they *do* with these student initiations? That is, what was the teacher's role with respect to the *content* dimension in sharing power and authority with students? Collaborative talk is considered to facilitate children's learning, their construction of knowledge, because it also makes it possible for teachers to be able to give feedback on these student responses. It gives them occasions to make their contributions be appropriate reactions to a learner's present needs (Pappas, 1997; Pappas & Barry, 1997; Pappas, Kiefer, & Levstik, 1999; Wells, 1998). Figuring out this aspect of classroom interaction became the next struggle for Hawa and Dorothy.

In studying children's early language development, Wells (1981, 1985, 1986) showed that those children who learned to talk most readily were those whose conversational partners were most willing and able to "lead from behind." In his words, "Letting the child take the initiative in selecting which aspect of the task or situation to attend to, these parents and other close adults in the child's life seemed intuitively to know how to accept and value the child's contributions and to sustain and extend his or her efforts at meaning-making" (Wells, 1993, p. 7). This approach is clearly based on Vygotskian (Vygotsky, 1978; Wertsch, 1991) notions of working in the learner's "zone of proximal development." It enables learners to appropriate or take over, not only the language of the culture, but also the cultural knowledge that is associated with the activities in which the talk occurs (Bruner, 1983).

Thus, to apply these ideas in the classroom, providing spaces for student initiations in responding to books creates opportunities for teachers to develop contingently responsive exchanges that are either at, or just beyond, children's current understandings (Wells 1986, 1990, 1998; Wells & Chang-Wells, 1992) These are teacher formulations that attempt to take into account students' present abilities and teachers' pedagogical intentions, but at the same time can be modified regarding teachers' agendas, in light of the feedback that children provide in their responses. Now, that is no easy matter—as we again recall what Anne said in the weekly meeting, "You don't know what they're going to say or how many are going to say it." Thus, the new challenge for Hawa and Dorothy, in their inquiries in sharing power with their students, was to create "uptake" strategies (Nystrand, 1997) that would be responsive to students' ideas or conjectures in the reading-aloud sessions. Examples 3 and 4 show Hawa's and Dorothy's struggles to accomplish this facet of collaborative talk.

Hawa's Struggles to Respond to Students' Meanings.   Example 3 is an excerpt of Hawa's reading of *Mufaro's Beautiful Daughters* (Steptoe, 1987). This is the first time that Hawa tried out the counting procedure, which is illustrated in the beginning of the example. Then, perhaps because she seemed to be caught up with the process dimension, it was difficult for her to be able to comment about students' efforts.

The book is about two beautiful daughters, Manyara and Nyasha, who traveled to meet a great king in the hope that one would be chosen to be his queen. Periodically, in the discussion, children voted and made predictions as to which daughter—the "bad" or "good" sister, as they decided to call them—would be successful in this quest. The excerpt begins with Hawa reading the text where Manyara, the "bad" girl, met an old woman, who tried to give her advice.

Example 3:
Hawa's Reading-Aloud of Mufaro's Beautiful Daughters

1	Hawa:	THE OLD WOMAN SPOKE. "I WILL GIVE YOU SOME ADVICE, MANYARA. SOON AFTER YOU PASS THE PLACE WHERE TWO PATHS CROSS, YOU WILL SEE A GROVE OF TREES. THEY WILL LAUGH AT YOU. YOU MUST NOT LAUGH IN RETURN. LATER, YOU WILL MEET A MAN WITH HIS HEAD UNDER HIS ARM. YOU MUST BE POLITE TO HIM." "HOW DO YOU KNOW MY NAME? HOW DARE YOU ADVISE YOUR FUTURE QUEEN? STAND ASIDE, YOU UGLY OLD WOMAN!" MANYARA SCOLDED, AND THEN RUSHED ON HER WAY WITHOUT LOOKING BACK. [holding up the book for students to see the illustrations, Hawa seems to be addressing a student who might not be attending to the book] Tara, I hope that you're enjoying the story.
2	Cf1:	She's not going to be a queen.
3	Hawa:	[still focusing on Tara] It's one of my favorites. You want to see it.
4	Cf1:	She's the bad girl.
....		[Several children are talking at once. A girl in the front row has raised her hand, and Hawa has called on her, but unfortunately the girl's talk is inaudible.]

5	Cf2:	(.... ....).
6	Hawa:	Oh, she might see her sister there already? [Then when two children begin to talk at once, Hawa gives each a number] One, two.
7	Cf3:	Have you read that story, but on your own?
8	Hawa:	Yes.
....		[There is more discussion on how many times Hawa has read the book and then she calls on Jonathan.]
9	Jonathan:	Um, by the time ... she thought that when she left her sister——left before the sister ... her sister probably left before her ... and she's still going to ... (....) before she took off.
10	Hawa:	Okay. Three, four, five. [assigning turns to three other children by pointing to those with their hands raised] Speak louder so that the people in the back can ah ... hear us....
....		
11	Hawa:	[She is now at another part of the book, showing another page of the book, and calls on a student who has a comment.] Yes?
12	Cm4:	You see that (...) right there?
....		[There is a short interruption as Hawa asks students to listen to their classmates.]
13	Cf5:	[pointing at the picture] You see like that house right there?
14	Hawa:	Right.
15	Cf5:	Maybe she has to go over there.
16	Hawa:	Could this be the——where the king lives? Or the prince?
17	Cs:	Yeah.
18	Cf6:	It looks like it's not far but the (...) line that you could go through, the path....
19	Hawa:	C, are you listening to what she's saying?
20	Cm6:	It looks like a street, Teacher. It looks like a street.
21	Cf6:	You go——you go....
22	Cf5:	Like a path.
23	Hawa:	Like a path, a street.
24	Cf5:	And the other girl didn't——the other girl didn't.
25	Hawa:	(...), Can you hear what she's saying up here? If you three have something to share, please share with all of us.
26	Cf2:	And the other girl, she's not going to know where the prince lives.
27	Hawa:	Vera, I haven't heard from you. Maria, I haven't heard from you today.
28	Cm4:	Maybe the evil sister probably took the wrong path.

29	Hawa:	She took the wrong path?
30	Cs:	Yeah.
31	Hawa:	Okay, maybe.
		{Fieldnotes, Videotape, 10/24/94}

We saw at the beginning of example, the use of the nomination-via-counting system that Hawa was trying out. Overall, Hawa seemed to be focusing mostly on how to manage the attention of her students, rather than on anything they might have said. There are several instances where she has checked what various children offered, and in doing so accepted their ideas. And, at the place where students are trying to puzzle out the paths in the illustration, she provided a contingent response to C5's comment by suggesting that the path might lead to where the king lives. Towards the end of the excerpt, C2 seemed worried that the other—or the "good"—girl might have taken the wrong path (line 26), which might mean that she won't get to the prince, and, in turn, by implication, would not win out as the queen. In line 28, C4 suggested an alternative proposal—namely, "maybe the evil sister ... took the wrong path," an idea that many of the children seemed to want to go along with. At the very end, Hawa tentatively accepted this possibility.

Thus, at this time of her inquiry, Hawa attempted to deal with the process dimension of sharing power with her students, wanting to hear from all, as can be seen by how many children contributed, even in this short excerpt. However, in doing so she was not able to address many of the meanings or ideas that students offered by adding her expertise to help them to find deeper responses and interpretations to the book she read. Even so, howver, we can see how much her students were already finding their voices, and seemed to be starting to be critical readers by considering several perspectives about what might be happening in the story, which was a major goal of Hawa's inquiry.

Dorothy's Struggles to Respond to Students' Meanings. As already noted, Dorothy also tried the nomination-via-counting system that ended up very successful for Hawa, but abandoned it to develop alternative strategies to cope with these simultaneous student initiations. Dorothy also had difficulties in finding the best ways to deal with students' initiations, so that these responses would lead to even more meaningful understandings. Example 4 provides an illustration of her struggles in this area.

Here, we focus on the classroom discussion, initiated by a student question, as Dorothy read *Darkness and the Butterfly* by Grifalconi (1987). Then we examine that episode in our weekly meeting conversation that occurred a few weeks later, when Dorothy shared the edited version that included that classroom footage. Thus, two types of discourse are provided here—first, classroom discourse from the videotape, then the discussion about it in our meeting.

In our meeting that day (present at the meeting were teacher–researchers Dorothy, Hawa, Sonia, and Sue, and university researchers Chris, Diane, and Shannon), we already saw other segments of the videotape. Now we noted on our editing sheet that the next part had to do with a boy's interruption of Dorothy's reading by asking, "Is that a poem?" As you see in the following excerpt—Example 4A—when the student asked about whether the book was a poem, the other students, who had some earlier curricular experience regarding poems, brought in their own ideas about their characteristics. Most argued that the present book was not a poem, but a story.

Example 4A: Excerpt of Classroom Discourse of Dorothy's Reading-Aloud Curriculum Genre, Shared at the Weekly Meeting

1	Dorothy:	"BUT LOOK AT THAT LITTLE BUTTERFLY, OSA; *SHE* MUST THINK SHE IS THE SMALLEST OF THE SMALL. DARKNESS PURSUES HER TOO——YET *SHE* FLIES ON!" SLEEPILY, OSA THOUGHT ABOUT THAT. "MAYBE SHE HAS A SECRET?" {AND} THEN SHE SHOOK HER HEAD. "BUT I HAVE NO WINGS TO FLY." OSA HEARD THE WISE {WOMAN CALL FORTH}: "YOU WILL FIND YOUR OWN WAY. YOU WILL SEE." OSA NODDED, AND BEFORE SHE KNEW IT, SHE FELL INTO A DEEP SLEEP....
2	Cm1:	That's a poem?
3	Dorothy:	Pardon me?
4	Cm1:	That's a poem. Or is that a poem or is it a story?
5	Dorothy:	Is this a poem or is it a story? What do you think?
6	Cm1:	# A story. #
7	Cs:	# Story. #
8	Dorothy:	Why do you think it's a——excuse me, why do you think it's a story? Who else thinks it's a story?
9	SCs:	[About 9 students raise their hands.]
10	Dorothy:	Cm2, why do you think it's a story?
11	Cm2:	It doesn't have <things> that rhyme.
12	Dorothy:	It doesn't have very many rhyming words.
13	Cm2:	It doesn't have stanzas.
14	Dorothy:	It doesn't——it's not written in stanzas, good.
15	Cm3:	It doesn't have four lines....
16	Dorothy:	Okay, do some stanzas have four lines? Do all stanzas have four lines in a poem?

17	Cs:	No.
18	Dorothy:	No, do all stanzas have rhyming words?
19	Cs:	No.
20	Dorothy:	Is it too long?
21	SCs:	# Yes. #
22	SCs:	# No. #
23	Dorothy:	Well, we haven't read very long poems, I agree. But poems can be very, very long. They can be longer than a story. (...) Do you think this story could be made into a poem?
24	Cs:	Yes.
25	Dorothy:	Probably so, probably so. {Edited videotape shared 03/29/95 from classroom videotape, 03/01/95}

Actually, although Grifalconi, the author and illustrator of the book, wrote this book as a story, she also included poem-like qualities in it, both in its format and in its lyrical phrasing. So, Cm1's question was probably a very reasonable one. And, the idea that there weren't any stanzas in the book is not really accurate because the text was written in a stanza-like fashion—with each line beginning with a capital letter, for example. However, this was probably not very noticeable to the students because usually there was only one stanza per page and they wouldn't have been able to see this capitalization or punctuation from their seats.

Dorothy subsequently looked at this book, and the student's question about it, quite differently since we examined it in our meeting, but in the upcoming excerpt of the meeting discussion, her attention was on other features of the interaction that involved her role in responding to students' initiations.

Example 4B: Excerpt from Weekly Meeting—Dorothy
Sharing Edited Version of Her Reading-Aloud Curriculum
Genre [Darkness and the Butterfly].

1	Diane:	I thought that was a really good wrap-up question, "Can this be made into a poem?" And all the kids answered, "Yeah, sure."
2	Dorothy:	Well they did——they did kind of do a little bit of that when we kind of went in and out of poetry. I couldn't get them to come up with a poem. We had a theme to send to the ... dental week or something and they just....
3	Chris:	[facing Dorothy] See, it's just that the kind of conversation would have been quite different if you had said, "Tell me why did

you——what makes you *say* that, what makes you think that
this might be a poem?"

4 Dorothy: Mmm, I'm getting too direct here [pointing to the video
screen]. The question is becoming looking for an answer instead
of just a comment and let them go in what direction
they——And I can hear that now, where I could never hear that,
I mean, I wouldn't——I thought that was good! [As Dorothy
talks, she waves her hand in front of her face as if to wave off her
own lack of hearing herself before now.]

5 Chris: Yeah, yeah.

6 Dorothy: I mean I'm beginning to see that because you cut them off
you're looking for yes or no, or the whole class responds....

7 Chris: Usually, yeah, usually there is a whole——yeah, there's a real
clue when the whole class is going "yeaaah" or "noooo" [lowers
her voice and makes it long, like a mechanical answer, and the
whole group laughs]. You know that "whoops, I'm definitely asking a pseudo-question here!" But you know there's some points
where that might be appropriate because you're trying to make
connections to other kinds of instruction, you know.

8 Hawa: Or sometimes you get them when they say "yeah" and you ask
them "why?" and they say, "uh, well, uh...."

9 Sonia: That's because they expect this, they expect....

10 Chris: Well, you know people call this procedural display and mock participation. In other words, kids know the routine but sometimes
there's no——and lots of teachers accept that they've understood and it's really just surface procedures so people call it procedural display and mock participation. It's that IRE where the
teacher does this, the kids say that, and teacher evaluates. It's
the kind of thing that you guys are trying to challenge.

11 Sonia: It's hard....

12 Dorothy: It's hard, but it's neat though [pointing to the video screen].
It's hard too because——I think this is the first time that I've
seen value in looking at my video. I can relate to things now and
actually I heard that and it sounded awful. I mean just the kids
says, "yesss" and before perhaps I would have thought, "Gee, is-
n't that good, they're all responding" [sort of with an exagger-
ated smile as if to show how silly that was].

13 Shannon: And they all got the right answer.

14 Dorothy: And not even the right and wrong answer but just that they
were....

15 Chris: Engaged.

16 Dorothy: [pointing to Chris] Yes, engaged. And somebody wasn't. Which
isn't as good as....

17 Chris: Yeah, a kid could be looking over there [Chris turns in her seat
to look away from the group] and said "yeah."

18	Dorothy:	Right.
19	Chris:	Well, maybe you can hear it because you have gone beyond in your inquiry in some way.
....		[The discussion then changed topic to see and consider the last segment of the video.]
		{Videotape of Weekly Meeting, 03/29/95}

Dorothy came to an important understanding about her interactions with students in her inquiry. That is, students' unison yes or no responses were no longer seen to be that comforting, or seen as evidence of student engagement to her. Instead of the development of more substantive meanings, this type of classroom interaction was now viewed by her as problematic and indicative of mostly mock participation and procedural display, (which Chris put a label to, drawing from some ideas in Bloome's, 1994, work). Thus, her making the effort to provide opportunities for her students' initiations around books was not enough. Her figuring out how best to contingently respond to students' initiations to sustain and extend them in the joint construction of collaborative talk was also important.

We can also see how much Dorothy valued the viewing the videotape of her interactions, because it enabled her to "hear" what, in the past, she had not heard. Thus, although she might have missed an important opportunity to respond to her student's question on this particular day in a way that might have contributed to her understanding her students' understanding of this multicultural book, which was at the core of her inquiry, with the help of the videotape she was given a chance to become more explicitly aware of what she had to do in the future to accomplish that goal in her inquiry.

Summary

In summary, both Hawa's and Dorothy's inquiries in the reading-aloud curriculum genre show how complex and difficult it is to move away from transmission-oriented teaching to make classroom interactions more collaborative. Both process and content dimensions of sharing teacher authority are interrelated in complex ways. The collaborative "dance" (Oyler, 1996b) requires the sharing of both student and teacher expertise in the joint coconstruction of meanings. The next section provides examples of these successful efforts.

COLLABORATING FOR NEW UNDERSTANDINGS

There were many instances where collaborative talk was accomplished in their classrooms, and where Hawa's and Dorothy's sharing of power and authority led to rich joint understandings about books. We first consider examples from Hawa's inquiry.

Collaborative Interactions and Discourse in Hawa's Read-Alouds

Example 5 illustrates how Hawa and her students figured out *Anansi the Spider* (McDermott, 1972). In this tale, Anansi set out on a long, difficult journey and was threatened by Fish and Falcon, but he was saved from terrible fates by his six sons. The focus of much of the conversation around the book was keeping track of these sons and how their special skills helped Anansi. Most of the example has to do with the part of the book when Anansi is being swallowed by Fish.

Example 5: Hawa's Reading of Anansi the Spider

1	Hawa:	…HE FELL INTO TROUBLE.
….		[Hawa shows the next pages, which is only illustration (with no text) where Anansi has fallen into the river and is being swallowed by a fish.]
2	Hawa:	What kind of trouble did he fall into?
3	Cm1:	Big.
4	Cf2:	In the water, in the water.
5	Hawa:	In the water?
6	Cs:	In the fish.
7	Hawa:	In the fish mouth?
8	Cm3:	He fell in the water (…).
9	Cf4:	Maybe he fell in the water and the fish is going to eat him.
10	Hawa:	Let's find out….
….		[There is a distraction with two girls putting things away. Students and Hawa reiterate where they were regarding the picture and Hawa begins reading.]
11	Hawa:	…OFF HE [ROAD BUILDER SON] WENT, MAKING A ROAD. THEY WENT FAST, THOSE SIX BROTHERS, TO HELP ANANSI. "WHERE IS FATHER NOW?" "FISH HAS SWALLOWED HIM!" "ANANSI IS INSIDE FISH." RIVER DRINKER TOOK A BIG DRINK. [turning he book around so that students can see the pictures]
12	Cs:	[almost gasping at the pictures] "Ohhh."
13	Cf4:	He swallowed the spider?
14	Hawa:	Did he swallow the spider?

15	SCs:	#Yes.#
16	SCs:	#No.#
17	Hawa:	The River Drinker? What is he good at swallowing? Clarissa?
18	SCs:	Spider.
19	Hawa:	If his name is River Drinker, what do you think he did?
20	Cm5:	Drink.
21	Hawa:	Clarissa?
22	Cm5:	He drinks water.
23	Hawa:	Do you agree with that, Clarissa?
24	Clarissa:	[Nods.]
25	Hawa:	Yeah?
26	Clarissa:	He drinked water out of the (...).
27	Hawa:	Okay. Let's find out. NO MORE RIVER. THEN GAME SKINNER HELPED FATHER ANANSI. HE SPLIT OPEN FISH.
28	SCs:	[Several children make noises that indicate disgust.]
29	Cm3:	How did they do that?
30	Cf4:	Probably the spider had fell in the water and then the fish he was drinking the water. But then when the water was going in his mouth the spider was going in (... ...).
31	Hawa:	That's an interesting thought.
32	Cf4:	How did they open the fish?
33	Hawa:	How did they open the fish? How did they get to the fish?
34	Cm5:	They wished the fish wouldn't have ate him.
35	Hawa:	Yeah. But, in order to get to the fish, they had to do something with the water.
36	Cm5:	Get it in the mouth.
37	Hawa:	So which son drank up the water, Clarissa?
38	SCs:	The spider.
39	Hawa:	And what was the spider that drank the water? What was his name? Remember? I heard you [Cm4] and Janie over there talking. I thought that maybe you were discussing.
40	Cm5:	River...River....
41	Hawa:	River Drinker.
		{Fieldnotes, Videotape, 11/07/94}

In the beginning of the example, Hawa had students examine the illustrations to see what trouble Anansi might have gotten himself into. These served as predictions. After Hawa read that indeed Anansi was swallowed by Fish, and that the son, River Drinker, then took action by taking a big drink, Cf4 asked if "he" swallowed the spider (line 13). Although it wasn't clear if this student was referring to Fish or River Drinker, students, with Hawa's help, tried to determine the role River Drinker played. Then, after Hawa read about another son, Game Skinner, who entered to help out in the story, another student—Cm3—again initiated another question in line 29 about how these sons accomplished these feats. Student Cf4 offered a possible solution to this question—an instance of cross discussion (Cazden, 1988; Lemke, 1990) between students, which we already mentioned, and which we found common in collaborative talk. Note in line 31 how Hawa accepted and gave value to this explanation—"That's an interesting thought." Then Cf4 also asked her own question, which Hawa accepted and also modified to help students again understand how River Drinker performed the necessary first step to open Fish and to save Anansi.

Thus, this example illustrated how frequently the reading-aloud discussions, initiated by students, became joint constructions in which Hawa played an important role, sharing her expertise, scaffolding students to become better responders to literature.

Many of Hawa's collaborative reading-aloud discussions were peppered by intertextuality. *Intertextuality,* as we have used it in our project, follows Bloome's (Bloome & Bailey, 1992; Bloome & Egan-Robertson, 1993) and Lemke's (1985) ideas. When teachers leave spaces for student initiation, children frequently make intertextual links in the classroom discourse; that is, they connect other books, songs, movies, and prior curricular information they studied, personal stories from home and community, and so forth, with the topic of discussion. According to Bloome, for these student offerings to be considered as instances of intertextuality, they must be proposed, recognized, acknowledged, and have social significance for the participants. Thus, intertextual links that begin from student initiation are characteristic of collaborative talk, which is something that Hawa, Dorothy, and the other teachers in the project attempted to promote.

Examples 6 and 7 provide examples of intertextuality in Hawa's classroom interactions. Example 6 shows a student's connection to another book that students had read. Hawa read part of the story, *The Vanganee and the Tree Toad* (Aardema & Weiss, 1983), and as she turned the page, she noted that a student had a comment.

Example 6:
Hawa's Reading of The Vanganee and the Tree Toad

1 Cm1:   Why does he have to (...)?

2 Hawa: Why does....

3 Cm1:   [pointing to the picture] The——whatever it is.

4 Cf2:   Toad.

5	Hawa:	Yeah, why does the toad have to sing?
6	SCs:	Or else they won't go to sleep.
7	Hawa:	They won't go to sleep. Oh, Clarissa, Clarissa. Maybe Clarissa will have some answers.
8	Clarissa:	The frog looks like the book——the book that last we read——that we read last time.
9	Hawa:	*The Lion and the* ....
10	Cf3:	No, *The Mouse and the Toad.*
11	Hawa:	*The Frog and the Toad?*
12	Cf3:	*The Horse and the*....
13	Clarissa:	*The Horse and the Dog.*
14	Hawa:	Okay, Clarissa, you made a connection there. Good thinking.... {Fieldnotes, Videotape, 3/21/95}

The example began with a student question about why the toad sang. Hawa did not answer this student question, but turned it over to other students, which is something that she frequently did (and which you will see Dorothy do as well). Hawa accepted several students' answers, but then noted that Clarissa might have another possibility. Clarissa, however, had something else to offer—namely, that the frog in the present book is like another book they read. Hawa and Cf3 took turns trying to come up with the particular book Clarissa might have had in mind, and were finally successful. Hawa then gave her credit for this intertextual connection—"good thinking"—which was probably why these student-initiated intertextual comments were so common in the reading-aloud classroom discourse.

Example 7 illustrates an intertextual link to a previous minilesson in writing prompted by Hawa, but which occurred as a result of a student initiation that involved asking about particular wordings used in the text of *Magnet Magic* (Adams, Mitchner, & Johnson, 1987).

Example 7: Hawa Reading Magnet Magic

1	Hawa:	[Hawa is in the middle of reading the book] "LET'S SEE. IT'S SOMEWHERE ON THIS TABLE," SAID MR. SMITH. HE STARTED MOVING THINGS ALL AROUND. "OH, HERE IT IS," HE CRIED. HE HELD UP SOMETHING SHAPED LIKE THE LETTER U.
2	Cf1:	Teacher, why did he cry?
3	Hawa:	Why did he cry?
4	Cm2:	[laughs]

5	Hawa:	Cm2, why are you laughing?
6	Cm2:	Because she said——said … "why did he cry?"
7	Jeanna:	[putting her hand to her throat with sound coming out of her mouth] He——he like screamed out. Screamed out like crazy. Not cried but screamed.
8	Hawa:	Not cry, like cry, Jeanna's saying. Like when we're writing, you know how I told you sometimes you can use different words to ah.…
9	Jeanna:	You don't have to just put "I screamed." You could put "he cried."
10	Hawa:	So it is just an expression.
11	Jeanna:	It's just another word for——it's just another word for um "screamed."
12	Hawa:	"Screamed," okay. Or "I said." Instead of the writer——the author saying "I said" all the time or "Mr. Smith said," he said "he cried."
		{Fieldnotes, Videotape, 02/02/95}

Hawa's reading was interrupted by Cf1's question about why he (Mr. Smith) "cried." Again, we see that Hawa directed the student question for the whole class to consider, and then dealt with Cm2's laughter about the question. Jeanna took on the question with a wonderful explanation (and demonstration) of the how the author's meaning of "cried" needed to be interpreted as "screamed." Hawa then confirmed Jeanna's ideas, and elaborated by pulling in the intertextual connection to a previous minilesson she had with the students about how they could make their story writing more interesting by using different words for "said." She was ably aided in this effort by Jeanna, and together they made the point again that this was an instance of the author's using "cried," a synonym for "screamed," instead of using "said." Thus, here the teacher was responsible for the intertextuality, but it happened and was contingently responsive to both student initiation and student explanation.

Collaborative Interactions and Discourse in Dorothy's Read-Alouds

Dorothy's data also had many instances of student initiations serving as intertextual links or connections, because she, like Hawa, gave value to such initiations. That is why they occurred so frequently. In Example 8, two cases of intertextuality during the reading of *Diego* (Winter, 1991) are illustrated—one prompted by Dorothy, which was enthusiastically taken up by the students, and one that connected to another book that was offered by a student.

Example 8: Dorothy Reading Diego

1	Dorothy:	DIEGO DIDN'T LIKE EVERYTHING HE SAW. THAT'S WHY HE HELPED THE POOR PEOPLE FIGHT THEIR WAR FOR EQUALITY. THEY WERE FIGHTING FOR FAIR WAGES AND A BETTER LIFE. DIEGO LOVED HIS PEOPLE MORE THAN ANYTHING, ALMOST … Do we know somebody else that we were just talking about?….
2	Cm:	Benito Jaurez!!
3	Dorothy:	Benito Juarez. How was he the same as Diego?
4	Cm1:	Because he was in Mexico….
5	Cm2:	And he believed in freedom.
6	Dorothy:	Freedom for who?
7	Cs:	The people!
8	Dorothy:	Freedom for the poor people.
9	Richardo:	Remember we read this story before when he saw something and he like draw something——draw it in real life.
….		[Several children's faces seem to show they don't understand or recognize what book he's talking about.]
10	Dorothy:	You know what you might do? I have some of the books out and some that we've read in bags back here. Would you like to do that? Sometime when you have free time, perhaps tomorrow, you can come and try and find the book you were talking about and share it with us. Just like Leon found a book that was by the same author and brought it. That's a very——that's a *nice* connection. Could you remember to do that for us?
11	Ricardo:	(… …).
12	Dorothy:	Okay. Because I'm not sure I remember the name of the book you're talking about. Maybe——perhaps you can find it.
13	C:	(… …).
14	SCs:	Oh yeah.
15	C:	I remember that.
16	Dorothy:	Okay. Well we each kind of remember the book.
17	C:	He colored whatever he saw … like flowers.
18	C:	He mashed the colors up.
19	Dorothy:	So what's going to happen is Ricardo is going to do the research for us. He's going to get——find that book.
20	C:	(…) look (… …).
21	Dorothy:	But you might not remember it. But that's what we're looking for. But I'm sure that when you see it, you'll remember it. [Directing her attention to Ricardo] That's a big help. [Returning to the book, reading the last pages of the book]. … DIEGO

RIVERA BECAME A FAMOUS ARTIST. HIS PAINTINGS MADE
PEOPLE PROUD TO BE MEXICAN. THEY STILL DO.

22 Miguel: I am!
                {Fieldnotes, Videotape, 03/22/95}

So, the first intertextual link was instigated by Dorothy. One boy quickly
seemed to know what she was thinking about and yelled out, "Benito
Juarez," who was a recent curricular topic students had talked about. Dorothy then asked for them to relate him to Diego. Two students offered
ideas, namely, that "he was in Mexico" and that "he believed in freedom."
Dorothy again asked for elaboration on this latter freedom idea, to which
most students responded in unison.

Then, perhaps spurred by Dorothy's intertextual example, Ricardo initiated his own connection. His was another book in which a character also
painted "real life." Initially, students did not seem to recognize this book,
but Dorothy took his possibility seriously by suggesting that he try to find
the book so he could share it at a later date. Then, another student said
something, which—although it was unfortunately inaudible—was successful in jarring the memories of other students, who seemed now to
know what book Ricardo was talking about. Once more, note how Dorothy
validated Ricardo's intertextual offering—"that's a *nice* connection," and
"that's a big help." At the end we added Miguel's response (to the author's
last words in the book) announcing that he is also be proud to be a Mexican. This response was important to Dorothy, because it seemed to bolster
her students' self-esteem about their identities as Mexicans or Mexican
Americans. This was one of the reasons she shared so many multicultural
books that included Mexican and Latino themes or characters.

The next and last example illustrates the ways in which Dorothy and her
students jointly constructed various possible interpretations of the book,
The Little Band (Sage, 1991). Although this is a short (as a student had
pointed out during the discussion), and somewhat simple and understated
book, it was fertile in evoking many responses from students. It is about a
mysterious little band (depicted in the illustrations as six young girls of diverse ethnic backgrounds) that marched into a town one day, delighting
all who heard its music. The band never stopped or spoke to anyone as it
wound through the town and then marched out of it, but the memory of its
music lingered on so that nothing was ever the same again.

Dorothy finished the book and a long discussion ensued. It started when
Anna asked a question, and then, because other students did not address it
and instead called out other questions, Dorothy spent time dealing with
process and management issues. Anna ended up reiterating her question
several times, and then, with Dorothy's prompting, called on several classmates for their ideas. Dorothy then asked the class if there were other
questions. In Example 9, note how Dorothy tried to get students to answer

the many questions they posed about the book, how she supported their efforts to offer, clarify, and justify different hypotheses about this little band.

Example 9: Dorothy Reading The Little Band

1	Dorothy:	Does anybody else have a question about the book?
2	David:	Why didn't they want to talk to people?
3	Dorothy:	Oh, why didn't they want to talk to people?
4	Cm1:	They were just marching.
5	David:	(... ...) the people were asking them (... ...). I don't——I don't understand that.
6	Dorothy:	Okay, but he's saying——can I repeat this and you tell me if it's right?
7	David:	[nodding yes]
8	Dorothy:	So they can hear you. Why didn't this marching band who was expressing themselves——why didn't they answer the people? People actually——can you give an example?
....		[David helps Dorothy find a page where the mayor wants to give a speech of welcome to the little band. Dorothy reads this part and then asks the whole class if they have any ideas to David's question. Students provided several possibilities——"maybe they were in a rush," "maybe they were concentrating on their work," "maybe they wanted peace." Then, an extended discussion took place among several of the students and me around this latest idea of wanting peace, and then Jeremy initiated another question to consider.]
9	Jeremy:	How come they picked *that* town (... ...)?
10	Dorothy:	How come *who* picked that town?
11	Jeremy:	The band.
12	Dorothy:	The band. The little band. What do you think?
13	Jeremy:	How come——how come they only went through ... through that town? How come they didn't go somewhere else?
14	Dorothy:	Maybe they have ideas. Maybe your classmates have ideas.
15	Cm2:	Maybe they didn't know (... ...).
16	Dorothy:	They might not have known of another place?
17	Cm2:	Yeah.
18	Dorothy:	Jeremy, where did you think this band came from?....
....		[There is a short discussion between Dorothy and students away from this question and then Dorothy reiterates her question for Jeremy.]
19	Jeremy:	From another town because the people were shocked.

20	Dorothy:	Oh, so you think they didn't come from that town. They came from someplace else. So you want to know——what did you want to know again?
21	Jeremy:	Why did they only go to that town?
22	Dorothy:	Okay. [picking up the book] Let's look at this back page for a moment.
23	C:	Where did they come from?
24	C:	Where did they go?
....		[Dorothy holds up the book and points out on the back how the band must have come on the path between two hills. She follows the path with her finger to the place where the band is depicted on the front of the book. She poses a question for the whole class.]
25	Dorothy:	Do we know where they come from? Like Jeremy asked.
26	Cs:	(... ...).
27	C:	Mrs. O'Malley, Mrs. O'Malley, why did they go *only* to that town?
28	Dorothy:	Do we know if they only went to that town?
29	Jason:	No. I have a (...).
30	Dorothy:	Okay, Jason.
31	Jason:	(... ...) another town (... ...) Who *are* they? Because (... ...).
32	Dorothy:	Good point! He was establishing the fact that even though we don't know where they come from ... the exact specific name of the town ... we know that they were from another town because ——why, Jason?
33	Jason:	Because (... ...).
34	Dorothy:	Oh, they wouldn't be asking those questions. Good for you. But that still doesn't settle that question for Jeremy.
....		
35	Cm3:	Why didn't the author tell the names of the kids?
36	Dorothy:	Why didn't tell the names of the children?
37	Cf4:	Maybe he didn't think of it.
38	Dorothy:	Maybe he didn't think of it.
39	Jeremy:	[standing up] Maybe they are from another country. Maybe they are from a different country. They talked to them in English and so they didn't understand them.
40	Dorothy:	Oh, he doesn't have them coming from a different town, but he has them coming from a different country. That's a point. ... {Fieldnotes, Videotape, 03/29/95}

Overall, this example illustrates the joint construction of knowledge of the various possible interpretations of the book. Because the text provides very little explicit information about the motives or characteristics of the little band, Dorothy and the students had to pose these questions about the book themselves and then discovered answers to them together.

In the beginning of the long discussion that occurred after the reading, which was not provided here, Anna commented that she didn't understand the book, and then when Dorothy asked her to clarify what she didn't understand, Anna posed the first question: "Why did they go and play for them?" Because almost all of the students had their hands up and were calling out other questions about the book, Dorothy first had to deal with this process-management feature of the discussion if she hoped to address the *meaning* or content of Anna's—and other students'—questions. Dorothy, therefore, spent time here to get them to pay attention to Anna's question, and then had Anna call on her classmates for their ideas. Thus, Dorothy's technique to have her students elicit ideas from each other to answer their questions can be see throughout the excerpts found in Example 9.

In the beginning of Example 9, David wanted to know why the little band didn't want to talk to the townspeople. Dorothy worked on checking or making sure what he was asking and even repeated it so all could hear. Note how she asks David's permission and input in posing his question correctly, and also how she asked David for the underlying rationale or evidence from the book for his question.

She also played an important role in helping Jeremy find answers to his question about why the band picked *that* town. She checked again to make she and others knew what his question was and encouraged others to suggest possibilities. Following up on C2's idea, she went back to Jeremy to ask where he thought the band came from. Again, Jeremy was asked to elaborate on the substance of this related question, and he explained why he was sure that they came from another town because the townspeople seemed shocked to see them. Subsequently, Dorothy also used the front and back of the book to pose another related question—"Do we know where they come from?" This led to Jason's idea, most of which was unfortunately inaudible, but was picked up by Dorothy. They must have come from another town because the townspeople wouldn't have asked so many questions. Note how Dorothy modeled how to think about, and give value to, Jason's contribution and at the same time pointed out that Jeremy's question was still unanswered.

Then, at the end of the example, a boy asked why the author didn't tell the names of the kids (of the little band). Again, Dorothy accepted it by repeating it. A girl suggested that maybe the author just didn't think of it, and then Jeremy suggested that they might have come from a different country and because the townspeople talked to them in English, the little band might not have understood them. Dorothy followed up, accepting this possibility by contrasting this new idea with others they already considered.

Thus, this is a good example of how collaborative talk reflects the sharing of both teacher and student expertise. Students were given many spaces to ask and answer their own questions about the book, but Dorothy frequently contingently responded to their contributions by helping them better understand the logic and basis for their hypotheses. She had them sometimes go back to what the text provided, and offered new related questions that sustained and extended the meanings and interpretations they offered.

RETHINKING TEACHER STYLE IN THE READING-ALOUD CURRICULUM GENRE

Although there have been studies about teacher styles in reading-aloud curriculum genre, we have very little research that focuses on the routes that teachers take to shed their transmission-oriented, IRE instructional way of teaching an alternative style that is sensitive to the voices of their students. In most studies, researchers either chose the books for the teachers to read, or let the teacher choose books to read, but who then are only observed or audio or videotaped one time. In the latter case, there is no information as to why a particular book was selected, or what a teacher's purpose might be in reading the book to students. Thus, Hawa's and Dorothy's inquiries offer new insights into the complex nature of teacher style in book-sharing experiences.

As Hawa and Dorothy began to encourage students' ideas and interpretations, they were challenged with how they would deal with simultaneous student response. Each teacher developed her own procedural strategies, which underscored the fact that there is no one way to orchestrate this kind of student participation. Thus, other teachers attempting to develop more collaborative reading-aloud sessions need to find their own ways to accomplish this process dimension of sharing authority with students.

According to Wells (1990), to be literate is "to have the disposition to engage appropriately with texts of different types in order to empower action, thinking, and feeling in the context of purposeful social activity" (p. 379). Wells proposed and describes several modes of engagement with text to further explicate this definition of being literate. He argued that the epistemic mode of engagement—where "meaning is treated as tentative, provisional, and open to alternative interpretations and revision" (Wells, 1990, p. 369)—fully exploits the potential of literacy because it empowers the thinking of those who use it. We believe that the content dimensions of the collaborative talk of the reading-aloud curriculum genre in Hawa's and Dorothy's classrooms illustrate this type of epistemic engagement. Because of these teachers' efforts and choices in their inquiries, students developed new ways of being, new repertoires with which to coconstruct and reenact knowledge (Green & Dixon, 1994).

Hawa: Because I shared my authority with my students, they became more in charge, initiated more reading on their own. They became more independent readers, I think, because of their active participation during the reading-aloud times. In fact, because I noticed that those who were good responders were the ones who were choosing to read more and more outside of the sessions, I set up what I called a monitoring system for those who didn't talk much during a reading-aloud time. If I saw someone who had not talked during the reading-aloud, I talked to him or her afterwards about it. Frequently, I would read to them the book I would be reading next and we would talk ahead of time about possible ways these children could contribute in the subsequent whole-class interactions. In this way, more and more students became engaged in our book discussions.

Other things happened too. Children on their own set up their own author studies, groups of them getting out books from the library, urging other students who didn't have a library card to get one, and so forth. And, at the end of the year they asked to have a couple days where they—the students—could lead their own whole-class read-aloud sessions. Thus, I felt that the collaborative nature of the reading-alouds I conducted spilled out into other parts of the day.

I have continued many things I started in my inquiry. I still encourage children to share their ideas, and I still do the follow-up monitoring because I am even more convinced that students' participation in the read-alouds is closely related to their becoming independent readers. I am also using audiotaping as a tool to help me understand the dynamics of classroom discourse and my role in it.

Dorothy: The collaborative discussion emerged because I worked so hard on my role. Even if I would say, "What do you think?," that puts them on the spot. I thought about this a lot and I tried to think how I might say things differently. I tried to prepare comments that would lead it wide open for the students and not put them on the spot. My difficulty was trying not to ask questions to get my answer from them. The timing was everything and the right words from me so that they weren't thinking, "What's she looking for?" But instead it would be a regular conversation, so they thought, "I have to make her understand this."

I also tried to facilitate more talk among the students. I would get them to call on each other, and that got better and better as we went along. I just tried to stay out more. I worked on this outside of the reading-aloud sessions. I would remind [the class] that someone was talking, and students began to be more aware of that, trying to get eye contact knowing when it could be their turn, holding their thoughts till then, even though sometimes they said they had forgotten their point.

Also, I had made the mistake in the beginning of cutting off students when more than one student said the same thing. I began to say that it is okay that someone has said the same thing, that it gave credence to the point someone had made. Some students would talk only if someone else had already said the same thing—even if that might not have even been his or her point. It was repetition in English for the Spanish-speaking students, giving them opportunities to practice these things. This language development was an issue in my inquiry too, a part of the multicultural theme, because it was an issue in the school, especially for that year.

So we got explicit on these outside experiences and then they developed this way of interacting during the reading-aloud times. I just didn't want to say too much about these process issues during the reading times because I felt it would affect the authenticity of the content of our discussion there.

The teacher meeting where the child asked if the book was a poem is still with me. It (and the other teacher meetings) had such an impact on me. I see that meeting and others more important even now than on that day. Because it has been captured now in writing in this chapter and in my own in the other book made me reflect on it over and over and over again. We are supposed to be lifelong learners, but how often do you carry something away, especially when it's been enacted as an adult and you move on and still think about it? It is amazing that it has influenced me in other contacts, for example, when I interact with children when I substitute now [Dorothy retired at the end of her year of inquiry], and even when I am with adults where there are occasions to present myself.

REFERENCES

Aardema, V., & Weiss, E. (1983) *The Vanganee and the tree toad.* New York: Puffin Books.

Adams, P., Mitchner, C. P., & Johnson, V. (1987) *Magnet magic.* Cleveland, OH: Modern Curriculum Press.

Bartolome, L. I. (1994). Beyond the methods fetish: Toward a humanizing pedagogy. *Harvard Educational Review, 64,* 173–194.

Bloome, D., & Bailey, F. (1992). Studying language and literacy through events, particularity, and intertextuality. In R. Beach, J. L. Green, M. L. Kamil, & T. Shanahan (Eds.), *Multidisciplinary perspectives on literacy research* (pp. 181–210). Urbana, IL: National Conference on Research in English.

Bloome, D., & Egan-Robertson, A. (1993). The social construction of intertextuality in classroom reading and writing lessons. *Reading Research Quarterly, 28,* 305–333.

Bruner, J. (1983). *Child's talk: Learning to use language.* New York: Norton.

Brusca, M. C. (1991). *On the Pampas.* New York: Henry Holt.

Cazden, C. B. (1988). *Classroom discourse: The language of teaching and learning.* Portsmouth, NH: Heinemann.

Cochran-Smith, M. (1984). *The making of a reader.* Norwood, NJ: Ablex.

Cummins, J. (1994). From coercive to collaborative relations of power in the teaching of literacy. In B. M. Ferdman, R.-M. Weber, & A. G. Ramierz (Eds.), *Literacy across languages and cultures* (pp. 295–331). Albany: State University of New York Press.

Dickinson, D. K., & Keebler, R. (1989). Variations in preschool teachers' storybook reading styles. *Discourse Processes, 12,* 353–376.

Dickinson, D. K., & Smith, M. A. (1994). Long-term effects of preschool teachers' book readings on low-income children's vocabulary and story comprehension. *Reading Research Quarterly, 29,* 104–122.

Elster, C. (1995). Importations in preschoolers' emergent readings. *JRB: A Journal of Literacy, 27,* 65–84.

Golden, J. (1990). *The narrative symbol in childhood literature: Explorations in the construction of text.* Berlin, Germany: Mouton de Gruyter.

Green, J. L., & Dixon, C. N. (1994). Talking into being: Discursive and social practices in classrooms. *Linguistics and Education, 5,* 231–239.

Green, J. L., Harker, J., & Golden, J. (1986). Lesson construction: Differing views. In G. W. Noblitt & W. T. Pink (Eds.), *Schooling in the social context: Qualitative studies* (pp. 46–77). Norwood, NJ: Ablex.

Grifalconi, A. (1987). *Darkness and the butterfly.* New York: Scholastic.

Gutierrez, K. D. (1994). How talk, context, and script shape contexts for learning: A cross-case comparison of journal sharing. *Linguistics and Education, 5,* 335–365.

Halliday, M. A. K., & Hasan, R. (1985). *Language, context, and text: Aspects of language in a social-semiotic perspective.* Victoria, Australia: Deakin University Press.

Kilbourn, B. (1991). Self-monitoring in teaching. *American Educational Research Journal, 28,* 721–736.

Kreisberg, S. (1992). *Transforming power: Domination, empowerment, and education.* Albany: State University of New York Press.

Lemke, J. L. (1985). Ideology, intertextuality, and the notion of register. In J. D. Benson & W. S. Greaves (Eds.), *Systemic perspectives on discourse: Selected theoretical papers from the 9th international systemic workshop, Vol. 1* (pp. 275–294). Norwood, NJ: Ablex.

Lemke, J. L. (1990). *Talking science: Language, learning, and values.* Norwood, NJ: Ablex.

Martinez, M., & Teale, W. (1993). Teacher storybook reading style: A comparison of six teachers. *Research in the Teaching of English, 27,* 175–199.

McDermott, G. (1972). *Anansi the spider.* New York: Holt.

Morrow, L. M. (1988). Young children's responses to one-to-one story readings in school settings. *Reading Research Quarterly, 23,* 89–107.

Nystrand, M. (1997). *Opening dialogue: Understanding the dynamics of language and learning in the English classroom.* New York: Teachers College Press.

Oyler, C. (1996a). Sharing authority: Student initiations during teacher-led read-alouds of information books. *Teaching and Teacher Education, 12,* 149–160.

Oyler, C. (1996b). *Making room for students in an urban first grade: Sharing authority in room 104.* New York: Teachers College Press.

Pappas, C. C. (1997). Reading instruction in an integrated perspective: Collaborative interaction in classroom curriculum genres. In S. Stahl & D. A. Hayes (Eds.), *Instructional models in reading* (pp. 283–310). Mahwah, NJ: Lawrence Erlbaum Associates.

Pappas, C. C. & Barry, A. (1997). Scaffolding urban students' initiations: Transactions in reading information books in the reading-aloud curriculum genre. In N. J. Karolides (Ed.), *Reader response in the elementary classroom: Quest and discovery* (pp. 215–236). Mahwah, NJ: Lawrence Erlbaum Associates.

Pappas, C. C., Kiefer, B. Z., & Levstik, L. S. (1999). *An integrated language perspective in the elementary school: An action approach.* New York: Longman.

Peters, R. S. (1966). *Ethics and education.* London: George, Allen & Unwin.

Ramirez, A. (1988). Analyzing speech acts. In J. L. Green & J. O. Harker (Eds.), *Multiple perspective analyses of classroom discourse* (pp. 135–163). Norwood, NJ: Ablex.

Sage, J. (1991). *The little band.* New York: Scholastic.

Sharer, P. L. (1992). Teachers in transition: An exploration of changes in teachers and classrooms during implementation of literature-based reading instruction. *Research in the Teaching of English, 26,* 408–445.

Smith, F. (1985). *Understanding reading.* New York: Holt, Rinehart & Winston.

Steptoe, J. (1987). *Mufaro's beautiful daughters.* New York: Lothrop, Lee, & Shepard.

Stevenson, S. (1992). *The princess and the pea.* New York: Dell.

Teale, W. H., & Martinez M. G. (1996). Reading aloud to young children: Teachers' reading styles and kindergartners' text comprehension. In C. Pontecorvo, M. Orsolini, B. Burge, & L. Resnick (Eds.), *Children's early text construction* (pp. 321–344). Mahwah, NJ: Lawrence Erlbaum Associates.

Vygotsky, L. S. (1978). *Mind in society: The development of higher psychological processes.* Cambridge, England: Cambridge University Press.

Wells, G. (1981). *Learning through interaction: The study of language development.* Cambridge, England: Cambridge University Press.

Wells, G. (1985). Preschool literacy-related activities and success in school. In D. R. Olson, N. Torrance, & A. Hildyard (Eds.), *Literacy, language, and learning: The nature and consequences of reading and writing* (pp. 229–255). Cambridge, England: Cambridge University Press.

Wells, G. (1986). *The meaning makers: Children learning language and using language to learn.* Portsmouth, NH: Heinemann.

Wells, G. (1990). Talk about text: Where literacy is learned and taught. *Curriculum Inquiry, 20,* 369–405.

Wells, G. (1993). Reevaluating the IRF sequence: A proposal for the articulation of theories of activity and discourse for the analysis of teaching and learning in the classroom. *Linguistics and Education, 5,* 1–37.

Wells, G. (1994). The complimentary contributions of Halliday and Vygotsky to a "language-based" theory of learning. *Linguistics and Education, 6,* 41–90.

Wells, G. (1998). Some questions about direct instruction: Why? To whom? How? And when? *Language Arts, 76,* 27–35.

Wells, G., & Chang-Wells, G. L. (1992). *Constructing knowledge together: Classrooms as centers of inquiry and literacy.* Portsmouth, NH: Heinemann.

Wertsch, J. V. (1991). *Voices of the mind: A sociocultural approach to mediated action.* Cambridge, MA: Harvard University Press.

Willinsky, J. (1990). *The new literacy: Redefining reading and writing in the schools.* New York: Routledge.

Winter, J. (1991). *Diego.* New York: Knopf.

Young, R. (1992). *Critical theory and classroom talk.* Clevedon, England: Multilingual Matters.

Chapter 7

Bridging Into English Through Reading-Alouds: More Than a Curricular Routine in a Bilingual Third Grade

Liliana Barro Zecker

Caitlyn Nichols

Linda Montes

Sonia Torres Pasewark

The reading-aloud curriculum genre is a common routine present in most elementary classrooms in the United States (Dickinson, Hao, & He, 1995; Martínez & Teale, 1993). The events in reading-aloud comprise the text read by the teacher of course, but also the complex talk that is jointly constructed between teacher and students as the written text is discussed or talked about (Teale & Martínez, 1996). Teachers have been observed to conduct read-alouds of storybooks in very different styles, modeling for

---

The introduction chapter of this book provides the theoretical and methodological background for the larger collaborative school–university action-research project and this chapter about Sonia's inquiry on reading-alouds. See also the last chapter, which further discusses the implications of Sonia's inquiry—as well as those of the other teacher researchers.

students different ways of approaching, responding to, and thinking about literacy events in general, and texts in particular (Dickinson & Keebler, 1989; Dickinson & Smith, 1994; Martínez & Teale, 1993). These observations indicate the importance of classroom discourse as a powerful tool that can realize the notion of literacy learning as cultural apprenticeship. This oral text, which is constructed in the reading-aloud routine, has the potential to make the unspoken aspects of literate ways of thinking explicit to young children (Reder, 1994; Wells & Chang-Wells, 1992).

This chapter is about Sonia Torres Pasework's inquiry on how to use the reading-aloud curriculum genre to help her Spanish-speaking third graders to understand and appreciate English as a second language. As she read books in English, she hoped to bridge the children's abilities to become truly bilingual. Studies of discourse in bilingual classrooms have described the varied strategies that members of such communities use to accomplish communication (Martin-Jones, 1995). Among these strategies, *code switching,* or the ability to alternate between two language systems, has received special attention, given its wide use. The switching between two languages and other inter-comprehension strategies, such as use of gesture or prosodic (stress or intonation) cues, enables participants, whose linguistic repertoires vary considerably, to achieve mutual understanding during the course of conversation (Arthur, 1996; Martin-Jones, 1995).

The research on code-switching strategies in bilingual classrooms has changed greatly over the past 2 decades due to a shift from a quantitative approach to a more pragmatic one that uses microethnographic analyses (Martin-Jones, 1995). Early studies of code switching primarily documented the frequency with which teachers spoke students' first languages during instructional time. Later, more attention was paid to the different linguistic functions that were employed in one language versus another. These studies described which communicative acts (e.g., directives, clarifications, etc.) were typically associated with one of the available languages (Guthrie & Guthrie, 1994). For example, some studies showed that students' first language was more commonly used when teachers checked for understanding and clarified concepts, but directives and metastatements were predominantly given in students' second language (Martin-Jones, 1995).

Such a framework, however, proved insufficient to capture other important features of classroom talk. It described individual communicative acts without considering the complex flow of classroom discourse, the ways in which students and teacher came to an understanding. As a result, more recent investigations of code switching in bilingual classrooms have emphasized the need for microethnographic studies that document the ways in which teachers and students accomplish negotiation of meanings in the particular context of specific bilingual teaching–learning events (Martin-Jones, 1995).

This chapter examines how Sonia, a Mexican-American, first-year teacher dealt with three major issues in using the reading-alouds in English as a bridge to foster her third-grade students' learning of the language and response to literature: how she handled concerns of translation and code switching; how she reconsidered the kinds of questions she asked her students; and how she attempted to address various racial and gender stereotypes.

BACKGROUND AND EARLY DIFFICULTIES IN DEVELOPING THE READING-ALOUD CURRICULUM GENRE

This was Sonia's first year as a teacher. She was assigned a third-grade bilingual classroom that contained a higher incidence of special-needs students (those with learning disabilities, behavioral problems, or who were recent arrivals) than any of the other third grades in the school. Sonia's group of 17 students was also markedly imbalanced genderwise because she had 4 girls and 13 boys. All students were categorized as *A* students, indicating little- or low-level of English-language proficiency, but this language ability among students was still quite variable. Some of the children seemed to be quite comfortable when receiving instruction in English, but many could not understand or respond to simple everyday commands, if given in English. Sonia was aware of the particular characteristics of her class as a group and, although she was excited to work at this school, she felt that this grouping was both unfair to her, as a first-year inexperienced teacher, and to the students.

Sonia: I had strong ties to the community and the school since I had lived in the neighborhood and attended the school as a student. That made a big difference in the way I approached my job and my students. I remember coming back and smelling the same smells, looking at the same classrooms where I had been a student. It was a weird feeling. The difference was that, before I could not complain about what I did not like, now I could change things. Although I always spoke Spanish at home with my parents, I had never been in a bilingual classroom. I don't think bilingual education, as it is done now in the Chicago schools, is the best possible thing that can be given to these children. These children need to learn English, to learn about other worlds. They already know about their own culture—the Mexican Cinco de Mayo and Mother's Day. Now they live here, and this is the world that they need to be prepared to face.

As a new teacher, I was hesitant about the different approaches I could take to achieve my overall goal, which was to help my students bridge into English. I was frustrated and angry about the wide gap that separated my education as a teacher at the university and the reality of my urban classroom. By October, I was desperate and unfocused. At the beginning, I tried different things everyday. My inquiry, the reading-alouds, helped me focus more on what I wanted to do regarding teaching them English.

The choice of books for the read-alouds constituted a major dilemma for Sonia. It was hard for her to find high-interest books that had vocabulary and text-structure levels commensurate with the wide-ranging English proficiency of her students. Management of the reading-aloud routine was also problematic. As her students' attention and interest dwindled, management of seating arrangements, turn-taking in the discussions, and inappropriate behaviors took precedent over the educational purposes she had for the read-aloud.

Sonia: As a first-year teacher, they tell you that you are supposed to do this and that, but you tend to fall back into what seems easier. I had heard about different kinds of questions, but had never seen them put into practice. I student taught with a teacher who used very traditional methods, and that's the way it had been when I was student at the school. I did not think about what I was asking or why I was asking. I just tried to get some answer, just feeling my way through it. However, it was good that we discovered how to improve ourselves as teachers through discussion with each other in our weekly meetings as we shared our dilemmas.

The university researchers (as well as the other teacher researchers) provided Sonia with some book suggestions to use with her group: Some worked better than others. Other teachers involved in the project also brought up class-management issues that arose as they tried to craft more collaborative teaching–learning interactions with students in their own classrooms. In their experience, class discussions became more enthusiastic, but noisier, as more students wanted to participate. During the weekly project discussions, these colleagues shared with Sonia the strategies they were using to make reading-alouds manageable, nonchaotic situations that encouraged participation and allowed spaces for children's voices.

As already indicated, Sonia dealt with various multiple issues over the course of the year. It became clear that more than merely bridging her students' learning of language per se was involved. As Sonia's students became more proficient in English, the discursive practices in the routine changed remarkably. There was a noticeable modification in the patterns of English and Spanish code-switching structures in the reading-alouds. More important, the discussions began to foster higher levels of literate engagement with the text at hand because Sonia altered her questioning practices and, thus, the kinds of response to text that she modeled for her students (Wells & Chang-Wells, 1992). Finally, reading-alouds seemed to take a new character as Sonia selected books to fuel discussions that would challenge social and racial stereotypes. In that sense, read-alouds evolved into language–learning situations that questioned cultural and gender power beliefs (Edelsky, 1994).

CHANGES IN PATTERNS OF CODE SWITCHING

At the beginning of the school year, Sonia's interaction with her students during reading-alouds was characterized by code switching that consisted mainly of literal translation of the book text. Sonia seemed to be aware to the importance of her students to understand vocabulary and initially she tended to translate the text of the books word by word. Often, she posed questions designed to elicit vocabulary items, the kind of classroom talk genre described by Heath (1986) as *label quest,* which is highly frequent in bilingual classrooms (Arthur, 1996).

Sonia's need to make sure that her students comprehended all that was read to them resulted in a high incidence of literal, *pseudoquestions,* ones for which she already knew the answers (Dillon, 1994; Ramirez, 1988). She frequently read a section of the text and immediately asked her students questions about the information that had just been provided. For example, Sonia read *The Biggest Pumpkin Ever* (Kroll, 1984), a book with English text. For each page, Sonia first read the text in English and then translated into Spanish. The book tells the story of two mice, Clayton and Desmond, who tend to a pumpkin to make it grow as big as possible. The mice try a variety of strategies to make the pumpkin grow: feed it sugar water and fertilizer, cover it with blankets on cold nights, and so on. After Clayton wins the town pumpkin contest for its size, Desmond carves the biggest jack o'lantern ever on Halloween night. As Sonia read and translated the text, some the following questions were posed in Spanish to her students:

- ¿Quién es éste?/Who is this one? (asking the children to identify one of the mouse characters)
- ¿Qué le pasó a al calabaza?/What happened to the pumpkin?
- ¿Quién le echó el agua?/Who watered it?
- ¿Qué mas le echaron?/What else did they put in it? (asking about the sugar water mentioned in the book)
- ¿Quién está cuidando a la planta de día?/Who is taking care of the plant during the day?
  {Fieldnotes, 10/26/94}

Like these, all of Sonia's questions were initially directed to check the students' literal comprehension of the text. These questions did not model for the students the more reflective kinds of responses that would link the text to their experiences or would explore their hypotheses about the story line or characters. This early classroom talk about text seemed low level and unsophisticated; it did not evoke high-level elaborations from the students.

However, researchers of classroom discourse in bilingual classrooms have observed that the kind of code switching that is directed to facilitate audience understanding and participation via literal translation, like the one used by Sonia, is commonly observed during the early years of second-language learning and can be an effective communicative resource for successful teaching–learning interactions (Jiménez, García, & Pearson, 1996; Martin-Jones, 1995).

> *Sonia: I remember my first reading-aloud; I would read a sentence and then I would immediately translate. I felt they were just not getting it. At the beginning, I was doing a lot of translating, taking a line and translating it into Spanish. That was frustrating for them as well as for me. They complained, especially those students who were more fluent in English, that the reading-alouds were too long. One of my students told me once, "Teacher, you talk too much. You are saying the same in English and in Spanish. It's just too long." Then I was reading a page and then doing the translation after the page. Later, I would read them a page in English and, without translating, I would then ask them questions in Spanish. And then eventually, I just read the whole thing in English and asked questions in English. I think that showed progress for me as well as for them.*

As the year progressed, direct translation became less frequent in Sonia's reading-alouds. These changes in code switching use have been noted by other studies in bilingual classrooms, and they seem to be more marked among students enrolled in bilingual programs that have primarily transitional goals, such as the one in this particular school (Martin-Jones, 1995).

Students Begin to Collaborate in English Translations

Gradually Sonia's reading-aloud discussions were more idea driven as opposed to literal, and she began to share responsibility for the translations with her students. In time, Sonia sometimes read the whole text in Spanish and then in English and students began to negotiate with Sonia the language that they wanted to use first to read the book. Moreover, Luis, one of Sonia's most proficient English speakers, began to share the role of translator with Sonia. The following excerpt is from Sonia's reading aloud of the *The Desert Mermaid/La Sirena del Desierto* (Blanco, 1992), a book with wonderful illustrations that captured the students' interest. The book included text in both English and Spanish. (Note that italics mark code switching into English.)

Example 1

1   Sonia: ¿En inglés o en español?

2   Cs: ¡En español!

3   Sonia: ¿Qué tal los dos?

4   Cm: ¡Los dos (...)!

5   Luis: ¡Yo lo traduzco!

6	Sonia:	*You wanna translate? Okay!*
7	Luis:	Yeah.

….

8	Sonia:	Okay, este va a ser el plan: Yo lo voy a leer en inglés y luego Luis o quien quiera me lo puede traducir, okay?
9	Luis:	¡Yo lo traduzco!
10	Sonia:	Hugo, me pones ese lapiz ahí? *Thank you. Okay, this book is called* THE DESERT MERMAID, LA SIRENA DEL DESIERTO. *The story is written by Alberto Blanco. That's the author. That's the author. The author is Al….*
11	Luis:	Alberto Blanco!
12	Cf1:	Blanco?
13	Sonia:	*Yeah! Very good, Luis! And the pictures——it is illustrated by Patricia Reva. Patricia Reva is the illustrator. What's the illustrator, Luis?*
14	Luis:	El que dibuja las cosas.
15	Cm1:	El lus——el ilustrador.
16	Sonia:	*Very good.* El que dibuja las cosas.

Translation

1	Sonia:	In English or in Spanish?
2	Cs:	In Spanish!
3	Sonia:	How about both?
4	Cm1:	Both (…)!
5	Luis:	I translate!
6	Sonia:	*You wanna translate? Okay!*
7	Luis:	Yeah.

….

8	Sonia:	Okay, this is going to be the plan: I am going to read it in English and then Luis, whoever wants to, can translate it, okay?
9	Luis:	I translate!
10	Sonia:	Hugo, can you put the pencil there? *Thank you. Okay, this book is called* THE DESERT MERMAID, LA SIRENA DEL DESIERTO. *The story is written by Alberto Blanco. That's the author. That's the author. The author is Al….*
11	Luis:	Alberto Blanco!
12	Cf1:	Blanco?
13	Sonia	*Yeah! Very good, Luis! And the pictures——it is illustrated by Patricia Reva. Patricia Reva is the illustrator. What's the illustrator, Luis?*
14	Luis:	The one who draws the things.

| 15 | Cm1: | The lus——the illustrator |
| 16 | Sonia: | *Very good.* The one who draws the things.
{Fieldnotes, videotape, 12/05/94} |

Luis was very proud of his capabilities as translator and was often consulted by students and Sonia alike about how to say different things in the other language. During the rest of the read-aloud, he was able to translate most of the main ideas without making use of the Spanish text in the book, only hesitating with specific vocabulary terms such as *amuleto* (luck charm).

Later during the school year, other children started to volunteer as translators or interpreters as they became more proficient in English. This happened frequently if the books included both English and Spanish versions. Although their knowledge of English was quite limited for spontaneous translation, they realized that they could use the Spanish text as a scaffold to guide their English renditions.

CHANGES IN QUESTIONING PATTERNS

As word-by-word or phrase-by-phrase translation became less dominant within the reading-aloud routine, Sonia began to shift her ways of questioning students and eliciting responses to the text. Although vocabulary discussion was always an important aspect of the talk surrounding the books, Sonia's questions moved away from mere checking of literal understanding. She now posed queries that modeled more critical responses to text and constructions of new meanings. Her questions asked students to make predictions, to relate ideas in the books to their to own experiences, and to reflect on characters' feelings. Example 2 is from a discussion on *The Rainbow Fish* (Pfister, 1992)—which tells how the most beautiful fish in the ocean discovers the real value or beauty and friendship. Rainbow Fish had many wonderful, shiny scales, with which he would not part. As a result, he became the loneliest fish in the ocean until he began to share his scales with other fish. In doing so, he was no longer the most beautiful fish, but he learned how to be happy. Next, Sonia tries to get students to examine the fish's personality in the beginning of the book and why he did not play with the other fish. (Again, as previously, italics mark code switching into English.)

Example 2

| 1 | Sonia: | ¿Cómo era el pez? ¿Cómo era el pez? Javier, ¿Cómo era el pez? ¿Cómo era el pez? |
| 2 | Javier: | De arcoiris, de colores. |

3	Hugo:	Chico ... aburrido ... enano ... feo.
4	Javier:	Tenía las escamas de todos los colores....
5	Sonia:	Pero, ¿qué tipo de personalidad?
6	Cm1:	Bilingüe.
7	Sonia:	Eh, Luis ¿Qué tipo de personalidad traía el pescado? ¿Silvia?
8	Cs:	(... ...).
9	Silvia:	Bueno.
10	Cm2:	Mira, teacher, como brillan las escamas (...) desde acá brillan.
11	Sonia:	Juan, ¿Cúal personalidad tenía?
12	Cs:	(... ...).
13	Silvia:	Era bueno.
14	Cf1:	Mala, teacher.
15	Silvia:	Bueno.

....

16	Vilma:	Es bueno y malo.
17	Sonia:	¿Él jugaba con los otros peces?
18	Cs:	¡No!
19	Sonia:	*He didn't play with them right? Why do you think he didn't want to play with them?*
20	Cm1:	*Because,* se le ensucian las escamas.
21	Sonia:	*Why do you think he did not want to play with them?*
22	Cm2:	Porque luego se le caen (...) en el mar las escamas.
23	Sonia:	*Maybe.*

Translation

1	Sonia:	What was the fish like? What was the fish like? Javier, what was the fish like? What was the fish like?
2	Javier:	Like a rainbow, of all colors.
3	Hugo:	Small ... bored ... dwarf ... ugly.
4	Javier:	It had scales of all the colors....
5	Sonia:	But, what type of personality?
6	Cm1:	Bilingual.
7	Sonia:	Eh, Luis, what kind of personality did the fish have? Silvia?
8	Cs:	(... ...).
9	Silvia:	Good.
10	Cm2:	Look teacher how the scales shine (...) from here they shine.
11	Sonia:	Juan, what personality did it have?

12	Cs:	(... ...).
13	Silvia:	It was good.
14	Cf1:	Mean, teacher.
15	Silvia:	Good

....

16	Vilma:	It was good and mean.
17	Sonia:	Did he play with other fish?
18	Cs:	No!
19	Sonia:	*He didn't play with them, right? Why do you think he didn't want to play with them?*
20	Cm1:	*Because,* its scales get dirty.
21	Sonia:	*Why do you think he did not want to play with them?*
22	Cm2:	Because then its scales fall (...) into the sea.
23	Sonia:	*Maybe.*
		{Fieldnotes, videotape, 4/03/95}

Sonia did not get what she had expected initially from the students here, but all her attempts were directed to make them reflect on the Rainbow Fish's personality and the reason for his behavior. Later, Sonia continued to try to scaffold her students' understanding about Rainbow Fish's feelings and the consequences of his actions. When she asked them if they thought that Rainbow Fish was going to be happy without the scales, the following discussion ensued:

Example 3

1 Sonia:	*Pedro said something very important. He said the fish thought he was* muy fregón *and he is going to be happy once he gives his scales away. Why do you think he is going to be happier when he gives his scales away?*
2 Cs:	(... ...).
3 Sonia:	*Why?* [pointing at Silvia to answer]
4 Silvia:	Porque van a ser sus amigos y....
5 Sonia:	*Who's going to be his friends?*
6 Cs:	#Todos los pescados.#
7 Cs:	#Todos los peces.#
8 Sonia:	*I'm just asking Silvia!*

9 Silvia: Los pecesitos van a jugar con él porque son felices con una sola escama.

10 Sonia: *Okay, good.*

....   [Sonia continues to probe later during the discussion.]

11 Sonia: *What would you do if you had something beautiful but lots and lots of it, would you share it?*

12 Cs: *#Yes!#*

13 Cs: *#No!#*

14 Sonia: *No? Just a little bit? How about you, Sara? How would you share it?*

15 Sara: Sí, sí … porque me miran así y después me dicen, "¿Me puedes dar uno?" y yo digo, "No." Y se sienten mal.

16 Sonia: A ver Pedro. ¿Qué dijo el pulpo?

17 Pedro: Que dé eso brilloso, que le dé a cada uno de los pescados y luego se va a hacer bueno.…

18 Cm1:   (…).

19 Pedro: ¡Feliz! ¡Se va a ser feliz!!

20 Sonia: *That's right! You got it, Pedro!*

Translation

1 Sonia: *Pedro said something very important. He said the fish thought he was very proud and he is going to be happy once he gives his scales away. Why do you think he is going to be happier when he gives his scales away?*

2 Cs: (… …).

3 Sonia: *Why?* [pointing at Silvia to answer]

4 Silvia: Because they are going to be his friends and.…

5 Sonia: *Who's going to be his friends?*

6 Cs: #All the fish.#

7 Cs: #All the fish.#

8 Sonia: *I'm just asking Silvia!*

9 Silvia: The little fish are going to play with him because they are happy with just one scale.

10 Sonia: *Okay, good.*

....   [Sonia continues to probe later during the discussion.]

11 Sonia: *What would you do if you had something beautiful but lots and lots of it, would you share it?*

12 Cs: *#Yes!#*

13 Cs: *#No!#*

14 Sonia:	*No? Just a little bit? How about you, Sara? How would you share it?*
15 Sara:	Yes, yes … because they look at me like this and then they tell me "Can you give me one?" and I say, "No." And they feel bad.
16 Sonia:	Let see, Pedro. What did the octopus say?
17 Pedro:	To give away that shiny stuff, to give it to each of the fish and then that would make him good.…
18 Cm1:	(…).
19 Pedro:	Happy! That would make him happy!
20 Sonia:	*That's right! You got it, Pedro!*
	{Fieldnotes, videotape, 04/03/95}

Sonia scaffolded the discussion in a way that enabled some of her students to articulate not only their comprehension of the text, but also their interpretation of it, as shown by Sara's comments near the end of the excerpt. This kind of interchange of ideas was still heavily supported by Sonia because she needed to ask and rephrase very specific questions to get her point across. Yet, her questions during this discussion model a response to text that was very different from the way she elicited answers from students at the beginning of the school year. Her questions now were less focused on the factual information included in the text and referred more to the motives of Rainbow Fish, the rationale behind octopus' advice, and how Rainbow Fish's behavior elicited a new response from the other fish. Sonia also managed to make the students reflect on how the story line could connect to the reality of their own experiences about sharing with others and making friends. In this way, Sonia's line of questioning provided more open spaces for the sharing of her students' interpretations and, at the same time, modeled a type of engagement with text that required them to react to it and go beyond the information given.

In the example, Sonia reinforced Pedro's responses very emphatically. Pedro was a learning-disabled student who experienced marked difficulties in reading and could not read independently in either English or Spanish. He received help from a reading specialist, but was still developing basic word identification skills typical of a much younger child. As his comments show in this example, and in examples to follow, he participated in reading-aloud discussions very enthusiastically, making key contributions that demonstrated good comprehension of the text and to make important connections between the text and Sonia's queries. In that sense, for Pedro, reading alouds constituted a bridge into the world of literature and literate thinking, allowing him to participate in literacy engagements through talk (Wells, 1990; Chang-Wells, 1992).

BUILDING COMMUNITY AND ADDRESSING SOCIAL AND GENDER ISSUES

At the beginning of the school year, a rotation among third-grade classrooms in which students received instruction by separate teachers on specific aspects of language arts (reading, writing, grammar, and drama) made Sonia's schedule extremely fragmented and confusing for the children. Sonia requested changes that would allow her to spend more time with her students and build some continuity within the curriculum. She wanted her students to experience the classroom as an environment of social and cognitive support in her class (Henson, 1993). Sonia spent a considerable amount of time building the feeling of the classroom as a community wherein everybody had the right to participate and the obligation to respect others. In Example 4, Sonia discussed a storybook with the students and had to discipline Javier, who had a history of disruptive behavior that often interfered with the flow of classroom activities.

Example 4

1	Sonia:	Okay, aquí va el caballo Silver Star y la va a llevar para, al templo de los pájaros cantores [pointing to book]. ¿Por qué creen que la va a llevar … Javier!
2	Javier:	Pues le digo que no me toque y adrede lo hace. [blaming his behavior on a classmate]
3	Sonia:	¡No! Yo te estoy viendo! *He is not touching you! You move! … You move!* Es la segunda vez. Hugo, hazte un poquito para allá por favor. Tú, Luis, también.
4	Luis:	¿Por qué no lo separa mejor, maestra! [asking Sonia to ask Javier to leave the group]
5	Sonia:	Javier tiene que aprender a cómo portarse con todos los demás niños. Él también es parte del grupo, okay?

Translation

1	Sonia:	Okay, here goes the horse Silver Star and it's going to take her to, to the singing birds' temple. [pointing to book] Why do you think it's going to take her … Javier!
2	Javier:	I tell him not to touch me and he does it on purpose. [blaming his behavior on a classmate]
3	Sonia:	No! I am watching you! *He is not touching you! You move! … You move!* This is the second time. Hugo, move that way please. You, Luis, too.
4	Luis:	Why don't you better separate him, teacher! [asking Sonia to ask Javier to leave the group]

5   Sonia: Javier has to learn how to behave with all the other kids. He is
                part of the group too, okay?
                {Fieldnotes, videotape, 12/05/94}

Sonia's comments about Javier having to learn to be part of the group, which she had reiterated in many occasions, reinforced the idea of the group's ability, as well as responsibility, to adjust in order to make things work for everybody. Although these kinds of interchanges frequently interrupted the flow of reading-aloud discussions in this class, Sonia never hesitated to address these issues.

Sonia was also concerned about her students' views about racial stereotypes and gender roles. As her questioning style began to foster more elaborate discussions and responses to literature, her goals on this dimension became more evident. Sonia took advantage of every possible opportunity to foster reflection about patterns of social interaction, the importance of being accepting and nonprejudiced, and the need to be open minded.

The following excerpt illustrates how important this goal was for Sonia. It took place during a read-aloud as Sonia tried to reorganize seating arrangements in the group to minimize students' distractions.

Example 5

1   Sonia: *Very good! Okay. Do you know what? Everyone is talking at the
                same time.* Todos están hablando al mismo tiempo y *right now
                isn't beauty shop time.* Ahorita no es tiempo de peinarse el pelo,
                okay? ¿Por qué las niñas están en una esquina?
2   Cm1:   ¡No sé!
3   Javier: ¡Así *debe* ser!
4   Sonia: ¡No, así no *debe* ser!
5   Cm1:   Pues si otro (...).
6   Sonia: Las niñas se pueden sentar donde quieran.
7   Cm2:   ¿Y ellas por qué están juntitas?
8   Cs: (...).
9   Sonia: ¿Ahí están bien? ¿Ahí se quieren quedar?
10 Javier: Unas niñas, unas niñas de un lado y los niños apartados. ¡Ay!
11 Sonia: Las niñas, las niñas se pueden sentar allí. Okay, está bien, ellas
                quieren sentarse allí. Es su decisión.

Translation

1   Sonia: *Very good! Okay. Do you know what? Everyone is talking at the
                same time.* Everyone is talking at the same time and *right now*

		isn't beauty shop time. Now it is not the time to comb our hair, okay? Why are the girls in a corner?
2	Cm1:	I don't know!
3	Javier:	That's the way it *should* be!
4	Sonia:	No, that's not the way it *should* be!
5	Cm1:	But if other (...).
6	Sonia:	The girls can sit wherever they want.
7	Cm2:	Why are they all together?
8	Cs:	(...).
9	Sonia:	Are you all right there? Do you want to stay there?
10	Javier:	The girls, the girls on one side and the boys separate. Ay!
11	Sonia:	The girls, the girls can sit there. Okay, it is all right, they want to sit there. It's their decision. {Fieldnotes, 02/07/95}

Initially, Sonia interrupted her reading-aloud to question the girls' seating arrangement, noticing that as they were combing each other's hair, they were distracted. Yet, as one of the boys in the classroom remarked that sitting in a corner was "the way it *should* be" for girls, Sonia elaborated on his remark, highlighting the fact that girls can make their own decisions. She argued that they could sit in the corner or "wherever they want," emphasizing their power to make choices and challenging the social-order stereotype that girls can be told what to do.

Sonia also took advantage of discussions that dealt with racial differences to challenge her students' views. In the next example, Sonia used a comment made by Luis during a reading-aloud discussion that led to talk about different car brands. At this particular point, students were talking about the Volkswagen bug, a popular car in Mexico.

Example 6

1	Luis:	Teacher, de aquí para allá hay chinos! [pointing in a sweeping motion that indicated south of the school neighborhood]
2	Sonia:	¿Cómo?
3	Luis:	Japoneses, de aquí para allá. Dice mi mamá que tienen unos carros muy chicos.
4	Cm1:	¿(...) muy grandes, verdad?
5	Luis:	No, (...).
6	Sonia:	Okay, toda la gente puede tener un carro de diferente tipo.

7 Cm2:   Como lo chiquito.

8 Cs: (... ...).

9 Sonia: Luis, la maestra tiene un carro japonés pero yo soy mejicana.

10 Cm: (... ...).

11 Sonia: No importa qué tipo de carro maneja la gente, okay? *It doesn't matter, it doesn't matter.*

Translation

1 Luis: Teacher, from here to there, there are Chinese people! [pointing in a sweeping motion that indicated south of the school neighborhood]

2 Sonia: Pardon?

3 Luis: Japanese, from here to there. My mom says that they have very small cars.

4 Cm1:   (...) very big, right?

5 Luis: No, (...).

6 Sonia   Okay, people can have different types of cars.

7 Cm2:   Like a little one.

8 Cs: (... ...).

9 Sonia: Luis, the teacher has a Japanese car, but I am Mexican.

10 Cm2:   (... ...).

11 Sonia: It doesn't matter what kind of car people drive, okay? *It doesn't matter, it doesn't matter.*

{Fieldnotes, videotape, 01/11/95}

Sonia took advantage of this discussion to reinforce the idea that different people—Chinese, or Japanese, or Mexican, and so forth—are entitled to different choices, and that things like the type of car they drive are not to tied to their ethnic backgrounds. Situations like the ones described in the two examples just presented were not uncommon in Sonia's class, and she consistently challenged her students' preconceptions when the opportunity arose, especially in terms of gender–power relationships and racial stereotypes. She felt that the cultural background of her students, very similar to the one that she had experienced growing up, warranted special attention to these issues.

The goal of challenging some of her students' ideas about racial and gender roles began to guide Sonia's book choices during the last part of the school year, even though she did not seem to realize how much she keyed into these issues when they arose. She commented that it was through discussion with the university researchers that she became aware of this goal.

During the second semester, Sonia's list of books for reading alouds included *The Rainbow Fish* (Pfister, 1992), *Stellaluna* (Cannon, 1993), *The Paper Bag Princess* (Munsch, 1980), *Kokko's Kitten* (Petterson, 1982), and *The Fourth Little Pig* (Celsi, 1992). Each of these stories, through plot and characters' interactions, emphasizes the importance of accepting and expanding one's horizons to new and diverse ways of thinking. In different ways, these stories can question typical views of gender and racial roles, as well as power relationships in contemporary Western society.

CRITICALLY EXAMINING GENDER ROLES IN *THE PAPER BAG PRINCESS*

Sonia: I think these issues came through because they are very important for me personally. My students really got into gender issues and tried to justify what they felt. It was interesting to see how the way 9-year-olds really believe some things about boy and girls, men and women. They see themselves in these roles. The boys see themselves in these roles and the girls see themselves in these roles. I felt they had a really hard time accepting I was the boss because to them, bosses can only be men. I was really adamant about questioning some of their ideas on certain things. Then, when we read The Paper Bag Princess, *it was interesting that they couldn't accept that this woman in the story was telling this guy to get lost. Why would a woman do that? Isn't that what she lives for? They go home and they see their Power Rangers and then 2 or 3 hours of soap operas, and in these soap operas the male–female relationships are very marked. They also are such typical stereotypes of race; the servants are black. All the women have the same role. It is only a happy ending if the young, innocent, beautiful girl married her knight in shining armor. And the girls believe it and that's what they shoot for.*

When I was their age and lived in this community, I thought this was the world. I can see myself in these girls and boys. But there are other worlds, other ways of thinking that are different and that these children need to know.

Sonia read *The Paper Bag Princess*, a story that highlights the idea of women being strong and independent in their decision making, later during the school year. The story tells about Prince Ronald, who rejects his bride-to-be, Princess Elizabeth, because she looks dirty and ugly after she fought the dragon who had burned down Ronald's kingdom and taken him prisoner. Sonia probed and questioned them throughout the read-aloud to consider Elizabeth's decision to leave Ronald after he indicated that he valued her appearance more than her character. Students were very involved and seemed to be genuinely interested in the story. The next two excerpts from this reading-aloud session (one of Sonia's longest)—Examples 7A and 7B—illustrate their examination of these issues. Sonia's comments were in English even when her students' contributions were predominantly in Spanish. Because most of the discussion takes place in

English, a separate translation is not included for these next two examples, but instead line-by-line translations are provided next to Spanish statements. Example 7A occurs towards the end of the story.

Example 7A

1	Sonia:	Let's see. ELIZABETH WALKED RIGHT OVER THE DRAGON AND OPENED THE DOOR TO THE CAVE. THERE WAS PRINCE RONALD. HE LOOKED AT HER AND SAID, "ELIZABETH, YOU ARE A MESS! YOU SMELL LIKE ASHES, YOUR HAIR IS ALL TANGLED AND YOU ARE WEARING A DIRTY OLD PAPER BAG. COME BACK WHEN YOU ARE DRESSED LIKE A REAL PRINCESS. [Sonia shows the illustrations to the whole group] See that?
2	Cs:	Ooooh! (... ...).
3	Sonia:	Why?
4	Cm1:	(...) cansando al dragón. {(...) tiring the dragon.}
5	Sonia:	He's, I don't know, I don't like him. Let's see what happens. [she reads but interrupts herself to pose a question] "RONALD," SAID ELIZABETH.... What do you think Elizabeth is going to do? Do you think Elizabeth is going to come back and get all pretty and beautiful? [gesturing as if fixing her hair]
6	Cm1:	#Yeah, yeah, yeah!#
7	Cs:	#(... ...).#
8	Sonia:	Maybe? Yes? No? Maybe not, maybe yes.
9	Cs:	(... ...).
10	Silvia:	Sí, sí. {Yes, yes.}
11	Sonia:	Why do you think so?
12	Cm1:	I don't think so.
13	Cm2:	Why should she get married?
14	Cm3:	Va a venir (...). {She or he is coming (...).}
15	Sonia:	That's true. Okay, listen to what Silvia has to say. This is very important. Jairo? She said that Elizabeth was going to go back home, and put, you know, get beautiful, put——fix her hair, wash her face....
16	Cm1:	Put make-up.
17	Sonia:	Put some make up on, put on a nice dress.
18	Silvia:	(...) bien arreglada. {(...) made up nicely.}
19	Sonia:	Right, so Prince Ronald will love her.
20	Cm1:	#But (...) what's going to happen?#
21	Cm2:	#Pero (...) casa (...) está, está bien fea.# {But (...) house (...) is——is very ugly.}

| 22 | Sonia: | I don't know. Well, why is she dirty? |
| | | {Fieldnotes, videotape, 04/10/95} |

Sonia offered her view of Ronald—"I don't like him"—regarding how Ronald treated Elizabeth, who got so messy saving him from the dragon Then, as she began to read more, she stopped and asked students if they thought Elizabeth would come back like a princess, "all pretty and beautiful." Students seem to have mixed opinions about this, but Silvia's answer seems to indicate that the most appropriate resolution of the conflict was for Elizabeth to improve her appearance.

There was a lot of overlapping talk after the end of Example 7A, with many students expressing their ideas at once. Sonia asked them to predict if the story would end in marriage between Ronald and Elizabeth, and most students seemed to think that would be the case. Sonia then read the rest of the story, getting to the last paragraph: "RONALD," SAID ELIZABETH, "YOUR CLOTHES ARE VERY PRETTY AND YOUR HAIR IS VERY NEAT. YOU LOOK LIKE A REAL PRINCE, BUT YOU ARE A BUM!" A nobody. THEY DIDN'T GET MARRIED AFTER ALL.

At first there was some discussion of the meaning of *bum*, which students initially interpreted as *ugly*. Sonia clarified the meaning of the word by saying that a bum was someone who "is worried about how he looks more than getting a job or being responsible … not nice." Sonia then queried her students about what they thought were Elizabeth's reasons to leave him. One of the boys joked that "maybe she did not understand English," a comment with undertones about the social values and stature assigned to speakers versus nonspeakers of English. Another student answered that "maybe she was crazy." Sonia further prompted this latter child to explain more but he did not, and so she once more reread the end of the book adding, "See? She was happy!"

Example 7B shows how she subsequently summarized the whole story in an attempt to make Elizabeth's feelings and decisions more obvious to the children.

Example 7B

1	Sonia:	Look! Look! Listen! Listen! [showing illustrations] Right here in the beginning she's all in love with the prince, "Ooh, you are so beautiful, oh la la!" Right here. And then the dragon goes and you know, burns everything and takes the prince away. I mean, the dragon was going to eat the prince, right?
2	Cm1:	(… …).
3	Sonia:	But in the end, the prince tells her, "Oh, you're so ugly." Why do you think Elizabeth got mad?

4	Luis:	Cause it was not she—it was not her fault.
5	Cs:	It was the dragon's fault.
6	Sonia:	Okay, it was the dragon's fault but what did Elizabeth do?
7	Cs:	#(......).#
8	Pedro:	#Well, le salvó la vida.# {#Well, she saved his life.#}
9	Sonia:	*That's it!* [pointing excitedly to Pedro] Pedro, you got it!!
10	Cm1:	¿Quién? {Who?}
11	Sonia:	*You got it!* Say what you just said.
12	Pedro:	Le salvó la vida. {She saved his life.}
13	Sonia:	Who ... who saved whose life?
14	Pedro:	La señora. {The lady}
15	Sonia:	Saved whose life?
16	Pedro:	Del señor. {The man's.}
17	Sonia:	That's right! The princess, Elizabeth. Elizabeth saved the prince's life! See? How does she do that?
18	Luis:	Cachando a ese dragón. {Catching that dragon.}
19	Sonia:	Right, she use her....
20	Luis:	Imagination.
21	Sonia:	She used her....
22	Cm1:	Her brain!
23	Sonia:	She used her brain.
24	Cm1:	Estaba pensando. {She was thinking.} [banging on his head with his hands]
25	Cm2:	Que—cómo cansarlo. {That—how to tire it out.}
26	Sonia:	Right, she used her brain.
27	Cm1:	Estaba pensando cómo (......). {She was thinking how to (......).}
28	Sonia:	To think of ways to tire the dragon so she could save the prince. Pedro was right. So she could save the prince. And then, when she saves the prince, what does the prince say, Pedro?
29	Pedro:	She—the prince says, oh, que esta fea. { ....oh, that she was ugly.}
30	Sonia:	Yeah! The prince said, "You are ugly."
31	Pedro:	Y ... al principio, y al principio como (......) todo eso. {And ... at the beginning, and at the beginning how (......) all that.}
32	Sonia:	That's right. So wouldn't you be mad?
33	Cs:	(......).
34	Cm1:	(...) le dijo (...). {(...) told him/her (...).}

35	Sonia:	Yeah, real smart. Now let me ask you, Vilma, Silvia, Mimi....
36	Cm2:	Las tras comadres. {The three girlfriends.}
37	Sonia:	Yeah, let me ask you, if you had a boyfriend ... do you think this would be? A girl could tell a man, "Get out of here!" Right?
38	Javier:	Yo le diria apártate de mi camino. {I would tell him get out of my way.}
39	Sonia:	That's right. What would you do, Vilma? Very good Javier! What would you do if you saved your boyfriend's life?
40	Javier:	Ella no entiende, teacher. {She does not understand, teacher.}
41	Sonia:	We'll help her. Vilma ... she understands.
42	Cm1:	Sí? {Yes?}
43	Sonia:	[speaking loudly and slowly] Vilma, if you had a boyfriend—if you had a boyfriend and you saved his life but you got all dirty [gesturing as if she got something smeared on her face] and he said, "Oh, I don't want you anymore," wouldn't you be mad?
44	Vilma:	#[Shakes her head slightly indicating "no."]#
45	Cs:	#[Other children are talking at once.]#
46	Sonia:	No? You wouldn't be mad?
47	Vilma:	[Shakes her head again.]
48	Sonia:	Javier, help me, help me [pointing to Vilma] so that Vilma understands what I'm telling her. Vilma, if you had a boyfriend and you saved him....
49	Javier:	Y si tu tuvieras novio (...).... {And if you had a boyfriend (...)....}
50	Cm1:	Y lo has salvado.... {And you have saved him....}
....		[Two of the students sitting next to Vilma are translating for her too.]
51	Sonia:	And, if you saved his life but you got dirty, you know, but you got all dirty and he told you, "Ooooh, you are dirty!" Would you stay with him?
....		[Children continue to translate for Vilma as Sonia talks but what they say is inaudible.]
52	Sonia:	Tell her, Javier, tell her what I just said.
53	Javier:	(...) le salvó la vida (...) muy fea (...) y maestra, que salió allí. {(...) saved his life (...) very ugly (...) and teacher, that got out of there.}
54	Cm1:	[translating for Vilma also] Y estuvo bien fea y con toda la ropa arrugada aquí en la frente. {And she was very ugly and all her clothes were wrinkled here in the forehead.} [touching Vilma's forehead, and saying something about being dirty on her face as the illustrations in the book and Sonia had shown]

55	Vilma:	No.
56	Sonia:	No? You wouldn't stay with him?
57	Vilma:	[Shakes her head "no."]
....		[Students are talking amongst themselves. It is time for the class to go to lunch.]
		{Fieldnotes, videotape, 04/10/95}

Students' responses to Sonia's questions seemed to indicate that Elizabeth's reasons to leave Ronald were not immediately obvious to them. They did not agree wholeheartedly, at least initially, with the book and with Sonia's condemnation of Ronald's attitude and behavior toward the female figure in the text. Even when Sonia's prompts led Pedro to recognize Elizabeth's strength and commitment because she saved the prince's life, nobody articulated the idea of the prince being unfair and selfish in return. Only after Sonia posed her question repeatedly, emphasizing the key elements, did Vilma seem to consider that Elizabeth's was the right decision.

Sonia: I was not surprised at my students' reactions during this discussion. It is unfortunate but most of them see these attitudes taking place on an everyday basis. Sometimes, I think that all my efforts did not accomplish my goals; I did not help them change their minds. The boys and the girls still thought that this is the way the world is and is supposed to be. But, other times, especially now that I look back I think that maybe our discussions made some difference. Maybe they planted some seeds that would stay with them.

THE MULTIFACETED POSSIBILITIES
OF THE READING-ALOUD CURRICULUM GENRE

The Paper Bag Princess session best represents the transformations in form and content that characterized the reading-aloud curricular routine in this third-grade classroom. Patterns of code switching shifted and were transformed as the flow of communication demanded it. Code switching was not limited to a specific set or categories of speech acts, but rather accommodated participants' particular needs as they focused on meaningful discussions. Thus, this finding validates the need for a more microethnographic approach to study of code switching, that is, one that considers actual language use in bilingual classrooms (Martin-Jones, 1995).

In general, the frequency of Sonia's code switching from English to Spanish decreased as she used more and more English, not only in the texts she read, but in her ways to guide the discussions of them. Even when most of her students continued to use Spanish to answer her questions or express their ideas, she was able to respond to their initiations in ways that scaffolded their learning of English. When necessary, Sonia did resort to Spanish translation as an intercommunication strategy, but it became a less frequent mode of communication. Moreover, when possible, Sonia shared English translation responsibilities with students as they gained greater proficiency in English. In this way, she provided opportunities for them to engage in English use and to model it for their peers. The reading-aloud routine, therefore, was then an effective curriculum genre that successfully supported second-language learning among this group of students.

As her students became more proficient in English, there was a shift in the kinds of questions that Sonia posed to them during the reading-aloud discussions. Initially, most of her questions were directed to check for literal comprehension and vocabulary knowledge. Later, Sonia was able to model and support initiations that required a more involved response, providing her students with opportunities to offer and reformulate their ideas, via classroom talk, through what Wells (Wells, 1990; Wells & Chang-Wells, 1992) termed an epistemic mode of engagement of text.

Sonia: I am not sure that they left my third grade knowing all they should, or achieving at the level that they should. However, they made big strides in their ability to understand English, to follow a discussion, but I wish I had had more time to work on reading and writing in English. Many were starting to use English more fluently, with less fear. My greatest accomplishment, I think, was showing them that it was possible for them to learn both languages, to speak and understand both. That's what they need if they want to succeed. I think they felt much better about themselves at the end of the year, and that is important. I heard their voices and also helped them lose their fear to try their English voice.

Finally, Sonia utilized reading-aloud discussions to nudge her students into taking a critical stance with respect to gender and racial preconceptions. She respected her students' positions as these issues were raised during reading-aloud discussions, but she never missed the opportunity to challenge their ideas or to present alternative views. In a sense, Sonia, via read-aloud discussions, was able to realize the kind of language-learning situation that Edelsky (1994) described as the true, but elusive, goal of progressive language education. That is, this is the aim that ties language use to question, to reflect upon, and thus to make possible changes in "people's societal positions, their structured privileges, their greater or lesser power, and the interests of the group they represent" (p. 255).

In summary, it is important, as research on reading-aloud continues, to critically examine this curricular routine from what many view as merely a common literacy practice that somehow fosters literacy learning. Reading-alouds can function in very different ways depending on the text that is read, a particular teacher's goals, and the context of a particular classroom community—the ways and the extent to which students are given opportunities to offer their own ideas as they coconstruct meanings with the teacher.

REFERENCES

Arthur, J. (1996). Code switching and collusion: Classroom interaction in Botswana primary schools *Linguistics and Education, 8,* 17–33.

Blanco, A. (1992). *La sirena del desierto/The desert mermaid.* San Francisco, CA: Children's Book Press.

Cannon, J. (1993). *Stellaluna.* San Diego, CA: Harcourt Brace Javonovich.

Celsi, T. (1992). *The fourth little pig.* Austin, TX: Raintree Steck-Vaughn.

Dickinson, D., Hao, Z., & He, W. (1995). Pedagogical and classroom factors related to how teachers read to 3– and 4–year-old children. In K. Hinchman, D. Leu, & C. Kinzer, (Eds.), *Perspectives on literacy research and practice. Forty-fourth yearbook of the National Reading Conference* (pp. 212–221). Chicago, IL: National Reading Conference.

Dickinson, D. K., & Keebler, R. (1989). Variations in preschool teachers' storybook reading styles. *Discourse Processes, 12,* 353–376.

Dickinson, D. K., & Smith, M. A. (1994). Long-term effects of preschool teachers' book readings on low-income children's vocabulary and story comprehension. *Reading Research Quarterly, 29,* 104–122

Dillon, J. T. (1994). *Using discussion in classrooms.* Buckingham, England: Open University Press.

Edelsky, C. (1994). Education for democracy. *Language Arts, 71,* 252–257.

Guthrie, L. F., & Guthrie, G. P. (1994). Teacher language use in Chinese bilingual classroom. In S. Goldman, & H. Trueba (Eds.), *Becoming literate in a second language* (pp. 205–231). Norwood, NJ: Ablex.

Heath, S. B. (1986). Sociocultural contexts of language development. In D. Holt (Ed.), *Beyond language: Social and cultural factors in schooling language minority students.* Los Angeles: Evaluation, Dissemination and Assessment Center, California State University.

Henson, J. (1993). The tie that binds: The role of talk in defining community. In K. M. Pierce, & Gilles, C. J. (Eds.), *Cycles of meaning* (pp. 37–57). Portsmouth, NH: Heinemann.

Jiménez, R., García, G. E., & Pearson, P. D. (1996). The reading strategies of bilingual Latina/o students who are successful English readers: Opportunities and obstacles. *Reading Research Quarterly, 31,* 90–112.

Kroll, S (1984). *The biggest pumpkin ever.* New York: Scholastic.

Martin-Jones, M. (1995). Code-switching in the classroom: Two decades of research. In L. Milroy & P. Muysken (Eds.), *One speaker, two languages: Crossdisciplinary perspectives in code-switching* (pp. 90–111). Cambridge, England: Cambridge University Press.

Martínez, M., & Teale, W. (1993). Teacher storybook reading style: A comparison of six teachers. *Research in the Teaching of English, 27,* 175–199.

Munsch, R. (1980). *The paper bag princess.* Toronto, Canada: Annick Press.

Petterson, F. (1985). *Kokko's kitten.* New York: Scholastic.

Pfister, M. (1992). *The rainbow fish.* New York: North-South Books.

Ramirez, A. (1988). Analyzing speech acts. In J. L. Green & J. O. Harker (Eds.), *Multiple perspective analyses of classroom discourse* (pp.135–163). Norwood, NJ: Ablex.

Reder, S. (1994). Practice-engagement theory: A social-cultural approach to literacy across languages and cultures. In B. M. Ferdman, R.-M. Weber, & A. G. Ramirez (Eds.), *Literacy across languages and cultures* (pp. 33–74). Albany, NY: State University Press.

Teale, W., & Martínez, M. (1996). Reading aloud to young children: Teacher's reading styles and kindergarteners' text comprehension. In C. Pontecorvo, M. Ossolini, B. Burge, & L. Resnick (Eds.), *Children's early text construction* (pp. 321–358). Mahwah, NJ: Lawrence Erlbaum Associates.

Wells, G. (1990). Talk about text: Where literacy is learned and taught. *Curriculum Inquiry, 20,* 369–405.

Wells, G., & Chang-Wells, G. L. (1992). *Constructing knowledge together: Classrooms as centers of inquiry and literacy.* Portsmouth, NH: Heinemann.

Part III

Drama Curriculum Genres

Two teacher researchers completed inquiries that focused primarily on drama.

In chapter 8, Hank Tabak, university researcher, collaborated with Paul Fowler to relate Paul's study on the use of drama. For several years, Paul was the school's literature enrichment specialist—also know as the "books on wheels guy"—who shared stories with children in K to 4th-grade classrooms. Then, due to a faculty down-sizing, he found himself as the teacher of a contained sixth grade. He had successfully used drama with the K to fourth-grade children, and also with older children in afterschool programs, so he was eager to try out more longterm drama projects in this new teaching context. His first efforts to implement drama structures were problematic for many reasons. However, later in the year, he found more success in facilitating student improvisations of realistic fiction. Both kinds of experiences are presented and illustrated in the chapter.

Chapter 9 begins with relating Bernadine Braun's efforts to make her reading-aloud sessions more collaborative. Bernadine felt that having her special education students initiate their responses to books during read-alouds was requisite to their being able to subsequently dramatize them, which was the major focus of her inquiry. Dian Ruben and Jane Liao, university researchers, worked with Bernadine to give an account of these experiences. Throughout, Bernadine struggled to find the "right balance" of teacher control to help her students engage in literacy learning through drama. Using information from her colleagues at the weekly project meetings, she found ways to facilitate successful drama activities for her students. She again had difficulties when students attempted to dramatize plays they wrote on their own. Despite all of these ups and downs, children —especially two older sisters who were unable or unwilling to participate in many class activities at all in the beginning of the year—benefited from drama activities.

Both chapters describe and discuss what is involved when teachers attempt to incorporate drama-curriculum genres to support literacy learning. Paul illustrates what happens when a "beginning" teacher launches drama activities, and Bernadine's chapter shows how an experienced special education teacher challenged some of her underlying philosophies and expectations about her students as learners when she tried drama to engage them more completely in literature.

Chapter 8

Trying Out Roles for Learning: Finding the "Right" Drama Approach for Sixth Graders

Henry Tabak, Jr.

Paul Fowler

Drama, as one of the oldest literary forms, has been used to educate for thousands of years. In the absence of written language, ancient societies performed dramatic rituals to pass on traditions, sacred beliefs, taboos, mores, and history to their members, and to cope with everyday human experience (Brockett, 1968).

Creative drama still has an important role in education. Besides learning about artists, drama offers students opportunities to function as artists (Heathcote, 1980). The benefits of drama are many. For example, Conard (1992), based on her analysis of a range of studies using creative drama in the classroom, argued that because drama is multidimensional—requiring the use of the affective, cognitive, and psychomotor domains—it can serve as a critical vehicle for learning and integrating the language arts other curricula. In addition, because drama is a cooperative enterprise (O'Neill, 1988), it promotes collaboration among students (McCaslin, 1980; Moffett, 1983; O'Neill & Lambert, 1982).

The introduction chapter of this book provides the theoretical and methodological background for the larger collaborative school–university action-research project and this chapter about Paul's inquiry on drama. See also the last chapter, which further discusses the implications of Paul's inquiry—as well as those of the other teacher researchers.

As a mode of learning, drama represents a particular semiotic means by which students can actively identify with and imagine roles and situations so as to enable them to explore issues, events, and relationships (O'Neill & Lambert, 1982). According to O'Neill & Lambert, drama is seen not merely as a handmaiden in the teaching of various curricular subjects such as history or science, but also as a critical two-way process that occurs when it is employed in education. In their words, "Other subject areas will provide drama with a serious and worthwhile content and, in many cases, a powerful context for the make-believe, while drama strategies will enliven and illuminate these areas of the curriculum" (p. 16).

As a response to literature, drama provides opportunities for children to become characters, as well as critics, as they construct and evaluate different interpretations of books they have read (Wolf, 1994). As different students take on various roles, they hear how others might have understood a situation, a scene, and then begin to appreciate the potential multiple meanings of language (Bakhtin, 1981, 1986; Halliday, 1978). They consider the points of view that different readers-as-actors bring to and take from texts (Rosenblatt, 1978). Moreover, students become more explicitly aware of the social dimensions of literacy; that is, they begin to appreciate the expectation of the reciprocity or dialogue between readers and writers in written discourse (Cazden, 1992; Nystrand, 1986, 1987; 1997; Nystrand & Wiemelt, 1991; Wells, 1998).

Thus, drama provides a process of *transmediation* (Harste, 1993; Smagorinsky & Coppock, 1995). It is a way by which students can read the signs of a literary text, collaborate with others in constructing a meaning of those signs, and then create a new representation of that meaning in a different sign system that fuses oral language with gesture and action. As Moffett (1983) argued, drama is a different mode of thinking and abstracting; it is a different tool to embody ideas. Drama becomes, then, an important part of students' cultural "tool kits" (Wertsch, 1991); it offers another mediational means for them to make meaning.

Paul: I got hooked into drama around 1990 when I was prodded into playing Fred, the warm-hearted nephew of Scrooge, in a musical called "Mr. Scrooge." Although I studied English literature at undergraduate school and had read many books, I never really dug very deep into the characters. However, in doing this play, I had to know about my character and read the script with a more critical eye than I had never done before. I was always thinking about what motivated Fred and I had to consider all these things when I said every line. I had to interpret the inflection on each word. "Mr. Scrooge" was a story that I would have laughed at as an undergraduate as being basic and boring; however, I, in actually doing it, learned how deep you can look into the simplest of stories and how my understanding of the people and myself grew enormously for the experience. It changed the way I look at learning. Drama was an eye opener in the sense that it showed multi-

ple ways to a character, other characters, or the words or lines being read. Meanings get created by the person who is saying the lines. Reading becomes more of a fluid, live enterprise. I have found that it is hard sometimes for kids to respond this way, say even through journal responses. Drama helps them to have more of an authentic and thoughtful response to what they are reading. It helps them consider different possibilities.

For a couple of years, I had been the teacher doing the "books-on-wheels" program at Andersen. I went to preschool to fourth-grade classrooms and shared good children's literature with these students. In this capacity, I had employed various creative drama techniques to help my students develop richer responses to the books I read to them. Although I felt I had been successful in using drama with these students and in some short-term experiences with some of the older students at school, I still had questions about how best I might use it more effectively, and I had planned to do my inquiry around ongoing tensions I still felt.

Then, 1 month or so into the school year, there were staff cuts, and I became—for the first time—the teacher of a self-contained sixth-grade class of 27 students (11 girls, 16 boys; 18 Latinos, 5 African Americans, and 4 Anglo children). Although I was very nervous about the challenge of developing the whole curriculum for these sixth graders, and of course, the issues of classroom management and discipline that came with the assignment, I was also excited to study how to use drama at this level. I had taken a class with Cecily O'Neill where I had read Drama Structures *(O'Neill & Lambert, 1982), and I was thrilled with the opportunity to try out the ideas in my classroom. Thus, I continued to do my inquiry around drama, but of course my questions and context were now quite different.*

Many of Paul's early drama efforts drew on ideas from the *Drama Structures* (O'Neill & Lambert, 1982) book. However, although the objectives and purposes of these drama exercises had great potential for promoting Paul's aims, his experiences to implement them with his students were difficult. Many of these difficulties were compounded by the challenges he faced as a "beginning" teacher. His use of student improvisations of scenes of adolescent literature later on in the year was much more successful. Thus, we offer examples of both types to characterize the major features of his inquiry in the use of drama to promote his students' learning.

STRUGGLES TO PROMOTE THE "MANTLE OF THE EXPERT" IN DRAMA

Part of the sixth-grade history and social studies curriculum at Andersen is the study of early civilization. Paul decided to experiment with ideas in "The Lost Valley" drama structure from the O'Neill and Lambert book. This unit invites students, through dramatic play, to reconstruct the life and work of a primitive society by participating in tasks such as shelter

building, hunting or gathering, preparing defenses, organizing tribal cele-
brations, and so forth.

*Paul: I had hoped to help my students take on a variety of expert roles so
that they would learn how important it is for them to cooperate with one another to build their understanding of how all aspects of a society are interrelated. I launched the drama, trying to use the actual words of the book,
which I had memorized the night before:*

> Welcome to the Scientific Research Institute. I am really pleased that you are
> the people who have finally been chosen for this experiment. ... [F]or the next
> year we shall be living as the members of a primitive tribe, without the bene-
> fits of the twentieth century. We shall have to cope with unusual problems, I
> am sure, but lessons learned may help us to find out more about such people
> and may be of benefit to us in our present-day situation. Now, you may have
> lots of questions you didn't have a chance to ask when you can to the inter-
> views. I'll try to answer them for you here. (p. 87)

*Well, this first session in early December went great. After some initial
confusion, students began to ask questions, ones which were not that unlike
the ones that O'Neill and Lambert depicted. And, as they suggested, in responding to student comments, I tried to stress the idea of experts, people
who would be chosen for the experiment for their various expertise.*

Thus, a key goal in Paul's drama inquiry was to help his students take
on the "mantle of the expert," which is a core concept in both O'Neill's
(1988) and Heathcote's (Heathcote & Herbert, 1985) work. However,
despite the success of the first drama exercise, quite a few of the students became increasingly confused about their roles as experts in
drama sessions.

For example, again using an exercise from the same drama structure in
the book, Paul told his students that team members, who now worked in
various groups around expert tasks, would attempt to explain the project
to a wider public audience. As preparation for the news reporters, Paul
asked some of his students to give him an example of a question they might
ask them. Two students gave examples, and then Kendall asked Paul,
"Shouldn't we have some kind of *expert* to tell us what kind of stuff they
have down there when we get there?" Paul quickly replied, "*You* are the experts! Like the cooking group are the experts on what's going to be there
to cook. They're the only ones that know!" (Fieldnotes, 01/26/95)

Although Paul stressed many times that the students in the various
groups were to see themselves as experts, many still did not seem to understand what this meant in terms of make-believe. Example 1 shows a discussion during that same session. Paul went around to check the progress of
the various groups, and just finished a conference with the doctor and vet-
erinarian group, which consisted of four boys. Paul now got the attention

of the whole class and asked Samuel, who was a member of this group and who had a poster he and his group had been working on, to tell the class what he might say to the fictional reporters who would come on Monday. Samuel started out slowly, but Paul's support helped him to elaborate. By asking about the mushroom that Samuel said they would likely encounter in their journey back in time, Eva also nudged Samuel to consider information that had not as yet been thought of. However, although Eva's challenge seemed initially useful by pointing out more dimensions to that group's role as experts, later on she showed that she wanted the "real" answer, not any make-believe one.

Example 1

1	Paul:	You just told me about something that they [reporters] might ask you. Show everybody your poster.
2	Samuel:	[He stops drawing and then holds the poster above his head for everyone to see.]
3	Paul:	Okay, so when the reporters come ask you about that poster, what are you going to tell them?
4	Samuel:	It was in the garbage can.
5	Paul:	[patiently responding among student giggles] Okay, what are you going to tell them about that mushroom [which is depicted on the poster]?
6	Samuel:	That we found it ... where....
7	Paul:	Why is that mushroom important?
8	Samuel:	[with authority] Because it kills people! #And....#
9	Paul:	#Okay.#
10	Samuel:	The animals that eat it, they die.
11	Paul:	Okay ... [after asking other students who are talking to be quiet, he continues] So you're telling me as a group we need to know about that mushroom because it's poisonous, and we have to avoid it.
12	Samuel:	Yeah, it kills the animals.
13	Paul:	And it'll kill us too if we eat it.
14	Samuel:	Yeah.
....		[During this latter exchange, Eva has had her hand raised. After addressing other remarks about the poster to Samuel, Paul asks students to be quiet, and then he acknowledges her.]
15	Eva:	I've got a question for that mushroom group. If it kills people, like, like when you eat it, and it gets to your stomach, do you die right there? Er, how?

....   [Paul refers the question to Samuel, who didn't seem know how
               to answer. After getting students to be more quiet, Paul asks
               Eva to repeat her question.]

16 Eva: You said the mushroom was poisonous. When you eat it and it
               goes to your stomach, would you die right there?

17 Samuel: Yeah.

18 Julio: [another member of his group] No, it takes a couple of minutes.

19 Eva: He doesn't know!

20 Paul: Oh, I think he knows. He's the expert!

21 Eva: Well then....

22 Paul: Samuel, Samuel, I'm sure you know that. Will people die right
               away, or....

23 Samuel: Yeah!

24 Paul: Will they....

25 Samuel: Yeah, people will die right away because it has poison on it.

26 Eva: Will it wait until it hits your stomach, or will you die right away
               when you eat it when it's still in your throat?

....   [Samuel hesitates and other students talk, remarking that he
               doesn't know the answer. Paul quiets students down and gets
               Eva's permission to paraphrase her question.]

27 Paul: Ummm, Samuel, she just wants to know if you will die as soon
               as it touches your lips, or will it wait until it reaches your stom-
               ach and*...

28 Samuel: No, it'll take like 5 minutes.

29 Paul: So five. So basically almost as soon as you....

30 Eva: Where did he get the answer from?

31 Paul: He's the expert! He's the expert! Just like you're the expert of
               something.

               {Fieldnotes, videotape, 01/26/95}

It was unclear throughout Example 1 if the interactions were perceived by
Paul and students as a drama rehearsal for the upcoming television cover-
age where various team members would explain facets of the expedition,
or if they were just discussing, as a class, issues to think about as part of
preparation for the upcoming drama. That is, it was not apparent when
Paul and the students were "in role."

Although Samuel and his doctors- and vets-group members had done
some work on presenting their expertise at the upcoming program, it was
also apparent that much had not been thought out. Thus, Paul's asking
why the mushroom on the poster was important (line 7) was critical be-

cause it helped Samuel (and his group and other expert groups) to think about the kind of preparation that would be necessary as experts if they were to be persuasive. After a slow start, Samuel did offer that the mushroom would kill people and animals (lines 8 & 10). Paul then expanded Samuel's ideas in line 11, "we need to know about that mushroom because it's poisonous, and we have to avoid it."

Eva (in line 15) also prodded Samuel and his group to elaborate by asking how fast the poison would affect its victim. When Samuel and Julio give different answers, she exclaimed, "He doesn't know!" Paul then stepped in to defend Samuel by stating, "He's the expert!" However, Eva was unrelenting in her insistence on more details (see line 26 and Paul's paraphrase of her question in line 27), but when Samuel offered "5 minutes" as the time the mushroom would cause death, she demanded, "Where did he get the answer from?" Once again, Paul's response to her was that Samuel was the expert "just like you're the expert of something."

Thus, on one hand, Paul and Eva seemed to help Samuel (and the rest of the class) realize that trying on roles did entail intellectual effort by being more aware of the kinds of questions that fictional reporters might ask to members of the expedition. This enterprise, then, would not only make the upcoming drama more successful, but would also spark issues and concerns to follow-up in their inquiries in their social studies curricular content. On the other hand, it seemed also evident that Eva (as well as many other students) seemed confused about what this mantle of expert consisted of in drama, versus in the research she might be doing outside of drama. Unfortunately, Paul's mere reiterations of "you're the expert" did not foster students' understandings in this way.

Paul: I just didn't make things explicit enough for the kids. In the Drama Structures *book, O'Neill and Lambert expect that students are learning ongoing background in the subject they are going to dramatize. They also assume that students will be made aware of this link. Because I didn't make it clear about this link—which O'Neill and Lambert called a two-way process—between studying the subject matter on early civilization societies and the drama, students didn't get the rationale for what we were doing in drama sessions. Moreover, in their book, O'Neill and Lambert also provided resources for "The Lost Valley" structure. These would not have been appropriate in my case because these were on very primitive societies and gauged for high school students. But I should have realized that I needed to bring into the classroom the relevant reading materials for enriching the social studies content inquiry, which then would have embellished the drama, and on and on, back and forth between the two.*

Moreover, I was ineffective in explaining the role of expert in drama. I never even had a good minilesson to elucidate what I really meant by "you're the expert," which I realize now I just kept repeating over and over again. So, students continued to be befuddled and frustrated. Besides my not fostering the kind of learning I had hoped to encourage, many gave up al-together and caused me even more management difficulties.

Thus, Paul's first efforts to use this drama structure from the book to encourage his students to try on the expert role were problematic. His attempts to encourage similar roles in implementing drama structures in a later unit on "Disasters" resulted in not much more success, for about the same kind of reasons. However, in a subsequent unit on "Power," as well as other subsequent thematic units during the year, he began to experiment with student improvisations of scenes of realistic fiction. Finally, Paul felt more success and confidence using drama because it helped his students greatly in their interpretations of literature.

RESPONSE TO LITERATURE: DRAMA TO FOSTER MULTIPLE MEANINGS

Paul: I turned to drama improvisations of realistic fiction because I began to remember why I had initially wanted to do drama with students in the first place. I started with some new questions for my inquiry that recalled how much I learned in my own personal theater experience. Can drama provide a doorway to greater involvement and understanding of literature? Can drama help connect literature to students' lives? Finally, how do I get the very peer-oriented and self-conscious sixth graders to step outside themselves to take on the role of a character who might be very different from them?

Also, because I was having so many problems of class management, I thought that dramatizing a chapter or passage from a book would be more of a short-term or "bounded" experience that could happen during a period. I also chose to try this new venture by having the drama be more related to a particular piece of literature at a time when I had only half of the students in class. Also, when I began to realize that many of my problems were also due to the fact that most students had never been exposed to drama before this year, I decided to introduce students to some of Spolin's (1975) theater games even before we tried the literature improvisations. Thus, there were lots of reasons why the latter drama episodes worked out much better.

As already noted, Paul did have successful drama experiences with his students, mostly centering around improvisations of realistic fiction. Through drama, his students developed authentic responses to this literature by gaining opportunities to have rich transactions with texts. Rosenblatt (1988) spoke of the "efferent/aesthetic continuum" on which both readers and writers take a stance on literature that reflects their purpose in communication. In her theory, she utilizes an iceberg as an analogy to describe this continuum—the tip of the iceberg, the efferent stance, represents facts to be "retained, used, or acted on after the reading event" whereas the rest of the iceberg, the aesthetic stance, stands for "the experiences, the qualities of the structured ideas, situations, scenes, personalities, and emotions called forth" (p. 5).

Drama especially enhanced this latter aesthetic stance, the "lived-through" meanings of the text, allowing students to enter the world of the characters depicted in the story by interacting with others in role. As Rosenblatt (1988) stated (p. 5), "This meaning evoked during the aesthetic transaction constitutes 'the literary work,' the poem, story, or play. This evocation, and *not the text,* is the object of the reader's 'response' and 'interpretation' both during and after the reading event."

Drama helped Paul's students in two major ways: First, through improvisation, students formulated multiple interpretations of the same text, and second, while in role they became actor-as-writer participants by creating new dialogue and different extensions of characters and plot. Thus, to reiterate the previous analogy, students were guided to focus on the rest of the iceberg instead of just concentrating on the tip. Dramatic scenes of *Bingo Brown and the Language of Love* (Byars, 1989) show the nature of these student transactions.

CREATING MULTIPLE TEXTUAL INTERPRETATIONS THROUGH IMPROVISATION

Paul's students were able to delve deeply into the texts by taking on the roles of the characters and by acting out short scenes. Each improvisation displayed a unique interpretation of the same text. The interactions between Paul and students prior to their improvisations, and then immediately afterwards in wrap-up discussions, were critically important in fostering these multiple interpretations of the *Bingo Brown and the Language of Love* book (and others).

Bingo Brown, who just completed the sixth grade and can't wait to become a man, discovered that he must go through a few more trials and triumphs before growing up. In the examples, Paul had just read aloud the first six (of nine) pages of the opening chapter, "The Groundhog Mustache." It was dinnertime in the Brown household, and Bingo's mother complained to her husband about the trouble she's had with the billing department at the telephone company. Bingo's father was busy making dinner and seemed more interested in eating than in hearing about the telephone company. Bingo's mom furiously exclaimed that the company has overcharged them $54.29 for seven calls to Bixby, Oklahoma, and that they don't even know anybody living there! Bingo gasped when he heard his mother's comment, because he is the one who made the calls. Bingo's girlfriend, Melissa, moved to Bixby. When he received a postcard from her with her phone number on it and the message "call me," he approached his mother and asked her if it would be all right if he called Melissa. It turned out that at that time his mother was preoccupied studying for her real estate exam and told him it would be okay for him to call. Bingo sheepishly apologized for the misunderstanding and the family finally sat down to eat the cold stir fry his father prepared for dinner.

Paul: As I thought about this scene, I decided that my role would be that of coach, cheerleader, and advisor. I would definitely not force my ideas on them about how to play the characters unless I felt they had taken something too far. However, I would guide them if I thought they had seriously misinterpreted a character's motivations. I entered into the scene skeptically because I had been so unsuccessful at getting children to open up to the world of pretend. I was pleasantly surprised at the results.

On the first day that we improvised the scene, we did it four times. The first time that students acted out the part, they were hesitant. By the fourth rendition of the scene, after watching, thinking, and talking about the scene, it jelled to the point where the students lost self-consciousness on the first try. It was clear, though, even during the first improvisation, that students could take on a role. I was surprised only the extent to which that they immersed themselves in it. After I read the scene, I asked if anyone would be willing to take the chance and take the role of either Bingo, the mother, or the father. Three kids reluctantly took the parts: Louise took the part of mother, Willie became the father, and Jack became Bingo.

Before the first improvisation began, Paul asked Willie about his character's actions and motivations. Although the following interactions in Example 2 may seem trivial at first glance, Paul's questions, and his decision to let Willie alter the storyline, gave the message to students that multiple meanings were to be explored.

Example 2

1 Jack:	[sitting down next to Willie, playfully wiping his own upper lip with his index finger] I got a mustache.
2 Paul:	[pointing to Willie] All right, what are you doing at first, Dad?
3 Willie:	Well at first I'm going to be at dinner, and I'm going to go [cupping both of his hands around his mouth and raising his voice], "Dinner's ready!"
4 Paul:	What are you doing before you call, while they're over there doing the scene?
5 Willie:	Ah, waiting.
6 Paul:	You're just waiting?
7 Willie:	Well, what am I supposed to do?
8 Paul:	I don't know. What do you think you should do?
9 Willie:	(... ...).

10 Paul:	What do you think he's doing before he calls and says "dinner's ready"? What do people do before they say dinner is ready? Does your mom just sit there and wait, and all of a sudden say [in a louder voice], "Huh! Dinner's ready!" Or, what does your mom do? Or, dad? Whatever?
11 Jack:	[whispers to Willie] <Set the table.>
12 Willie:	[smiling and giggling, looking from Jack to Paul] No, I ain't setting the dinner table, the table is already set.
13 Paul:	Okay, the table's already set, so what else could you be doing to get that dinner ready?
14 Patricia:	[standing nearby, listening to the conversation] Cook it!
15 Willie:	Dinner's just sitting in the stove all ready now (... ...).
16 Paul:	[pointing at Patricia] Patricia's got a great suggestion.
17 Willie:	We're letting all the dinner cool, because it's too hot.
18 Paul:	Oh, I see. Okay, fine. All right.
19 Patricia:	[walking over to Willie] Aren't you going to cook it first?
20 Willie:	[getting a little frustrated, speaks louder] But it's already cooked!
21 Paul:	Okay, fine. I just thought you might——well … well, all right. {Fieldnotes, videotape, 05/17/95}

The significance in this example is that Paul did not demand that Willie follow the events of the text by cooking dinner as Bingo's father did in the story. Also he did this even though Patricia suggested that Willie, as the father, should. Willie wanted to be seated at the table waiting for the meal to be served, and Paul was open to letting him explore this new twist in his character's action. Also, by allowing Willie the freedom of modifying the storyline, Paul expressed a teaching stance of being a facilitator or guide. As he indicated earlier, Paul decided that his role would be coach, cheerleader, and advisor. He demonstrated that his students did not have to follow the text literally; they were encouraged to experiment with multiple interpretations, and with other potential meanings. This approach of Paul's contributed to the success of the *Bingo Brown* and other literature improvisations.

Paul: It is unreasonable to expect that students will be able to jump into a role the first time that they act out a scene. They need to see the scene develop, see how the parts are interpreted by others, and simply see it enough times to be able to take on the attitude of the character. During this 45-minute period, Jack played the role of Bingo in the first and third times that we did the improvisation. I watched Jack develop from a person just trying to remember what his character was supposed to be thinking and saying to a person who clearly became his character. Jack's ability to interpret and de-velop Bingo's character was ever evident during and after his initial impro-visational attempt.

After the first improvisation, Paul asked his students what they thought about the performance, in a wrap-up discussion: "Tell me some good things, positive things, and some things that could be improved." Such follow-up discussions are key not only for further successful improvisations, but also provide the means to add another layer of multiple meanings, thereby enhancing interpretation. Here, Eva, Jack, Willie, and George became involved in a discussion about Jack's rendition of Bingo's character. Eva remarked that she liked the way Jack played Bingo because he was honest. George quickly disagreed, claiming that Jack was trying to avoid telling the truth. Example 3 shows more of this discussion while different ideas were considered. Jack offered even another thesis that is different from this honest-versus-dishonest interpretation regarding Bingo's personality.

Example 3

1	Jack:	But he forgot about that. He didn't lie. He just said, "Who would have made fifty-four dollars and twenty-eight cents worth of phone calls to ... that ... Oklahoma." But then he remembered, so he didn't lie.
2	George:	[to Jack] He was gonna lie.
3	Jack:	[in a louder voice] No, he didn't.
4	George:	[also with a raised voice] He was!
5	Jack:	[his voice rising in pitch] He wasn't a liar!
6	George:	He was trying to pull it off——pull it off....
7	Jack:	Yeah, but....
8	George:	When he said # <who would make phone calls to Oklahoma for fifty-four dollars and twenty-eight cents.> #
9	Jack:	#yeah, but that was like his forgetful side.# Like he said, [raising his voice in wonderment] "Who would have made fifty-four dollars and twenty-eight cents...."
10	Willie:	[having heard enough of this conversation, taking on a teacherly role] #Okay, okay! Does any other people want to do this thing? Does anyone else want to try?#
11	Jack:	#(... ...) <but then he remembered>.# {Fieldnotes, videotape, 05/17/95}

Through improvisation Jack (and all the other students involved) lived through his (their) characters' experiences offered by Byars' text. Jack's idea that Bingo has a "forgetful side" was not mentioned in the part of the book that Paul read aloud, although it did surface later on in the story through some of Bingo's subsequent actions. Jack could have been drawing on his own personal experience in this interpretation, and we can only speculate on whether or not the improvisation helped him "read between the lines" to predict or infer another side of the Bingo character. But what seems evident in his, and all the other students', improvisations was their heightened ability to probe more deeply into their characters' motivations, and by doing so create multiple interpretations of the same text. We were also surprised about how salient the actual amount of the telephone bill appeared to be for the students. From a Rosenblatt perspective, by acting out their characters' experiences, situations, scenes, personalities, and emotions, Paul's students empathized with Byars' characters, and for a brief time actually became them. That is, they participated in the tensions, conflicts, and resolutions of the story.

ACTOR AS WRITER: CREATING NEW DIALOGUE AND PLOT EXTENSIONS THROUGH IMPROVISATION

Closely interrelated to Paul's students understandings of multiple aesthetic interpretations of a text, was their learning to create dialogue and plot extensions through improvisation. In this way they became writers of new text. According to Moffett (1983), drama is "the matrix of all language activities, subsuming speech and engendering the varieties of writing and reading" (p. 61). In particular, dialogue is a major means of developing thought and language. It especially highlights Bakhtin's (1981) sense of "dialogue" by emphasizing how much the social dimensions of language are enacted. When students are creating new dialogue in drama, they are involved in *joint thinking,* or social negotiation, and must cooperate with one another even if they disagree. While they are improvising a scene, they are incorporating the points of view, attitudes, ideas, and modifications of ideas of their coactors, even when they openly reject them.

Example 4 happens when students were about halfway through their second improvisation. Jack was playing the father, Willie was Bingo, and Eva was Bingo's mother. Besides the fact that all the dialogue was spontaneous and new in this particular segment, students also created a novel plot elaboration by demanding that Bingo pay for the phone bill from his allowance. This was not in the part of text that Paul read, but is subsequently in the book. So, in some ways students wrote the rest of the chapter.

Example 4

1   Jack: [stands up, pulls out a chair from the kitchen table and points to it, then in a commandingly bellowing voice addresses Willie/Bingo] Sit down!

2	Willie:	[quickly sits down and hesitantly whines] What? Oooaaww!
3	Jack:	[sits down, looks directly into Willie's eyes and menacingly points his index finger at him] You're going to have to pay for this phone bill.
4	Willie:	[digging in his pockets] Here! Here! Here! [hesitates, realizing he doesn't have any money and points back over his shoulder, probably to his imaginary bedroom] Why don't you take it from my allowance?
5	Eva:	[crosses around the back of the "kitchen table" and sits down directly across from Wayne, adjacent to Jack, and gets close to Jack's face, shouting] No allowance!
6	Jack:	[shaking his index finger in front of Willie's face] No allowance for 2 weeks!
7	Willie:	[banging both of his hands on the table in frustration whines] Nooo!
8	Eva:	[looking at Jack, waving her hand in a downward motion in disbelief] Two weeks? [then looks at Willie] No allowance until you pay back the fifty-four dollars and twenty-eight cents.
9	Willie:	[pointing back over his shoulder to his imaginary room] I have fifty-four dollars and twenty-eight cents. I have more than that in my bank! (... ...)····
10	Jack:	[in a loud voice] Where did you get the money?
11	Willie:	[in frustration, also in a loud voice] Allowance!
12	Jack:	[in disbelief] Allowance? I never gave you $54.
13	Willie:	But, but, (... ...)····
14	Jack:	You don't even know how to save yet!
		{Fieldnotes, videotape, 05/17/95}

It is clear in this improvisation that the amount of the bill was prominent. Students debated how this large bill was seen as Willie's/Bingo's responsibility, and then about how this could be accomplished. In line 3, Jack, as father, stated that Willie as the Bingo character would have to pay the bill. At first, this Bingo offered money from his pocket, but then suggested his allowance as a source of payment. We do not know that if this latter move on Willie's part was motivated by the fact that he realized that he did not have anything in his pocket to offer as money, or whether the whole turn in line 4 was created in role. Students awareness of how much $54.28 might represent for sixth graders, especially the economic status of these particular urban students, was then demonstrated when Eva first argued for no allowance in line 5 and modified it to "no allowance until you pay back the fifty-four dollars and twenty-eight cents" in line 8 when Jack as father indicated that Bingo would lose a mere 2 weeks' worth of allowance to cover the bill. Thus, Eva is showing her sense of money matters, as well as Jack is, who questions whether Willie's Bingo could have ever saved that amount (in line 12), or whether he knew to save at all. Thus, although the idea of using Bingo's allowance to pay for the bill is something that Byars includes later in the book, the students here are creating new almost sinister undercurrents about who this Bingo character might be like. These actors build on each other's contributions to extend the plot and character motivation, thereby reflecting not only their grasp of issues of credibility regarding money issues, but also their ability to foreground a sense of mystery that the actual text never provides. Consequently, these changes in the improvisations demonstrated how drama can make more explicit the reader–writer connections that underlie text construction (Tierney & Pearson, 1984; Tierney & Shanahan, 1991).

SOME FURTHER REFLECTIONS: DRAMA AS COLLABORATIVE MEANING MAKING

We learned at the end of the year, through interviews with Paul's students, that most of them had meager prior experience in the form of the creative drama he tried out in the beginning of his inquiry. That fact itself may have contributed to some of the difficulties he had in trying out the drama structures during this early period. For example, O'Neill and Lambert (1982) cautioned:

> Some students may have never experienced play of this kind and may be unwilling or unable to pretend. Drama is unlikely to develop successfully unless the students are prepared to make believe ... to share their make-believe with others while working together, and to maintain and extend their make-believe by appropriate action, role, and language. (p. 12)

Thus, if Paul had found out from his students about their backgrounds regarding drama, he might have modified what he had done accordingly, or might even have offered to them ahead of time some other dramatic exercises (such as the Spolin theater games that he subsequently used before the literature improvisations). In this way, his students would have been better initiated in the realm of make-believe for learning.

However, we all think most of the early problems Paul confronted were more due to confusion on the part of students taking on the mantle of the expert, rather than on their inability to make believe in this context. In other parts of the curriculum, students were encouraged to be experts on various inquiries, and getting the right answers to their questions in their research did matter. According to O'Neill and Lambert, drama is also inquiry, but its functions are realized differently. Hence, the potential of drama as a creative semiotic tool for students to explore and learn about issues, events, and relationships was extremely limited during the early part of the year.

Paul: There were so many reasons why my early drama attempts failed. First, problems arose simply because of my lack of experience in the contained classroom. I had to juggle so many new facets of teaching to implement the drama structures successfully. I felt that every day was a trial by fire. There was also the fact that I did not make it clear enough to my students how the drama experiences would be linked to our other social studies classwork on ancient civilizations. And, related to this, I just wasn't effective in explaining what I meant about their being experts. I could have had some minilessons to elucidate this notion, but I didn't do it. The two-way process that O'Neill and Lambert talk about just never happened.

In contrast, Paul felt that the improvisations of literature were very important to his students' learning. O'Neill and Lambert (1982) claimed that drama:

> ... works from the strength of the group. It draws on a common stock of experiences and in turn enriches the minds and feelings of individuals within the group...The most significant kind of learning [it promotes is their] understanding about human behavior, themselves, and the world they live in. (p. 13)

For example, in all four improvisations from the book about Bingo Brown (as well as from other drama experiences of this kind), students successfully worked together to create unique interpretations of the same text. They learned additional information about the characters in the story by taking on roles and interacting with one another. Students played off one another and used each others' individual characterizations to formulate viable, interesting, collective textual interpretations. In doing so, they also helped each other to see the same characters through a variety of different lenses, and in some instances may have even gained new insights on the human condition in general. Indeed, Barton & Booth (1990) argued that drama enables children to apply their own experiences to a text, allowing for their own "subjective worlds to come to play, helping them understand the meanings of the story as they live through the drama experience" (p. 136). Thus, drama requires that students create personal and negotiated responses; it unlocks the collaborative comprehension of a story.

Paul: My attempts to include drama, in this first year of teaching sixth grade, in many ways added to my confusion and frustration. Nevertheless, I am so glad I propped open a doorway of discovery that I can keep pushing open further in future teaching to come. Just like my success with Mr. Scrooge years ago, I had a success with Bingo Brown. I discovered how much drama could enhance the discussion of the literature in the classroom. I found out that I could also learn a lot about my students' lives and beliefs through drama. I have continued to build upon this experience by using drama to help kids gain a greater appreciation of literature and of themselves.

REFERENCES

Bakhtin, M. M. (1981). *The dialogic imagination.* Austin: University of Texas Press

Bakhtin. M. M. (1986). *Speech genres and other late essays.* In C. Emerson & M. Holquist (Eds.) & M. Holquist & C. Emerson (Trans.). Austin: University of Texas Press.

Barton, B., & Booth, D. (1990). *Stories in the classroom: Storytelling, reading aloud and roleplaying with children.* Portsmouth, NH: Heinemann.

Brockett, O. G. (1968). *A history of the theater.* Boston: Allyn & Bacon.

Byars, B. (1989). *Bingo Brown and the language of love.* New York: Puffin Books.

Cazden, C. B. (1992). *Whole language plus: Essays on literacy in the United States and New Zealand.* New York: Teachers College Press.

Conard, F. (1992). *The art in education and a meta-analysis.* Unpublished doctoral dissertation, Purdue University.

Halliday, M. A. K. (1978). *Language as social semiotic.* London, Edward Arnold.

Harste, J. C. (1993, December). *Multiple ways of knowing: Curriculum in a new key.* Paper presented at the National Reading Conference, Charleston, SC.

Heathcote, D. (1980). From the particular to the universal. In K. Robinson (Ed.), *Exploring the theatre and education* (pp. 7–50). London: Heinemann.

Heathcote, D., & Herbert, P. (1985). A drama of learning: Mantle of the expert. *Theory into Practice, 24,* 173–180.

McCaslin, N. (1980). *Creative drama in the classroom.* New York: Longman.

Moffett, J. (1983) *Teaching the universe of discourse.* Portsmouth, NH: Boyton/Cook.

Nystrand, M. (1986). *The structure of written communication: Studies in reciprocity between writers and readers.* Orlando, FL: Academic Press.

Nystrand, M. (1987). The role of context in written communication. In R. Horowitz & S. J. Samuels (Eds.), *Comprehending oral and written language* (pp. 197–214). San Diego, CA: Academic Press.

Nystrand, M. (1997). *Opening dialogue: Understanding of the dynamics of language and learning in the English classroom.* New York: Teachers College Press.

Nystrand, M., & Wiemelt, J. (1991). When is text explicit? Formalist and dialogic conceptions. *Text, 11,* 25–41.

O'Neill, C. (1988). The Wild things go to school—Drama in reading: A co-operative enterprise. *Drama Contact, 12,* 3–4.

O'Neill, C., & Lambert, A. (1982). *Drama structure: A practical handbook for teachers.* Portsmouth, NH: Heinemann.

Rosenblatt, L. M. (1978). *The reader, the text, the poem: The transactional theory of the literary work.* Carbondale: Southern Illinois University Press.

Rosenblatt, L. M. (1988). *Writing and reading: The transactional theory* (Technical report No. 13). University of Berkeley, CA: National Center for the Study of Writing.

Smagorinsky, P., & Coppock, J. (1995). The reader, the text, the context: An exploration of a choreographed response to literature. *JRB: A Journal of Literacy, 27,* 271–298.

Spolin, V. (1975). *Theatre game file.* St. Louis, MO: Cemvel.

Tierney, R. J., & Pearson, P. D. (1984). Toward a composing model of reading. In J. M. Jensen (Ed.), *Composing and comprehending* (pp. 33–45). Urbana, IL: ERIC Cleeainghouse on Reading and Communication Skills.

Tierney, R. J., & Shanahan, T. (1991). Research on the reading writing relationship: Interactions, transactions, and outcomes. In R. Barr, M. L. Kamil, P. Mosenthal, & P. D. Pearson (Eds.), *Handbook of reading research* (Vol. 3, pp. 246–280). White Plains, NY: Longman.

Wells, G. (1998). Some questions about direct instruction: Why? To whom? How? And when? *Language Arts, 76,* 27–39.

Wertsch, J. V. (1991). *Voices of the mind: A sociocultural approach to mediated action.* Cambridge, MA: Harvard University Press.

Wolf, S. A. (1994). Learning to act/acting to learn: Children as actors, critics, and characters in classroom theatre. *Research in the Teaching of English, 28,* 7–44.

Chapter 9

Finding the Right Balance: Using Drama to Promote Special Education Students' Engagement in Literacy Learning

Dian Ruben

Jane Liao

Bernadine Braun

Barton and Booth (1990) argue that *story drama,* the exploration of meanings of a story through improvised action, enables children to apply their own experiences to the story text. It allows for their own "subjective worlds to come into play, helping them understand/the meanings of the story as they live through the drama experience" (pp. 135–136). Drama requires that students create personal responses to a story; it unlocks "internal" comprehension of it.

The introduction chapter of this book provides the theoretical and methodological background for the larger collaborative school–university action-research project and this chapter about Bernadine's inquiry on drama. See also the last chapter, which further discusses the implications of Bernadine's inquiry—as well as those of the other teacher researchers.

Recently, Guthrie (1996; Guthrie, Schafer, Wang, & Afflerbach, 1995) argued that our teaching of reading solely in terms of a cognitive competency in schooling has not been successful. Instead, what is needed is the creation of classroom social contexts where literacy engagement is developed—that is, where all students are able to become self-determining community members involved in an ongoing effort for understanding. Literacy engagement is important, he says, "because it links traditional notions of cognitive competence to learners' personal and motivational needs, to the social milieu in which these may be fulfilled, and to the potential of literacy as an avenue for gaining knowledge" (p. 435–436). Drama in the classroom provides a context that engenders literacy engagement in this way. Drama is a cooperative enterprise that promotes collaboration among students (McCaslin, 1980; Moffett, 1983; O'Neill 1988). Moreover, through drama, students can actively identify with, and imagine, roles and situations, enabling them to explore issues, events, and relationships (O'Neill & Lambert, 1982). Moreover, research has indicated that dramatizations increase children's abilities to recall, connect, and integrate events in stories (Pelligrini, & Galda, 1982; Saltz & Johnson, 1974).

Traditional teaching methods for learning disabled and other special needs students have mostly consisted of meaningless drill and practice that focuses on their deficits or weaknesses (Rhodes & Dudley-Marling, 1988). Because this deficit model has emphasized students' inadequacies, such practices have had a devastating effect on the lives of many of these children (Hollingsworth & Reutzel, 1988; Poplin, 1988a, 1988b; Sears, Carpenter, & Burstein, 1994). Isolated, rote learning, controlled completely by the teacher, does not allow for connecting students' prior knowledge or learning and therefore encourages passivity in learners. In such a view of teaching and learning, there are no opportunities for these students to take on the "mantle of the expert," which Heathcote & Herbert (1985) argued, drama can offer.

Bernadine: My inquiry began by trying to use drama to foster my students learning–sequencing skills and vocabulary. My students' parents do not see the need for literature in the home, or reading to their children. Thus, because their access to literature is so limited at home, and because I believe that good literature helps students in building their vocabulary, I wanted to enlarge on this area of the language arts—their exposure to and their active participation in literature.

This chapter tells about Bernadine's inquiry to use drama to help her special needs students to become engaged in literacy. It meant that Bernadine and her students had to take on new roles—in drama—and in the everyday relationship of teacher and students.

Because her present inquiry in drama paralleled, in many ways, the process she had undergone during the previous year to promote interactive, collaborative reading-aloud sessions, and because she felt that the nature of these exchanges served as an important springboard for subsequent drama efforts, we begin with examining issues regarding student and teacher roles in these read-aloud activities. Then, we share Bernadine's struggles to implement story-drama activities with various books she read to her students. Throughout her inquiry, finding the right balance of control to support her students' literacy engagement was a major concern. We illustrate her difficulties and successes here, and in the last section, where we document students who write and act in their own plays. Many of her changes represented a challenge to traditional deficit assumptions that underlie teaching–learning for special education students.

DEVELOPING READING-ALOUD SESSIONS THAT FOSTER STUDENT-INITIATED RESPONSES

The year before this inquiry Bernadine, and some of her other colleagues in the teacher–researcher group had done inquiries to make their reading-aloud sessions more collaborative. Bernadine moved considerably from her role as an inquisitor, but was still working on this facet of her teaching because she believed that her students' efforts in offering their own responses to a book would be an important prerequisite to the drama activities she hoped to do with that book.

Bernadine: The previous year I received a one-word answer or a shrug of the shoulders to my questions during my reading-aloud sessions. I attributed many of these reactions to the fact that I was not asking enough open-ended questions or not waiting for an answer. I began to see that I needed to change if I wanted them to respond more and to initiate discussion. As I changed, they began to change by asking their own questions and stating their opinions about aspects of the books I was reading.

In the year of the inquiry, I was still working on making my read-alouds more collaborative. When I reread fairy tales in order to use them for dramatic play, the children were finally becoming uninhibited enough to make comments as we went along. They were even relating story events to things that happened in their lives.

Thus, during the year of her inquiry, Bernadine showed success in developing more interactive read-alouds where students' voices could be heard. For example, in January they did a dramatization of *Jack and the Beanstalk* (de Reniers, 1990), which was one of several versions of this tale that they had read aloud. In one of these latter sessions—in Example 1—it is apparent that students are comfortable in interjecting their ideas about the book. In the beginning, for instance, Julissa's comments about what the giant eats indicated her comfort. Then, she also responded, along with Arnie, to Jack's hair in an illustration. Arnie subsequently had questions about the beanstalk and the clouds, which reminded Melissa of a story she heard about a giant who fell from the sky.

Example 1

1	Berna.:	HERE'S A STORY ABOUT A BOY NAMED JACK, BOLD AS BRASS, SHARP AS A TACK. IT'S ALSO ABOUT A GIANT——NOT VERY BRIGHT, BUT MEAN AND *BIG*. IN JUST ONE BITE HE CAN SWALLOW A PIG BUT WHAT THIS WICKED GIANT LIKES MOST ARE BOYS——AND GIRLS——BROILED, ON TOAST....
2	Cs:	[in disgust] Eeeeeuuw!
3	Julissa:	I'd rather have cooked pig. Cooked pig is good!
4	Berna.:	[Bernadine is finishing up reading the part where the beanstalk has appeared and is showing the illustrations on that page. The left-hand page depicts the night before——Jack had a hard time sleeping and left his bed in shambles. The right-hand page has Jack——with his spiky hair standing out high from his head——putting his clothes on as he notes the beanstalk outside his window.] ... JACK JUMPS UP, PUTS ON HIS CLOTHES, THEN GOES TO THE WINDOW. WHAT DOES HE SEE? SOMETHING LEAFY AND GREEN ... IS IT A TREE? NO. IT'S——....
5	C:	It is a tree.
6	Berna.:	Is it a tree?
7	Cs:	No. It's a beanstalk.
8	Julissa:	#Look at this hair! Look at his hair!#
9	Berna.:	#It's a beanstalk.#
10	Arnie:	[loudly] Look at his bed!
11	Berna.:	Yeah, look at his bed.
12	Julissa:	Look at his hair!
13	Arnie:	[pulling his hair up] His hair looks like this.
14	Berna.:	Yes, his hair looks like that.
....		[Bernadine finishes reading the next page, which shows a two-page illustration of the beanstalk.] ... "THE MAGIC BEANS MY MOTHER THREW INTO THE YARD TOOK ROOT AND GREW AND GREW AND GREW UP TO THE SKY."
15	Arnie:	Ms. Braun, he has to climb all the way to the top?
16	Cs:	No.
17	Arnie:	He'll fall. Does he have to fly all the way to the top?
18	Berna.:	He could.
19	Arnie:	Is it a magic cloud?
20	Berna.:	Is it a magic cloud?
21	Cs:	No.
22	Arnie:	It could be....

23	Berna.:	It could be because the giant's house is on it....
24	Stan:	But that's a fake....
25	Berna.:	Could a giant's house sit on a cloud?
26	Cs:	#Yes.#
27	Cs:	#No.#
....		
28	Melissa:	Excuse me ... my friend went to Puerto Rico. She was in Mex——<Gloria>, she went. to Puerto Rico. This giant fell from the sky. I'm not joking.
29	C:	<You> never seen no giant.
30	Melissa:	Excuse me! Uh my——<Gloria> went to Puerto Rico ... and she saw a giant fall from the sky....
31	C:	(...).
32	Melissa:	Down to the ground.
....		[The conversation goes into another direction.]
		{Fieldnotes, videotape, 01/10/95}

Many student initiations occurred in this instance of the reading-aloud curriculum genre. Although most of the them just gave a response of disgust on hearing the giant eating boys and girls, Julissa offered her own view that cooked pig would be better. Later on in the story when Jack awakened to find a beanstalk growing, she also commented several times about Jack's hair. Bernadine did not follow up on these, but she did affirm Arnie's demonstration of how his hair looks like Jack's. Bernadine said that she did not take up on Julissa's response here because Julissa knelt on her chair and contributed in an inappropriate way, which was something she was working on from her Individualized Education Plan (IEP). However, Bernadine's lack of response to Julissa's responses did not discourage her altogether because she provided her ideas subsequently (not included here).

Subsequently, Arnie asked questions about Jack's climb or flight to the top of the cloud. His ideas about the cloud possibly being magic—or fake, as Stan suggested—were followed up by Melissa's story about a giant falling from the sky. In a cross discussion (Lemke, 1990) between herself and other classmates who questioned her tale, she maintained that it was "true."

Thus, most of the reading-aloud of the book seemed to be a collaborative one. Students generated many good interpretations of their own, ones that Bernadine hoped they could build on in the drama of the book a couple days later. However, as she began to orchestrate these drama experiences for this book as well as others, she faced the same kinds of difficulties regarding control as she battled in developing more student-

centered reading-alouds. That is, in the beginning she became very directive during these play episodes. She struggled to find the "right" balance
so that students would be given opportunities for engaging in the book, in
this mode of expression, by offering their ideas in dramatic action as actors, characters, and critics (Wolf, 1994).

BALANCING TEACHER CONTROL
IN DRAMATIZING STORIES

Frequently, less able readers have difficulties in participating in literacy
discussions—they don't speak or voluntarily engage in conversation about
books (Wollman-Bonilla, 1994). Bernadine already experienced this reluctance in her reading-aloud sessions. However, as she realized that the ways
in which she had typically run them were, to a great extent, responsible for
her students' lack of talk, she began to alter her control of the talk. As a result, students initiated more of their own ideas; they learned to speak up
while Bernadine provided spaces for their comments and showed them
that she valued their efforts.

When she began to implement drama activities, Bernadine's control
was in full force again. For example, in the acting of a Rumplestilskin story,
she directed every aspect of the activity, telling students their parts, where
to sit or stand, what to do, and what to say.

To Stan:	That's not how the story goes. You keep forgetting your lines. Do it again.
To Julissa:	You're going to brag to the king that your daughter can spin straw to gold.
To Arnie:	King, call your knight. Put her in the room. Take her to the new room with more straw. {Fieldnotes, videotape, 02/14/95}

Earlier, when Bernadine and students dramatized the *Jack and Beanstalk* book (a couple of days after the reading-aloud session discussed
around Example 1), Bernadine gave up some her regulating behavior.
However, this might have been more of an inadvertent release of control
on her part because she ended up taking the role of the giant, making her
too busy to manage everything. Example 2 hints at some of the possibilities that children might have pursued in their acting roles, but also illustrates how hard it was for Bernadine to let them go in improvising or
adding new dimensions to the characters or action. The example begins
with the giant (Bernadine) seated at a table on which "money" had been
placed. The wife (Julissa) places food on it for the giant to eat, with Jack
(Konrad) hiding in the oven (under a desk). Note that the dialogue of the
drama is marked with quotation marks.

Example 2

1	Julissa:	"Here you go." [placing food on table]
2	Konrad:	[knocks on the desk several times, but Bernadine does not respond so he goes out from under the desk and stands behind her]
3	Berna.:	[reacting] "Fee, Fie, Foe, Fum...."
4	Konrad:	[takes the cue and returns to hiding in the oven (under the desk)]
5	Berna.:	[counting the money prop on the table] "Now I lost count." [steps out of character, addressing the Konrad-Jack character] Now we're back at your house. Cecilia, [playing Jack's mom], are you ready?
6	Konrad:	[leaves the giant's house and goes to Jack's house bringing a prop representing gold that students had constructed ahead of time] "I've brought gold."
7	Cecilia:	"Get some more."
8	Berna.:	Is that how the story goes? [telling what Cecilia/Jack's mom should say] Go to the village and get some food.
9	Konrad:	[he leaves and goes to another part of the room to get food]
10	Berna.:	[directing both Cecilia and Konrad] Now go to bed.
11	Cecilia and Konrad:	[pretend to be asleep]
12	Konrad:	[to Bernadine] And then I wake up, right?
13	C:	Is she sleeping too? [referring to Jack's mother]
14	Berna.:	Yeah, she's sleeping too. [to Konrad/Jack] #Then you go back up....#
15	Konrad:	#[begins knocking on the giant's door]#.
16	Julissa:	#[lets Konrad/Jack in]
17	Berna.:	[stomping around] "I smell that boy again."
18	Konrad:	[on hearing the stomping, goes into hiding]
19	Julissa:	"You're thinking wrong."
20	Berna.:	[sits down and pretends to eat]
21	Konrad:	[knocking on the desk and when there's no response, comes out and talks to Bernadine out of role] You heard a knock.
22	Berna.:	"Who's knocking? What's that knocking?"
23	Julissa:	"I don't know? It's nothing."
24	Konrad:	[talking to Julissa, out of role] You went out and opened the door and no one was there.
25	Berna.:	Is that how the story goes? So there wasn't any knocking, was there?

{Videotape, 01/12/95}

There were some cases in this example where Bernadine interacted with Julissa as having an equal status as a character, giving her little supervision. This might have been why Konrad felt he had the freedom to go into another direction in line 6 when he stated that he brought gold, which Cecilia then followed up on in line 7. However, Bernadine pulled them back to the storyline, and told Cecilia (Jack's mom) what she should say to Jack, and then directed them both to go to sleep. That is, a very different version *could* have been created here and would have been interesting to follow: Jack might have responded that there was no more gold and that he had taken it all; or he might have gone directly back to the giant's house to claim the hen, etc. In other words, the children might have constructed some other adaptation of the storyline that showed their own interpretations to it. Yet, Bernadine insisted that they follow the literal rendition here, and this also happened later (line 24) when Konrad wanted Julissa (giant's wife) to open the door because of the knocking, which he earlier instigated (line 21) and even got Bernadine to go along if even for a short while (line 22).

Thus, although Bernadine frequently allowed for elaborations or extrapolations in student interpretations to the story during the reading-aloud discussions, she was insistent that students follow the literal meaning of the story during the dramatization of the book. She seemed to interpret students' deviations from the story line as their inability to follow the sequence of the story events, and not as occasions for improvisation on their part. Thus, when children strayed away, she controlled its unfolding, thereby making it almost impossible for the children to engage in the book creatively.

Despite Bernadine's frequent controlling behaviors, there were instances of give and take in this particular drama experience so that afterwards both Bernadine and students alike felt that it was fun. And, there were some indications that she was beginning to think differently about her students' abilities to dramatize a story. She seemed to appreciate Konrad's attempts to improvise, "You were having as much fun as I was." She was impressed with the way that Cecilia had prepared and enacted her role: "You did real well writing out your part, Cecilia. … You did a good job writing down that script. … I didn't think you could write it all down and get it all read off. … But you did."

Seeking Advice from Colleagues at Weekly Meetings

In February, some edited parts of the *Jack and the Beanstalk* drama in the classroom were shared at two of our weekly meetings. Although Bernadine wanted students to learn sequencing from dramatizations, she was also concerned about the fact that some of the students—especially Cecilia and her sister, Ana, who as eighth graders would be graduating at the end of the year—were unwilling or unable to be actively involved in drama or in many of the other activities in class. In fact, Cecilia's participation in the play acting was a first-time experience for her, and Bernadine was extremely excited about her participation.

In the first weekly meeting Bernadine remarked that her students spontaneously performed or acted out all the time, but did not seem to want to participate in the drama of the books that much. Michael, one of her colleagues with a degree in drama, suggested some strategies for her.

Example 3A

1 Michael: Do it very subtly. [chuckling] You try at all costs——even when you're working with adults——you don't as the director or facilitator (... ...). It starts off with just reading the poem, reading the poem, reading the poem ... until people spontaneously, just the kids, react to it. Because that's where ... (...) ... because what they're doing is not the play, they're playing at (...). And then it just comes out of that. And as the facilitator one of the things you can do is (... ...). Do you know what I mean?

2 Chris: So in other words, take the initiations, even during the discussions and not make it maybe a separate thing from the post (...) to the drama. But see how you can facilitate from the discussion itself #and as they initiate something, you let them go with that particular part.#

3 Michael: #Right. It's a very natural thing.# For example (... ...) ... ... so then maybe they'll want to make it into a game, you know. If you are the facilitator and you want to make it into a game, you want to make it <click>. You say, "How many different kinds of vocal responses can you think of for each (...)?" so that the kids can <pour> forth all kinds of physical actions that maybe go with it. Or maybe you as facilitator can read the poem and periodically the kids would ... stop and make the sound effects ... just like you did with the (...). Then they're not timid because they've already done it. They did it naturally. They did it without being asked. Then that's putting a little bit more structure on them ... but without taking the play out of it.

{Videotape, weekly meeting, 02/07/95}

Thus, here Michael suggested transitional strategies to serve as bridges to separate story dramatizations. That is, as children are engaged in discussion while she read a book (or poem), Bernadine, as facilitator, could wait for more spontaneous actions from the children first, on which she could then follow up. Subsequently, Michael suggested (not included here) that he thought if she tried this, students might become more confident. Bernadine seemed to consider these ideas of trying to fuse the drama into the reading-aloud, which also meant that she would have to relinquish more control on those occasions when students evoked drama responses.

Then in the next meeting, discussion of Bernadine's research continued. This time, Chris Pappas, a university researcher, tried to clarify from Bernadine whether students' learning a literal sequencing of events in stories and becoming more confident in participation were, in fact, two facets of her drama inquiry, and whether they might be working against each other. Dian commented that students might develop more confidence if they did not have to rely so much on Bernadine during drama episodes. Some suggestions are made and considered, and then Paul, who was also doing an inquiry on drama in his classroom, offered more.

Example 3B

1 Chris: Do you want in this acting, in this drama, for it to be a literal presentation of that particular book or is it more an occasion for you to help some of these kids that you said are having difficulty in presenting ... and finding some ways for them to be more free and to see what happens if they did that?

....

2 Berna.:   What I want from this play acting is that they recall in sequential order what is going on. Now, I don't care what they say. If they say whatever they want to say (... ...). But what I'm trying to do is to get them to recall in sequential order what's going on ... what went on in the book ... because they have a very hard time when we're doing anything that has recall in a sequential order. And this part of my inquiry is to see if they can recall these. You know, like when Jack was under the desk and he came out and he said to me something about (... ...) ... and it was completely out of the story. That never happened. And if it did happen, it could've come at the end but not where he put it in the story. It's just ... a recall in sequence of the action, not necessarily the words, but the action part of the story.

....

3 Dian: I think the question becomes whether these kids have the confidence to believe they can do this. And I think there is a lot of reliance on you because if they——they'll get quiet and they'll say nothing for a while, and you will help them along. You'll tell them what's happening and I think that they need——if they were able to recall and do it in a sequence, it would boost their confidence that they can do this. So they could do it without your urging or without your giving them the words. So uh....

....   [Various suggestions are offered and then Chris offers an idea.]

4 Chris: I wonder if you did things like had them make pictures first ... of what the sequence of the story is. Take a piece of paper and

       fold it so that there are like six little sections and you tell them what the picture is in the very beginning and at the end and then they fill in the others. And then maybe use that as the means by which——that they could ... re-enact it. I don't know.

5 Berna..: Well it's worth a try. I tried listing the sequence on the board of the action. That helped a little. It wasn't as good as it could have been, but it did help a little.

....

6 Chris: So ... anybody else have some suggestions?

7 Berna.: I'm hoping for any ideas because I've tried so many things....

8 Paul: I was just gonna say ... as long as they have maybe different experiences. Where sometimes you can be real specific about it, "This is gonna be——we're trying to get this in order." And there are experiences when it's not quite so rigid.

9 Berna.: Oh, there are many ways that are not as rigid as this is. Again, how do I say it? If they don't have a specific guide to follow they get to a point where they're frustrated and feel that this just isn't what you want and so they don't do anything. Then they don't get the experience of what we're doing ... at all and this is frustrating for me.

10 Paul: Is it possible that it's frustrating for them because it's frustrating for you? If you like went with it and said, "Okay, we're just gonna kind of go with it." You know, and whatever and wherever they take it, they take it. Maybe they wouldn't feel so pressured as long as you could kind of facilitate it ... for some kind of smoothness, you know.

11 Berna.: It's a possibility. I had noticed that since we've been doing the storybooks and acting out that in the play time, their free time, they're more free. They come up with the puppets and they do things.

       {Videotape, weekly meeting, 02/28/95}

It was clear from Bernadine's response (line 2) to Chris's question about the focus of her inquiry that Bernadine felt that fostering students' sequencing abilities through drama was an integral feature of her inquiry that she did not want to give up. She specifically noted in line 2 how the Konrad-Jack character's diversions from the story line seen in Example 2 were inappropriate and gave evidence of students' lack of recall of the sequential order. Dian, then, offered that she thought that if students could enact the drama without Bernadine's constant urging and telling, they would begin to rely more on themselves and become more confident. Chris suggested that perhaps they could make their own *storyboard* (what is sometimes called a version of a "sketch-to-stretch" activity, Harste & Short, 1988; Pappas, Kiefer, & Levstik, 1999) that would somehow help students generate the sequence of the story as preparation of the drama.

Then Paul (lines 8 & 10) suggested that Bernadine provide two kinds of experiences and be explicit with students about the distinction between them—ones where order is required, and ones where actions need not be so rigid, and Bernadine and the students could be more free and "kind of go with it."

Subsequently, Bernadine attempted to incorporate these two ideas. She implemented the storyboard activity that students created to assure their understanding of the sequence of story events and also as a vehicle or tool to prepare them in dramatizing the stories. She began to allow students to have opportunities to be more free to improvise. In doing so, Bernadine's role in supporting students' drama experiences became less controlling and more collaborative.

Trying Out Storyboards

These changes could be seen in their acting out of *Horton Hatches the Egg* (Seuss, 1940), which occurred a few days after the second teacher meeting. The book is about an elephant, Horton, who is persuaded to sit on an egg for Mayzie Bird while she is off to a life on the beach. Bernadine got the students to generate their own storyboards for the book. During the construction of these storyboards, Bernadine was fairly directive in telling the students what should go in each of the eight sections, although she did take suggestions from them. Students made their own pictures of the events they identified for the story and Bernadine allowed them a lot of leeway in how these were to be depicted on their papers.

As will be seen in Example 4, the storyboards enabled Bernadine to consciously give up control by encouraging the students to refer to them when they became hesitant and looked to her for answers or directions. Example 4 shows students' dramatization at the beginning of the story when Mayzie Bird, played by Stan, asked Horton, who was Polly, to sit on her egg.

Example 4

1 Berna.:   [to Darla] Do you have your storyboard so you know where we're going? Okay, it's all up to you. Go ahead Mayzie.

2 Polly: [walks over to where Mayzie Bird (Stan) is sitting on the egg]

3 Stan: "Will you sit on my egg?"

4 Polly: "No, I have some work to do." [stands in front of Stan for several seconds awaiting his reply]

5 Stan: [looks at Bernadine and seems to want her to help]

6	Berna.:	[does nothing]
7	Polly:	[Is becoming impatient as she pats her foot and drums on her thigh with her fingers. Finally she turns partially around and addresses Bernadine.] Ms. Braun ... [in an exaggerated manner suggesting increasing impatience]
8	Stan:	I don't know what to say next.
9	Cf1:	You talk to her. You convince her.
10	Cf2:	Say please....
11	John:	You beg her!
12	Stan:	"Please, can you sit on my egg?"
13	Polly:	"No, I have some work to do."
14	Stan:	[looks at Bernadine with a nervous smile]
15	Berna.:	[no response.]
16	Polly:	[whispers to Stan] (... ...).
17	Stan:	"I'm tired of sitting on this egg. I'll come back in a little while."
18	Polly:	[whispering] "Go, bye."
19	Stan:	[leaves and goes to another part of the room]
20	C:	[off camera] You're at the beach.
21	Berna.:	Excuse me. He knows where he's going.
22	Darla:	[enters the scene and hesitates]
23	Berna.:	What happens next? If you forget, look at your storyboard.
24	Darla:	[walks over and looks at storyboards they had made that are laying on a desk nearby. She and Konrad, John, and Stan are hunters in the story. As the boys enter with guns drawn, she joins them.]
		{Fieldnotes, videotape, 03/02/95}

Students soon realized that they have freedom from Bernadine's usual directive nature and end up having much fun in this enactment of the book. They helped each other—for example, when several of them (lines 9–11) help Stan out when he said that he did not know what to say next, and later when he was at a loss and Polly whispered to him to prompt him (16 & 18). In addition, Bernadine treated them quite differently from their earlier experiences, too, by telling Darla that "it's all up to you" (line 1) and by remarking to the student in line 21 that Stan "knows where he's going." Thus, here she shored up students' confidence by letting them know that she believed that they have the competence to dramatize the book on their own. As a result, they slowly began to act and to make decisions on their own.

Bernadine was quite active in helping the students choose props and create the storyboards ahead of time. Then, she made concerted efforts in asking for students' input, but when the dramatization started, her stance became that of a facilitator by repeatedly guiding students back to their storyboards when they seemed unsure. Her changes regarding control enabled them to take on the mantles of expert (Heathcote & Herbert, 1985); they had opportunities to engage with the text by understanding the meanings of the story as they lived through the drama experience. Bernadine found a way to balance the explicitness and freedom for these special education students (Zucker, 1993) so that they were able to learn the sequencing of story events and ways to develop and improvise their own interpretations of the book.

Bernadine: Using the storyboards put the responsibility on the children. I did not have to be in charge so much. I could have students refer to them. As will be seen, I did not think about this aid for when they did their plays. I don't know why. I guess I was so used to directing everything to ensure a reasonable outcome that it was very hard for me to let the children produce plays that were in my eyes unacceptable. It was not always clear where I should step in and help or when I should let them follow their own ways.

WRITING AND DRAMATIZING THEIR OWN PLAYS: EXPLORING THE TEACHER'S ROLE IN SCAFFOLDING THE PROCESS

Towards the end of the year, students in three groups created their own plays and dramatized them, and the challenge of balancing control for Bernadine emerged again. Group 1, a group of five boys, based their play on the movie, "The Lion King." They focused on incidents happening at Pride Rock (the point where the lion could view his entire kingdom), which were mostly fighting. There was little dialogue, but Arnie (who played the father lion, Mufasa) and Konrad (who played the young lion, Simba) frequently discussed and decided on their respective lines throughout their performances of the play. The three other boys (Paul, Stan, and John) were the hyenas and played minor roles in this production. The boys had not written a script, but basically reconstructed the story from memory as they went along. As a result, they provided a very confused version, often mixing up different parts of the movie.

Bernadine: I asked them to write any play that they wanted. They could come up with something from their imagination, whatever. They were enthusiastic about it, but not in the way that I would have liked for it to be. It went along, but they just didn't want to write anything down. I kept asking. I wanted a script from each one [group] so that I would have something to support what they're doing. They had been thinking about it, rehearsing and trying different things, but when you saw it the 8th or 10th time, you would see that they had changed everything. I mean, this was nothing like what they told me they were going to put on. And, they got to a point where they were out of control.

Bernadine insisted continually that they produce a script, but they resisted. Without input and scaffolding from Bernadine, this group was unable to complete any adequate performance; its production consisted of everyone just rolling around the floor "fighting." They did make efforts to script their performance, but their skills were not at a level at which they could accomplish much without help. Bernadine gave her students the invitation to create their own plays, and they excitedly took it up, but she had moved completely to an almost hands-off stance for most of the process.

She approached the two other groups in a similar fashion. Group 2 worked on the play "The Dead Cheerleaders," which seemed to be based on a horror movie. An entire football team (John, Arnie, Konrad, and Stan) was killed and somehow the cheerleaders (Melissa, Polly, and Darla), who were the major protagonists in this production, had some kind of power to bring them back to life. The play took place in a graveyard and the girls made headstones as props and painted their faces to look gory. This group was not successful in writing a script either. These members ad-libbed their lines during each performance without any direction or input from Bernadine as to how they might develop ways to improve these renditions.

Group 3's play was based on the story "The Little Mermaid," and was performed mostly by the two eighth-grade sisters, Cecilia and Ana, who played all of the parts. There was an evil queen who had a crystal ball and held the mermaid hostage, who was subsequently saved by the mermaid's father, and they ran away with a goldfish and live happily ever after. This is the only group who created a script, one that they dictated to Dian, from which they practiced and read during their performances.

This was the first time these two girls had performed before an audience (except for Cecilia playing a role in the drama of *Jack and the Bean-stalk*—see Example 2), and they did a fair job, even though they partially covered their faces with their script pages as they read their lines. Following feedback, they improved with each performance.

Thus, with the exception of Dian's support in Group 3's efforts, the students rarely received any scaffolding in their play endeavors. However, although Bernadine did not involve herself much in these matters, she did have a debriefing after one of the initial performances, in which she had students evaluate their acting. On this occasion, she provided some support and direction for them. The "Lion King" play was discussed first and illustrated the kind of self-critique that was done.

Example 5A

1	Berna.:	What did you think about the play?
2	Polly:	It was not that good.
3	Berna.:	Oh, you have to tell me why. You can't just say, "It wasn't good." You have to tell us why.
4	C:	Because it was too much fighting.
5	Berna.:	It was too much fighting. All right. {Videotape, 04/25/95}

So, Bernadine's invited discussion, and although she accepted and reaffirmed their assessments of performances, she insisted that they provide a rationale for their criticism. Later (not provided here), she asked questions—"Would that make it better?" and "What do you think?"—that encouraged students to think about suggestions.

This stress on rethinking was frequent when the actors themselves were evaluating their own performances. For example, when Konrad offered "saying it louder" as a self-critique, Bernadine responded with "Yeah, that would help a lot," letting them know that their own evaluations were legitimate and worthwhile. However, when John said, "it stinks," and Stan exclaimed that "it sucks!," Bernadine rejected the criticism as not being specific and not helpful to the participants.

Example 5B

1	Berna.:	No! Don't tell me it stunk and it sucked! I want to know what can you do to make it better!
2	Arnie:	You know ... you could——don't be scared ... prepare more....
3	Paul:	Don't try to play the two parts ... uhm ... together.
4	Berna.:	Okay, let's not——who's got paper? Get a paper, write this down so you don't forget. Somebody in your play. Write it down!
5	Cs:	[John, Arnie, and Konrad all get paper to write on]
6	Berna.:	[quietly repeats Paul's suggestion]
7	Arnie:	[repeating softly each of the words as he writes them down] (... ...) to ... gether ... together!
8	Berna.:	Right! All right, what else was a suggestion?
9	C:	(... ...).
10	Berna.:	Someone suggested that you speak louder. All right, put that down.

11   Konrad: [writes "spec" ("speak"). ...]
                  {Videotape, 04/25/95}

Most of the self-evaluation was genuine and relevant, but centered on the process dimensions of acting—except for Paul's idea that the content of two parts of the "Lion King" story should not be mixed up. Bernadine's insistence of their writing down these ideas showed that she felt that they were important enough to consider for future reference and use.

Later on in the critique discussion, as the class moved to evaluate the other two plays, Paul suggested that they write a script of "Lion King" and "read the thing" and have further talk with Arnie concerning what they should do about their play. Unfortunately, there was little follow-up on these assessments or suggestions, which were created in the discussion session. Moreover, there were few comments in the debriefings concerning the meanings of students' plays. These would have provided opportunities to engage in text negotiation of interpretation, which is the major advantage of doing the dramatizations or improvisations in the first place (Wolf, 1994). Yet, although there was only minimal scaffolding, it was scaffolding nonetheless, so that Bernadine was beginning to find her way to provide the right balance to support her students engagements of text through drama.

THE IMPORTANCE OF PROVIDING SUPPORTIVE FEEDBACK FOR SPECIAL NEEDS STUDENTS

Sawyer (1991) argued that special needs students need opportunities to communicate or engage through print so they can be provided supportive feedback. How to do this—to balance the teacher control—was an underlying theme in Bernadine's inquiry. She became successful in accomplishing this in the reading-aloud curriculum genre and then in dramatizing stories, where she began with too much control to find a balance. She started at a different place when students were given opportunities to create and dramatize their own plays—an almost complete "go with it" approach—that was devoid of her scaffolding, present in the other literacy and drama routines.

In reflection and analysis of the data in Bernadine's inquiry, we all have been surprised why we did not consider ways to supply this assistance in these latter drama ventures at the time. Why didn't we think of storyboards, for example, which were so successfully used in students' earlier drama experiences of stories? Although all three play groups relied on prior knowledge of a plot from a movie, we seemed to have been caught up with students' excitement and newly developed confidence that they *could* fashion new renditions.

> *Bernadine: I know that I went to the extreme on the group plays and that I'll have to find ways to get back to the middle somehow. Again I don't know why I didn't think about the use of storyboards for the plays. But nobody thought of them—university researchers didn't, I didn't, even the children didn't. Where were we? I guess it shows how harried we were when we were in the midst of it!*
>
> *But this was also a success story, especially for the two girls, Ana and Cecilia, who would not participate in the beginning of the year. They would sit and watch and never initiate. They would never answer questions in class; they would never ask questions themselves. And yet they wrote the script. It was all their words, and they got up and they said it all the way through. I was so happy. This was a breakthrough, a huge step for them just to get up in front of us. Ana was up there—it was the first thing she had ever participated in, ever!*
>
> *I had wanted students to learn sequencing skills in my inquiry, and the drama helped with that, and [with] the emotional side, too. The kids went looking for books, they acted out in their free time. It did other things—it related more to their life skills, their being more responsible for self.*

In her inquiry, Bernadine challenged some of her own underlying philosophies and expectations about her students as learners. Bernadine had many years of teaching special needs children and was steeped in the traditional views that see instruction for students with learning disabilities as one of remediating their underlying ability deficits (Poplin, 1988a, 1988b; Zucker, 1993). For this reason, her journey was fraught with difficulty. Yet, at the same time, her expertise from these long years of experience also enabled her to be successful in finding the right balance to help students to become literate. Drama enabled Bernadine to construct social contexts where literacy engagement occurred. Students' cognitive competence of learning sequencing skills and vocabulary were linked to their own personal, motivational needs. Thus, these drama activities became contexts where the potential of literacy as an avenue for gaining knowledge was possible.

REFERENCES

Barton, B., & Booth, D. (1990). *Stories in the classroom: Storytelling, reading aloud and roleplaying with children.* Portsmouth, NH: Heinemann.

de Reniers, B. S. (1990). *Jack and the beanstalk: Retold in verse for boys and girls to read themselves.* New York: Macmillan.

Guthrie, J. T. (1996). Educational contexts for engagement in literacy. *The Reading Teacher, 49,* 432–445.

Guthrie, J. T., Schafer, W., Wang, Y. Y., Afflerbach, P. (1995). Relationships of instruction to amount of reading: An exploration of social, cognitive, and instructional connections. *Reading Research Quarterly, 30,* 8–25.

Harste, J. C., & Short, K. G. (1988). *Creating classrooms for authors: The reading-writing connection.* Portsmouth, NH: Heinemann.

Heathcote, D., & Herbert, P. (1985). A drama of learning: Mantle of the expert. *Theory into Practice, 24,* 173–180.

Hollingsworth, P., & Reutzel, D. (1988). Whole language with LD children. *Academic Therapy, 23,* 477–481.

Lemke, J. L. (1990). *Talking science: Language, learning, and values.* Norwood, NJ: Ablex.

McCaslin, N. (1980). *Creative drama in the classroom.* New York: Longman.

Moffett, J. (1983) *Teaching the universe of discourse.* Portsmouth, NH: Boyton/Cook.

O'Neill, C. (1988). The Wild Things go to school—Drama in reading: A co-operative enterprise. *Drama Contact, 12,* 3–4.

O'Neill, C., & Lambert, A. (1982). *Drama structures: A practical handbook for teachers.* Portsmouth, NH: Heinemann.

Pappas, C. C., Kiefer, B. Z., & Levstik, L. S. (1999). *An integrated language perspective in the elementary school: An action approach.* New York: Longman.

Pelligrini, A. D., & Galda, L. (1982). The effects of the dramatic-fantasy play training on the develop children's story comprehension. *American Educational Research Journal, 19,* 443–452.

Poplin, M. (1988a). The reductionist fallacy in learning disabilities: Replicating the past by reducing the present. *Journal of Learning Disabilities, 21,* 385–448.

Poplin, M. (1988b). Holistic/constructionist principles of the teaching/learning process: Implications for the field of learning disabilities. *Journal of Learning Disabilities, 21,* 401–416.

Rhodes, L. K., & Dudley-Marling, C. (1988). *Readers and writers with a difference: A holistic approach to teaching leaning disabled and remedial students.* Portsmouth, NH: Heinemann.

Saltz, E., & Johnson, J. (1974). Training for thematic-fantasy play in culturally disadvantaged children: Preliminary results. *Journal of Educational Psychology, 66,* 623–630.

Sawyer, D. J. (1991). Whole language in context: Insights into the current debate. *Topics in Language Disorders, 11,* 1–13.

Sears, S., Carpenter, C., & Burstein, N. (1994). Meaningful reading instruction for learners with special needs. *The Reading Teacher, 47,* 632–638.

Seuss, Dr. (1940). *Horton hatches the egg.* New York: Random House.

Wollman-Bonilla, J. E. (1994). Why don't they "just speak?" Attempting literature discussion with more and less able readers. *Research in the Teaching of English, 28,* 231–258.

Wolf, S. A. (1994). Learning to act/acting to learn: Children as actors, critics, and characters in classroom theatre. *Research in the Teaching of English, 28,* 7–44.

Zucker, C. (1993). Using whole language with students who have language and learning disabilities. *The Reading Teacher, 46,* 660–670.

Part IV

Other Language
and Literacy Curriculum Genres

This last section covers the "miscellaneous" language and literacy inquiries of four teacher researchers. Two inquiries incorporate the read-aloud curriculum genre (covered in Section II), with additional curricular routines not seen before. The other two inquiries also introduced new curriculum genres.

In chapter 10, university researchers Liliana Barro Zecker, Caitlyn Nichols, and Linda Montes, collaborated with Sonia Soltero to give an account of Sonia's exploration of the "language richness" of her Spanish-speaking kindergartners. To understand the sources of these students' language competence and to further help them become reflective thinkers, Sonia invited them to be informants of the curriculum that she and they coconstructed. Several curriculum genres—reading-aloud and social studies or geography lessons—were involved in her inquiry as she and her students created "conversations" to make explicit, and further build on, the funds of knowledge that underlie these young children's linguistic and cognitive capabilities. Most of these conversations were collaborative ones, but tensions or dilemmas also occurred in the process. Sonia's reflection on her questioning and other interactional strategies to foster her students' critical thinking can be found throughout the chapter.

Chapter 11 is about the pretend-reading curriculum genre that Dee (Demetrya) created for her kindergarteners. Noting that her boys were especially unmotivated or uninterested in literacy activities or the books in the library classroom, Dee set up a period each day for all of the children to reenact books that were read to them. Dian Ruben and Jane Liao worked with Dee to relate the struggles and successes in this enterprise. They il-

223

lustrate the very collaborative nature of these emergent readers' pretend reading. They also document the issues that were involved in Dee's scaffolding and assessing the reading efforts of students who had diverse, and ever-changing, abilities.

Similar to Sonia's inquiry, Renuka Mehra's inquiry encompasses several curriculum genres. In chapter 12, Jane Liao and Dian Ruben collaborate with Renuka to discuss how Renuka attempted to create ways to provide individualized instruction within various group-reading experiences. After her first steps are regarded by her as not helpful, Renuka used reading-alouds, reader-response journal writing, and small-group extension activities as ways for her second graders to respond to a novel study. All three routines are examined and illustrated in the chapter to show Renuka's successes and vulnerabilities as she tried to support individual students' literacy understandings in group settings.

In chapter 13, Shannon Hart and Diane Escobar worked with Sue Jacobson to report on Sue's inquiry to develop literature-discussion groups for her fourth graders. Students, who at the beginning of the year were not used to sharing their own responses to literature, ended up being able to come up with their own questions for examination and discussion with their peers. Although Sue ultimately was successful in creating literature-discussion groups in which students had *real* conversations about literature, the road in developing them was sometimes rocky. This journey is depicted by four major stages, ones in which various process and content issues in the literature groups are addressed.

All four chapters describe and discuss various literacy routines. Sonia's and Renuka's inquiries are complex because several curriculum genres are involved—the reading-aloud curriculum examined in Section II—as well as new ones. Dee's inquiry on the pretend-reading curriculum genre and Sue's study on her literature-discussion groups provide other routines to support and scaffold student-literacy learning. As with the other chapters in this book, the chapters in this section again explore the issues that emerged as teachers developed collaborative styles of teaching.

Chapter 10

Exploring "Language Richness" in a Bilingual Kindergarten Classroom: The Possible Forms and Power of Collaborative Talk

Liliana Barro Zecker

Caitlyn Nichols

Linda Montes

Sonia White Soltero

For many years, the low literacy levels attained by language-minority students have been explained in the context of a deficit theory or cultural deprivation (Bartolome, 1994; Delgado-Gaitán, 1987). Often, these students' failures to achieve higher levels of educational achievement were attributed to a mismatch between their home and community and

---

The introduction chapter of this book provides the theoretical and methodological background for the larger collaborative school–university action-research project and this chapter about Sonia's inquiry on her students' language richness. See also the last chapter, which further discusses the implications of Sonia's inquiry—as well as those of the other teacher researchers.

the discourse and socio-cultural patterns of interaction in the classroom (McCollum, 1991; Moll & Greenberg, 1990). More recently, some investigators argued that ethnolinguistic minorities fail to attain higher literacy levels because they often do not receive enough explicit instruction to allow them to master the "register of the mainstream" (Delpit, 1995; Reyes, 1992). Other investigations, specifically concerned with the low literacy levels attained by many Latina or Latino students, pointed out that, while the cultural and socioeconomic backgrounds of this group are different from those of the majority population, these students have available rich funds of knowledge and possess vast linguistic, cultural, and intellectual resources to fully support their literacy learning (Moll, 1992).

Learning, as defined in sociocultural terms, is a negotiation or coconstruction of shared meanings and knowledge in the context of social interaction (Edwards & Mercer, 1989). Language, the main tool of semiotic mediation, plays a crucial role in the expression and building of these understandings among the members of a community (Vygotsky, 1978; Wells, 1994; Wertsch, 1991). This perspective calls for a departure from traditional transmission-based instructional models to more social–transactional ones in which learners become "informants" of the curriculum (Wells & Chang-Wells, 1992). Within that framework, teachers are to be facilitators of learning, context makers who scaffold students' progress into more advanced and complex forms of knowledge based on the specific cultural, linguistic, and cognitive resources of their students (Hiebert & Fisher, 1991; Tharp & Gallimore, 1988). Building on these principles, Willinsky (1990) uses the term *New Literacy* to describe a more collaborative and participatory instructional approach to literacy instruction, one that would empower students by forging close links between their understandings and the literacy curriculum.

In recent years, the definition of literacy has been extended to make its nature as a higher mental function or a *way of knowing* more explicit. Wells and Chang-Wells (1992) defined literacy or literate behavior as a way of engaging cognitively and affectively with the world. "To be fully literate is to have the disposition to engage appropriately with texts of different types in order to empower action, thinking, and feeling in the context of purposeful human activity" (p. 147).

But what constitutes appropriate engagement with text, and what is text? Wells and Chang-Wells (1992) claimed that literacy requires individuals to have the ability and disposition to engage with texts *epistemically,* that is, to participate in engagements in which "text is treated, not as a representation of meaning that is already decided, given, and self-evident, but as a tentative and provisional attempt on the part of the writer to capture his or her current understanding in an external form so that it may provoke further attempts at understanding as the writer or some other reader dialogues with the text in order to interpret its meaning" (p. 140). They also extended the definition of *text* "to any artifact that is constructed as a representation of meaning using a conventional symbol system" (p. 145). Moreover, they emphasized the importance of recognizing classroom discourse as text. They argued that the practice of engaging epistemically with oral text—that is, engaging in talk that fosters expression, reflection on, and reformulation of meanings—realizes the notion of literacy learning as cultural apprenticeship in that it introduces children to literate thinking by making this mainly silent and covert mental ability explicit to them. Such a view, then, has important implications for the role that classroom talk—what is said, who says it, and how it is said—plays in the early literacy learning.

Thus, language as a meaning-mediating tool has an important role, especially when teachers move away from teacher-dominated structures typical of transmission-oriented approaches to more collaborative classroom interactions—and talk—that provide open spaces for students' voices (Cazden 1988; Wells, 1993, 1994; Young, 1992).

Sonia White Soltero, an Argentinean-U.S.-trained teacher who is fully bilingual, informally observed the language richness of her 21 Spanish-speaking kindergarten students (most came from low-income Mexican families who had recently immigrated to the United States, although there were also a few children from Puerto Rican families). This chapter describes the ways in which knowledge was coconstructed and explored in this bilingual classroom as Sonia sought out and built on her students' linguistic and conceptual resources.

Sonia: I wanted my inquiry to be an exploration of my students' "language richness." My Chicago students seemed to display a language richness that impressed me. Their vocabulary and ability to understand language and express themselves defied the myth about children from immigrant families who live on the boundaries of poverty, not possessing complex language skills, especially those required to succeed in school. I was interested in understanding their "language richness" better and making evident to them the vast funds of knowledge that seemed to be supporting their development. My goal was to capitalize on their language and cognitive resources to help them grow as reflective thinkers. I wanted them to value their own knowledge and to feel free to express and build on it in the context of the classroom.

CLASSROOM TALK AS CONVERSATION

"Living in particular classrooms leads to particular ways of communicating and acting, which in turn leads to particular ways of being, ways of doing, and ways of knowing" (Green & Putney, 1996, p. 1).

As the school year progressed, Sonia and her students began to craft specific ways of communicating, especially during specific curriculum genres such as read-aloud and social studies discussions. "Conversations," as Sonia called them eventually, became central in these routines. She felt that constructing this kind of talk was time consuming and often difficult, but eventually, allowed her to forge a learning–teaching relationship that was truly collaborative.

Sonia: It took some time and conscious effort on my part to make conversation a major way of classroom talk. Often, children come to school with a set of preconceived ideas about school culture. They have specific expectations about how school is supposed to work, their roles as students, and the roles of adults as teachers. Most often the expected behavior entails a traditional view of education; children sit passively listening while the teacher teaches. In this scenario, children have very little to contribute, because it is assumed that they don't know anything (at least they don't know anything that is of any importance), and teachers educate and instruct, because it is assumed that they know everything.

During the first month or two of my inquiry, I struggled to change my students' views on what they thought school ought to be. Many of the students, who later became eager informants, were at first quite puzzled and even a bit nervous about the way I conducted classroom discussions (which I later, and more appropriately, began to call "conversations"). Our discussions were not mere conversations; they had structure and specific purposes. I encouraged them not only to share their experiences, but also to explore and become more aware about how they acquired new knowledge outside the classroom.

My questioning strategies were, at first, regarded with skepticism by the children. They, understandably, were not all together sure about the true intentions of my questioning. Did I really want to know the answer? Was I really interested in what they had to say? Later, I realized that children are used to adults questioning them for purposes other than getting to an answer or explanation, such as a parent or teacher asking a child after he or she has broken something, "Why did you do that?" or "What do you think you are doing?" After some time, the students began to anticipate our conversations and my questioning line. Many times, students and I engaged in discussions that almost seemed like they were guiding themselves, taking lives of their own.

Sonia identified conversations as playing a crucial role in realizing her efforts to explore and extend her students language richness and to foster their growth as reflective thinkers. These conversations became the tapestry or canvas on which new knowledge was woven. They brought to the foreground students' knowledge and contributions and, in turn, led to rich coconstruction of new meanings as Sonia built on her students' expertise by sharing her own (Wells, 1998; Wells & Chang-Wells, 1992). Conversations were central to the classroom culture and served as a forum for the redefinition of new ways of being, new ways of doing, and new ways of knowing, and of what counted as academic knowledge (Green & Putney, 1996; Gutierrez, Rymes, & Larson, 1995). Furthermore, these conversations constituted powerful oral literate events, making possible the explicit unfolding of epistemic modes of engagement as students and teacher expressed their meanings, reflected on them, and transformed them (Wells, & Chang-Wells, 1992).

However, not every conversation constituted fertile ground for the transformation of knowledge or for the making explicit of epistemic modes of engagement with text. That is, Sonia faced various dilemmas as she struggled to find ways to encourage her students to contribute their funds of knowledge. Often it was difficult for her also to find the appropriate means to scaffold or guide their progress into higher levels of understanding. Thus, both successful and problematic conversations in various curriculum genres are provided to illustrate the range of Sonia's inquiry on language richness.

NEW WAYS OF BEING AND DOING: VALUED INFORMANTS

The linguistic and cognitive resources of language-minority students have often been either ignored or assumed to be in conflict in the demands of schooling in general, and literacy learning in particular (Delgado-Gaitán, 1987; McCollum, 1991; Moll & Greenberg, 1990). Sonia referred to that notion as a myth that she was ready to challenge. It has been argued that interactions between students and teachers reflect the patterns of cultural and power relationships in the society at large. As patterns of teacher–student communication change, they have the potential to transform the more traditional and well-entrenched relationships in the broader society (Cummins, 1994). During the conversations that realized many of her curricular routines, Sonia was able to communicate to the students that she was genuinely interested in their contributions and that they possessed valuable information. They had new opportunities for being, doing, and knowing in the classroom as valued informants. The following examples illustrate how Sonia's responses to students' initiations acknowledged them as important, active participants in the discussions, and how their contributions became the basis of newly elaborated knowledge.

Is Mexico in South America?

Example 1 comes from a small-group discussion during a unit about travel and maps. On the previous day, Sonia suggested that the students ask their families about their histories, mainly as they related to where parents and siblings had been born. Students now shared this information.

Example 1

....		[Vicente is telling about his brother being born in Mexico.]
1	Lidia:	(...) eso es Sudamérica.
2	Sonia:	(... ...) Mexico en Sudamérica?
3	Eddie:	No, Sudamérica es otro país.
4	Sonia:	¿Sudamérica es otro país?
5	Lidia:	No, es otra ciudad.
6	Sonia:	¿Es otra ciudad?
7	Cm1:	No, es un estado.
....		[Sonia gets up and shows them a map of the Americas that she had shared with them on a previous day. She asks students to point to South America. After one of them does, Sonia asks them to look for another map that shows South America (there is one on the chalkboard) where students are able to locate it.]
8	Sonia:	Sigamos, Vicente nos está contando que su hermano nació en Mexico. Lidia dijo que era Sudamérica, pero Sudamérica no es un país, o una ciudad, es parte de un continente donde hay muchos países.

Translation

....		[Vicente is telling about his brother being born in Mexico.]
1	Lidia:	(...) that is South America.
2	Sonia:	(... ...) Mexico in South America?
3	Eddie:	No, South America is another country.
4	Sonia:	South America is another country?
5	Lidia:	No, it is another city.
6	Sonia:	It is another city?
7	Cm1:	No, it is a state.
....		[Sonia gets up and shows them a map of the Americas that she had shared with them on a previous day. She asks students to point to South America. After one of them does, Sonia asks them to look for another map that shows South America (there is one on the chalkboard) where students are able to locate it.]
8	Sonia:	Let's go on. Vicente is telling us that his brother was born in Mexico. Lidia said that it was South America, but South America is not a country or a city, it is part of a continent where there are many countries.

{Fieldnotes, videotape, 03/16/95}

This discussion illustrated how Sonia responded to students' initiations, creating spaces for their voices as they shared their hypotheses about South America. Rather than cutting the discussion with a "No, South America is another continent," she repeated their initiations in question form, marking the importance of considering them carefully. At the end, she highlighted Vicente's and Lidia's contributions to the discussion and responded to them contingently (Wells & Chang-Wells, 1992), extending their knowledge by sharing her expertise.

Green and Putney (1996) claimed that within the culture of each classroom, the ways in which its members communicate molds not only learning opportunities, but also shapes shared knowledge of what it means to be a member, and what is valued as academic content in each classroom community. The example illustrates how students' roles were some of the valued contributors, regardless of the correctness of their initiations.

Stealing from Mexico and Wetbacks

Example 2 supports those observations with more examples of the nonjudgmental ways in which Sonia responded to her students' comments, the ways in which she extended them, and more importantly, how students' meanings determined the content of academic knowledge. It again contains excerpts of the conversation that ensued around the topic of maps and travel. Sonia and half of her class (the others were at computer class) sat around a table facing a bulletin board that showed a map of North America.

Example 2

1 Sonia: Aquí dice México. Esto es Estados Unidos, esto es México. [pointing to them on the map]

2 Esteban: Pero de todos modos México no es——no es chiquito, cuando ellos robaron——la tierra, todavía es grande, México.

3 Sonia: México era grande antes. ¿Y quién le robó la tierra?

4 Esteban: Los de aquí.

5 Sonia: Ooooh. ¿Y quién te contó?

6 Esteban: Mi papá.

7 Sonia: Tu papá. ¿Y tú sabes qué parte era de México que ya no es? [She waits but there is no response.] ¿Qué parte sería esa? Esto es México. [pointing on the map] ¿Cuál era la parte que era de México antes?.

8 Esteban: Esto——era—era——era de aquí pa' allá. [pointing towards the map]

9	Sonia:	¿Para abajo?
10	Esteban:	(••• •••).
11	C1:	Aquel no era, Maestra.
12	Sonia:	Pero Estados Unidos está acá arriba. Esos son otros países. [pointing to countries south of México on the map]
13	Cf:	Aquel, Maestra, aquel.
14	Sonia:	Yo creo que acá arriba, acá, esta era la parte que tu papá te contó que era de México....
15	Esteban:	A lo mej——a lo mejor——es——este es un lugar famoso porque también hay un——un país que es famoso por—— porque ahí los mexicanos no——no pueden pasar a través de——de la línea (•••).
16	Sonia:	¿No pueden pasar?
17	Esteban:	No.
18	Sonia:	¿A dónde?
19	Esteban:	La——la línea es de Est——es parte de Estados Unidos.
20	Sonia:	¿Acá en la——en la——en el límite? ¿Justo acá, en esta línea?
21	Esteban:	Uhum.
22	Sonia:	¿No los dejan pasar?
23	Esteban:	Ya <mi tío> lo atraparon el año pasado.
24	Sonia:	¿Quién sabía eso?
25	Esteban:	Mi papi me lo contó y también...
26	Sonia:	¿Qué te dijo? [She waits but there is no response.] ¿Quién sabía de eso que——uy, vamos a esperar a Vicente y Mariela porque están jugando. El papá de Esteban le contó a él que hay partes acá, en el límite con México y Estados Unidos, que no dejan entrar a los mexicanos. ¿Por qué sería eso? ¿Por qué no los dejan entrar?
27	Cm1:	Porque no•....
28	Sonia:	¿Por qué será?
29	Cm1:	Porque•....
30	Mariela:	Ell——ellos no son de este país.
31	Sonia:	¿Porque los mexicanos son de México y no son de Estados Unidos?
32	Cf1:	#Maestra•....#
33	Sonia:	#Pero ustedes están acá, y ustedes son de México•....#
34	Cf1:	#Maestra ... maestra ... mi papá vino a los Estados Unidos.#
35	Cm:	#A mí si me dejan entrar, y soy de Chicago.#
36	Sonia:	Porque naciste en Chicago. ¿Y por eso te dejan entrar? Hmmm. ¿Quién mas nació en Chicago? ¿Quién nació en México?

37	Cs:	[Raise hands and talk all at once.]
38	C:	#Yo nací en Chicago.#
39	C:	#Yo nací acá.#
40	C:	#Yo igual.#
....		[Sonia names some of the ones born in Chicago and some of the ones born in Mexico. Then she questions some of them who have not volunteered information. Some do not know and Sonia tells them to ask their mothers. Then Sonia poses another question.]
41	Sonia:	¿Y sus mamá y papá, dónde nacieron?
42	Cf:	En México, mi mam——mamá y mi papá nacieron en México.
43	Esteban:	Mi tio es mojado.
44	Sonia:	¿En *Mojado*? [Because they were talking about being born *in* Mexico and reluctant to believe the children would know the word "mojado" (wetback) in Spanish, Sonia initially responded to the child's comment as if "mojado" were the name of a place in Mexico.]
45	Cs:	[laughter]
46	Cf1:	Caminando … se fue caminando porque un amigo de mi mamá lo dijo.
47	Sonia:	¿Qué?
48	Cf1:	Que … e … e … e——que mojado quiere decir que se vienen caminando, de allá.
49	Sonia:	Hmmmm, y se vinieron caminando ¿Y por qué le dicen mojado? [She waits but there is no response.] ¿Porque se mojó?
50	Cs:	No.
51	Esteban:	Pero mi papá dice que——se vino, yo creo.…
....		[Sonia asks Cs not to touch the microphone, to sit down in their chairs and calls some names, especially as Esteban wants to keep talking.]
52	Esteban:	Yo creo que——yo creo que——yo creo que se vino en un taxi de México.
53	Sonia:	¿En un taxi de México? [with emphasis as "Can this be?"]
54	Esteban:	A lo mejor.
55	Sonia:	¿En un taxi de México? Aquí está Chicago, acá arriba. Tuvieron que cruzar toooooodo esto para ir a México. [pointing on the map] ¿Se habrá ido en un taxi?
56	Cs:	(... ...).
57	Esteban:	(...) en lugar de en un taxi, a lo mejor se fue en un avión.
58	Sonia:	Hmmmm. Okay, estamos hablando——Esteban nos contó que alguien le había dicho que a la gente que se cruza caminando le

		dicen mojado. ¿Alguien sabe por qué? [She waits but there is no response.] ¿Qué quiere decir mojado?
59	Cm:	Que están mojados.
60	Sonia:	Que se mojó. Porque muchas personas que viven en México, cruzan por un río y se mojan. Pero le dicen mojados, pero no es una cosa muy linda que le dicen. Cuando le dicen mojado no es——no es algo lindo, es algo que no….
61	Cf:	Que no lo deben repetir.
62	Sonia:	Es un insulto. ¿Saben lo que es un insulto?
63	Cm1:	¡Maestra!
64	Sonia:	¿Qué es un insulto?
65	Cm1:	¡Maestra!
66	Sonia:	Cuando yo le digo a alguien "Eres un tonto," eso es un insulto.
67	Cs:	[laughter]
68	Sonia:	Si alguien te dice, "Eres un mojado." ¿Eso qué es?
69	Cs:	Un insulto.
70	Cf:	Es una grosería.
71	Sonia:	Es una grosería, uhum. Okay, aquí tenemos el globo, el globo terráqueo se llama.

Translation

1	Sonia:	Here it says Mexico. This is the United States, this is Mexico. [pointing to them on the map]
2	Esteban:	But yet Mexico is not——is not small, when they stole——the land, it is still big, Mexico.
3	Sonia:	Mexico was big before. And who stole the land?
4	Esteban:	Those from here.
5	Sonia:	Ooooh. And who told you?
6	Esteban:	My dad.
7	Sonia:	Your dad. And do you know what part was Mexico's and it is not any more? [She waits but there is no response.] What part would that be? This is Mexico. [pointing on the map] Which was the part that was Mexico's before?
8	Esteban:	This was——was——was from here to there. [pointing towards the map].
9	Sonia:	Going down?
10	Esteban:	(… …).
11	C1:	That one was not, Teacher.
12	Sonia:	But the United States is up here. These are other countries. [pointing to countries south of Mexico on the map]

13	Cf:	That one, Teacher, that one.
14	Sonia:	I believe that up here, here, this is the part that your dad told you was Mexico's....
15	Esteban:	Maybe——maybe th——this is a famous place because there is also a——a country that is famous bec——because, there, the Mexicans cannot——cannot go in through——through the line (...).
16	Sonia:	They cannot go in?
17	Esteban:	No.
18	Sonia:	Where?
19	Esteban:	The——the line is of U——is part of the United States.
20	Sonia:	Here in the——in the——in the border? Right here, on this border?
21	Esteban:	Uhum.
22	Sonia:	They don't let them in?
23	Esteban:	And <my uncle> was caught last year.
24	Sonia:	Who knew that?
25	Esteban:	My daddy told me and also....
26	Sonia:	What did he tell you? [She waits but there is no response.] Who knew about that——ooops, let's wait for Vicente and Mariela because they are playing. Esteban's dad told him that there are parts here, in the border with Mexico and the United States, that they do not let the Mexicans in. Why would that be? Why don't they let them in?
27	Cm1:	Because they don't....
28	Sonia:	Why would that be?
29	Cm1:	Because....
30	Mariela:	The——they are not from this country.
31	Sonia:	Because the Mexicans are from Mexico and they are not from the United States?
32	Cf1:	#Teacher....#
33	Sonia:	#But you are here, and you are from Mexico....#
34	Cf1:	#Teacher ... Teacher ... my dad came to the United States.#
35	Cm:	#They let me in, and I am from Chicago.#
36	Sonia:	Because you were born in Chicago and because of that they let you in? Hmmmm. Who else was born in Chicago? Who was born in Mexico?
37	Cs:	[Raise hands and talk all at once.]
38	C:	#I was born in Chicago.#
39	C:	#I was born here.#

40	C:	#Me too.#
....		[Sonia names some of the ones born in Chicago and some of the ones born in Mexico. Then she asks some of them who have not volunteered information. Some do not know and Sonia tells them to ask their mothers. Then Sonia poses another question.]
41	Sonia:	And your mom and dad, where were they born?
42	Cf:	In Mexico, my mo——mom and my dad were born in Mexico.
43	Esteban:	My uncle is wetback.
44	Sonia:	In *Wetback*? [Because they were talking about being born *in* Mexico and reluctant to believe that the children would know the word *mojado* (wetback) in Spanish, Sonia initially responded to the child's comment as if *mojado* were the name of a place in Mexico.]
45	Cs:	[laughter]
46	Cf1:	Walking … went walking because a friend of my mom's said that.
47	Sonia:	What?
48	Cf1:	Tha … a … a——that wetback means that they come walking, from there.
49	Sonia:	Hmmmm, and they came walking, and why do they call him wetback? [She waits but there is no response.] Because he got wet?
50	Cs:	No.
51	Esteban:	But my dad says that——he came, I believe….
....		[Sonia asks Cs not to touch the microphone, to sit down in their chairs and calls some names specifically as Esteban wants to keep talking.]
52	Esteban:	I believe that——I believe that——I believe that he came in a cab from Mexico.
53	Sonia:	In a cab from Mexico? [with emphasis as "Can this be?"]
54	Esteban:	Maybe.
55	Sonia:	In a cab from Mexico? Here is Chicago, up here. They had to cross aaaaall this to get to Mexico. [pointing on the map] Would he have gone in a cab?
56	Cs:	(... ...).
57	Esteban:	(...) instead of a cab, maybe he went on a plane.
58	Sonia:	Hmmmm. Okay, we are talking——Esteban told us that some-one had told him that the people that cross by walking are called wetbacks. Does anybody know why? [Waits but there is no response.] What does wetback mean?
59	Cm:	That they are wet.

60	Sonia:	That he got wet. Because many people that live in Mexico cross through a river and get wet. But they call them wetbacks, but it is not a nice thing to say. When they call them wetback it is not, it is not something nice, it is something that is not....
61	Cf:	That should not be repeated.
62	Sonia:	It is an insult. Do you know what an insult is?
63	Cm1:	Teacher!
64	Sonia:	What is an insult?
65	Cm1:	Teacher!
66	Sonia:	When I tell someone, "You are a dummy," that is an insult.
67	Cs:	[laughter]
68	Sonia:	If someone tells you, "You are a wetback," what is that?
69	Cs:	An insult.
70	Cf:	It is a rude comment.
71	Sonia:	It is a rude comment, uhum. Okay, here we have the globe, the earth globe it is called.

{Fieldnotes, videotape, 02/28/95}

It is obvious that children felt comfortable in their roles as valued informants, but the most salient feature of the conversation excerpt has to do with what counted as academic knowledge in this classroom. The topics of land appropriation and immigration issues are, in general, not part of kindergarten social studies curricula. Yet, these were some of the meanings that maps and the boundaries of countries triggered for these students and, in the culture of this classroom, they were allowed to discuss, explore, and extend them as Sonia used them as a springboard to build more elaborated discussion and knowledge. She allowed for their initiations to become the core of the discussion. She frequently responded to them with phatic markers (i.e., ooohs, humms) (Halliday & Hasan, 1976) or with a combination of phatic markers and some other comments, signaling that she was listening to their ideas attentively (lines 5 & 49). She guided Esteban through an exploration of his own ideas as she asked him to reflect on where he got that information about Mexican land being stolen (line 5), or if what he was saying was plausible as she wondered about his father coming from Mexico in a cab (line 52). She marked his comments as valued contributions that were the source of subsequent discussion. Students were also allowed to try to make explicit the meaning of "wetback" as they contributed their own knowledge of the term (lines 46 & 59). Subsequently, she explained to them its origin (line 60), and the insult connotations that the word can have, to help them better understand the term (lines 60–71).

NEW WAYS OF KNOWING:
BECOMING CRITICAL THINKERS

Sonia: I wanted my students to feel valued contributors to the classroom knowledge. More importantly, I felt my mission as a teacher was to educate them as "critical thinkers." That is something more profound than making them "just functionally literate." People talk about making these children functionally literate so that they can fill out forms and get a job, but by doing so they are imposing on them their low expectations. My students demonstrated skills and abilities that were very high. They need to be able to think critically, to make their own decisions, to be able to speak their own minds, and they can do it if we allow them to.

The conversations in the next examples illustrate how Sonia asked her students questions that helped formulate their ideas more completely. Her responses to their initiations fostered self-questioning about the content and source of the knowledge they shared with the group. It was during these particular instances of classroom talk that epistemic modes of engagement with text, typical of literate thinking, became particularly apparent.

The Houses Are Sinking

Example 3 was also taken from one of classroom discussions around the topic of maps and traveling. Again, half of the group was at computer class, so Sonia had the other half of the class sitting around a table in front of a bulletin board where there were a variety of large maps.

Example 3

1	Sonia:	¿Cómo se llama esta parte de Mexico?
2	Cs:	[provide no answer]
3	Sonia:	Baja California.
....		[Sonia then points to the word, MEXICO, on the map. Someone comments about the letters being really apart as they spread across the map.]
4	Esteban:	Las casas se andan hundiendo.
5	Sonia:	¿Cómo sabes?
6	Esteban:	(.... ....) los programas.
....		[Sonia asks if anybody else has seen the news and asks them if they know why the houses are sinking.]
7	Lidia:	Se abrió la tierra.

8	Vicente:	No ... que se quebró.
9	Esteban:	Cada día cae agua.
10	Sonia:	¿Cada día *cae agua*? ¿Cómo se dice que *cae agua*?
11	Esteban:	Cae lluvia.
....		[There is talk about floods, water rising, etc. Esteban talks about people walking in the water. Lidia talks about watching the news. Sonia asks her if she saw something about the floods.]
12	Lidia:	No ... pero ví que nevaba mucho.
13	Esteban:	En Canadá se esta deshaciendo el hielo.
14	Sonia:	¿En Canadá se esta *deshaciendo* el hielo? [using a lot of gesture]
15	Eddie:	(...) derrite.
16	Sonia:	¿Por qué será? ¿Por qué se está derritiendo el hielo en Canadá?
17	C:	#(...) sol.#
18	C:	#(...) calor.#
19	Sonia:	¿Qué está viniendo? ¿Qué....
....		[Cs continue to talk about winter ending and spring starting.]

Translation

1	Sonia:	What do you call this part of Mexico?
2	Cs:	[provide no answer]
3	Sonia:	Baja California.
....		[Sonia then points to the word, MEXICO, on the map. Someone comments about the letters being really apart as they spread across the map.]
4	Esteban:	The houses are sinking.
5	Sonia:	How do you know?
6	Esteban:	(... ...) the programs.
....		[Sonia asks if anybody else has seen the news and asks them if they know why the houses are sinking.]
7	Lidia:	The ground opened.
8	Vicente:	No ... it cracked.
9	Esteban:	Each day water falls.
10	Sonia:	Each day *water falls*? How do you say that *water falls*?
11	Esteban:	Rain falls.
....		[Sonia talks about floods, water rising, etc. Esteban talks about people walking in the water. Lidia talks about watching the news. Sonia asks her if she saw something about the floods.]

12	Lidia:	No ... but I saw that it snowed a lot.
13	Esteban:	In Canada the ice is falling apart.
14	Sonia:	In Canada the ice is *"falling apart"*? [using a lot of gesture]
15	Eddie:	(...) melts.
16	Sonia:	Why would that be? Why is the ice melting in Canada?
17	C:	#(...) sun.#
18	C:	#(...) heat.#
19	Sonia:	What is coming? What....
....		[Cs continue to talk about winter ending and spring starting.] {Fieldnotes, 03/14/95}

Sonia often responded to her students' initiations with questions such as, "How do you know?" (line 5) and, "Why would that be?" (line 16). In asking students to consider the source and content of their knowledge, she provided them with ample opportunity to reformulate it or at least to pose hypotheses (i.e., the earth opening or cracking, water or rain falling) when they tried to explain how the flood occurred.

Sonia often nudged students to express their knowledge in better or clearer ways. One of the prevalent strategies that Sonia implemented to explore and build on her students' linguistic and cognitive resources was what we called *semantic extensions* or *elaborations*. During these elaborations, Sonia concentrated on word meanings. In this example, this was observed as she encouraged them for more precise word usage that led to "raining" and "melting" in lines 10 and 14. Sonia's emphasis on word meanings went beyond mere labelling of the "How-do-you-say ... ?" or "What-do-you-call-this?" type so common in early-childhood classrooms. Rather, her approach extended the students' knowledge to semantically related terms or domains. Her scaffolding enabled them to consider related meanings in extended semantic webs or fields; together they created *lexical collocations* (Halliday & Hasan, 1976). That is, in the discussions, she made links to topic-related words or vocabulary (e.g., weather words, airplane words).

Thinking About Word Meanings in *El Avión de Angela*

Example 4, an excerpt from the discussion that took place during the reading aloud of *El Avión de Angela* (*Angela's Plane*) (Munsch, 1988), includes several instances of lexical extensions and illustrates how Sonia was able to utilize her students' ideas as a springboard to expand their knowledge base. Sonia used the book, and a big poster on the bulletin board that showed the interior of a plane.

Example 4

1   Sonia: [reading from the book] YO ME LLAMO ÁNGELA Y SOLO TENGO CINCO AÑOS Y NO SE NADA DE VOLAR AVIONES. "DIOS MÍO, QUÉ LÍO!" CONTESTÓ LA VOZ. "ENTONCES ESCÚCHAME MUY BIEN ÁNGELA: AGARRA EL TIMÓN Y DA VUELTA HACIA LA IZQUIERDA." [addressing the group] ¿Qué querrá decir el "timón"?

2   Ramón: El volante.

3   Sonia: El volante. [she points to the book] ¿Cómo sabías que el timón era el volante?

4   Cm1:   Porque … era así. [moves hands like steering, then looks at Ramón]

5   Sonia: Ramón, ¿por qué?

6   Ramón: Porque estaba pensando.

7   Sonia: Aah! Ramón estaba pensando porque el escuchó lo que estaba diciendo el cuento. Le dijeron: "AGARRA EL TIMÓN." Tiene que ser el volante, no?

….   [Later on, the conversation moves on to plane crashes and what the children know about planes.]

8   Sonia: Vamos a hablar un poquito de cuando hay accidentes de aviones.

9   Cm1:   Cuando chocan.

10   Sonia: Cuando chocan con otro avión pero cuando se vienen abajo, ¿cómo se llama eso?

11   Cm2:   Estrellar.

12   Sonia: Se estrellan.

….   [A few minutes, later Sonia turns to the nearby poster and uses it a basis of conversation.]

13   Sonia: Y pueden mirar por la ventana. Y acá, acá está la parte donde.…

14   Cm1:   Manejan!

15   Sonia: Manejan … eeeh.…

16   Mariela: Esos dos son los jefes.

17   Sonia: ¿Son los jefes?

18   Mariela: Sí.

19   Cs: No.

20   Sonia: Son los.…

21   Cs: Los pilotos!

22   Sonia: Los pilotos, aha. Y sí, son como los jefes.

23   Cf1:   Mi hermano tiene aviones de——de juguete.

24   Sonia: Si tienen aviones de juguete en casa, los pueden traer mañana. Los van … a traer mañana, para verlos.

25	Esteban:	Yo tengo un avión que es——es de la ... de la Army.
26	Sonia:	De la Army! Porque hay distintos tipos de aviones....
....		[Sonia refers them back to poster and asks them what type of plane the one in the poster is.]
27	C:	#(...) llevan gente.#
28	C:	#Los de la army.#
29	C:	#Llevan tanques.#
30	Esteban:	#Llevan comida para los pobres.#
31	Sonia:	¿Cómo sabes? [asking Esteban]
32	Esteban:	Porque——porque pasan en las noticias.

Translation

1	Sonia:	[reading from the book] MY NAME IS ANGELA AND I AM ONLY FIVE YEARS OLD AND I DON'T KNOW ANYTHING ABOUT FLYING PLANES. "OH, MY GOD, WHAT A MESS!" ANSWERED THE VOICE. "THEN, LISTEN TO ME VERY CAREFULLY, ANGELA: TAKE THE WHEEL AND TURN LEFT." [Sonia addresses the group] What would *timón* (wheel) mean?
2	Ramón:	The wheel.
3	Sonia:	The wheel [she points to the book] How did you know that the timón was the wheel?
4	Cm1:	Because ... it was like this [moves hands like steering, then looks at Ramón]
5	Sonia:	Ramón, why?
6	Ramón:	Because I was thinking.
7	Sonia	Aah! Ramón was thinking because he listened to what the story was saying. They told her: "TAKE THE *TIMON*." It has to be the wheel, right?
....		[Later on, the conversation moves on to plane crashes and what the children know about planes]
8	Sonia:	We'll talk a little bit about when there are plane accidents.
9	Cm1:	When they bump.
10	Sonia:	When they bump with another plane, but when they come down, what do you call that?
11	Cm2:	Crash.
12	Sonia:	They crash.
....		[A few minutes later, Sonia turns to the nearby poster and uses it a basis of conversation]
13	Sonia:	And you can look through the window, and here, here is the part where....

14	Cm1:	They drive.
15	Sonia:	They drive … uuuh.…
16	Mariela:	Those two are the bosses.
17	Sonia:	The bosses?
18	Mariela:	Yes!
19	Cs:	No.
20	Sonia:	They are the.…
21	Cs:	The pilots.
22	Sonia:	Aha, the pilots. And yes, they are like the bosses.
23	Cf2:	My brother has——has toy planes.
24	Sonia:	If you have toy planes at home, you can bring them tomorrow. You are going … to bring them tomorrow … to look at them.
25	Cm1:	I have a plane that is——is from the Army.
26	Sonia:	From the Army? Because there are different types of planes.…
….		[Sonia refers them back to poster and asks them what type of plane the one in the poster is]
27	C:	#(…) carry people.#
28	C:	#Army planes.#
29	C:	#Carry tanks.#
30	Esteban:	#Carry food for the poor.#
31	Sonia:	How do you know? [asking Esteban]
32	Esteban:	Because——because they show them on the news. {Fieldnotes, videotape, 02/12/95}

During this conversation, on lines 1 through 7, Sonia attempted to make explicit the self-inquiry processes by which Ramón could have arrived to the definition of *timón* (wheel). Later, she steered the conversation to the discussion of specific word meanings as she marked the differences between "bump" and "crash," and clarified that plane drivers are not "bosses," but "pilots." When students initiated comments about the different types of planes they know in lines 27 through 30, Sonia helped them to reflect on their sources of knowledge as she asked Esteban "How do you know?" on line 31. Thus, using the students' contributions to the discussion, Sonia managed to push the boundaries of the semantic domain at issue to include new or better understandings of these words. The examples illustrate how, with her questions and responses to their initiations, Sonia is not as much interested in getting the right responses, but in scaffolding them into more exact formulations of their knowledge, and in fostering their reflections on the sources of that knowledge.

Sonia: I was always impressed by my students' knowledge of vocabulary and how much they were able to learn from what was going on at home. While most of parents in the families in my class had very limited experience with literacy and schooling, my students were able to articulate their ideas successfully and build on them as they interacted with me and with each other, provided the right kind of interactions and discussion framework. I was able to convey to them that thinking about a possible response was more important than having the correct response. It was during these discussions that I was able to learn the most about them, and then let my curriculum be informed by their expertise.

NEW WAYS OF BEING A TEACHER: THE STRUGGLES OF COLLABORATION

The transition from traditional transmission-oriented instructional models to more collaborative ones, that take into account students' linguistic and cognitive resources, demands a transformation of classroom culture. The discussion so far explained, and illustrated with examples, how this transformation both requires and results in new ways of being, acting (doing), communicating, and knowing, for teachers as well as for students. Taking on this new role can be problematic from the teacher's perspective. Sharing power with students does not mean that teachers relinquish their positions as experts and decision makers; teachers are still in charge (Oyler, 1996) and are responsible for the scaffolding of students into higher and more complex levels of knowledge. However, the juggling of her roles as facilitator and expert sometimes created struggles for Sonia. As some of the following examples show, they required ongoing and on-the-spot crafting and tuning up.

While her classroom history, discourse, and learning unfolded, Sonia wrestled, not only to build collaboration through talk, but also to build talk that would lead to higher levels of knowledge. It was not a matter of just fostering conversations for the sake of conversation or the mere sharing of experiences; fruitful classroom talk was not "any talk." Sonia, in her role of facilitator and context maker, had the overall responsibility to make conversations educationally significant. In that position, she often had to make decisions about which and whose knowledge or ideas counted as a valuable initiation worth pursuing. As she opened up spaces for students' voices, she faced questions such as: "What is an acceptable initiation?" and, "What constitutes educationally significant conversation?" Obviously, many factors have an impact on what we have termed *acceptability issues*: the interplay of teacher's and children's personalities, physical time and space constraints, curricular pressures, and so forth.

Sonia: There were many times of tension while trying to find the most appropriate ways of responding and fostering collaboration during our con-

versations. For example, one day everybody came and talked about Selena, the singer who had died. That was a very important topic for them, but how could I connect it to what we were studying that day? Sometimes, students would bring things that were completely disconnected, that had nothing to do with what we were discussing, like comments on the soap operas that they watched on television in the evening.

In time, our conversations became longer and more involved, and with this came the dreaded management issue. The children were so eager to contribute, and to be heard by me and their peers, that many times they would seemingly go off in tangents that either had little or no relevance at all to the topic at hand. I again struggled with trying to accept and encourage children's initiations while trying to contain the conversations within time and topic relevance constraints. This was a difficult task for me. I felt I had no time to find out if, indeed, there was no relevance to our discussion in a child's initiation. Many times, the child's contributions were related, but two- or three-times-removed from our conversation; nevertheless in the child's mind it was valid and had relevance. Sometimes because of the time constraints, I had to cut children off by making statements such as: "Are we discussing that now?" or "Can we talk about that later?"

Difficulties in Exploring Dog Breeds

The next two examples reflect classroom activity and discourse that typify Sonia's efforts to guide conversation in the right direction, scaffolding as meaning unfolded, nudging, and prompting, while juggling her role of being the expert and facilitator at the same time. Example 5 illustrates the type of "on-line" call that Sonia often had to make as she was trying to open the floor for a discussion that did not take off, maybe because it did not interest students or was too difficult for them to follow. This conversation occurred during a big-book read-aloud that mentioned a Pekinese dog. Sonia interrupted the read-aloud and posed a question to the group sitting around her on the rug.

Example 5

1	Sonia:	Hay distintos tipos de perros. ¿Qué tipos de perros hay?
2	Cs:	(... ...) color.
3	Sonia:	Hay distintos tipos de perros: pekinés, collie, poodles. ¿Qué otro tipo? ¿Qué otro tipo de perro hay?
4	Cm1:	Uno negro.
5	Cf1:	Una perra.
6	Sonia:	Si, hay perros y perras.

Translation

1	Sonia:	There are different types of dogs. What kinds of dogs are there?
2	Cs:	(... ...) color.
3	Sonia:	There are different types of dogs: Pekinese, collie, poodle, what other type? What other types of dogs are there?
4	Cm1:	A black one.
5	Cf2:	A female dog.
6	Sonia	There are dogs and female dogs.
		{Fieldnotes, 11/18/94}

Sonia attempted to start a conversation that would explore, and probably extend, children's knowledge about different kinds of dog breeds. She queried them about the topic twice, on lines 1 and 3, about different types of dogs. She nudged some more by providing them with some examples (line 3), but finally left the discussion there, after acknowledging their contributions about male and female dogs as different dog categories. Sonia considered this particular conversation to be a good example of how she too, as a teacher, took risks by presenting possible topics of exploration to her students without knowing exactly how they would react. She considered this risk-taking aspect of her inquiry, and the ability to be flexible to reroute conversation, as important parts of adjusting to a new way of being a teacher in ongoing collaboration with her students.

Difficulties of Relevance: "Miramar"

Example 6 illustrates how, on two different occasions, Sonia, as the teacher in charge, had to make decisions about what was an acceptable topic of conversation and which initiations were too far removed from the original theme. In an excerpt from a discussion around maps and travel, one of the boys in the group mentioned, while looking at a map on the board, that he had seen a car on fire as he was driving on the highway with his father. Then, Lidia brought up a fire in a soap opera.

Example 6

1	Lidia:	En la novela "Marimar" se quemó un jacal.
2	Cs:	[all talk at once about this episode]
3	Sonia:	¿Qué es un "jacal?" [Sonia is not familiar with the word.]
4	Mariela:	Eso es de Mexico!
5	Sonia:	¿Una casa en Mexico?

6	Cs:	¡Maestra! ¡Maestra!
....		[Esteban and Vicente go to the Lincoln Logs box and bring them to Sonia.]
7	Esteban:	Como de esto....
8	Sonia:	Oh! ¿Hecho con qué?
9	Esteban:	De madera.
....		[The conversation continues as Lidia starts explaining the plot of the soap opera.]
10	Lidia:	Ajá. Angélica le dijo a Renato que——le dijo a Renato, "Ya sabes qué tienes que hacer...." Y——y hizo así, entonces esta——al esta....
....		[Other children try to correct Lidia's retelling.]
11	Lidia:	Y le escribió una carta y——porque, porque esta Angélicano quería que Marimar se casara con ella porque....
12	Sonia:	Ah, bueno después me cuentan de "Marimar."
13	Cm1:	Maestra, ella, ella en el taxi. [continuing with "Marimar" plot]
14	Sonia:	Okay, ya no vamos a hablar de eso ... yo no quiero hablar de eso ahora.

Translation

1	Lidia:	In the soap opera "Marimar," a jacal burned down.
2	Cs:	[all talk at once about this episode]
3	Sonia:	What is a "jacal"? [Sonia is not familiar with the word.]
4	Mariela:	That is from Mexico.
5	Sonia:	A house in Mexico?
6	Cs:	Teacher! Teacher!
....		[Esteban and Vicente go to the Lincoln Logs box and bring them to Sonia.]
7	Esteban:	Like this....
8	Sonia:	Oh! Made of what?
9	Esteban:	Of wood.
....		[The conversation continues as Lidia starts explaining the plot of the soap opera].
10	Lidia:	Ajá. Angélica told Renato that——told Renato, "You know what you have to do...." And ... and did like that, then this——to this....
....		[Other children try to correct Lidia's retelling.]
11	Lidia:	And wrote a letter ... because——because this Angélica didn't want Marimar to marry her because....
12	Sonia:	Ahh, well, you tell me later about "Marimar."

13 Cm1:   Teacher, she, she in the taxi. [continuing with "Marimar" plot]
14 Sonia: Okay, we are not going to talk about that ... I don't want to talk
                about that now.
                {Fieldnotes, videotape, 03/14/95}

Conversation about maps and travel triggered a student's comment about a car on fire. This lead to Lidia's initiation about a *jacal* (log cabin) burning in a soap opera episode ("Marimar"). Talk then turned to "Marimar," but "Marimar," something that her students often liked to talk about, and Sonia apparently had not found to be particularly conducive to new learning, was not an acceptable topic to Sonia. She did not hesitate to put an end to that conversation. She made the same decision 2 days later, as the group got ready to share information about each child's family's history, and children spontaneously started talking about the previous night's episode of "Marimar."

Example 7

1 Sonia: Hoy no vamos a hablar de novelas. [speaking very firmly] Hoy no
                quiero que me digan nada de novelas.

Translation

1 Sonia: Today we are not going to talk about soap operas. [speaking
                very firmly] Today, I don't want you to tell me anything about
                soaps.
                {Fieldnotes, 03/16/95}

In these two examples, Sonia decided to cut the conversation about the soap opera short, because, even when of interest to the children and related to their everyday life outside school, she judged it inappropriate or nonfertile for the educational goals she had at the time.

COLLABORATIVE TALK AND ITS TRANSFORMATIVE POTENTIAL

The vignettes discussed demonstrate how crafting new teaching–learning relationships framed within the New Literacy perspective proposed by Willinsky (1990) can be realized in urban environments, populated by students whose abilities were traditionally dismissed as being at odds with the requirements of formal schooling. When Sonia explicitly took on her inquiry to explore her students' language richness, which she also termed their "funds of knowledge" (Moll, 1992), these kindergarteners learned to act as valued informants of the curriculum. They displayed high levels of knowledge, which were then further developed and reflected on, when guided by their teacher. Sonia's year-long inquiry journey as a teacher researcher exemplifies that coconstructing a classroom culture *with* students—one in which students are provided with opportunities to engage with texts epistemically—is a dynamic, ever-changing craft that can occur in urban classrooms. Granted, fostering more collaborative learning–teaching situations that respect students' ways of knowing is not free from struggle (Pappas, Zecker, & Soltero, 1996). It requires reworking of many givens of traditional, transmission-oriented classroom life, including questions about whose knowledge gets valued, who does the talking, and what is worthwhile to talk about. Collaborative teacher–student interactions and conversations result in new and more authentic ways of knowing by validating students' capabilities (Green & Putney, 1996; Gutierrez et al., 1995). These efforts give us the promise of possible even broader transformations in the cultural and power patterns that define the current society in which our children are growing (Cummins, 1994; Pappas & Zecker, 1996).

REFERENCES

Bartolome, L. I. (1994). Beyond the methods fetish: Toward a humanizing pedagogy. *Harvard Educational Review, 64,* 173–194.

Cazden, C. B. (1988). *Classroom discourse: The language of teaching and learning.* Portsmouth, NH: Heinemann.

Cummins, J. (1994). From coercive to collaborative relations of power in the teaching of literacy. In B. M. Ferdman, R.-M. Weber, & A. G. Ramirez (Eds.), *Literacy across languages and cultures* (pp. 295–331). Albany: State University of New York Press.

Delgado-Gaitán, C. (1987). Mexican adult literacy: New directions for immigrants. In S. Goldman & H. Trueba (Eds.), *Becoming literate in English as a second language* (pp. 9–33). Norwood, NJ: Ablex.

Delpit, L. (1995). *Other people's children.* New York: The New Press.

Edwards, D., & Mercer, N. (1989). *Common knowledge: The developing of understanding in the classroom.* New York: Routledge.

Green, J., & Putney, L. (1996, February). *What counts as literate actions in a bilingual classroom: Exploring individual-collective development.* Paper presented at the Research Assembly of the National Council of the Teachers of English Midwinter Conference, "A Vygotsky Centennial: Vygotskian Perspectives on Literacy Research," Chicago, IL.

Gutierrez, K., Rymes, B., & Larson, J. (1995). Script, counterscript, and underlife in the classroom: James Brown versus *Brown v. Board of Education. Harvard Educational Review, 65,* 445–471.

Halliday, M. A. K., & Hasan, R. (1976). *Cohesion in English.* London: Longman.

Hiebert, E., & Fisher, C. (1991). Task and talk structures that foster literacy. In E. Hiebert (Ed.), *Literacy for a diverse society* (pp. 141–156). New York: Teachers College Press.

McCollum, P. (1991). Cross-cultural perspectives on classroom discourse and literacy. In E. Hiebert (Ed.), *Literacy for a diverse society* (pp. 108–121). New York: Teachers College Press.

Moll, L. C. (1992). Literacy research in community and classrooms: A socio-cultural approach. In R. Beach, J. L. Green, & T. Shanahan (Eds.), *Multidisciplinary perspectives on literacy research* (pp. 211–244). Urbana, IL: National Conference on Research in English.

Moll, L. C., & Greenberg, J. (1990). Creating zones of possibilities: Combining social context for instruction. In L. C. Moll (Ed.), *Vygotsky and education* (319–348). New York: Cambridge University Press.

Munsch, R. (1998). *El arion de Angela (Angela's airplane)*. Toronto, Canada: Annick Press.

Oyler, C. (1996). *Making room for students: Sharing teacher authority in Room 104.* New York: Teachers College Press.

Pappas, C. C., & Zecker, L. B. (1996, December). *Breaking free: The political significance of collaborative talk.* Paper presented at the Annual Meeting of National Reading Conference, Charleston, SC.

Pappas, C. C., Zecker, L., & Soltero, S. W. (1996, February). *Relating Latino kindergarteners' funds of knowledge to school literacy curriculum: Struggles in scaffolding.* Presentation at the Research Assembly of the National Council of the Teachers of English Midwinter Conference, "A Vygotsky Centennial: Vygotskian Perspectives on Literacy Research," Chicago, IL

Reyes, M. de la Luz (1992). A process approach to literacy instruction for Spanish-speaking students: In search for the best fit. In E. Hiebert (Ed.), *Literacy for a diverse society* (pp. 157–171). New York: Teachers College Press.

Tharp, R. G., & Gallimore, R. (1988). *Rousing minds to life: Teaching, learning and schooling in social context.* New York: Cambridge University Press.

Vygotsky, L. (1978). *Mind in society: The development of higher psychological processes.* Cambridge, England: Cambridge University Press.

Wells, G. (1993). Reevaluating the IRF sequence: A proposal for the artiulation of the theories of activity and discourse for the analysis of teaching and learning in the classroom. *Linguistics and Education, 5,* 1–37.

Wells, G. (1994). The complimentary contributions of Halliday and Vygotsky to a "language-based theory of learning." *Linguistics and Education, 6,* 41–90.

Wells, G. (1998). Some questions about direct instruction: Why? To whom? How? And when? *Language Arts, 76,* 27–35.

Wells, G., & Chang-Wells, G. L. (1992). *Constructing knowledge together: Classrooms as centers of inquiry and literacy.* Portsmouth, NH: Heinemann.

Wertsch, J. V. (1991). *Voices of the mind: A sociocultural approach to mediated action.* Cambridge , MA: Harvard University Press.

Willinsky, J. (1990). *The New Literacy: Redefining reading and writing in the classroom.* New York: Routledge.

Young, R. (1992). *Critical theory and classroom talk.* Clevedon, England: Multilingual Matters.

Chapter 11

Fostering Young Readers: Creating Contexts for Kindergartners' Reenactments of Books *in* the Classroom

Dian Ruben

Jane Liao

Demetrya Collier

Research has indicated that many young learners acquire important understandings about written language by being read to and by being encouraged to reenact or pretend-read books on their own (Cochran-Smith, 1984; Doake, 1985; Holdaway, 1979; Panofsky, 1994; Pappas, 1993; Sulzby, 1985, 1996; Sulzby & Teale, 1991; Taylor, 1983). Although there has been research into the reading-like behavior of the early emergent reader, most of it was done in the context of the home, or by individually taking children out of the classroom for their reenactments to books. Also, most of these studies focused on children who have had histories of being read to. However, Dee's inquiry involves her efforts to provide her

---

The introduction chapter of this book provides the theoretical and methodological background for the larger collaborative school–university action-research project and this chapter about Dee's inquiry on pretend reading. See also the last chapter, which further discusses the implications of Dee's inquiry—as well as those of the other teacher researchers.

kindergartners, for most of whom at-home book-sharing experiences had
been limited, with daily opportunities to reenact books of their choice *in*
the classroom.

*Dee: Over the many years teaching all-day kindergarten, I noticed that
girls are usually easier to nudge into my class library center, but that boys often enter school with reluctance or little motivation to engage in reading activities. I saw this same behavior around reading this year for most of my 14
boys (out of 22 students), and I really thought I had to do something about it,
so that these boys (and my girls as well) would be interested in seeing themselves as readers. So, after my afternoon reading-aloud sessions (I read
aloud in the morning, too), I set up a time I called "pretend reading," and encouraged my students to "read" the books I had been reading in the classroom. At the beginning of the year, some of them had memorized a book, but
were reluctant to reenact it. So, I used "pretend" reading to better convince
them to try to retell the book in their own words, and that would count as
reading. I did do pretend reading in previous years when I encouraged children to go to the library. But this year it was a very specific emphasis. I had
never concentrated on it in the way I did in my inquiry, that is, setting a special time to have students read in this way, and for me to study it.*

Dee hoped that through these experiences of repeated pretend reading
of books she had read, her students would form a range of literate understandings that Holdaway (1979) characterized as a *literacy set.* One important area of knowledge of this literacy set is children developing a
familiarity with written dialect of book language, as opposed to typical
spoken language registers (Elster, 1995; Pappas, 1993; Pappas & Brown,
1987; Purcell-Gates, 1986; Sulzby, 1985, 1996; Wells, 1985, 1986). Also,
pretend readings enabled her students to learn essential strategies for
handling written language—for example, self-correction and predictive
operations—as well as to help them begin to acquire knowledge of the conventions of print, such as the directionality and phonetic principles of
print and concepts of word (Clay, 1979). Moreover, pretend reading has
been shown to enhance children's motivation for print, their enjoyment
and appreciation of the special rewards for reading and writing, which was
Dee's initial concern about her students' literacy development. Thus, Dee
believed that by creating contexts for pretend reading activities she would
have pleasurable goals for her students that would succeed in melding literacy learning and engagement in many significant ways (Dahl & Freppon,
1995; Turner, 1995).

This pretend-reading curriculum genre became a very complex social
and collaborative enterprise. Children sometimes found a spot by themselves in the classroom library or at one of the tables and read out loud
their approximations-to-text (McKenzie, 1977) of the many books that
were available to choose from. However, more frequently two or more chil-

dren met together to read a book and then helped each other in the reenactment process. They demonstrated for each other the directionality principles of written text, or how to point at each word. They also provided for each other wordings (based on their understandings of the meanings of the text and illustrations) that might not as yet become stabilized in the text renditions of their classmates. As Dee roved among individual students or buddies or small groups of children, a major part of her study centered around how she could best scaffold her students' ever-changing levels of emergent reading. As she noted in an end-of-the-year conversation about her inquiry, it was a struggle because she had not, until then, been explicitly aware of how children might really acquire the early emergent processes of reading (i.e., Holdaway's literacy set).

In the first part of this chapter we discuss and illustrate interactions of the kinds of successful collaborative arrangements that were created in the pretend-curriculum genre. In doing so, we show the ways that various male students became emergent readers and the assistance that Dee and classmates provided to support their efforts, because her concern for these students was the major impetus of her inquiry in the first place. Then, in the next section we more specifically address Dee's struggles to scaffold her students' developmental needs in becoming readers.

COLLABORATING TO DEVELOP STRATEGIES TO READ

Jimmy's Reading of *The Napping House* Book

All of Dee's students became readers, but, as already noted, this was accomplished through the help of others. Example 1 illustrates Jimmy's efforts to read *The Napping House* (Wood, 1984), which was a favorite book of the children. The book concerns a slumbering mouse, a snoozing cat, a dozing dog, a dreaming child, and a snoring granny on a cozy bed, all of whom are awakened by the bite of a wakeful flea. Jimmy is an African-American child who joined Dee's class in October. His reading of this book occurred late in the school year (March), but it represented an important first experience at seeing himself as a reader. Until then, he was often seen talking about the pictures in books with his classmates, but Jimmy usually chose very easy books for which he made no real attempts at pretend reading. He did especially like a book version of "Old MacDonald's Farm" because he could rely on his memory of the song to get through. However, he did not try at all to treat his recall of lines of the song as approximations to the text. Thus, before this reading of *The Napping House*, Jimmy did not seriously take on the role of reader. For example, the *Old Macdonald's Farm* book just provided a stimulus for him to sing the song he knew.

In the beginning of Example 1, Dee read the book to Jimmy and then with her input and students' input, he began to read on his own. Although

Dee and his classmates did aid him as they chimed in with suggestions, he was also insistent in giving his own rendition and in displaying his own understanding of the text.

Example 1

Text	Jimmy, Dee, and Other Readers	
And in that house there is a bed, a cozy bed in a napping house, where everyone is sleeping.	1 Dee:	Okay, see ... #AND IN THAT HOUSE THERE IS A BED ... A COZY BED IN A
	2 Jimmy:	NAPPING HOUSE# #AND IN THAT HOUSE THERE IS A BED... A COZY BED IN A NAPPY HOUSE#
	3 Dee:	WHERE EVERYONE IS....
	4 Jimmy:	SLEEPING [in a louder voice, then turns page] IN THE NAPPY HOUSE....
And on that bed there is a granny, a snoring granny, a snoring granny on a cozy bed in a napping house, where everyone is sleeping.	5 Dee:	Now who's on the bed? [pointing to the picture]
	6 Cm:	THE GRANDMA.
	7 Teresa:	A DOZY GRANDMA.
	8 Dee:	What kind of bed is it?
	9 Angel:	A COZY BED.
	10 Dee:	In what kind of house?
	11 Cs:	A NAPPING HOUSE.
	12 Dee:	Where everyone is doing what? [looking directly at Angel but seems to be expecting responses from the group]
	13 Cs:	SLEEPING.
And on that granny there is a child, a dreaming child on a snoring granny on a cozy bed in a napping	14 Jimmy:	[turning the page] (... ...).
	15 Dee:	What is the granny doing?
	16 Guill:	SNORI....

house, where everyone is sleeping.	17 Dee:	SNORING. And what kind of bed are they on?
	18 Angel:	#COZY#
	19 Jimmy:	#COZY#
	20 Teresa:	COZY BED.
	21 Dee:	What type of house?
	22 Jimmy:	NAPPY HOUSE.
	23 Dee:	Where everyone is....
	24 Jimmy:	#SLEEPING#
	25 Cs:	#SLEEPING#
	26 Dee:	Okay.
	27 Jimmy:	AND THE NAPPY HOUSE.... IT WAS NAPPY ... IN THE NAPPY HOUSE ... IT WAS ... EVERYBODY SLEEPY.
And on that child there is a dog, a dozing dog on a dreaming child on a snoring granny on a cozy bed in a napping house, where everyone is sleeping.	28 Dee:	Okay, now who's on top of the dreaming child now?
	29 Jimmy:	(...).
	30 Angel:	DOG....
	31 Dee:	What kind of a dog? A DOZING DOG.
	32 Teresa:	AND THE CAT....
	33 Jimmy:	No! Hey, don't tell me.
	34 Dee:	Okay, we're not going to tell you.
	35 Jimmy:	IS A NAPPY——IN A NAPPY HOUSE ... ... ALL THE PEOPLE SLEEPING IN A HOUSE. [putting his hand to his head and looking down as if to say, "I know that's not exactly what it says, but I did it."]

....

{Fieldnotes, videotape, 03/28/95}

Jimmy was first supported by Dee's reading *with* him, but then at line 4, his louder voice signaled that he was ready to read alone. However, between lines 6 and 13, he lost his role as single reader. During this period, Dee scaffolded what the text might be, by asking questions about the pictures, and other students participated in the reading by responding with approximations. After that, Jimmy attempted to regain his role as reader, but his efforts were so softly said that he could not be heard. Then along with Angel, Jimmy offered "cozy" to Dee's question about what kind of bed they were on, which Teresa extended to "cozy bed." Subsequently, he made a second effort as a single reader at lines 22 and 24, and especially at line 27 where he recapped the text they had been working on. Subsequently, at line 33, Jimmy indicated that he wanted to read on his own as he refused classmates' help with "No! Hey, don't tell me." Dee affirmed his right to be the lone reader at line 34, and Jimmy continued to persevere to make sense of the text.

Later, during the same reading (not provided here), other emergent literacy skills became apparent as Jimmy continued to reenact the book. He began to look more at the print, pointing at words with his finger, even though he was aware that he was not reading the actual words of the print. Again he collaborated and interacted with his peers and Dee. He used their feedback to self-regulate his use of language, and at the same time continued to insist that his classmates not tell him words in upcoming text. Moreover, as a reader, he began to self-correct his rendition of the text, frequently repairing initial wordings with ones that were semantically closer to the meanings of the text. Thus, being around his classmates, who saw themselves as readers, finally affected him in becoming a solo reader, and following this reading, Jimmy began to initiate reading more often.

The type of collaboration seen in Example 1 was typical with other students in Dee's classroom, although it was particularly significant for Jimmy because this was his first time at successful pretend reading. Dee's efforts with Jimmy and the other young emergent readers were one of the many occasions of small literacy-club meetings (Smith, 1988) that occurred during this curriculum genre, in which she shared her expertise in guiding and assisting her students to learn to read by reading (Pappas & Brown, 1987).

Reading Daddies

Another favorite book of the children was an informational book entitled *Daddies* (Greenspun, 1991). This book had wonderful black-and-white photographs of fathers (from a range of ethnic and racial backgrounds) with their children, involved all kinds of everyday, heartwarming, family experiences. The text of the book consists of only six sentences, with each page having only one or a few words depicting the actions in the photographs. Because of its content and format, this book early became an important one in supporting the pretend reading of all of the children, but especially the boys. The next two examples illustrate how they used this book.

Example 2 shows the kinds of approximations that children constructed for this book, as well as the collaborative assistance classmates provided. As the example begins, Ramon read the third sentence of the book and then tackled the beginning of the next sentence, all of which were accomplished with lots of Larry's help.

Example 2

Text	Ramon and Larry Reading	
Daddies give hugs	1 Ram.:	[pointing to the words]
and kisses,		DADDIES GIVE HUGS AND
		KISSES. [turns page
tickles and giggles,		and looks to Larry for
piggyback rides.		help as he points to
		the words above the
		picture]
	2 Lar.:	[pointing to words]
		#TICKLES (... ...).#
	3 Ram.:	#TICKLES (... ...).#

.... [Larry leaves for a moment as Ricardo joins Ramon. Larry returns and resumes his aid by reading each page, which Ramon then repeats.]

Daddies teach how to	4 Lar.:	<DADDIES KNOW HOW TO DO IT.>
	5 Ram.:	<DADDIES KNOW HOW TO DO IT.>
	6 Lar.:	I mean DADDIES KNOW HOW TO READ.
	7 Ram.:	DADDIES KNOW HOW TO READ.
	8 Lar.:	DADDIES GIVE SMILES.
	9 Ram.:	DADDIES GIVE SMILES. [turns the page]

{Fieldnotes, videotape, 11/15/94}

In the first part of the excerpt, Ramon offered a fairly accurate reading of the text. Subsequently, Larry and Ramon created a rendition that was farther from the wordings of the text. The page they attempted to read had the beginning of the sentence ("Daddies teach how to ...) that tells all the things that Daddies teach (... swim, and dive, ski, catch and throw, win, and lose."). At line 4, Larry generated a broad statement that captured the general meaning of the sentence. Then, in line 6, he repaired that to provide more specific information, namely, "Daddies know how to read," and then he added, "Daddies give smiles" in line 8. These latter efforts seemed to be based on the bottom, right-hand photograph showing an African-American father reading books to his two children at a library, and what he may have recalled of other wordings in other parts of the book ("Daddies … read stories" in the first sentence of the book and "Daddies need … smiles" from the last sentence). In this last part of Example 2 (and throughout the reading of the book), Ramon often merely repeated what Larry constructed (see lines 5, 7, and 9 above). Nevertheless, although Larry provided an immense amount of support for Ramon's reading of *Daddies* on this occasion, Ramon was still considered to be the reader. Ramon expected and wanted Larry's help, but at other times he frequently indicated to Larry, mostly by pushing Larry's hand, that he could read—and did read—portions of the book on his own.

Just a week later, the *Daddies* book was again featured in a critical way. Angel found this book a very personally salient one and had asked Dee if he could read it later to the whole class. When she gave him permission to do so, he practiced on his own and then pretend read it to his classmates during the last few minutes of the reading period. In Example 3, we have indicated the wordings of text found on the left- and right-hand side pages with a slash mark, and we have included Dee's minimal contributions in parentheses. Throughout his reading, he physically struggles with the book (because of its size) to show the pictures to his audience and point to the words of the book.

Example 3

Text	Angel's reading
Daddies/ hold babies,	DADDIES HOLD BABIES.
[picture]/ push strollers,	DADDIES PUSH STROLLERS [calls a name to get the student's attention]
share feelings,/	DADDIES [turns book around so Dee can see words] ([Dee: SHARE … I can't see the rest of it. Oh, FEELINGS. Okay.]) DADDIES SHARE FEELINGS.
read stories.	DADDIES READ STORIES [looking up to watch his audience]
Daddies have shoulders to stand on,/	DADDIES HAVE SHOULDERS TO SIT——TO STAND ON.

bellies to sit on,	DADDIES HAVE BELLIES TO SIT ON.
backs to climb on,	DADDIES (... ...).
hands to hold.	DADDIES (... ...). [calls out a student's name]
Daddies give hugs/	DADDIES GIVE <HUGGLES>.
and kisses,	DADDIES GIVE KISSES [calls a name]
tickles and giggles,/	DADDIES (...) GIGGLES.
piggyback rides.	DADDIES HAVE—DADDIES GIVE PIGGY-BACK RIDES [calls a name]
Daddies teach/	DADDIES TEACH
how to	HOW TO——
swim,/ and dive,	DADDIES ... TEACH HOW TO DIVE.
ski,/ [picture]	DADDIES SKI.
catch/ and throw,	DADDIES (...) HOW TO CATCH AND THROW.
win,/ and lose.	DADDIES KNOW HOW TO WIN AND LOSE.
Daddies take us/ to parades,	DADDIES TAKE US TO PARADES [calls a name]
and home again,/ [picture]	AND HOME ——AND HOME AGAIN.
on picnics, /	DADDIES TAKE US TO PICNICS.
to parties,	DADDIES TAKE US TO PARTIES [calls a name]
to the zoo. /picture	[skips a page]
Daddies need/ hugs and	DADDIES GIVE US <HUGGLES>.
kisses,	DADDIES GIVE KISSES.
smiles,/ and tickles,	DADDIES [turns book to Dee for help] ([Dee: AND TICKLES.]) AND TICKLES.
jokes,/and giggles, and	DADDIES GIVE GIGGLES.
"I love you."	I LOVE YOU.

{Fieldnotes, videotape, 11/25/94}

Angel's performance here was a confident one where he asked for help from Dee only twice—in the beginning on "share feelings," and towards the end on "tickles." Several of his reading behaviors were modeled from Dee's style of reading aloud—for example, his attempts to point to the words as he read (although it was not in one-to-one correspondence with the words of the text), show the pictures, and call out the names of class-mates who he felt were not paying attention to his reading. In his reading, he transformed the verbs, direct objects, or places that were expressed as a series in the sentences of the text into full-fledged sentences, all starting with "Daddies." Except for this modification, his text represented a close reading of the book. This particular pattern of approximation (i.e., adding the subject of "Daddies") was used by many of the children in reading this book (e.g., see Example 2).

Although many of children were already showing active participation in reading through reenacting books, Angel's initiation to read the book to the whole class spurred more excitement in pretend reading in the students. They were also much more eager to read to others as they began to visit other classes to read, or to the principal (to whom they read daily), or to Dian and Jane, or to other university researchers who might visit the class, or, indeed, to anyone who might enter the room at that time of day. Moreover, from that point, Dee altered the structure of the pretend-reading curriculum genre by setting aside time at the end for several students to read-aloud to the class. In doing so, Dee also raised the ante in their having the opportunity to read to the class—they had to practice ahead of time—and she began to let students take books home for that purpose, something she had been reluctant to do earlier.

Andre's Reading of *When I Was Sick*

It was perhaps these whole-class student-led reading sessions that provided the impetus for Andre to finally partake in pretend reading. Andre was a Latino student who Dee was especially concerned and puzzled about. She was constantly showing his dictations or writing to our project group to show how capable he was, but she could not understand his complete lack of interest in reading. So, on a day in February, when his hand was up to offer to take a turn to read, Dee was both thrilled and surprised. Andre had chosen the book, *When I Was Sick* (Hillman, 1989), to read. As was regular practice, he went to the front of the class and stood beside Dee. As is seen in Example 4, Angel soon offered to help him, to which Andre agreed. When Angel joined Andre, he stood right next to him, and although Andre was the main reader, they often read together.

Example 4

1	Andre:	WHEN I WAS SICK....
2	Dee:	(... ...). [distracted with another student]
3	Andre:	[turns the page]
4	Cs:	(... ...).

5	Dee:	[She takes the book and tries to close it because children are noisy, causing it to fall to the floor.] Wait a minute. We don't have a good audience. Let's just stop. [#reaches for the fallen book#]
6	Andre:	[#reaches for the fallen book#]
7	Angel:	Ms. Collier, you want me to help him?
8	Dee:	Help him? Stand here. [motioning to Angel to stand next to Andre] [to Andre] Do you need help?
9	Andre:	Uhhuh.
10	Dee:	Yeah!
11	Donald:	He said "no."
12	Dee:	He said "yeah." [to Angel] Okay, let's let him read first.
13	Andre:	[has the book open now reading] (... ...).
14	Donald:	WHEN I WAS SI....
15	Angel:	[takes the book and closes it to point to the words of the title on the cover, while Andre reads along] #WHEN I WAS SICK.#
16	Andre:	#WHEN I WAS SICK.# [opens the book and reads from the title page] WHEN I WAS SICK.
17	Dee:	Show the pictures.
18	Andre and Angel:	[both holding the book and reading together] WHEN I WAS SICK, I DIDN'T WANT TO EAT (...).
19	Andre:	THINNER [holding up the book to show the pictures]
....		[Dee stops the reading to get students to be quiet and be more attentive. After a few seconds, the two boys begin to read again.]
20	Angel:	#WHEN I....# [pointing to each word]
21	Andre:	#DIDN'T WANT TO# EAT....
22	Angel:	No!. WHEN I WAS SICK I——I DIDN'T WANT....
23	Dee:	Okay. I GOT THINNER ... AND....
24	Angel:	AND....
25	Dee:	THINNER. Okay, let's let Andre show the pictures. [taking the book, turning it for Andre]
26	Andre:	[#holds up the book for the students to see#]
27	Dee:	#And let's see if Andre can try and read some of it for us.#
28	Angel:	[#sits down on a chair next to Andre#]
29	Andre:	[finds a chair and sits down next to Angel]
30	Dee:	You know what? I think you two should read together all the time.
....		[Andre finishes reading the book, sometimes alone, sometimes with Angel's and Dee's assistance. Andre shows the pictures of

the last page, with much clapping (and "wolf" sounds) from the class. Then, as the rest of the class leaves the group, Dee turns to talk to Andre and Angel.]

31	Dee:	You know what I want you to do? I want him to——you know what I'd like for you two to do? [to Andre] I would like for you to sit down with Angel?
32	Andre:	[nods head "yes"]
33	Dee:	He wants to help you to read....
34	Andre:	(...).
35	Dee:	Do you mind if he sits with you?
36	Andre:	(... talking ...).
37	Dee:	It's okay? You did a real good job. I'm very proud of you ... <that> you want to read. Okay?
38	Angel:	One page was <wrong> at the back.
39	Dee:	I know, but I like the way you were pointing to the words and telling him what the words were. So you two can be partners, okay? Any time the library is open you can sit together. [while surrounded by many students who are getting ready to go home, she addresses Andre] Yeah, this is going to be your new buddy, okay? Your new friend.

{Fieldnotes, videotape, 02/02/95}

This was a red-letter day for Andre. First, he finally showed interest and readiness to be a reader by volunteering to take a turn to read the *When I Was Sick* book, *and,* a classmate offered to be his reading buddy! Realizing that this was Andre's first day to be the reader, Angel asked if he could help, and Dee assented when she saw that Andre agreed to it. Quite soon, though, Dee began to think beyond this particular reading by suggesting the idea of the two boys becoming more permanent reading buddies (line 30). Then after the book was read, she talked to Andre and Angel again about this reading-partners arrangement. Being careful again that Andre was a willing partner, Dee praised each of the boy's efforts, and argued that they could continue this collaboration, to which they both assented. In fact, even though the school day was almost finished, that partnership was observed immediately. Andre and Angel went over to a table with the book. They were joined by Jimmy and Donald. Angel started the reading, pointing to the words, then Jimmy and Donald chimed in. For a while, Andre just watched, but then he and Angel read together or Andre read with Angel's assistance, with Donald quietly reciting the words as well, and Jimmy just listening. Andre and Angel closed the book when they were done, and the four boys began to talk about the dragons they made in class that day.

Thus, Andre, an extremely reluctant reader, finally joined the literacy club (Smith, 1988). Dee and Angel—as well as his classmates' applause at the end—provided the support for Andre's maiden voyage. Although Angel and Dee provided wordings or prompted how and when to show the pictures, Dee made sure that Andre had the major role as reader.

More on Andre's Reading (of *Spring Green*)

The next example occured a couple of months later when Dee, sitting on the floor, asked Andre to come to read to her. He brought *Spring Green* (Selkowe, 1985). His motivation to read was much higher and he was often observed engaging in reading books on his own, or with Angel or other classmates. As is seen, in reading this book he used pictures a lot to create an interpretation of the text, but he also began to point to words and to figure out word-to-word correspondence and other medium aspects of print (Pappas, Kiefer, Levstik, 1999). *Spring Green* is about a duck, Danny, who goes here and there to find something for the green contest at Woody's spring party. During this journey, Danny met many of his friends who will be at the party too, as he considered and rejected different objects to take as his contribution to the competition. This was a much more complex book than *When I Was Sick*; consequently, Andre's approach in reading the book and Dee's manner of support are different. Before Example 5 began, Ramon joined Andre and Dee. Together they read the title on the front of the book and the title page, each time pointing to the words.

Example 5

Text		Andre, Dee, and Ramon
Page 1: left-hand side "Oh dear, oh dear, oh dear." Danny waddled back and forth and all around.	1 Andre:	[turning to the first page, looking at the bottom of the right-hand page] THE DUCK—— THE DUCK FOUND [He
Page 1: right-hand side "Are you looking for something you've lost?" T.J. asked him. "No, I'm looking for something for something I can't find."		looks back over to left-hand page, pointing at about the middle.
	2 Dee:	Okay, what——wait a minute. Show me where you're going to start reading at? Where do you start?

3 Andre:	[points to the upper corner of the left-hand side of the page]
4 Dee:	Okay.
5 Andre:	THE DUCK WAS RUNNING AND THEN THE DUCK FOUND THE BALL. [moving over to the right-hand page, running his fingers across the words on the first line] THEN THE DUCK SAW A HOLE [puts his finger back to the beginning of the line] SAW....
6 Ramon:	[points, picking up his finger for each word] You should point to one word at a time like that.
7 Dee:	He's not doing that though.
8 Andre:	THEN THE DUCK SAW LIKE A—LIKE A....
9 Ramon:	Oh, he saw one of those <things>. [pointing to a small animal called T. J. in the text coming out of a hole in the picture]
10 Andre:	LIKE A——LIKE A [pausing to think]
11 Ramon:	I forgot what it was.
12 Dee:	What?
13 Andre:	LIKE A [still thinking]
14 Ramon:	A skunk.
15 Dee:	Not you. [to Ramon]
16 Andre:	No, this ain't no skunk.
17 Dee:	Who's reading the

		story?
18	Andre:	[points to himself]
19	Dee:	[to Ramon] Let him interpret the story.
20	Andre:	LIKE ONE——LIKE A FERRET—— LIKE A FERRET.
21	Dee:	A ferret? Okay.
22	Andre:	(...) cause they got a nose like this. [pointing to the T. J. animal in the picture] You ever saw one?
23	Dee:	I think once. I think they were talking about the ferret on television the other day because, you know, because we don't have a lot of them around anymore.
24	Andre:	Oooh, I saw that movie about Kindergarten Cop. You saw that?
25	Dee:	Kindergarten Cop? But we're not talking about Kindergarten Cop now. You're doing your storybook for me.
26	Andre:	Okay. AND THEN HE WAS COMING OUT [looking at the pictures again] THEN (...) HIDE-AND-GO-SEEK. AND THEN HE WAS LOOKING AROUND.
27	Dee:	[pointing to the T. J. animal] So this animal here, what you call a ferret, is playing hide-and-go-seek with

the duck? Oh, okay.
.... [Andre reads the whole book using the pictures exclusively to tell a story.]

28 Dee: Okay, good! So, what
             we have to do the next
             time we look at that
             story, we have to look
             at the words, okay?

29 Andre: (...) have to take it
             home and learn how to
             read it.

30 Dee: You want to take this
             one home to learn how
             to read it? What does
             it say? [pointing to
             the title] SPRING
             GREEN. We'll start
             with the title. The
             title of the book is
             called SPRING GREEN.
             You want to take this
             one home today?

31 Andre: Yeah.

{Fieldnotes, videotapem 04/04/96}

In the beginning of the example, *medium* aspects of print were addressed (Pappas et al., 1999) That is, when Andre began to read the first page, his attention was on the right side of the book, and then to the left (line 1), so Dee had him reexamine which page should be read first. Also, when he just brushed his fingers across the words of the book, Ramon stated that Andre should point to one word at a time, and showed him how to do it.

In the rest of the example, the focus was on the *message* aspects of the book (Pappas et al., 1999). Of course, there is little relationship between what Andre read and the actual wordings or meanings of the text because Andre used mostly the illustrations for his text construction. Andre spent a lot of time trying to decide what to call the animal that the duck met. It is not clear from the illustration what this animal character (in clothes in the picture) is, nor is there any clue to its identification from its name, T. J. When Andre hesitated to come up with a name, Ramon suggested that it is a skunk (line 14), which Andre emphatically rejected. Dee mediated this debate by affirming Andre's role as the reader, and therefore the interpreter, of the book. Finally, in line 20, Andre offered "ferret" as the animal in his story, which Dee accepted. He then provided an explanation of why he thought it was a ferret—"they got a nose like this"—and then asked Dee if she had ever seen one. Dee reported that she had, but when she mentioned that she saw something about ferrets on television, Andre apparently thought she was referring to the movie "Kindergarten Cop," which included a ferret. Dee, not knowing of this connection, cut off this potential intertextual link (Bloome & Bailey, 1992; Bloome & Egan-Robertson, 1993) and had Andre redirect his attention back to the book. In line 26, Andre agreed to do so, and continued his reading by creating new actions in his story, which Dee checked because Andre used a couple of ambiguous "he's." Again, this was clearly not the actual plot of book, but Dee accepted Andre's interpretation of it based on the pictures.

After Andre's read the book, Dee praised his efforts, but also insisted that the next time "we have to look at the words" (line 28). Although she had him read the title from print, her intent was for him to construct a text that was closer to the actual meanings of the book, and not to depend so much on the pictures. When Andre asked to take the book home and to "learn how to read it," Dee agreed. Indeed, since it was now April in the school year, Dee no longer left the choice to take books home (or not) completely to the students. She made the taking of books home a regular routine for Andre and many of the other children, and she began to speak to parents when they came to school to bring or pick up their children about their need to read these books at home and to encourage their children to practice or pretend read them. When it was clear that this home support might not be available for certain children, she found time during the day to make sure that she read the books the children would take home.

Summary

As the examples show, most of the reenactments of books during the pretend-reading curriculum genre were collaborative in nature. Students supported each other, seeming to know the appropriate amount and kind of help needed. They learned to ask for aid from peers, but they were also quite good in letting others know when they did not want assistance.

In addition, Dee had many opportunities to successfully assist individual readers—all children, not only Jimmy and the other Latino on whom boys we focused in this section—by providing the important one-to-one support and encouragement that these young, emergent readers required. These kinds of interactions enabled Dee to help her young readers to develop ways to express their ideas and interpretations of books, and to take up her feedback as she responded to their efforts (Wells, 1986). For instance, in the last example, Dee determined that it was okay for Andre to interpret the book mostly through the pictures, and she effectively sustained his doing so for *this* time for *this* book. She then raised the expectations for him in reading that book, telling him that the next time he had to "look at the words," that is, try to approximate the wordings of text's message (and related illustrations). She also let him know that she would be there to help him in this next step in reading. Thus, students' learning to read progressed through all of these efforts on Dee's part.

> *Dee: Unfortunately, the Andre and Angel partnership (that began with the* When I Was Sick *book) didn't last long. Angel just read with so many other classmates, and he also read a lot with Ramon. Maybe, as a teacher, I should have done more to pull Andre back into reading. I did somewhat, as the example shows, but just not enough.*
>
> *My greatest regret was in my failure to develop a more formal assessment tool to use from the beginning of my inquiry, and therefore I wasn't able to document and make valid comparisons over the year. I got started by taking my own fieldnotes, trying to write down the children's strategies and abilities. These did help me in deciding what to do for individual children, but I had trouble in being more diligent, consistent, and detailed in my notetaking. I sometimes missed important data about their progress so that a few of the children, like Andre, weren't followed up as they could have been. But, it is a real dilemma. I didn't want to put pressure on him just because he's not performing like the other children. Yet, I didn't want him to lag so much from the others either. Scaffolding all the children, as it shows, was really hard.*

STRUGGLES AT SCAFFOLDING

Although Dee felt she was successful overall in helping her students become readers, her attempts to best scaffold her students' levels of reading were not always so easily accomplished. Dee's efforts at assisting her students required an awareness of each of her students' developmental level, what emergent literacy skills each already possessed, including how an individual child viewed himself or herself as a reader. It was sometimes difficult to know exactly how to contingently respond to children's present levels of reading when their abilities and understandings in making sense of print were constantly changing (Wells, 1986; Wells & Chang-Wells, 1992). That is, to find, and not cross, the fine line in which her expertise could serve as the "best fit" (Reyes, 1991) for fostering particular children's constructions of their own knowledge was an ongoing challenge. In the next section we show interactions with two girls, at either end of the emergent-literacy continuum, to examine and illustrate some of the difficulties Dee faced in providing the appropriate scaffolding for her students.

Samantha

The first example focuses on Samantha's reading of *I Like Me* (Carlson, 1988). Samantha, a Latina child who was nearly a year older than most of Dee's other students, got lots of literacy support at home and owned many different types of books. Here, Dee and Samantha were seated on the floor with several other girls nearby. During Samantha's reenactment of the text, she often looked at Dee, signaling that she did not know a particular word. Because she knew many sight words and had already acquired many other understandings of the medium aspects of written language (the phonetic principle, directionality, word-to-word correspondence, and so forth), Samantha was not comfortable to follow the pretend-reading route that we saw employed by the boys in the previous section. Her attempts were primarily print governed as she treated the text as an object of deciphering (Ferreiro & Teberosky, 1982; Juel, 1988; Sulzby, 1985, 1996). She tended to point to each word and wanted perfect reading from print. Example 6 depicts how Samantha relied on Dee for help, and Dee's struggle to support her efforts. We begin about the sixth page of the book, until which Samantha had little trouble in reading. The illustrations identify the "I" in this book as a pig character.

Example 6

Text	Samantha's Reading (with Dee's aid)	
I like to take care of	1 Samantha:	I [looks at Dee]
me.	2 Dee:	LIKE
	3 Samantha:	LIKE TO [looks at Dee]
	4 Dee:	TAKE
	5 Samantha:	TAKE OF [looks at Dee, pointing to "care," but skips it]
	6 Dee:	CARE
	7 Samantha:	CARE OF ME.
I brush my teeth.		I BRUSH MY TEETH.
I keep clean and		I KEEP MYSELF CLEAN.
	8 Dee:	Okay. I KEEP CLEAN AND
I eat good food.	9 Samantha:	I EAT GOOD FOOD.
When I get up in the	10	WHEN I GOT UP IN THE
morning,		MORNING,
I say, "Hi, good		I [looks at Dee]
looking!"	11 Dee:	SAY
	12 Samantha:	SAY <HUH>
	13 Dee:	HI
	14 Samantha:	HI [looks at Dee]
	15 Dee:	GOOD LOOKING
	16 Samantha:	GOOD LOOKING.
I like my curly tail		I LIKE MY CURLY TAIL,

my round tummy,			ME. ...
	17	Dee:	MY
	18	Samantha:	MY [looks at Dee]
	19	Dee:	ROUND
	20	Samantha:	ROUND TUMMY
and my tiny little feet.	21	Dee:	AND
	22	Samantha:	AND MY
	23	Dee:	TINY
	24	Samantha:	TINY
	25	Dee:	LITTLE
	26	Samantha:	LITTLE FEET

{Fieldnotes, videotape, 02/02/95}

Dee's challenge, here, was to determine how to scaffold Samantha's present skills to learn new ones without simply supplying unknown words. Early in the year this might have been acceptable to help launch Samantha as a reader, as was seen in Jimmy's and other students' emerging efforts in the previous section, but was this appropriate for Samantha? For much of the book, Dee practically gave Samantha the words of the text, one word at a time. In the beginning, the initiation for help came from Samantha as she looked to Dee for the next word she was unable to decode (e.g., see lines 1–7), but later on Dee merely jumped in at Samantha's least hesitation (e.g., lines 21–26).

Adding to Dee's dilemma was her knowledge that Samantha's mother wanted her to read "real" words and told Dee that she corrected Samantha's "mistakes" in reading at home. Seemingly, Dee took a similar emphasis here. On line 7, Samantha gave a perfectly good approximation of the text—"I keep myself clean" for the book's "I keep clean." Although Dee said "okay" to Samantha's rendition, she gave her the message that it was incorrect by repeating the book's language (line 8). Moreover, because Dee was so quick to provide the actual wordings of the book, there were lost opportunities for Samantha to self-correct her reading. For example, in line 16 Samantha correctly read, "I like my curly tail," and then began another part of that sentence of the book ("my round tummy") with "me." Dee quickly corrected this offering, leaving Samantha with little chance to self-correct this miscue (see also lines 12–14). Thus, Samantha thought that reading was getting all of the words correct, and Dee, here, did little to show reading in a different way by modeling strategies that Samantha could use when she was stuck—to use the context more to predict what a word might be, or to read around an unknown word and then consider what that word might be, and so forth—that would better facilitate her development as a reader.

Teresa

On the same day of Samantha's reading (Example 6), Dee read with Teresa, an African-American child who was a very beginning emergent reader. As Example 7 showed, Dee was nearly totally accepting of whatever Teresa provided as approximations of *Imogene's Antlers* (Small, 1985), a book about a girl who woke up to find that she grew antlers during the night.

Example 7

Text	Teresa's Reading (with Dee's Aid)	
On Thursday, when Imogene woke up, she found she had grown antlers.	1 Teresa:	(... ...) ... I HAD THESE THINGS ON TOP OF MY HEAD.
	2 Dee:	Okay.
Getting dressed was difficult,	3 Teresa:	MY SHIRT GOT CUT ——MY SHIRT HAD (...) [bends down very close to the book, looking intently].

.... [There are many interruptions as several students come over to Dee asking questions.]

Text	Teresa's Reading (with Dee's Aid)	
and going through a door now took some thinking. Imogene started down for breakfast... but got hung up.	4 Teresa:	(... ...) OUT OF THE DOOR. [turns page] SHE SLIDE DOWN THE STAIRS.[turns page] SHE HUNG ON THE THING.
	5 Dee:	Okay, this is the light fixture [pointing to the picture]
"OH!!" Imogene's mother fainted away.	6 Teresa:	IT WAS [looking intently at the left-hand page while pointing to words on the right hand page]
	7 Dee:	[pointing to the words on the right-hand side page] IMOGENE'S MOTHER FAINTED AWAY.
The doctor poked, and prodded, and scratched his chin. He could find nothing wrong.	8 Teresa:	[turns page] AND THE DOCTOR CAME.
	9 Dee:	Okay.

.... [Teresa reads the next page and then they are disturbed by other children. Teresa continues to read, but realizing that she had skipped a page, she goes back to it.]

Her brother, Norman, consulted the encyclopedia, and then announced that Imogene had turned into a rare form of miniature elk! Imogene's mother fainted again and was carried upstairs to bed.	10 Teresa:	THE BROTHER WAS THINKING——THE BROTHER WAS READING A BOOK. HE HAD TO DO HIS HOMEWORK.
	11 Dee:	Oh, okay. That's a good interpretation of that. What's happening here?[pointing to the next page]
	12 Teresa:	THE MOTHER FELL OUT.
	13 Dee:	Okay, she fainted again.
Imogene went into the kitchen. Lucy, the kitchen maid, had her sit by the oven to dry some towels. "Lovely antlers," said Lucy.	14 Teresa:	[turns the page and points to the middle of the right-hand side page] THE MOM....
	15 Dee:	Okay, over here [pointing to the left-hand side page] Start at this page, from left to right.
	16 Teresa:	THE MOMMY PUT TOWELS ON THE THING. IT WAS WET. SHE PUT IT ON.

{Fieldnotes, videotape 02/02/95}

Teresa was usually reluctant to use finger pointing as she read. However, during this reading, she pointed to words on each page, but her pointing and reading did not reflect any word-to-word correspondence, and sometimes she did not begin on the left-hand side page before the right. Thus, Dee modeled the pointing of words (for example, in line 7, when she read the words on a page) and explained about the need for attending to the left-hand page first when she turned pages (in line 15).

Although Teresa pointed to words frequently in this reading, and had a reading-like intonation (Sulzby, 1985, 1996), she primarily concentrated on the pictures to create her reenactment of the book—for example, when Teresa read about a shirt being cut in line 3, and the sliding down the stairs in line 4, because such actions were depicted in the illustrations. As already noted, Dee often just accepted these picture-governed ideas, often by saying "okay" or sometimes commenting more, such as when she remarked in line 11 how she thought Teresa's interpretation of her reading about the brother's reading was a good one (in line 10).

Although Teresa's rendition showed that she was capable of creating a text that conveyed meaning, many features of Teresa's message also showed an immature level of construction. For example, in the first couple of pages she used first person pronouns—"I" and "my"—but then switched to third person ones. She also used the general noun, "thing," several times—in lines 1, 4, and 16. Dee offered some vocabulary words for the middle one, "light fixture," which was a chandelier shown in the picture, but was not mentioned in the text.

Because Teresa was mostly attempting to create a reading from the pictures, and still had a lot to learn about the medium aspects of written language, Dee might have focused more on the message or meanings of the text in her interactions with her. For example, instead of saying "okay" to Teresa's offering in line 1, Dee might have asked if she knew what "these things" were, perhaps pointing to the antlers in the pictures to see if Teresa could learn a new lexical term that was significant in the story. As a result, Teresa might have been able to use that wording throughout the book instead of "thing" (e.g., in line 16). Dee might have intervened differently in line 11, too, maybe by getting Teresa to look at an alternative interpretation to the one that she gave (by suggesting that maybe the brother attempted to look into the books to find out the cure for Imogene's present predicament instead of just doing his homework). Or, Dee might have done more of what she did in the last part of line 11—get Teresa to consider what was happening next in the book, and then connect what Teresa approximated ("The mother fell out" in line 12) with the meanings and vocabulary of the book ("she fainted again"). Thus, as with Samantha, Dee missed opportunities to better scaffold Teresa's level of reading performance.

Of course, it is so easy to reflect on better responses after the fact, and for the most part Dee was quite successful in offering appropriate support, as the examples in the previous section illustrated. However, these two examples are provided here to illustrate the challenges Dee faced in fostering reading for Samatha and Teresa, as well as all of the other children in this urban kindergarten

Dee: I think that the hardest part of my inquiry was trying to assess and best scaffold all of the students when their understandings where changing all of the time. For Samantha, I tried to get her to take risks to make meaningful miscues, and not simply to become a word caller. For Teresa, who had had no preschool experience and got little or no support at home, I tried to support Teresa's imagination and enthusiasm to read by making sure that she did not choose books that were too difficult for her and that she tackled mostly ones that I had read aloud to the class several times.

ALL CHILDREN CAN BECOME READERS

At the beginning of the year, many of the children in Dee's urban-kindergarten classroom were reluctant readers, especially the boys. At the end of the year, all of her students saw themselves as readers, engaged in reading-like behavior—they saw reading as socially valued. Although there were varying abilities in reading among the children, they developed increasingly sophisticated strategies to figure out words and to create orally "writtenlike language" (Sulzby, 1996). Even though few read from print at the end of school year, they still learned many concepts and principles of written language and acquired a lot about the nature of "book language" (Pappas & Brown, 1987)—they learned how books work and what readers do. Thus, even the few ESL learners in the class profited from the reenactments because they could try out their own English versions of books that they heard Dee and their classmates read-aloud. That is, having repeated opportunities to self-control and self-repair language approximations was valuable in supporting their second-language learning (Carger, 1993; Shonerd, 1994).

We argued that these students' achievements were primarily accomplished collaboratively. Dee constructed a curriculum genre where students were encouraged to reenact books of their own choosing *and* she insisted that she and their peers could help each other in these literacy experiences. Dee's approach in her inquiry demonstrates that all children—even those who were not yet interested or motivated in such literacy practices—possess emergent skills on which a teacher can sustain and build. However, as she learned, such an enterprise involves a constant struggle to find the best forms of scaffolding.

Throughout the year, Dee modified the structure of the pretend-reading curriculum genre, for example, adding a time for her students to read to the whole class. This change and others—for example, the creation of certain reading buddies, and the practice of taking books home to practice—frequently began as student initiations that she refined and extended. Teale and Sulzby (1986) argue that we need to "legitimize all children's abilities to develop and build their own roots of literacy" (p. 13). Dee believed in, and acted out, this premise. Turner (1995) noted that, although there has been much debate and research as to which are the most effective literacy tasks and experiences to foster children's literacy development, much less attention has been directed towards their motivational effects. Clearly, Dee's pretend-reading curriculum genre provided the kind of classroom contexts that positively affected her students' effort, persistence, and concentration, thereby fostering their literacy understandings. Thus, reading became a valued social practice and students became better and better at it.

Dee: I think that more than anything, my inquiry confirmed my belief that my kids have the same abilities as children in the suburbs. You don't have to change your expectations about their learning. They just need to be stimulated the right way. Of course, a major part of my inquiry was trying to determine exactly what that "right" way was for my students, who were so diverse in their interests and who had different initial and ever-changing capabilities in reading. My inquiry into pretend reading has taught me that boys could be motivated to be readers even if they enter kindergarten with reluctance. I learned how to get students to stay involved in their pretend-reading routines. One was to let students continue Angel's idea of reading-aloud to the class. The demand was so great that I had to have a sign-up sheet to schedule them all in. A by-product of this was that students wanted to take books home to practice reading in preparation to their scheduled turns. I had not allowed that initially, but I did so when they seemed so motivated and excited. In addition, students came up with the idea of reading to other classes, and even to the principal, which we did.

I also learned that I need to think more about the books I read and made available for the children. Except for the Daddies *book, I didn't expose the children to informational books until toward the end of the year. Also, I have to think more about using some of the books I did use.* When I Was Sick *and other books like it are troubling me now. They did help to launch some of the children in reading, but then many kids also got stuck in reading them, afraid to risk reading a more complex, richer, and better piece of literature. So, I have to think more about this. I certainly need to get more books for the classroom library.*

REFERENCES

Bloome, D., & Bailey, F. (1992). Studying language and literacy through events, paricularity, and intertextuality. In R. Beach, J. Green, M. Kamil, & T. Shanahan (Eds.), *Multiple disciplinary perspectives on language and literacy research* (pp. 181–210). Urbana, IL: National Conference on Research in English.

Bloome, D., & Egan-Robertson, A. (1993). The social construction of intertextuality in classroom reading and writing lessons. *Reading Research Quarterly, 28,* 305–333.

Carger, C. L. (1993). Louie comes to life: Pretend reading with second language emergent readers. *Language Arts, 70,* 542–547.

Carlson. N. (1988). *I like me!* New York: Puffin Books.

Clay, M. (1979). *Reading: The patterning of complex behaviour.* Portsmouth, NH: Heinemann.

Cochran-Smith, M. (1984). *The making of a reader.* Norwood, NJ: Ablex.

Dahl, K., & Freppon, P. A. (1995). A comparison of inner-city children's interpretations of reading and writing instruction in the early grades in skills-based and whole language classrooms. *Reading Research Quarterly, 30,* 50–74.

Doake, D. B. (1985). Reading-like behavior: Its role in learning to read. In A. Jaggar & M. T. Smith-Burke (Eds.), *Observing the language learner* (pp. 82–98). Newark, DE: International Reading Association.

Elster, C. (1995). Importations in preschoolers' emergent readings. *Journal of Reading Behavior, 27,* 65–84.

Ferreiro, E., & Teberosky, A. (1982). *Literacy before schooling.* Exeter, NH: Heinemann.

Greenspun, A. A. (1991). *Daddies.* New York: Philomel.

Hillman, J. (1989). *When I was sick.* Crystal Lake, IL: Rigby.

Holdaway, D. (1979). *The foundations of literacy.* Sydney, Australia: Ashton Scholastic.

Juel, C. (1988). Learning to read and write: A longitudinal study of 54 children in first and second grade. *Journal of Educational Psychology, 80,* 437–447.

McKenzie, M. (1977). The beginnings of literacy. *Theory into Practice, 16,* 315–324.

Panofsky, C. P. (1994). Developing the respresentational functions of language: The role of parent-child book-reading activity. In V. John-Steiner, C. P. Panofsky, & L. W. Smith (Eds.), *Sociocultural approaches to language and literacy: An interactionist perspective* (pp. 223–242). Cambridge, England: Cambridge University Press.

Pappas, C. C. (1993). Is narrative "primary"? Some insights from kindergartners' pretend readings of stories and information books. *JRB: A Journal of Literacy, 25,* 97–129.

Pappas, C. C., & Brown, E. (1987). Learning to read by reading: Learning how to extend the functional potential of language. *Research in the Teaching of English, 21,* 160–184.

Pappas, C. C., Kiefer, B. Z., & Levstik, B. S. (1999). *An integrated language perspective in the elementary school: An action approach.* New York: Longman.

Purcell-Gates, V. (1986). Three levels of understanding about written language acquired by young children prior to formal instruction. In J. Niles & R. Lalik (Eds.), *Solving problems in literacy: Learners, teachers and researchers. Thirty-fifth yearbook of the National Reading Conference* (pp. 259–265). Rochester, NY: National Reading Conference.

Reyes, M. de la Luz. (1991). A process approach to literacy instruction for Spanish-speaking students: In search of a best fit. In E. F. Heibert (Ed.), *Literacy for a diverse society: Perspectives, practices, and policies* (pp. 157–171). New York: Teachers College Press.

Selkowe, V. M. (1985). *Spring green.* New York: Lothrop, Lee & Shepard.

Shonerd, H. (1994). Repair in spontaneous speech: A window on second language development. In V. John-Steiner, C. P. Panofsky, & L. W. Smith (Eds.), *Sociocultural approaches to language and literacy: An interactionist perspective* (pp. 82–108). Cambridge, England: Cambridge University Press.

Small, D. (1985). *Imogene's antlers.* New York: Scholastic.

Smith, F. (1988). *Joining the literacy club.* Portsmouth, NH: Heinemann.

Sulzby, E. (1985). Children's emergent reading of favorite storybooks: A developmental study. *Reading Research Quarterly, 20,* 458–481.

Sulzby, E. (1996). Roles of oral and written language as children approach conventional literacy. In C. Pontecorvo, M. Orsolini, B. Burge, & L. B. Resnick (Eds.), *Children's early text construction* (pp. 25–46). Mahwah, NJ: Lawrence Erlbaum Associates.

Sulzby, E., & Teale, W. (1991). Emergent literacy. In R. Barr, M. L. Kamil, P. B. Mosenthal, & P. D. Pearson (Eds.), *Handbook of Reading Research, Vol. II* (pp. 727–757). White Plains, NY: Longman.

Taylor, D. (1983). *Family literacy.* Exeter, NH: Heinemann.

Teale, W., & Sulzby, E. (1986). *Emergent literacy: Writing and reading.* Norwood, NJ: Ablex.

Turner, J. C. (1995). The influence of classroom contexts on young children's motivation for literacy. *Reading Research Quarterly, 30,* 410–441.

Wells, G. (1985). Preschool literacy-related activities and success in school. In D. R. Olson, N. Torrence, A. Hildyard (Eds.), *Literacy, language and learning: The nature and consequences of reading and writing* (pp. 229–255). Cambridge, England: Cambridge University Press.

Wells, G. (1986). *The meaning-makers: Children learning language and using language to learn.* Portsmouth, NH: Heinemann.

Wells, G., & Chang-Wells, G. L. (1992). *Constructing knowledge together: Classrooms as centers of inquiry and literacy.* Portsmouth, NH: Heinemann.

Wood, A. (1984). *The napping house.* San Diego, CA: Harcourt.

Chapter 12

Creating Ways to Individualize Teacher Response in Various Group Reading Experiences for Second Graders

Jane Liao

Dian Ruben

Renuka L. Mehra

Renuka: In September I had my 28 second-grade students involved in a space unit. Many of them had been with me when I taught them in first grade, but I had new students as well. As students were engaged in their own solar-system research projects, I was aware that their literacy abilities were quite diverse—ranging from those who were emergent readers to those who were reading at a third-grade level. However, although some were unable to read conventionally the various books we used, they were all able to share the knowledge they had learned about space. This unit led me to be concerned with finding ways to provide instructional activities where

---

The introduction chapter of this book provides the theoretical and methodological background for the larger collaborative school–university action-research project and this chapter about Renuka's inquiry on individualized reading instruction within collaborative group contexts. See also the last chapter, which further discusses the implications of Renuka's inquiry—as well as those of the other teacher researchers.

279

student knowledge (no matter what level) was recognized and shared while
still being able to address my students' very different instructional needs. In
my inquiry, I wanted to figure out how I could still have reading experiences
in a collaborative way—because I believed that it was important that chil-
dren interact with their peers and me to construct knowledge together—and
also to combine the goal of providing one-to-one instruction for students.

Renuka's inquiry involved creating experiences so that she could individualize reading instruction within group instructional settings. She wanted
to take on the role of *teacher as responder* (Lindfors, 1980), scaffolding
her individual students to move beyond their current limits, but she also
wanted other students to be involved in providing this support. Thus, collaboration among students was also an important facet of her role of responder. That is, believing that readers needed other readers to become
active and critical readers, she sought to create collaborative activities
that would promote inclusive learning. Exchanging others' ideas regarding the books to be read would contribute to the development of deeper
levels of understanding (Barnes, 1993; Hill & Hill, 1990).

Underlying Renuka's inquiry was an apprenticeship-learning model
(Rogoff, 1990) where learners had opportunities "to work collaboratively
under expert guidance and with more knowledgeable peers within an apprenticeship process" (Bayer, 1990, p. 11). Such a view promotes language
as an important tool—to help students make connections of new ideas to
prior knowledge and to foster their analyzing, clarifying, and evaluating various group members' conflicting points of view (Wells, 1990, 1998; Wells &
Chang-Wells, 1992; Wertsch, 1991). This perspective enables the co-con-
struction of meaning to be primary and makes the discourse, in which this
knowledge is collaboratively crafted, a vehicle for both validating and modifying students' understandings (Gavelek & Raphael, 1996; Pierce & Gilles,
1993; Wells, 1993, 1994; Wells & Chang-Wells, 1992).

TRYING OUT SMALL-GROUP READING

In the beginning she organized her 28 students of varying ability into
small heterogeneous reading groups of 5 to 6 members. One group per
weekday sat on the rug in a circle with Renuka, then each child took a
turn reading. She wanted to have literature circles, but had to resort to
using basal readers in this activity because of the lack of multiple copies
of trade books available to her. However, within a month or so Reuka
abandoned this arrangement when it came off like traditional teacher-directed, round-robin reading.

Her initial instructional goal for this grouping had been worthwhile.
She had felt that the small groups would enable her to individualize instruction and assess students' reading abilities, while still maintaining opportunities for students to interact with, and receive help from, their

peers. Unfortunately, sustaining the balance between providing teacher-led, one-to-one instruction and encouraging student colearning was problematic. Students' different ability levels in these groups, which Renuka viewed as a positive and essential facet in coconstructing knowledge, became extremely troublesome within this traditionally-structured reading activity.

The heterogeneity of the group acted against Renuka's desire to have students participate more in supporting the reading of their peers. On one hand, as higher-level readers jumped at the chance to assist by doing the reading *for* those peers who were having difficulties, Renuka had to ask them to let the less-able readers read on their own unless such aid was requested. On the other hand, the emergent readers were unhappy with the pace of reading; they felt that the group was reading too quickly, and frequently asked that it be slowed down. Moreover, because there was a need for Renuka to model appropriate ways for students to guide each other, most of the time she ended up providing most of the assistance for students or doing most of the reading when the basal passages were too advanced for most children's abilities. Thus, in many exchanges Renuka's role in group reading became dominant, and student-to-student interactions were minimized, making it impossible for her to realize her initial intent for her students to support each other. In addition, because group reading seem to emphasize correct reading, less attention was given to children's skills in comprehending or understanding the texts that the children were reading.

Thus, the *response* to literature, which Renuka initially had in mind when she began her inquiry, went off track as she and her students attended primarily on the decoding dimensions of reading. As a result, she decided to address oral reading instruction in another part of her reading program, and she returned to viewing individual instruction more within a response-to-literature approach as the goal of her inquiry. Subsequently, three other activities—interactive reading-aloud sessions, student-response journals, and small-group projects that served as extensions to a read-aloud book—were implemented with more success. This chapter describes these efforts to accomplish Renuka's aim to individualize instruction—or become a teacher-as-responder model—within group instructional formats.

PROVIDING INDIVIDUAL RESPONSE WITHIN THE TEACHER-LED READING-ALOUD CURRICULUM GENRE

As Renuka changed direction in her inquiry, she chose a particular time during the day (every day for 40 minutes) when some of her students were out of the room for a particular class. The remaining 18 students were still quite diverse in their abilities, so she felt that she might be more successful in trying out new ideas with this smaller group. Renuka's "new" inquiry was threefold: she studied her reading-aloud of *Ramona Quimby, Age 8* (Cleary, 1981); she examined how she individually interacted with students while they wrote journal responses to chapters of this book; and finally she worked with children in small-group extension projects after the book had been completed. In this section we focus on the reading-aloud sessions—the other two experiences are covered in the following sections.

During the previous year, she, and other teachers in the project, investigated how to develop more collaborative, interactive reading-aloud sessions. Thus, part of her present inquiry continued these prior efforts. Response-based approaches to literature deemphasize teacher transmission of literary knowledge as an object, and are also unlike skills methods that identify literal aspects of stories by having students summarize content or vocabulary (Cox, 1997; Many & Wiseman, 1992). Renuka's way of interaction in these reading-aloud sessions was to provide opportunities for students to initiate their views about, or reactions to, the story—to see literature as a lived-through experience (Rosenblatt, 1978). In doing so, she also created spaces for herself to contingently respond to specific students' contributions, thereby coconstructing meanings of a book (Wells, 1998; Wells & Chang-Wells, 1992). The goal, then, was to promote dicussions that served as "grand conversations" (Eeds & Wells, 1989) between Renuka and her students.

Creating Reading-Alouds for Considering Vocabulary and Content Within a Response Approach

In her reading-aloud sessions of the *Ramona Quimby* text, students eagerly initiated their own comments and questions. They also asked about particular vocabulary, as Example 1 illustrates. Here Renuka read chapter 6, about half way into the book, where Ramona came to school not feeling well. Ramona had oatmeal for breakfast, so when she saw the classroom jars of blue oatmeal (in which fruit-fly larvae were housed), she began to feel even worse. As the excerpt began, Renuka interrupted her reading to ask students to predict what was going to happen, and as part of their response, a student asked, "What is 'dreadful' mean?" As this was resolved, a prediction was offered, and then a student-initiated rationale for this prediction was presented, which Renuka addressed.

Example 1

1 Renuka: GO AWAY, BLUE OATMEAL, THOUGHT RAMONA, AND THEN
            SHE KNEW THE MOST TERRIBLE, HORRIBLE, DREADFUL,
            AWFUL THING THAT COULD HAPPEN WAS GOING TO HAP-
            PEN. What might that be?....

....		[Renuka asks then this of a particular child, Ana, who does not response; she then asks the class in general.]
2	Renuka:	What could that possibly, possibly be? That she is thinking something is dreadful … awful is going to happen.
3	Cm1:	What is "dreadful" mean?
4	Cm2:	She (... ...).
....		
5	Renuka:	What do you think is going to happen to Ramona? (***), what do you think is going to happen? Why don't you help each other here? (...)?
6	Cm:	It's gonna happen for....
7	Renuka:	Something dreadful she thinks is going to happen....
8	Cm:	Something bad.
9	Renuka:	And yeah....
10	Cm1:	Something awful?
11	Renuka:	[reading the text again] AND THEN SHE KNEW THAT {SOME-THING}——THE MOST TERRIBLE, HORRIBLE, DREADFUL, {AND} AWFUL THING THAT COULD HAPPEN WAS ABOUT TO HAPPEN. What was——what might that be? (...).
12	Cf:	Maybe what you just said, that what she thinks will happen *will* happen. Maybe it will happen to her.
13	Cm:	(... ...).
14	Renuka:	What do you think that might be, (...)? What do you think that might be?
15	Cf:	The teacher might call her a nuisance.
16	Renuka:	Oh, again?
17	C:	Again.
18	Renuka:	Do you think that will be awful for Ramona?
19	SCs:	Yeah.
20	Renuka:	I think she is going to feel terrible about that.
....		[There is a student interruption that is dealt with.]
21	Cf:	I think I know why the teacher maybe wants to call her that. Because she said, "go away blue oatmeal" right now.
22	Ramona:	Oh, she's——actually it's——you know what? When you look at——look at the line. [showing the actual print in the book and everyone moves in to see the book] Do you see that GO WAY, BLUE OATMEAL? Is that in quotation marks?
23	C:	Yeah. No.
....		[There is a discussion about the fact that there aren't any quotations marks, which includes examining the function of quota-

tion marks versus exclamation marks, and then Renuka returns to how to interpret the text that lacks the quotation marks.]

24	Renuka:	When you are saying something. But she's obviously not saying something because I don't see any quotation marks. So what do you think she's doing, "go away, blue oatmeal"?
25	Cs:	(··· ···).
26	Renuka:	She's thinking it because see what it says after that. GO AWAY, BLUE OATMEAL....
27	Kenneth:	Let me see it.
28	Renuka:	THOUGHT RAMONA.
29	Cs:	[Students are all looking at the book, talking at the same time.]
30	Renuka:	Right here [holding up the book]. GO AWAY, BLUE OATMEAL, and there's no quotations marks there, THOUGHT RAMONA. So she's——what is she doing? [pointing to her head]
31	Cm:	Thinking.
32	Ramona:	Okay. Let's see what happens. {Videotape, 02/02/95}

In this case, Renuka interrupted the reading to ask students to predict what might be going to happen next. In line 3, C1 asked about the meaning of "dreadful." Another student offered an answer (line 4), which unfortunately was inaudible, but might have had something about "bad"—which is mentioned by another student in line 8—or maybe even "awful" (line 10)—which C1 might have repeated as a question.

At any rate, students frequently asked their own questions about certain vocabulary or other aspects of the book, or just offered comments, because Renuka made the read-alouds a safe place. However, we included subsequent discourse in this example because it also showed how frequently she supported and contingently responded to various guesses students might have had. For example, in line 15, a child suggested that the dreadful thing that might happen next to Ramona could be that the teacher might call her a nuisance. This is a reasonable prediction because Ramona overheard her called this by the teacher in an early chapter, and the title of the chapter the class read was "Supernuisance." Renuka accepted this possibility, but when a student offered a rationale for this prediction in line 21—"I think I know why the teacher maybe wants to call her that. Because she said, "'go away blue oatmeal' right now"—Renuka worked to help them understand why this explanation might not be justified. Tactics such as going back to the author's words and even looking at the print itself to examine its punctuation showed how predictions could be evaluated. Thus, in these interactive reading-alouds, Renuka responded to individual students' ideas but also modeled various reading strategies that they could use in the future.

Students may have felt comfortable asking vocabulary questions in read-alouds because Renuka also posed her own when she thought that students might not understand a word that was critical to the story's meaning. However, Renuka's ways of asking about vocabulary did not lead to statements that defined unfamiliar words; instead they led to discussions about the story's content. Example 2 shows how this occurred about her asking about the word "exasperation." This happened at the very beginning of chapter 2 when Ramona's mother told Ramona to be nice to Willa Jean, the 4-year-old sister of her friend, Howie. Ramona stayed at their house after school each day until Ramona's parents picked her up, and Romana had trouble dealing with Willa Jean.

Example 2

1	Renuka:	What does it mean, "she asked in exasperation"? [reading again from text] "MOTHER, DO YOU HAVE TO SAY THAT EVERY SINGLE MORNING?" SHE ASKED IN EXASPERATION. Does anyone know that? What do you think? How does she feel about that, when her mother tells——every morning her mother tells her something?
2	C1:	Like a kid….
3	Renuka:	Now she feels like a little kid. But … does she want to hear that from her mother?
4	Cs:	No!
5	Renuka:	No she doesn't!
6	C2:	Like a big grown up!
7	Renuka:	That was one of the problems that she had, didn't she? She doesn't really want to be….
8	C3:	She doesn't really want to be eight….
9	C4:	Eight.
10	Renuka:	Eight and responsible for those jobs, right! And one of them was what? Taking care of whom?
11	Cs:	Willa Jean!
12	Renuka:	Willa Jean, okay. [continues reading] … SHE ASKED IN EXASPERATION. DEEP DOWN INSIDE WHERE SHE HID HER DARKEST SECRETS, RAMONA SOMETIMES LONGED TO BE HORRID TO WILLA JEAN. {Videotape, 12/08/94}

So here Renuka asked about the word "exasperation," but she asked it by eliciting students' views about what Ramona must be feeling and thinking in the context of the story so far. Renuka did it in a way that had students being concerned with both plot and character development. She accepted all student offerings—"like a little kid," "like a big grown-up," "she does-n't really want to be eight." In each case she sustained and extended them, thereby coconstructing new meanings. Thus, Renuka's responses to student guesses were not critical. Rather than tell students that their definitions were correct or incorrect, she often followed-up with her direct questions about a word meaning with questions about the information in the story. In this manner, she modeled how readers use context clues to help understand new vocabulary, and she engaged students' participation in the use of this reading strategy. Moreover, she found a way to do this by invoking an aesthetic response (Rosenblatt, 1978) from the students to the book.

Some Vulnerabilities in Teacher Scaffolding: Wanting Children to Discover the "Right" Answer

However, some of Renuka's questioning about content could be seen as being problematic. Although she rarely denied the validity of what children offered, she sometimes seemed to be waiting for them to come up with a particular answer she had in mind. This can be seen in the next example, which is also from chapter 2, a few pages after the part of the book that was discussed in the previous example, when Renuka asked about a "big problem in the story." Here, in Example 3A, to save space, we summarized students' responses and we concentrated on the ways that Renuka tried to push her agenda.

Example 3A

1 Reunka: AND EVEN THOUGH HER FAMILY UNDERSTOOD, RAMONA STILL DREADED THAT PART OF THE DAY SPENT AT HOWIE'S HOUSE IN THE COMPANY OF MRS. KEMP AND WILLA JEAN. Is that a big problem in the story? So far, does that seem to be a big problem?

2 Cm: Yes!

3 Renuka: Yes? Because what? How do you know it's a big part in the story? Or a big problem in the story? How do you know?

....   [Students venture a number of guesses that all seem to answer Renuka's question. They say that it's a problem because Ramona has to take care of Willa Jean; that people get tired and can't do that; that Ramona hates to do all the jobs she has to do now that she's 8, and particularly that she has to be nice to Willa Jean. None of these answers seem to satisfy Renuka.]

4 Renuka: I know she (Ramona) says that but how do we know that it's such a big problem for her? How does the author convey this to us? How does the author convey that to us?

....   [This question again draws responses similar to the ones sum-
               marized above——namely, Ramona has a problem about going
               to Howie's house because she has to take care of people and has
               to do all the jobs.]

5   Renuka: [interrupting and shaking her head negatively] You're repeating
               the same thing I just finished saying, again and again and again.
               You're not listening. Yes, it is a problem for her, she's already
               said that, and so have five others. But how does this author tell
               us, other than saying that [Ramona] has to take care of Willa
               Jean? How do we know that this is a big problem of Ramona?
               {Videotape, 12/08/94}

What is interesting is that Renuka told the children that they were "not listening" to her questions, when, in fact, that did not appear to be the difficulty at all. That is, it was more the case that Renuka seemed not to be able
to express clearly what she wanted them to consider. The children, however, were not put off by her remarks and continued to try to guess at what
Renuka's point might be. To each of several responses from students
about the content of the story, Renuka followed-up by incorporating that
student's answer and then repeated some variation on her question about
the author's methods or craft. When it appeared that the children were unable to arrive at the "right" answer she sought, she finally stated the answer herself—see Example 3B.

Example 3B

1   Renuka: How does the author tell us that it's irritating for Ramona to be
               taking care of Willa Jean? How do we get that message from
               her?

2   Cm: Willa Jean——I think Willa Jean is bad and is——she gotta
               ummmm … tell her how to learn things.

3   Renuka: Okay. And one time we learning a little bit about Willa Jean's
               personality, not an easy personality. But does the author bring it
               up again and again and again?

4   Cs: Noooooo!

5   Renuka: From the first chapter to this chapter, how many times have we
               heard that she does not like Willa Jean? A few times? Is she try-
               ing to convey that to us by telling us repeatedly?

6   Cs: [agreeing with Renuka as she shakes her head in a yes] Yes!

7   Renuka: Yes. She tells us in about three or four places in one chapter and
               now we're starting the second chapter and we hear about it
               again. So she is trying to tell us by writing about it again so that

we don't forget what problem it is that Ramona is facing with
Willa Jean.
{Videotape, 12/08/94}

Summary

Renuka worked on developing interactive reading-aloud sessions when her
students had ample opportunities to share their own reactions to the
book. She also had many occasions to respond to their efforts in ways that
demonstrated various modes of engaging a text as a reader. There were discussions of vocabulary, of content, and of how the content of the book related to children's own experiences. In addition, Renuka also included
attempts to make explicit to the children how an author signals to readers
important points (e.g., by repeating Ramona's feelings about Willa Jean).
By calling her students' attention to a variety of reading strategies during
the discussions, she was able to address the broad range of literacy abilities of her students.

In many ways, Renuka attempted to create a teaching approach that
Many and Wiseman (1992) recommend—to include or integrate the experience or aesthetic response to literature with the critical analytic or efferent stance so that students "at the same time bring to the reading event
understandings and capabilities which inform and enlighten the depth of
their aesthetic literary experiences" (p. 284). As Examples 3A and 3B indicated, sometimes there were vulnerabilities in this approach. Yet, her students never seemed to daunted by issues such as these and they always
jumped into the fray.

*Renuka: I guess it wasn't my intention to get them to my correct answer
in Example 3B, but, in retrospect, it certainly sounded like that I did do that.
My idea was to direct them to this big problem or main idea and have them
think it through. There were two things I think I probably had in my mind at
the time because I had readers so diverse. Some of them might never have
gotten the point in the story without some help; others may have needed this
attention to author craft. I was trying to demonstrate a strategy. Perhaps
here I let it go too long. When you are in it, making so many decisions, thinking on your feet, going back and forth negotiating with them on what they
think the meanings of the text might be, you don't always realize that it is going so long and that you might be running a point into the ground. And, I
guess I persisted because they persisted, and because there are so many instances that this approach had been so successful for us.*

Thus, in this very collaborative, assisted enterprise of reading- aloud,
the apprenticeship model was apparent as Renuka also urged her students
to adopt what Wells (1990) has characterized an *epistemic* orientation to

texts, one that sees meanings and interpretations as open and possible for revision. More of this was seen as she responded to her students as they made journal entries regarding the book.

RESPONDING TO STUDENT JOURNAL WRITING ABOUT THE BOOK

Another way Renuka attempted to be a teacher-as-responder and provide more individual assistance to her diverse literacy learners was to rove around the class and have miniconferences with her students while they wrote their ideas about *Ramona Quimby*. She frequently elicited aesthetic responses from them—favorite parts, predictions of what might happen next, relating experiences in their own lives, and so forth (Cox, 1997; Cox & Many, 1992).

Literature-response journals have been recommended because they can encourage students to actively foreground their personal responses to books (Rosenblatt, 1978). They serve a vehicle in which writing and reading come together, thereby motivating a range of student reactions or responses to literature (Wollman-Bonilla & Werchadlo, 1995). Journals provide a way for students to express their ideas, helping them to discover and examine their own thinking and transactions with texts (Schwartz, 1994). Journals also make it possible for teachers to recognize individual students' ideas, and at the same time to assist them to be better readers, which was a major goal of Renuka's inquiry.

Meeting the Needs of Individual Children

Renuka's conferences with children about their written responses frequently reflected her struggles to cope with the developmental levels of her students as she differentially reacted and attempted to support particular children's work. Conferences with Chandra and Dennis, who fell on the two ends of the developmental continuum regarding writing abilities, illustrate aspects of this dilemma.

Conferencing With Chandra.   Renuka finished reading aloud one of the later chapters (chapter 7, "The Patient"), and because they already read much of the book, Renuka had students choose their favorite parts so far to write about. With students who had more advanced abilities, she frequently sought more than an identification of what they liked. For example, in her conference with Chandra, who kept giving merely a summary of an event from chapter 2 that had to do with Ramona's day-care experiences at Howie's house, Renuka asked her to tell her *why* she liked it.

Example 4

1   Renuka: Okay, that's something you want to talk about. What are you go-
                ing to say about that part? What is it that you liked about that
                part?

2   Chandra: When I say....

3   Renuka: That was the part you liked. What did you like about it?

4   Chandra: I liked when they're playing dress up, but the mother said,
                "What are you doing on (...)?" Then Willa Jean said, "Dress up!"
                And she brought her some clothes and let Ramona have a ripped
                up shirt and then the boy have some slippers on so he could
                <swim> and he had on a suit and her dad's old hat and she had
                on a dress.

5   Renuka: And the last part was what?

6   Chandra: And they were getting married and she said, "Will you marry
                me?" and then she said, "You have to...."

7   Renuka: Now you've told me the story, actually you've told me——sum-
                marized the story for me. But what was it that you really liked
                about that part?

....   [The interchange continues with Chandra describing more
                about the story and Renuka asking yet two more times why
                Chandra has chosen this part of the story.]

8   Renuka: But why did you like that part?

9   Chandra: Because I——I was laughing about when he said that cause he
                said it funny.

10 Renuka: He said it funnily? So you liked that part because it was
                <stated> funny. So you're going to write about, briefly, about
                the part and then why you liked it, okay?

                {Videotape, 12/08/94}

As this example shows, Chandra persisted in summarizing the favorite
part, but Renuka kept having her provide a rationale or justification for
her choice.

Conferencing with Dennis.   To complete the same assignment,
however, Renuka adjusted her expectations for Dennis, who was a student who entered her class as an emergent reader and wrote with difficulty, using mostly invented spelling that often he himself had difficulty
deciphering. From him, she tried to elicit the description or summary of
the part he liked, which, when conferencing with Chandra, Renuka indicated was not enough.

Example 5

1	Renuka:	Okay, what is it that you're going to write about? The part that you liked best in the story?
2	Dennis:	Willa Jean.
3	Renuka:	Willa Jean? Okay, buy what about Willa Jean?
4	Dennis:	Uhmmmm … The part——here's a story that I did about Willa Jean that I couldn't finish.
....		[Dennis reads haltingly from what he has written. What he reads does not seem to be very coherent and he has difficulty reading it. Renuka has him find words that are familiar to him to facilitate further reading and discussion with him.]
5	Renuka:	Okay, point to some words that would tell me about something about the story [waiting about 30 seconds while Dennis looks for words].
6	Dennis:	[points to a word]
7	Renuka:	Okay, what's that word?
8	Dennis:	Dad.
9	Renuka:	Okay, what about Dad?
10	Dennis:	The Dad came in and says (...) and then he says that he's going to medical school....
11	Renuka:	Okay, that he's going back to school again?
12	Dennis:	[nods affirmatively]
13	Renuka:	Okay. And what was he going to do at school?
14	Dennis:	He was going to be an art teacher.
15	Renuka:	Okay. He was going to be an art teacher. Was that one of your favorite parts though?
		{Videotape, 12/08/94}

As his discussion continued with Renuka (not provided here), Dennis seemed to consider her last question, but did not affirm that this was one of his favorite parts. Consequently, in her subsequent interactions, Renuka had him identify a part that he remembered from the story, which she then followed-up on by asking him if that was one that was important to him.

Thus, throughout her roving conferences with her students of diverse ability, she accepted their responses, but then attempted to extend them by raising questions that made them think more about what they had written, assisting them go beyond their present efforts.

Promoting an Aesthetic Response: Relating Personal Experiences to Text Meanings

As already indicated, Renuka also asked students to relate ideas or events in the book to students' personal experiences. The prompt that evoked some of the richest responses from students was when she had them to write about a time they had been punished, which followed her reading of fourth chapter of the book ("The Quimby's Quarrel"). In this chapter, when Ramona and her sister refused to eat the tongue that the mother prepared, their parents told them that the two girls would be responsible for making dinner the following day. The end of the chapter showed the two sisters stating that they thought that having to make dinner themselves was unfair, and hoping that they might avoid this punishment by being extremely good the next day.

This was a day when all of the students were in class at this time because the computer class for some of them was cancelled. Renuka read to all of them and students who were usually there for this period had summarized the story so far. As her usual practice, Renuka circulated among the children as they wrote, conferring with them one-on-one. The two major questions she kept posing to them were: Did they feel bad about their own punishments? Did they learn anything from the experience?

Conferencing with Clarrisa. In Example 6, Clarissa (a high-ability student) read from her journal entry when Renuka dropped by.

Example 6

1	Clarissa:	WHEN I WAS PUNISHED. TUESDAY I GOT PUNISHED BECAUSE I WAS. (...) AT (...). I ALSO WAS HANGING AROUND WITH 13-YEAR OLDS AND I GOT A SMART ATTITUDE WITH THE TEACHER. AND THEY GOT——I GOT PUNISHED WITH (...). BUT THE NEXT DAY I WAS EXTREMELY GOOD.
2	Renuka:	Okay. So what is it that you made your mind about here? How did you feel about the punishment? Did you think it was right or appropriate?
3	Clarissa:	Well, yeah! But one thing I was glad.
4	Renuka:	You were glad you were punished?
5	Clarissa:	No! I was glad I did not get *whupped.* But I got punished.
6	Renuka:	At home or at school?
7	Clarissa:	At home.
8	Renuka:	Okay. And you think you're going to repeat something like that again?
9	Clarissa:	Never.
10	Renuka:	No? Why not? Why?

11	Clarissa:	Because I'd get in trouble again. My mom said the next time it happens I'll get whupped.
12	Renuka:	What did you learn from that?
13	Clarissa:	[looking down towards her notebook] Well, one thing it says in the Bible: If you don't hit your child and they do——well, you don't have to hit them every single little thing they do——but if you don't whup your child most of the time when they do something bad, that means you don't love your child. That's why my mom teaches or disciplines me. Punish them or do something to them.
14	Renuka:	So, you think you're learning something from the discipline.
15	Clarissa:	Yes.
16	Renuka:	Well, that's good. Because you're obviously taking some time to think about what you did and why you were punished.
17	Clarissa:	[Still looking down towards to her notebook, nods several times in agreement.] {Videotape, 01/09/95}

Thus, here, Renuka had students write about when they had been punished because this topic was one that was evident in the chapter she read (and would continue in the next chapter as well). However, once again Renuka did not settle on Clarissa just describing her offense and punishment, but had her and her classmates consider about it more deeply and more personally.

After the writing sessions, Renuka asked for volunteers to share their responses with their classmates. Most students were quite loud and eager in the bidding to be called on to tell their punishment stories. Renuka selected six to read. Dennis, who we met in Example 5, and with whom Renuka had not met during this journal-writing time, was chosen to present third.

Supporting Dennis' Sharing of His Journal Entry.   Renuka again scaffolded his ideas by having him elaborate on what he wrote, but what is notable in this exchange is that Dennis had little difficulty reading back what he wrote despite his use of mostly invented spelling to express his meanings. This is in contrast to his performance in Example 5, only 1 month later. Moreover, classmates seemed to follow Renuka's lead in cheering him on.

Example 7

1	Dennis:	[beaming and looking pleased with himself] I did both things. [meaning both parts of the assignment, writing about his experience being punished and making a prediction for the next chapter]
2	Renuka:	You did both things? Oh, wonderful, Dennis, oh!

3	Dennis:	Should I read both?
4	Renuka:	Yeah, please!
5	Cm:	Yeah, Dennis!
6	Dennis:	[reading word by word, pausing briefly between each word, but reading fluently without repeating or misreading the words] THE LAST TIME I WAS PUNISHED THAT WAS IN NOVEMBER AND I WAS PUNISHED FOR BEING BAD IN SCHOOL AND I COULDN'T PLAY MY NINTENDO.
7	Renuka:	How did you feel about that?
8	Dennis:	Um, I felt sad and I was crying.
9	C:	#I cried.#
10	C:	#I cried.#
11	C:	#I never cry!#
12	Renuka:	#Did you think about what you need to do about (...).# Sh—h—! I cannot hear Dennis, but I hear other voices! [redirecting her attention to Dennis] Yes?
13	Dennis:	Um, I couldn't play with nothing because I was put on punishment. And then I had to sit down so I couldn't play with none of my toys. I couldn't watch TV. (... ....). I think that the fifth one [fifth chapter] is going to be about the good Sunday [title is "Extra-good Sunday"] and they may not fight no more.
14	Cs:	[agreeing and appearing to cheer him on] Yes!
15	Renuka:	So you're thinking about a day when they don't fight. [sounding very impressed] That's very good, Dennis, for thinking of that. {Fieldnotes, videotape, 01/19/95}

In this journal-writing assignment, Renuka did not put any explicit requirements for the children to make connections between their own punishments and those of the characters in the book. However, she had them ponder their own punishments like Ramona did in the book, and this seemed to "level the playing field" for student responses. Thus, Renuka's classroom was made a safe place for students to present their thoughts to their classmates and teacher. When describing their own experiences to the class, emergent reader-writer students, such as Dennis, could be as capable as students with advanced literacy skills, such as Clarissa.

Summary

The journal-response activity that followed the reading-aloud chapters enabled Renuka to have another opportunity to take on role of teacher-as-responder. Because this was the first time these students did written journal responses, Renuka assigned prompts to elicit their ideas. However, she did provide a range of possibilities; some worked better than others in helping all students be able to express and share their responses successfully. Overall, though, in her conferences with individual students (or sometimes several students at the same table), she could provide the appropriate scaffolding to address her student-ability differences. In her interactions with them, she always raised the ante, leading from behind (Wells, 1986), trying to build on their developmental efforts. Moreover, many of these exchanges again promoted an epistemic orientation to engaging of the text. That is, in having them consider predictions or relate their own experiences with those of characters, for example, she facilitated their rethinking the meanings of the story, reacting to the potentialities of text interpretation.

Renuka: I was always asking, "Why?" when children gave responses. I think they know the "why" implicitly, but do not easily express it in their writing. Also I think they think they need to say so much more or say it in a particular way, say as in Chandra's case, when they could have simply written that they found it funny. They don't think that's somehow enough in their minds. Maybe they were so used to just summarizing or telling the story, maybe it is a developmental thing to first tell the story, or what they liked. I always tried to use the analogy of seeing a movie, telling why they liked what they had seen. I was always trying to get them to say "why" not just in journal response writing, but all the time across the curriculum.

I had had kids do written responses to reading in the past, but this was usually done in a very short-time manner. This, though, was a novel and this was the first time I had students write repeatedly as an ongoing responsibility. I gave them the prompts, but I really mixed them up. I had had diverse children, abilitywise, in previous years, but this class was nothing like that. It was even much more diverse. So I tried lots of different things to see what would work for all of the students.

SMALL-GROUP EXTENSION PROJECTS: STRUGGLES OF INTERVENTION VERSUS INTRUSION

At the end of reading the *Ramona Quimby, Age 8* book, Renuka launched small-group projects in which students had another opportunity to respond and extend their understandings and interpretations of the book. Renuka (and the student teacher she had at the time) spent a lot of time deciding on group membership.

Renuka: There were two major factors I had in mind in assigning students to groups. In each group I wanted to have one "mother hen" or leader with kids who would get along, and I wanted a mix of high- and low-ability students in each group. I had alternate groups planned in case these didn't work out, but my biggest fear was that we would have to completely rethink the groups.

I debated and debated how to group students—due to students moving, there were now 14 students—10 Latinas and Latinos, and 4 African Americans. It was such a juggling act. Some groups were easy because they congregated together. Others, I knew, would be able to hold forth in discussions of the book, but I wasn't sure about the other dimension of their having to negotiate their views with others in the group. Kids had strengths and were needy in different ways and they all had to hear each other and compromise to do the project work. Figuring that out regarding grouping was hard and not always perfect.

Four projects were created during a brainstorming session—the poem group, the TV group, the puppet group, and the play group. In some way, each project provided a means of *transmediation* (Harste, 1993; Smagorinsky & Coppock, 1995), where students could read the signs of a literary text, collaborate with others in constructing a meaning of those signs, and then create a new representation of that meaning in a different sign system. Each project offered students opportunities to engage in a different mode of thinking, to embody their ideas about the book in a new vehicle of understanding. Consequently, the extension projects once again enabled students to have an epistemic stance to the text—they could become aware of the potential multiple meanings of language (Bakhtin, 1981, 1986) by reconsidering their own interpretations of the book as they discussed and heard their group members' points of view.

When a teacher takes on the role as responder in these project contexts, he or she is constantly confronted with the question: Respond how? According to Lindfors (1990), it is frequently difficult to distinguish between "intervention" and "intrusion." In her words:

> When are we, in fact, helping (intervening) and when are we taking over (intruding)? I don't have any foolproof test for determining this. What one person sees as intervention, another sees as intrusion. Perhaps the best we can do is to be aware of the dividing line between intervening (helping) and intruding (taking over) is very thin and to ask ourselves regularly, "Am I intervening or intruding here?" (p. 304)

Renuka confronted this dilemma of intervention versus intrusion frequently throughout her inquiry, but it became much more problematic—and more apparent—in the small-group project work. We will focus on two of the four groups—the poem group and the TV group—to illustrate the complexities of group dynamics and collaboration and Renuka's response to their work. Certain issues emerged from these groups, and we show how Renuka attempted to support their work by describing and contrasting interactions.

The Poem Group

Although both groups did end up with successful, collaborative projects, the poem group seemed to have more difficulties. Initially, students favored limiting their foci to one chapter of the book, but there was disagreement as to what chapter to do—Angel, Dennis, and Marisol wanted to do "Rainy Sunday," the last chapter of the book, and Tomas wanted to do the next-to-the-last chapter, "Ramona's Book Report." Presumably to resolve this conflict, students eventually ended up writing about multiple chapters.

During that first session, Renuka asked them about how they planned to approach their project: "How are you going to make the poem?" There was little response to that. Dennis attempted an answer that focused the part he would play in reciting the poem. Renuka responded to this by reinforcing the group nature of this project. She told him, "It's not just you," and then reminded them all that they would all play a part in saying the poem together: "It's she and he and he and you. Everybody is going to have to say it together." {Videotape, 02/28/95}

Although Renuka stressed the cooperative nature of the group work, some of the things she suggested that the group do were difficult to achieve. For example, she recommended that someone reread some of the chapters, taking out the main points that could then be incorporated into the poem. The group interpreted this recommendation literally, as a direction to treat all chapters this way. This, in effect, placed most of the responsibility for leading the group work on the two more academically skilled members of the group (Angel and Marisol). Although this particular point may not have been a conscious decision on Renuka's part at this moment, it was consistent with one of the factors she considered in determining group membership, namely, that there would be a "mother hen" to supervise the work of the other children. At any rate, this decision and other guidelines, provided by Renuka to presumably facilitate a *group* effort, frequently supported instead a hierarchy within the group, with the more academically successful students devaluing and often ignoring the input from the less literate group partners.

Should the poem rhyme or not? In the beginning, Renuka suggested that the poem might or might not rhyme. The children quickly decided that it should rhyme, but they become quite stymied as to how to approach such a composing challenge. In Example 8, Renuka intervened and tried to help them in this effort. Dennis suggested that they look at main ideas from the chapters they had down on their papers, and then come up with a rhyme for them. As this excerpt began, Renuka had them think about what word could rhyme with "eight" to go with the first line, "Ramona Quimby, Age 8."

Example 8

1	Renuka:	What's the word that you want to rhyme with "eight"?
2	Tomas:	She was eight years old?
3	Cs:	Ummmm. [all appear to be thinking]
4	Renuka:	Oh, I can think of some.
5	Cs:	What?
6	Renuka:	But I'm not telling you. You tell me.
7	Angel:	[smiles]
8	Dennis:	Eight?
9	Angel:	<Six.>
10	Renuka:	[bringing her fingers to her ear and then drawing them away as she speaks] Rhyming words mean words that sound similar.
11	Angel:	Eight, eight....
12	Renuka:	It's like "eat," "hat," "mat," "pat," "rat." All those sound similar.
13	Angel:	"Ate," "eat," (...)....
14	Renuka:	#No-oo, "eat" and "eight" don't rhyme. And you decided that your group wants a rhyming poem, right?#
15	Dennis:	#"Cat" ... ... "hat" ... ... "at"....#
16	Angel:	Yeah.
17	Renuka:	How about I help you with one line and then you go for it yourself? And I don't know if I can come up with this. You have to help me. "Ramona Quimby, Age 8, Never came to school late."
18	Angel:	#[begins to write] What is it again? [looking at Renuka]#
19	Dennis:	#[rests his chin on his hand on the desk, putting his head close to Angel's arm to get a look at the paper that is nearly covered by Angel]#
20	Renuka:	Never ... came ... to ... school ... late. That's how you got it? "Never come to school ... late." Now what should the next line be? Did she meet somebody on the bus?
21	Cs:	Yeah.
22	Renuka:	Another word that rhymes with "late." Do you know another word?....
23	Angel:	"Eight"? "Eight"?
24	Dennis:	(... ...).
25	Renuka:	Do you know another word?
26	Angel:	"Eight"?
27	Renuka:	Another word for "friend." Do you know another word for "friend"?

28   Angel: Ummm.

29   Renuka: Because who does she meet on the bus?

30   Angel: That kid.

31   Renuka: Who....

32   Dennis: #Ummmm.#

33   Angel: #Danny.#

34   Dennis: The one they called the super foot.

35   Renuka: Okay. Let's see, "Ramona Quimby, Age 8, Never came to school late" ... ummmm. "On the bus, she met a mate."

36   Tomas: A "mate"?

37   Renuka: A "mate." Means it's a friend. Okay. Now ... I'm leaving you to that. I did my part which got that started. Now all you're doing is writing this because that's going to take a while. We already have a clue right here. This is telling us what those chapters are about. Take those and use one line to say something about them ... in a poem. And use that rhyming. Stick to that.

             {Videotape, 03/15/95}

Initially Renuka tried to help the group members come up with their own rhyming words and lines. However, after her reviewing what rhyming meant and seeing that they had trouble doing that, she finally provided two lines to rhyme with "eight." Thus, her quandry about how she could or should respond is clear here—the dilemma of intervention versus intrusion is apparent.

Although it was the group who chose the idea that the poem should rhyme, the project seemed like it was a teacher-directed assignment. Group members no longer felt that the rhyming aspect was something they decided on or that they could change. Very little progress occurred on the poem as this focus continued during several subsequent sessions. Only when the constraint of the rhyming was dropped, did group members feel freer and more able to accomplish the goal of writing a poem.

The TV Group

The TV-group collaboration had its difficulties, but there were less of them. Although this group also considered the whole book, the TV-project responsibilities for the nine chapters were easily and evenly divided among the three group members, Andre, Kenneth, and Jonathan. This group began listing interesting parts of each chapter, and in the following example they sorted out—with Renuka's help—how to go about the illustrations (the "TV screens").

Example 9

1	Renuka:	Maybe each one——like you read three parts, you read three parts, you read three parts. Divide the first three you take, the next three you take, and the next three you take. And you make an illustration of that. Let's go. I'll show you what I mean.
....		[Renuka and the three boys go with the paper to a spot on the floor.]
2	Renuka:	Okay, it's kind of like rolling a film.
3	Andre:	They are going to be like rolling?
4	Renuka:	Yeah. Like it'll keep going, it'll keep going ... and here they'll see your pictures. Got it?
5	Kenneth:	Yeah.
6	Renuka:	That's what I'm asking you to first decide. Who is gonna take which three parts to draw?
7	Cm:	Oh.
8	Renuka:	You decide as a group.
9	Andre:	I thought it was a chapter.
10	Renuka:	Right. Which three chapters is he going to take, and you....
11	Jonathan:	[mentioning a chapter] "The Extra-Good Sunday."
12	Renuka:	It has to be——maybe the first three, the middle, the last three. I don't know. [pointing to each of them] Or maybe last three, middle three, first three. But you need to decide that by looking at that sheet.
13	Kenneth:	We-we-we....
14	Andre:	Okay, we just put....
15	Kenneth:	...should have two pieces of information because umm....
16	Andre:	We just put ahhh....
17	Kenneth:	[listing chapters] "At Howie's House" and ummm ... "The First Day of School." He should have put ummm Ramona on the first day of school and when Howie was kicking——I mean when (...) was kicking the <seat>.
18	Renuka:	Well, you know what? You may add that if you get the first three parts. But as a group you decided that that was important. It's written down. If you were not participating in the group and did not say that at the time, it's not down on the sheet. That's why it's important that you participate, don't you think?
19	Kenneth:	[nods "yes"]
20	Renuka.	Yep. You got it. Okay.
21	Andre:	Should we put our initials on the (...)?

....   [There is more discussion as to who would be taking which
                     chapters. The boys start mentioning various chapters they
                     wanted to do, which are not the first three, middle three, last
                     three. Finally Renuka realizes what the boys are proposing.]

22 Renuka: No, no, no. Maybe I'm wrong on this. Help me out here. Okay,
               I'm thinking if he takes the first three, then he makes the first
               three chapters' pictures. If you take the middle three, then you
               make the——Are you gonna do that or are you gonna decide?
               I'll take chapters 2 and 6 and I'll take 5, 4, and 3 and I'll take....

23 Jonathan: Yeah, yeah, yeah.

24 Renuka: Any chapter?

25 Jonathan: Yeah.

26 Kenneth: I'll take "Supernuisance" and "Howie's House."

27 Renuka: Put a circle and put your initials in there. So we know.
               {Videotape, 03/15/95}

It is difficult to recognize any imbalance in participation in these interactions. Kenneth, who, because of frequent absences from school, sometimes had readjustment troubles with being included in classroom activities, was an active group member here. Because each took responsibility for three of the chapters, each contributed equally. Renuka intervened in a successful way, helping them launch the next steps of their project.

Thus, there are several areas of contrast regarding this TV-group work with the poem-group project. Unlike the poem group, the TV group was not required to *reread* the book. Moreover, being able to make illustrations—a concrete, nonwriting feature—supported the work of the TV group across sessions, which was quite different from the poem group, which had no such hands-on facet to their task.

Scaffolding of "throwing up."   The next and last example also shows how particular characteristics of the project task provided all three members to be actively engaged, and we again see Kenneth's efforts appreciated by Renuka and his classmates alike. Renuka was about to respond to Jonathan's script (to go along with one of his TV-screen illustrations), when Kenneth asked her what it sounds like when someone throws up.

Example 10

1 Kenneth: How does it sound when you throw up?

2 Renuka: You tell me.

3	Andre and Kenneth:	[make faces and disgusting sounds]
4	Renuka:	[smiling] Okay. Well, you know, if you're putting that in your thing then maybe you wanna mention that you can....
....		[A girl from another groups comes to talk to Renuka.]
5	Renuka:	Kenneth, when you——you're showing the part, you can say it that way.
6	Kenneth:	Okay.
7	Renuka:	You can say it in a dramatic way.
8	Kenneth:	You can——and you can say it to your audience and she went, "WOWWWWW," whatever you want!
....		[Renuka then directs her attention to Jonathan, who has revised a part of his script, which Andre thinks sound fine now. Kenneth has also been practicing "throwing up" and Renuka returns to more discussion on the topic.]
9	Renuka:	[to Kenneth] I bet your audience is gonna love that.
10	Kenneth:	[smiling broadly] She thrown up like——I saw somebody that throw up white vomit.
11	Renuka:	Well, depends on what they ate, right Kenneth?
12	Jonathan:	Uewww! (...) like pizza.
13	Kenneth:	Probably like uhmmm——it's something that she——I think it's yellow. And what do you call it?
14	Renuka:	I have no idea.
15	Kenneth:	I think——let's see. It's something like banana pudding.
16	Renuka:	[smiling but with a disgusting face] Ughhhh! Well! Custard you mean?
17	Kenneth:	Noooo.
18	Renuka:	[to Angel from the poem group who has come up to her, wanting help on spelling] You want to spell "nuisance"? I think Andre and Kenneth just discovered it so they can show you. [leaves group] {Videotape, 04/06/95}

While some might not think it is very educationally important to scaffold Kenneth's "throwing-up" sounds, it was an important facet of this group's performance of its project. We can also see how Jonathan revised his script as a result of Renuka's response, which is not present but only summarized in the excerpt. And, although not much was illustrated in this particular example about Andre's contributions, he was indeed an active participant when he reviewed the work of his group members and reported that it sounded fine to him.

Summary

The dynamics of the poem and TV groups were quite different, as well as Renuka's response and interactions with each group. Tomas and Dennis, the beginning reader-writer students in the poem group, still relied primarily on oral communication to gain information from, and to participate in, class. Thus, they freely verbalized as they attempted to compose lines of the poem, which would have helped the composition process, had the more literate members been more receptive to listening, responding to, and noting these two boys' suggestions. However, not only did Angel and Marisol appear to generally neglect the contributions of Tomas and Dennis, but they also often did not do their own composing within the group-project time. That is, because they seemed self-conscious about the fact that they did not know about rhyming and writing a poem very well, they did not model or demonstrate for Tomas and Dennis their processes to develop poem lines. Yet, this is one of the major advantages for mixed-ability, cooperative work and one of the reasons Renuka grouped these children as she did. Moreover, Angel, although he had high-level literate skills, seemed more dependent on Renuka's assistance than the two less literate boys, frequently seeking her guidance in his work on the poem, as can be seen in the last few interactions in Example 10 when he asked for her help in spelling "nuisance."

Nevertheless, Tomas and Dennis did develop valuable critical thinking and verbal skills because they had to work hard on advancing their arguments or points of view to their other two group members. They persisted, and these opportunities did facilitate their learning. And, once the group began to consider its performance of the poem, all members participated equally.

Thus, the projects provided another activity for Renuka to provide individual assistance within a collaborative-group format, and overall she was successful in doing so. However, as we have tried to illustrate, how to respond appropriately in these dynamic, ever-changing contexts is a complex challenge, fraught with ongoing dilemmas as to the best ways to support these young learners in becoming literate.

Renuka: It is so hard to juggle this intervention versus intrusion role. I hate it sometimes when I get in there because it's not my decision. I want them to know that they are responsible for each other in the group and somehow the decision that one makes has to be decided upon by the others. They have a hard time doing that because one or two of them decides and then they think that that's the group decision. So, I kept pointing that out. I think they got it eventually. I wanted to stay out of their groups this time as much as I could since I didn't get to do much of that during the other curricular activities. I wanted these groups to be student directed as much as possible.

Of course, I was frequently drawn in by them in their work. I felt I had to intervene—intrude?—in the poem group. They decided that the poem should rhyme, and although I showed them poems from the Shel Silverstein book, and we had read other poems, it was so hard for them. Then they got so that they thought it had to rhyme, which took me some time to realize. When I finally said that it doesn't have to be that way, they seemed to get "unstuck." The performance of this group was great and all participated. Despite the difficulties that Dennis and Tomas might have had in getting Angel and Marisol to pay attention their efforts, that process of these two having to articulate their views was what I was looking for in the group work, and I think they benefited from it.

The TV group did do better, despite the fact that Kenneth was out so much. He would be gone 2 days and then he would come back to try to enter the group work again. He would lose his script, and try to adjust to what the other two boys had been working on while he was gone. But then after the third day, he would be gone again. If these two boys seemed to marginalize him, I think it was because of these constant absences. Children really liked Kenneth and I think he really wanted to be in school, but family circumstances caused his frequent absences and he suffered for it.

In retrospect, I did intervene more than I had realized, and I guess I think how I did do that was useful and helpful for the students. I always tried to give them strategies. But organizing and monitoring successful collaborative-group work is really hard to do. One thing that helped, was that some of the groups did work a lot on their own. I had thought that the puppet group might have needed more of my help, but it functioned pretty well without me. So, although I roamed around, I was focused on what each group of kids might need from me, what I should keep an eye on. I did take anecdotal notes as I sat with them so I would know what to bring or what I thought they might consider next time. That helped. I had wanted to assess them as they participated in these groups and I think I managed to do that—and to respond to them when it was necessary—even though it was hard.

CONCLUSIONS

Overall, Renuka had success in her inquiry to develop ways to take on the role as a teacher-as-responder. However, it is important to point out how difficult this was to accomplish. Throughout, struggles to help or intervene versus to intrude or take over were present. These dilemmas were found in all three activities. In the reading-alouds she sometimes might have pushed too hard to have students "discover" her agenda. Some of her prompts were problematic for both students and Renuka in students' written-response journals. For example, she sometimes had students write summaries of portions of the book, which did not seem to be a very purposeful or authentic communicative act because it emphasized recall of the events in the book, about which everyone was knowledgeable. Thus, these summaries could be seen as more of an intrusion instead of interventions of students' own reactions to the book. However, sometimes these summaries were appropriate when the whole class ended up being present due to a cancellation of the computer class that a group of students regularly attended. These summaries also ended up being helpful to several groups in their projects because they were able to use them as beginning points for their group-project efforts. In the poem-group work, Renuka seemed to be reluctant to intervene so as not to be intrude, even though that group desperately needed her assistance. Her intervention in helping on the rhyming ended up being intrusion because that group continued on that course so long. They did get unstuck later, when Renuka finally said again to them that the poem did not have to rhyme.

Despite these difficulties, Renuka provided activities for students to engage in texts in a epistemic mode—they learned that written language could be seen as being tentative and provisional, ready for multiple and alternate interpretations and meaning. She developed ways to give individual assistance for a diverse group of literacy learners, which was the major aim of her inquiry.

REFERENCES

Bakhtin, M. M. (1981). *The dialogic imagination.* Austin: University of Texas Press.

Bakhtin, M. M. (1986). *Speech genres and other late essays.* Austin: University of Texas Press.

Barnes, D. (1993). Supporting exploratory talk for learning. In K. M. Pierce & C. J. Gilles (Eds.), *Cycles of meaning: Exploring the potential of talk in learning communities* (pp. 17–34). Portsmouth, NH: Heinemann.

Bayer, A. S. (1990). *Collaborative-apprenticeship learning: Language and thinking across the curriculum, K-12.* Mountain View, CA: Mayfield.

Cleary, B. (1981). *Ramona Quimby, age 8.* New York: Avon.

Cox, C. (1997). Literature-based teaching: A student response-centered classroom. In N, J. Karolides (Ed.), *Reader response in elementary classrooms: Quest and discovery* (pp. 29–49). Mahwah, NJ: Lawrence Erlbaum Associates.

Cox, C., & Many, J. E. (1992). Towards an understanding of the aesthetic response to literature. *Language Arts, 69,* 26–31.

Eeds, M., & Wells, D. (1989). Grand conversations: An exploration of meaning construction in literature study groups. *Research in the Teaching of English, 23,* 4–29.

Gavelek, J. R., & Raphael, T. E. (1996). Changing talk about text: New roles for teachers and students. *Language Arts, 73,* 182–192.

Harste, J. C. (1993, December). *Multiple ways of knowing: Curriculum in a new key.* Paper presented at the meeting of the National Reading Conference, Charleston, SC.

Hill, S., & Hill, T. (1990). *The collaborative classroom: A guide to co-operative learning*. Portsmouth, NH: Heinemann.

Lindfors, J. W. (1980). *Children's language and learning*. Englewood Cliffs, NJ: Prentice Hall.

Many, J. E., & Wiseman, D. (1992). The effect of teaching approach on third-grade students' responses to literature. *Journal of Reading Behavior, 24*, 265–287.

Pierce, K. M., & Gilles C. J. (Eds.). (1993). *Cycles of meaning: Exploring the potential of talk in learning communities*. Portsmouth, NH: Heinemann.

Rogoff, B. (1990). *Apprenticeship in thinking: Cognitive development in social context*. New York: Oxford University Press.

Rosenblatt, L. M. (1978). *The reader, the text, the poem: The transactional theory of the literary work*. Carbondale: Southern Illinois Press.

Schwartz, L. (1994). Reading response journals: One teacher's research. In G. Wells (Ed.), *Changing schools from within: Creating communities of inquiry* (pp. 99–127). Portsmouth, NH: Heinemann.

Smagorinsky, P., & Coppock, J. (1995). The reader, the text, the context: An exploration of choreographed response to literature. *Journal of Reading Behavior, 27*, 271–298.

Wells, G. (1986). *The meaning makers: Children learning language and using language to learn*. Portsmouth, NH: Heinemann.

Wells, G. (1990). Talk about text: Where literacy is learned and taught. *Curriculum Inquiry, 20*, 369–405.

Wells, G. (1993). Reevaluating the IRF sequence: A proposal for the articulation of theories of activity and discourse for the analysis of teaching and learning in the classroom. *Linguistics and Education, 5*, 1–37.

Wells, G. (1994). The complimentary contributions of Halliday and Vygotsky to a "language-based theory of learning." *Linguistics and Education, 6*, 41–90.

Wells, G. (1998). Some questions about direct instruction: Why? To whom? How? And when? *Language Arts, 76*, 27–35.

Wells, G., & Chang-Wells, G. L. (1992). *Constructing knowledge together: Classrooms as centers of inquiry and literacy*. Portsmouth, NH: Heinemann.

Wertsch, J. V. (1991). *Voices of the mind: A sociocultural approach to mediated action*. Cambridge, MA: Harvard University Press.

Wollman-Bonilla, J. E., & Werchadlo, B. (1995). Literature response journals in a first-grade classroom. *Language Arts, 72*, 562–570.

Chapter 13

The Rocky Road to
Grand Conversations:
Learning How to Facilitate
Literature-Discussion Groups
in Fourth Grade

Shannon Hart

Diane Escobar

Susan C. Jacobson

The "campus" of Jungman School during the 1994–1995 school year consisted of the main building and four mobile classrooms. These "classrooms" were installed in the early 1960s to serve as temporary classrooms to alleviate overcrowding in the main building. Designed to last only several years, children were housed in these trailers until the 1995–1996 school year. Our story takes place in one of those mobile classrooms, during the preceding year.

The introduction chapter of this book provides the theoretical and methodological background for the larger collaborative school–university action-research project and this chapter about Sue's inquiry on literature groups. See also the last chapter, which further discusses the implications of Sue's inquiry—as well as those of the other teacher researchers.

As you approach the mobile the first impression you get is the drabness of the trailer. The beige sides of the trailer are patched with layers of paint used to cover the graffiti, which appears several times a month. Gang insignia, declarations of love, and various names bleed through the light-gray paint that was used to cover them across the years. The trailer stands approximately 4 feet above the ground. Wooden steps were built to allow us to walk up to the door that is always kept locked. You must knock hard on the door, especially during the winter when the blower from the heater inside the trailer makes it nearly impossible to hear each other, let alone a knock on the door. Because the door has no window, one must tell the person on the other side who it is, and that person, often a student, must decide whether it is safe to allow entrance.

Once you enter the tiny trailer you are immediately bombarded by the stuff that adorns the walls and ceiling. Fourth-grade children's desks are together in groups of four or six, leaving just enough room to navigate between them. Every available space is filled with inspiring posters (e.g. "we all smile in the same language"), pictures created by students, and a list of classroom rules, and mobiles of students' artwork hang from the ceiling. As the seasons change, so do many of the pictures on the walls, yet the ambiance sends the same message: this trailer is inhabited by a teacher and students creating their own little world.

This chapter describes how the structure of the curriculum genre of literature-discussion groups evolved during the year as Sue attempted to foster student autonomy and the love of reading through genuine reflection and dialogue about novels.

WHY LITERATURE GROUPS?

Sue: When I was in college learning to be a teacher, I was taught a "new" way—that the best way to teach kids is to relate to them, not lecture them. So, I guess I've always wanted to teach this way, which is very different from the way many of my colleagues teach. And it's hard, too!

I also remember being taught in elementary school by a basal approach and I thought it was so boring. Because when I went home, Mom would read these really neat books at nighttime. And, I always wondered, "Why aren't these here at school?" Also, teachers would ask all these dumb questions, ones that were not fun. There were no questions where I could really talk about what I thought about books. That's why I decided to try out these literature groups as my inquiry. I thought that it would be another step toward teaching the way I thought it should be done. I would try to get kids to talk to each other; I would have a chance to talk to them, and we'd all get to read great books!

Literature-discussion groups (sometimes also referred to as literature circles, book clubs, conversational or peer-discussion groups, and literature-study groups) are a relatively new method for student-centered in-depth studies of literature in classrooms (Eeds & Wells, 1989; Hill, Johnson, & Noe, 1995; Leal, 1992; McMahon & Raphael, 1997; Samway & Whang, 1996; Short & Pierce, 1990; Wiencik & O'Flahavan, 1994). This method of literature study requires both teachers and students to assume new roles in the educational enterprise. Teachers must shed their roles as transmitters of knowledge to act as facilitators or guides (Freedman, 1993), while students assume the responsibility of group negotiation and interpretation of literature.

Literature groups rely on reader-response theory and a transactional approach to reading (Rosenblatt, 1976, 1978). According to Karolides (1997), "Readers are not passive spectators *of* the text but are active performers *with* the text" (p. 8). Transactions represent "lived-through" experiences with texts (Karolides, 1992; Rosenblatt, 1978). Such a process argues that meaning is both a bringing to and a taking from a text; meaning is created out of the reader–text interaction in a particular situation so that different interpretations are possible (Bruner, 1986).

The notion of literature discussion groups is also grounded in the sociocultural view of learning (Moll, 1990; Vygotsky, 1962, 1978; Wertsch, 1991), which emphasizes that learning activities take place not within individuals, but in transactions between them (Wells & Chang-Wells, 1992). As students learn how to interpret and critique literature within discussion groups, they are also learning how to understand the differing views and interpretations of others.

Moreover, literature groups are occasions for exploratory talk that supports learning (Barnes, 1992, 1993; Barnes & Todd, 1995). So much of reading instruction has stressed students' understanding the literal aspects of text or getting correct responses (Barr & Dreeben, 1991) that many students have difficulty in critically examining texts, considering other points of view, or constructing thoughtful responses to texts (Almasi, 1995). Literature groups, then, are seen as alternative arrangements to explore texts together. There are many more opportunities for students to express themselves more fully on topics they find interesting. In these grand conversations (Eeds & Wells, 1989), their *authentic* responses to literature—not ones that the teacher or an adult might have made—are promoted while students listen, examine, and consider the various multiple meanings of their peers.

EVOLUTION

How do you best facilitate genuine reflection and conversation among a group of fourth-grade students? This is the question Sue sought to answer throughout the year. In the process of answering this question she attempted to strike a most tenuous balance between teacher direction and student autonomy. One way that Sue tried to find this balance was through the structure and organization of the time devoted to literature groups. She worked to turn the responsibility for the working of the groups over to the students. This was not always an easy task, nor were the students always ready to take the responsibility. The move from one classroom structure to another does not happen overnight or without difficulties. Sometimes the conversations are not "grand" (Roller & Beed, 1994); sometimes the path toward developing literature-discussion groups can be rocky.

Coupled with her direct goal of genuine conversation about literature, Sue viewed literature groups as an opportunity to help her students acquire socialization skills. Much like one of the goals of cooperative learning (Hill & Hill, 1990), Susan hoped that the group work would foster the interpersonal skills that are necessary for good discussions of literature, but are also useful in all areas of school and life.

The entire morning was allotted for literacy activities. Typically, the literature groups happened midway through the morning. Before working in literature groups there was usually time to read the current novel together as a class. Several forms were used for this task, such as whole-group silent reading, small-group reading aloud, or buddy reading (two students taking turns reading out loud). There was also time during the morning for book extensions such as art activities or writing in student reader-response journals. The structure of activities (and time allotted for them) surrounding the literature groups' sessions varied, but they rarely affected how the literature groups themselves were organized or operated.

The students in Sue's room were heterogeneously grouped according to ability, with three to five students per group. In Sue's class of 22 students, all were Mexican American except two, a boy and girl, who were both African American. The time slated for literature groups (which occurred twice a week, mostly on Tuesdays and Thursdays) was usually broken into three phases. In the first phase, Sue typically reviewed the reading to be discussed and gave any special instructions that were necessary that day. The next phase involved the actual discussions revolving around specific questions or topics to be addressed by each group. The final phase was a whole-class debriefing about issues or questions raised in the small-group discussions. Although we may cover aspects of the first and third phases in this chapter, the second phase, or the actual literature discussions of student groups, is the major focus.

While the structure of the literature-groups curriculum genre changed across time, so too did the level of sophistication of student conversations. As the year evolved, students became more comfortable with the tasks of reading and discussing literature. Their own lives and experiences formed the basis of their interpretations of the books, and they slowly began to share these observations with their classmates. The issues raised by the students in these groups, such as racism and sexism, attest to their developing critical awareness.

There were four major stages of this evolution of creation of group literature discussions during Sue's year-long inquiry. Each stage had its own defining characteristics. For each stage, we describe the its structures and give examples of the level of student discussion and group dynamics. As you see, the path that this class traveled was not a straight and smooth one, but rather one with curves and bumps.

Sue: I had lots of difficulties in doing literature groups even though I was committed to developing them. For example, I had major problems in getting multiple copies of good literature for everyone. But, I was ready for branching out this way and dealing with the hassles. I was really sure that this was going to help my students be excited about books and become life-long readers. More than just getting good books, I really hoped that these groups would help the kids learn how to work together. It's so important for kids to know how to listen and how to share their ideas—that their ideas are even worth sharing—that I tried hard to make that an important part of this literature-group time.

STAGE 1: SLOW AND STEADY

Sue begins each year by giving herself and her students time to get to know one another. Thus, she did not begin her literature groups until the end of September. Most of the students who entered Susan's room in fourth grade had been together in third grade, where they had a more traditional teacher. For the most part, their experience with reading groups was confined to teacher-directed, basal-bound reading groups. In contrast, Sue did not lead the groups. Instead she floated from group to group, sometimes being a silent observer, other times actively participating. Because her students came from a more traditional experience, the first few months of the year were spent—frequently through reading-aloud sessions—helping them learn to read critically, to share their opinions, and to believe that their opinions were worth sharing.

The first novel read and discussed in literature groups was *Charlotte's Web* (White, 1952). This classic children's book about Wilbur the pig, who is rescued from slaughter by a creative and wise spider named Charlotte, is not a very difficult one for fourth graders and was familiar to most of the students. Students read a chapter or two ahead of the group-discussion period, and then usually wrote down their responses in their journals.

The structure imposed by Sue for the first attempt at literature groups was highly teacher directed: Each group was given a different question, written by Sue, on a sentence strip. After several minutes, Sue would announce that it was time for them to switch questions with the next group and then to discuss that question. This procedure continued until each of the groups had discussed each question.

The questions themselves were open-ended such as, "What word would you use to describe Wilbur?" and, "How would you feel if you were Charlotte and never received any attention for your work?" and, "If you could come up with a new 'problem' in the story, what would it be?" These early discussions tended to be fairly straightforward, each student taking a turn to answer the question. Their responses to the questions were generally limited to simple answers such as, "I think Wilbur was nice" and, "Wilbur was curious," or "I would feel bad if no one paid attention to my work," or "A good problem would be if Charlotte was the one going to be killed and Wilbur would have to save her." {Fieldnotes, 09/29/94}

Because this was the students' first exposure to the idea of group discussions of literature, it was quite obvious from these responses that they were not really discussions. They appeared to still be working in the traditional answer-the-question mode. For example, only when asked (by the university researchers or by Sue) did they elaborate and talk more about their ideas. Students themselves did not question each other, rather they seemed to accept what each person said and then move to the next person's answers.

Sue: I always start the year off by getting to know the kids. I do a lot of read-alouds and read individually with them to get to know where they are academically, as well as what their interests are. I didn't even start literature groups until the middle of September. I think I came up with some good questions for them to consider, but most of their answers were okay, but not very deep. I remember how discouraged I was with their progress in the beginning. Some days they seemed to do well with it, but there were other times when they just wouldn't work and all they did was play. Most of the students were reluctant readers. Most had had only basal experiences and they didn't know what the reading of literature could open up for them.

STAGE 2: ATTEMPTS TO BE MORE "HANDS OFF" ON CONTENT

By November, *Charlotte's Web* was completed and the class started a new book, *Sarah, Plain and Tall* (MacLachlan, 1985), which is the story of a motherless family who advertises for a wife and mother to come to live with them on the prairie in the 1800s. Sarah arrives from Maine and there are adjustments to be made on the part of each individual.

With a new novel came a new structure for the literature groups. During this stage, Sue moved away from the teacher direction that characterized the first stage and gave the students almost "free reign" in that she did not create specific questions for them to consider in their groups. Instead, students were encouraged to discuss topics that they thought were important.

This new structure was introduced on November 21. Sue began by explaining that they were going to discuss the book, but that this time, instead of using questions given to them on sentence strips as in *Charlotte's Web*, they were to come up with their own discussion questions.

In addition, in an attempt to move her students toward genuine discussion, Sue demonstrated what she meant by a discussion by trying to create a hypothetical situation that one of groups might have.

Example 1

1	Sue:	Now, for example, here is my group [pointing to the table of students sitting in front of her]. And I say, "You know what, I really liked this book. This was my favorite book." Then Tabitha might say, "I didn't like this book." [asking the class] Is it okay if Tabitha disagrees? It's all right, right? That's what starts a discussion. Because then I might say to Tabitha, "Well gosh, Tabitha, this was my favorite book, why didn't you like it?" Then she can say something back. She can say, "Well I didn't like it because I didn't like Jacob" or "I thought the book was boring." That's your opinion and you have a right to that opinion. So I can't say to Tabitha, "you're wrong, Tabitha."
		{Fieldnotes, videotape, 11/21/94}

For the most part, Sue attempted to show students that it was going to be okay that they might have disagreements or different opinions about the book, and that they must be respectful about these differences of opinion. However, unfortunately, she only offered as examples of "I like the book," or "it was my favorite book" responses. And, she modeled very simplistic rationales for these initial responses. There is no elaboration of why she didn't like Jacob that might refer to the author's characterization of the plot and so forth, or that if one says a book is boring, he or she has to provide strong arguments to back up this evaluation.

Perhaps that is why the subsequent group discussions tended to be problematic on two fronts. First, students didn't seem to be invested in the discussion, often leaving only a few members of the group to do all the talking. Second, the discussions continued to be stilted, each person saying what they liked or didn't like. Example 2 shows what typical discussions were like. The group consisted of two boys (Alejandro and Melvin) and two girls (Christina and Ana). As you can see, Melvin and Ana did the majority of talking about the topic of likes and dislikes:

Example 2

1	Ana:	What I liked was the characters because on every single page they um——they put like a new character in. Did you notice? They put like a new a character in——they put in Matthew, then Maggie, then Sarah. And like on every page they put a different character and ... [pausing a few seconds, but no one talks] You

		say something! [addressing Melvin, who was sitting across from her]
2	Melvin:	*You* say something! [pointing to Christina, sitting to his right]
3	Christina:	[says nothing, but stares back at Melvin]
4	Melvin:	[after several seconds, he speaks] I liked the book because ... um ... ... it was too long——no, it was short. That's why I didn't like it, it was too short.
5	Ana:	I liked the book because ... I think it was kind of interesting. It had——like, it talked about two different kinds of places. It talked about different characters, showed us some things that are like <made>. It showed us William the brother....
6	Melvin:	I liked the book because they were comparing William and Jacob, and Sarah and their old mother.
7	Christina:	No, they were comparing it to Jacob and Sarah.
8	Melvin:	No Jacob and what's his face ... William. {Fieldnotes, videotape, 11/21/94}

There was very little give-and-take interaction common to genuine discussions. Instead, Ana and Melvin seemed to be putting forth all of the effort just to think of things to say to fill the time. There were some hints of possibilities in their responses, though, but they never came to fruition. For example, maybe Ana was getting to something when she brought up the idea that there were new characters on every page, but she never tried to elaborate on this idea, and no one else seemed to be interested in following it up. Also, later, when Ana brought up different comparisons—different places, different characters, different "some things are made"—which Melvin then began to build on, by mentioning how he liked the way William and Jacob, and also Sarah and their other mother, were compared. However, these never went anywhere because Melvin and Christina subsequently just disagreed about what characters were being compared in the book. Thus, the content of the discussions was not very rich or "meaty."

Introducing "Rules" for the Process Dimensions of Literature Discussion Groups

Also during this session in November, Sue addressed process dimensions of this curriculum genre by introducing the idea of rules for literature-discussion groups. Before she turned the time over to their group discussion, she asked the class to brainstorm a list of "rules we might have to have in a group with a few other people." Sue wrote students' suggestions on the board, which eventually were transferred to a large piece of paper that was hung on the wall. Eight suggestions were made:

1. Help the group
2. Be fair
3. Listen to everybody's ideas
4. Work together
5. Be cooperative
6. Wait until people finish talking
7. Respect others
8. Don't hog the conversation

In an attempt to foster social skills and genuine conversation, Sue referred to these rules that students developed that day, throughout the rest of the year. Eventually she asked them to evaluate their groups about how well they worked as a group, based on these rules.

Later in this stage, the class began to read the book *Superfudge* (Blume, 1980). Sue moved even farther, from suggesting topics, to asking the students to "be creative and come up with your own topics of discussion. Whatever you think is interesting. Just remember to follow our rules. We're going to keep it to about 10 minutes so we don't run out of things to talk about. Then we'll see what you discussed and maybe bring them up to the big group." {Fieldnotes, 01/17/95}

Summary

Thus, in this stage, Sue tried to address both content and process aspects of literature-discussion groups. However, her advice about content was fairly vague, but she was more specific regarding process. That is, she encouraged her students to freely discuss any topic, but she had not abandoned her role of organizer, reminding them to follow the rules and specifying the amount of time allotted for discussion. It is important to note that Sue always remained in control of these latter aspects of the literature groups. It is within this structure that students had autonomy—in their realizing the rules in their groups, and in their deciding on what to talk about content.

Sue: Actually I tried to cover content more specifically with the kids. For example I had students involved in character studies. I tried a character-study table that asks about characters (Did what? When? Where? Why?) that students filled in. Also, I worked on their reader-response journal entries. In fact, one of the days we read Superfudge, *we had brainstormed a list of nine things, which we put on the board, that could serve as prompts to make these responses be more interesting. These included: telling something funny a character did, something that you didn't understand, compare characters, become the character, and so forth. However, although groups seem to be drawing on these a little from what they said in the whole-class debriefing sessions afterwards (one group specifically said that it used the character comparison), I noticed that they still seemed to be using the same old, "What did you like?," "What didn't you like?," "Who was your favorite character?" questions to guide discussions to a large degree when I roved around to observe groups. The discussions were boring—not real conversations. I think that's why I decided to change the format of group discussions by giving students the questions again. I just felt that the group discussions were just not rich enough, that they were not considering important themes and issues in the books.*

STAGE 3: SUE RETURNS TO MORE "HANDS-ON" REGARDING CONTENT; STUDENTS BEGIN TO DEVELOP BETTER CONVERSATIONS

By February the class was reading the book, *Bridge to Terabithia* (Paterson, 1977). Sue went back to controlling the discussion questions, as she had done in the beginning of the year, by giving each group a question on a sentence strip to discuss and pass. However, although this structure was similar to the early time, the level of student discussion was not. Instead of simply answering the questions, often with one-word answers as they expressed themselves at the earlier time, now students used these discussion questions to have real conversations about the questions, ones that were now also addressing important issues, such as sexism. Example 4 shows some of the discussion of a five-member group (Christina, Lisa, Melanie, Armando, and Felipe), which began with Lisa reading the question.

═══

Example 4

1	Lisa:	WAS IT FAIR FOR THE BOYS TO DECIDE NOT TO LET THE GIRLS TAKE PART IN THEIR RACE?
2	C:	Uh, no.
3	Armando:	It wasn't fair because girls can play. They can race too.
4	Melanie:	It was fair because they are the same thing. They should be treated equally and with respect.
5	C:	I know.
6	Armando:	Yeah. The only thing that is different is that they're a girl and he's a boy.
7	Lisa:	There's nothing——there's nothing wrong....
8	Melanie:	There's nothing different.
9	Armando:	I know.
10	Melanie:	Maybe they think that girls can't play because boys are better.

11	Lisa:	[very excited, at first she begins to raise her hand and then brings it down, now touching words on the sentence strip as if to make a point] Oh, probably, oh probably….
12	Armando:	Probably they think that girls….
13	Lisa:	SHHH! [putting her finger to her mouth]
14	Armando:	Probably they…. [he stops, smiles as if to say "whoops" and puts his hand over his mouth as Lisa continues]
15	Lisa:	Probably the boys think that girls don't race….
16	Armando:	Probably the boys think that she can't race, that probably that she runs too long [meaning slow?] and that (……). [his voice trailing off, sometimes talking into his hands]
17	Melanie:	Probably they think, #um#
18	Armando:	#[leans over her to address the camera] Hi!#
19	Melanie:	[pushing Armando away with her elbow continues] She can't play——that girls can't play because, um——they probably think that they're only supposed to be playing like hopscotch or jump rope.
20	Cf:	Yeah, jump rope.
21	Lisa:	And patty cake.
		{Fieldnotes, videotape, 02/07/95}

In the beginning, the group members—boys and girls alike—stated that they thought that is was not fair that girls could not race like the boys, but then they tried to give possible reasons why the boys might have felt girls should not participate. They got so excited in their exchanges that sometimes they forgot to follow the rule about letting people take turns (e.g., lines 11–15). Melanie even persisted to tell her ideas, even when Armando was doing antics toward the video camera. Moreover, as students offered different possibilities, it was clear that they were listening to each other as they built on and extended each other's ideas.

Thus, if a similar question had been posed earlier in the year, it is likely that the sentiments expressed might have been similar, but the student interaction likely would not have been nearly as complex. This sophistication developed, we believe, as the result of the students' increasing familiarity with the concept of discussion, as well as through their increasing ability to handle more challenging texts. Students also found this book extremely interesting, so the content of the book also might have sparked these better and more genuine conversations.

Sue: Well, I wasn't sure if it was good that I went back to giving the kids the questions to discuss, but when I asked them if they liked when I did it, they were enthusiastic about my doing it. They seemed even relieved in some sense.

I felt good about the discussions on Bridge to Terabithia. *They seemed much more excited in talking about it—so much so that we had to get back to some of our rules. They said that groups were too loud and complained that some people were hogging the conversation. I think before they wouldn't have cared that much if they hadn't had a turn. They struggled with that book like you wouldn't believe, but the story was so great that it just overtook that and they fell in love with it. They always referred back to it, everything was bridged to* Bridge to Terabithia. *Something would happen in the classroom and someone would refer to the book. It was constant. They also linked it to their own life experiences and to other books we read later. The teacher the next year read the book again and they still loved this story. We battled through that book because the language—the vocabulary—was difficult for them, but they wanted to it for themselves. The death issue in the book was very interesting to them.*

STAGE 4: COMING TOGETHER

The last stage of the evolution in Sue's inquiry on literature-discussion groups began in March, which was a pivotal month in her efforts to have students again have more control over the content dimensions of group discussions by introducing new procedures of process.

The month started with her reliance on the earlier structure of giving the students questions to discuss. It ended with students writing their own questions on sentence strips to pass to one another for consideration. This content variation on the structure, we believe, was the most successful one in terms of fostering student autonomy and genuine discussion.

Also, by the beginning of February, Sue began to notice that the groups were often dominated by one or two members. This was troublesome for her, because fostering social development through literature groups was always a tacit goal. She attempted to address this issue by initiating the idea of *roles* to use in the groups during discussion. Sue experimented with four jobs that different members would take on. The *Controller* (later changed to *Organizer*) was responsible for seeing that each person had a chance to answer a question. The *Writer* was to record each member's responses to questions. The *Reader* read the questions to the group and reported their responses during the whole-class debriefing time. Finally, in groups with four people, there was an *Encourager* whose job was to help the group stay on track and to compliment others' ideas. Through the roles, Sue hoped to encourage each group member to feel worthwhile, and at the same time to develop social skills.

When students began to read and discuss *The Whipping Boy* (Fleischman, 1986), Sue gave students sentence strips, and with her encouragement and telling them to not worry about spelling, students, for the first time, wrote their own discussion questions. This book is about a bratty prince and his whipping boy, who have many adventures when they inadvertently trade places after becoming involved with dangerous outlaws. Students' questions, for the most part, dealt primarily with the reading they had just done and were open-ended questions, or if they were phrased to elicit a simple answer, had a "why or why not?" tagged on them to make them more complex: "Do you think Prince Brat will help Jemmy? Why or why not?"; "Is the king worried about Prince Brat or not? Why or why not?"; "Would you run away just because you're bored?" "Do you think Jemmy wrote down the right message on the ransom note or was it really a rescue note?" {Fieldnotes, 03/31/95}

The act of writing their own questions seemed to encourage more sophisticated questioning of one another in the group discussions. For example, on the first day of the new structure, one group, while responding to the question, "Do you think Prince Brat will help Jemmy? Why or why not?" a student was heard asking each person to also add *how* he or she thought Prince Brat might help. As already noted, this was previously not a common practice. Before, individual responses usually tended to go unchallenged and were simply noted by others.

Using Student-Initiated Questions to Examine Personal and Social Issues

As the students became more accustomed to writing their own questions, the questions became more sophisticated, thereby facilitating more sophisticated discussions. In April, they were reading the book *Blubber* (Blume, 1974), a story about a girl named Jill who goes along with the rest of the fifth-grade class in tormenting Linda, an over-weight classmate who they have named "Blubber." Jill subsequently finds out what it is like when she, too, becomes a target of abuse from the class. Sue chose this book because there was a particular student who was overweight and was teased by other students in the class. She hoped that students' discussions of this book might help them become more sensitive and thoughtful about this issue. The quality of the student-written questions became increasingly better. For example, on 1 day the five questions written by the groups were:

- Do you think Jill and Linda will become friends? Why?
- What would you do if you were Wendy's friend?
- What if your friend started picking on a race? [It was established that "race" was referring to people of a particular racial group] What would you do?
- If you were Linda, would you tell your mother?
- If you were Linda's mom, what would you do if you found out that Jill and her friends were picking on Linda?
  {Fieldnotes, videotape, 04/13/95}

Thus, students moved away from "why or why not?" questions and were now constructing more "How would you feel?" or interpretive questions. Frequently, their questions asked students to put themselves in the places of the characters, thereby fostering discussions that touched on personal and more relevant issues such as racism and friendship. We believe that this transition to more personal topics is consistent with other research on peer-led groups where students are encouraged to set their own agendas for discussions (Almasi, 1995; Commeyras, 1994).

Example 5 covers one group's discussion of the question regarding race. Sue dropped in during its deliberation, unaware until then what question they were to consider, and also participated in the conversation.

Example 5

1	Kim:	[reading the question to group] WHAT IF YOUR FRIEND STARTING PICK ON ANOTHER RACE? WHAT WOULD YOU DO?
2	Sue:	Ooooh.
3	Cf:	Well I'll tell them to stop it. And then if they start picking on me more I'll tell my mother and my mother will probably call the police or something.
4	Lisa:	If they keep on picking on me, I will tell my mom 'cause if I (...) they wouldn't stop. I'd tell my mom so she can go and tell the principal.
5	Melvin:	I'll go and tell the principal and then they'll probably talk to their moms.
6	Felita:	Me, I would talk to the kid personally. And then if she——if she can't do nothing about it, I'll go to my parents.
7	Sue:	Did you hear what she said? Say what you said again. Who would you talk to first?
8	Felita:	I'd talk to the kid.
9	Sue:	[to the group] She'd talk to the kid first.
10	Lisa:	What if the kid doesn't want to talk to you?
11	Felita:	I wasn't making fun of the kid so why wouldn't they want to talk to me?
12	Lisa:	Well, like I was saying, if they (... ...).
13	Sue:	We can't hear you with your face in your arms.
14	Kim:	[rereading question for Lisa] IF YOU WERE——IF YOUR FRIEND STARTED PICKING ON ANOTHER RACE....
15	Lisa:	Oh yeah.
16	Cm:	If he's picking on your race and you wanted to talk with them to tell them to quit and that, he might not want to listen to you.

17	Sue:	Why wouldn't he want to listen to you?
18	Lisa:	Because he's another race?
19	Kim:	Yeah, because of the color of his skin. And they mostly don't like black kids and pick on them coming. They like——they'll say "oohh...."
20	Sue:	Who doesn't like black kids?
21	Kim:	Some people.
22	Sue:	I don't necessarily think that's true. I think it's all races because you know what I mean? I don't think it's just about black people.
23	Kim:	And the whites, they sometimes pick on white people, they tell them "Pollocks" and things.
24	Felita:	When you said——you ask me why wouldn't the kid talk to me? Maybe they think that I'm like him, that I'm probably be mean to him. But I would try to tell them I'm not like them (...). {Fieldnotes, videotape, 04/13/95}

Thus, there were differences of opinion about what people would do if a friend was picking on a person of a different race. Actually, within this discussion, the target of who is being picked on or of who the victim of racial harassment is, kept shifting. As a result, there very interesting insights into how the various students felt about this topic and how they were able to express their views to others.

It is important to remember that the racial makeup of this class was predominantly Mexican American. However, the existence of two African American students in the class seemed to encourage the examination of racism and difference to varying degrees at different times, in different contexts, throughout the year.

As already indicated, Sue chose to read *Blubber* because she hoped that it would lead to more understanding towards Tabitha, who was overweight. This hope was somewhat of a success because later in the after-group debriefing of the question, "Do you think Jill and Linda will become friends? Why?" Tabitha herself talks about how Ernesto changed his behavior towards her. Although it was hard to hear everything she said in this whole-class setting, we were all moved by what she said.

Example 6

| 1 | Tabitha: | I think (... ...). I think it's no accident that (...) we get along better (...) the happiness that me and Ernesto. Maybe they—— me and Ernesto——he hasn't been picking on me that much because.... |

2 Sue: He's not. I've noticed that too. And you've really been trying,
                right Ernesto?

3 Kayla: (*** ***) happiness.

4 Sue: Well, that's true too. The good things, right? See, Ernesto. You
                can do it. [begins to read another question to hear other sum-
                maries from groups] ....
                {Fieldnotes, videotape, 04/13/95}

Thus, in this last final stage of Sue's inquiry, literature-discussion groups
were quite successful, and Sue achieved many of her goals in her inquiry.
Students were learning to craft provoking and thoughtful questions and
they engaged in many genuine and grand conversations.

   *Sue: I was just so amazed at the kinds of questions that the kids wrote for
group discussions towards the end. And, the discussions were so much
more real ones, sort of chatting back and forth to each other. Students were
really learning from each other. They were also learning the important social skills. I think it is easier to be a talker than it is to be a listener. I saw
them becoming better listeners, which made them better talkers.*

   *I don't remember where I got the idea for the roles for the students. It was
probably from something I read in a book or at a workshop I attended on co-
operative groups, or I had a student teacher at the time and she might have
suggested it. Although they helped in the process, I think the roles part became stale, which may be why interest in having literature-discussion
groups waned toward the very end of the year. The next year I didn't use
roles at all because they seemed to become too burdensome.*

FINAL COMMENTS AND CONCLUSIONS

We attempted to portray some of the major challenges and triumphs experienced in one classroom. These were due to Sue's inquiry to try out various structures to help her students to love reading and to become
independent readers and thinkers. The balance between teacher input and
student autonomy continued to be a difficult one to strike throughout the
year. Sue's inquiry documents the development in the types of questions
students asked about their reading, and the confidence that they gradually displayed in their abilities to discuss and to critique.

   There are certain myths about urban schools and urban students. The
belief that "those kids" can't achieve is a hard one to shake. Sue addressed
that issue head-on in the end-of-the-year interview on her inquiry. When
she was asked how she thought what she learned could effect urban
schools, she responded, "I think anyone could benefit from it, it was very
simple: It was reading great literature with children. How could you not

benefit from that?" When asked how she responded to the argument that city kids don't have the backgrounds to be able to handle this type of work, Sue summed up her philosophy as: "[T]eacher expectations make the difference. It's the way the teacher presents it. If you make it seem hard and impossible, it will be. But if you take it slow, and do it step-by-step, you can do it." {Videotape, End-of-year interview, 07/21/95}

It is this step-by-step process we attempted to illustrate—to indicate the kinds of difficulties that arose for Sue in implementing the curriculum genre of literature-discussion groups, and how Sue attempted to address them in this rocky road to the grand conversations.

Sue: The funniest part of my inquiry on literature-group discussions is that I thought I invented this! I didn't know all that stuff had been written about. When Shannon, Diane, and Chris started giving me stuff to read about it, it was like, "Oh, is that what you call that?" I just thought it made sense to teach literature this way. Of course, there were many up and downs in my inquiry to figure it out for myself. But I have a passion for literature and I wanted my kids to have one, too. I hoped that discussions groups would help on this.

REFERENCES

Almasi, J. F. (1995). The nature of fourth graders' sociocognitive conflicts in peer-led and teacher-led discussions of literature. *Reading Research Quarterly, 30,* 314–351.

Barnes, D. (1992). *From communication to curriculum.* Portsmouth, NH: Boynton/Cook.

Barnes, D. (1993). Supporting exploratory talk for learning. In K. M. Pierce & C. J. Gilles (Eds.), *Cycles of meaning: Exploring the potential of talk in learning communities* (pp. 17–34). Portsmouth, NH: Heinemann.

Barnes, D., & Todd, F. (1995). *Communication and learning revisited.* Portsmouth, NH: Boynton/Cook.

Barr, R., & Dreeben, R. (1991). Grouping students for reading instruction. In R. Barr, M. L. Kamil, P. B. Mosenthal, & P. D. Pearson (Eds.), *Handbook of reading research* (Vol. 2, pp. 885–910). New York: Longman.

Blume, J. (1974). *Blubber.* New York: Dell.

Blume, J. 1980). *Superfudge.* New York: Dell.

Bruner, J. S. (1986). *Actual minds, possible worlds.* Cambridge, MA: Harvard University Press.

Commeyras, M. (1994). Were Janell and Nessie in the same classroom? Children's questions as the first order of reality in storybook discussions. *Language Arts, 71,* 517–523.

Eeds, M., & Wells, D. (1989). Grand conversations: An exploration of meaning construction in literature study groups. *Research in the Teaching of English, 23,* 4–29.

Fleischman, S. (1986). *The whipping boy.* New York: Troll.

Freedman, L. (1993). Teacher talk: The role of the teacher in literature discussion groups. In K. M. Pierce & C. J. Gilles (Eds.), *Cycles of meaning: Exploring the potential of talk in learning communities* (pp. 219–235). Portsmouth, NH: Heinemann.

Hill, S., & Hill, T. (1990). *The collaborative classroom: A guide to co-operative learning.* Portsmouth, NH: Heinemann.

Hill, B. C., Johnson, N. J., & Noe, K. L. S. (Eds.). (1995). *Literature circles and response.* Norwood, MA: Christopher-Gordon.

Karolides, N. J. (1992). The transactional theory of literature. In N. Karolides (Ed.), *Reader response in the classroom: Evoking and interpreting meaning in literature* (pp. 21–32). White Plains, NY: Longman.

Karolides, N. J. (1997). The reading process: Transactional theory in action. In N. J. Karolides (Ed.), *Reader response in elementary classrooms: Quest and discovery.* Mahwah, NJ: Lawrence Erlbaum Associates.

Leal, D. J. (1992). The nature of talk about three types of text during peer group discussions. *Journal of Reading Behavior, 24,* 313–338.

MacLachlan., P. (1985). *Sarah, plain and tall.* New York: Harper & Row.

McMahon, S. I., & Raphael, T. E. (Eds.). (1997). *The Book Club connection: Literacy learning and classroom talk.* New York: Teachers College Press.

Moll, L. C. (Ed.). (1990). *Vygotsky and education. Instructional implications and applications of sociohistorical psychology.* Cambridge, England: Cambridge University Press.

Paterson, K. (1977). *Bridge to Terabithia.* New York: Avon.

Roller, C. M., & Beed, P. L. (1994). Sometimes the conversations were grand, and sometimes .... *Language Arts, 71,* 509–515.

Rosenblatt, L. M. (1976). *Literature as exploration* (3rd ed.). New York: Noble and Noble.

Rosenblatt, L. M. (1978). *The reader, the text, the poem: The transactional theory of the literary work.* Carbondale: Southern Illinois University Press.

Samway, K. D., & Whang, G. (1996). *Literature study circles in a multicultural classroom.* York, ME: Stenhouse.

Short, K. G., & Pierce, K. M. (1990). *Talking about books: Creating literate communities.* Portsmouth, NH: Heinemann.

Vygotsky, L. S. (1962). *Thought and language.* Cambridge, MA: MIT Press.

Vygotsky, L. S. (1978). *Mind in society: The development of higher psychological processes.* Cambridge, MA: Cambridge University Press.

Wells, G., & Chang-Wells, G. L. (1992). *Constructing knowledge together: Classrooms as centers of inquiry and literacy.* Portsmouth, NH: Heinemann.

Wertsch, J. V. (1991). *Voices of the mind: A sociocultural approach to mediated action.* Cambridge, MA: Harvard University Press.

White, E. B. (1952). *Charlotte's web.* New York: HarperCollins.

Wiencik, J., O'Flahavan, J. F. (1994). From teacher-led to peer discussion about literature: Suggestions for making the shift. *Language Arts, 71,* 488–498.

Chapter 14

Transforming Curriculum Genres in Urban Schools: The Political Significance of Collaborative Classroom Discourse

Christine C. Pappas

Liliana Barro Zecker

Although all of the chapters in this book described teacher researchers' focusing on their own inquiry questions to develop literacy-curriculum genres that would foster their urban students' learning, several common threads emerged from all of these accounts. This chapter covers three major themes. First, it revisits New Literacy ideas as they were enacted in the studies. Second, it addresses, again, how changing the teacher–student power relationships to privilege both teacher and student voices in curriculum genres transforms the talk—it becomes a collaborative, dialogic discourse to support students' learning in powerful ways. Finally, it discusses the *political* significance of collaborative discourse in urban schools.

REVISITING NEW LITERACY IDEAS: EXAMINING EPISTEMIC AND INQUIRY ENGAGEMENT OF TEXT

We noted in chapter 1 that a major aim of New Literacy (Willinsky, 1990) is to make reading and writing more personally meaningful for students, and that to accomplish this goal, teachers must reevaluate the everyday instructional patterns of interactions they have with their students. Such a shift requires altering underlying power relationships between teachers and students while teachers attempt to challenge the traditional transmission-oriented educational model. In Willinsky's words:

> [T]o shift this meaning of literacy also necessarily alters the relationships between teacher and student. The teacher, as an authority on what needs to be known and done, begins to turn over more of this responsibility to the student and to the meaning that comes from somewhere within the students' work with literacy. In these terms, then, the New Literacy's proposal is to reshape the *work* of the classroom around a different form of reading and writing. The moral, psychological, and social worth of this literacy begins with the students as sources of experience and meaning. To alter the form of literacy in this fashion clearly entails redefining the role and relationship of teacher and student. (p. 7)

In all of the chapters, teachers made efforts to give students more responsibility and opportunity to control and to contribute the meanings of the texts they read and about which they wrote. These teacher researchers saw their urban students as valuable sources of experience and meaning; they actively attempted to include their urban students' various funds of knowledge (Moll, 1990, 1992). Thus, all of them worked at crafting interactions in which students' voices—their ideas, comments, questions— were encouraged and valued.

To enact New Literacy aims in the curriculum genres that were the sites of the teacher-researchers' sites of inquiry, the nature or status of knowledge itself was transformed. No longer was knowledge treated as fixed, objective, autonomous, or as some entity that is given, transmitted, and received to and by students (Nystrand, 1997; Wells, 1998). Instead, literate thinking was fostered through what Wells' (1990) called *epistemic* engagement of text—wherein "meaning is treated as tentative, provisional, and open to alternative interpretations and revision" (p. 369). Thus, there was an "inquiry" stance in classroom interactions (Lindfors, 1999). This epistemic mode of engagement or collaborative inquiry, enabled students to reexamine and reconsider both their ideas and others' ideas. This occurred because students did not have to worry about coming up with right answers or to try to remember exactly what teachers or textbooks said. Tentative *knowing,* which is at the learner's current understanding, leads to the potential of knowledge building and conceptual change (Nystrand, 1997; Wells, 1990, 1998; Wells & Chang-Wells, 1992).

Thus, all of the teacher researchers were successful in taking on collaborative styles of teaching that focused on student meaning. They all attempted to enact New Literacy ideas, which meant that they had to struggle to fashion ways that they would share power and authority with their urban students of diverse ethnolinguistic backgrounds. These efforts led to transforming literacy-curriculum genres, in which the nature of classroom discourse was altered so as to hear and respond to students' voices.

CREATING COLLABORATIVE, DIALOGIC CLASSROOM DISCOURSE: SUCCESSES AND DIFFICULTIES

The aims of the New Literacy to focus more on student meaning require that the traditional teacher-controlled *IRE pattern*—teacher *I*nitiating, student *R*esponding, and then teacher *E*valuating—that is inherent in a transmission-orientated educational model must be challenged (Cazden, 1988; Edwards & Mercer, 1987; Gutierrez, Rymes, & Larson, 1995; Nystrand, 1997; Young, 1992). In such IRE teacher–student interactions, the teacher has a fixed, strict agenda that allows for little room of deviation or student elaboration. There is a lack of open-mindedness where different points of view, exploratory ideas, or student approximations can be raised and examined (Barnes, 1992, 1993; Barnes & Todd, 1995; Freedman, 1993). Epistemic or inquiry modes of engagement of text are impossible. IRE activity structures are especially common in urban classrooms. Efforts to move away from such monologically organized instruction to develop collaborative discourse were a critical feature of all of the teacher-researchers' inquiries.

In chapter 1, ideas from Bakhtin's (1981, 1986) work were used to argue for classroom discourse where knowledge building would be promoted, where participants had particular occasions in which they would be able to solve problems by means of dialogic responsivity. Wells (1998) described these classroom encounters as:

> In order to make a useful contribution, speakers first have to interpret the preceding contribution(s) and compare the information presented with their own current understanding of the issue under discussion, based on their experiences and any other relevant information of which they are aware. Then they have to formulate a contribution that will, in some relevant way, add to the common understanding achieved in the discourse so far by extending, questioning, or qualifying what someone else has said. Other participants contribute similarly, turn by turn. (p. 29)

In collaborative, dialogic discourse, understanding develops because the contributions of others serve as "thinking devices" (Lotman, 1988). There is tension in the process as reflection and reformulation are promoted. There is a "cognitive worktable" created where both teachers and students attempt to link puzzle pieces together to fashion coherent, joint meanings (Almasi, McKeown, & Beck, 1996).

Many markers or features characteristic of collaborative talk were found in the classroom-discourse examples found in the various chapters. When teachers questioned, they were *authentic questions,* not the *pseudo-* or known-information questions that are so prevalent in IRE discourse patterns (Edwards & Mercer, 1987; Mehan, 1979; Nystrand, 1997; Ramirez, 1988; Shuy, 1988; Young, 1992). The excerpts were filled with *student initiations*—students own ideas, comments, or questions (Oyler, 1996a, 1996b; Pappas & Barry, 1997). Especially in reading-curriculum genres, many of these initiations consisted of *intertextual links* (Bloome & Bailey, 1992; Bloome & Egan-Robertson, 1993), where students juxtaposed other texts—other books, songs, movies, TV shows, personal stories from their home or community, and so forth. In addition, student initiations were frequently *language play or approximations* of conventional structures (Lindfors, 1999). Students also engaged a lot in *cross discussion*, where students talked to each other without teacher mediation (Lemke, 1990). There was a *range of teacher responses* to student contributions to scaffold their understandings. The teacher could revoice a hesitant student voice by reformulating that student's offering, thereby allowing him or her to retain some ownership and credit for the reformulation (O'Connor & Michaels, 1993). The teacher could contingently respond to students' initiations so that these student comments were sustained, demonstrating to students that their claims or expertise were valued. Or, teacher response to students' ideas could be extended by the teacher's introducing additional information or alternative interpretations so that students were challenged to go beyond their current understandings (Wells, 1990, 1993, 1994, 1998; Wells & Chang-Wells, 1992). Finally, there were many *tentative remarks offered by both teachers and students.* And, especially when students were given opportunities to offer their conjectures, or when their ideas represented partial or mistaken understandings, the teacher's contribution could serve as follow-up, feedback, or uptake (Lindfors, 1999; Nystrand, 1997; Wells, 1993, 1998).

Thus, these teachers had new roles in collaboration—they had to learn how to encourage and provide spaces for their students' initiations, and had to figure out how to ask different kinds of questions and different ways to respond to their students' ideas. How does all of this dialogic talk affect teachers' power and authority? Lindfors (1999) argued that when teachers promote and take seriously children's inquiry in classroom talk, they give up *control* but not *power*. In collaborative interactions and discourse, teachers actually become powerful in new, different ways. Thus, it is important to emphasize that, although the teacher researchers in this book engaged in what Oyler (1996a) termed "the dance of shared teacher authority," it does not mean that they no longer provided their expertise. When students have opportunities to contribute substantially in the discourse, it does not follow that their teachers have "given up" power, authority, or privilege. Authority is not a possession like that (Manke, 1997, Oyler, 1996a). It is not a fixed-amount entity where garnering it means that there is a corresponding loss for another (Lindfors, 1999). Instead, when teachers share authority, they learn to create new strategies or new "dance steps" to use in their interactions and relationships with their students (Oyler, 1996a; Oyler & Becker, 1997). Moreover, although there were common markers or features in the collaborative discourse in all of the curriculum genres and all of the classrooms, it is important to emphasize that individual teachers had to develop their own strategies. For example, they all got ideas to try out in their own classrooms to deal with particular difficulties in each inquiry from the project personnel (the other teacher researchers and the university researchers) at the regular weekly meetings, but not all ideas worked—they had to find *their own ways* to use with *their own students*.

Although the teacher researchers were successful in this enterprise, all of the chapters also showed that taking on such approaches in classroom discourse is fraught with difficulties and challenges. In IRE, monologically organized instruction, there is usually a preplanned agenda with basal or textbook lessons to implement. It does not matter who the student audience is; the same questions are used and teachers look for the same right answers. In contrast, there is no scripted sequence to follow in collaborative, dialogic discourse. Certainly, teachers have important educational purposes or goals for these interactions, but they have to "go with the flow"—they have to wait for what students bring to the social, cognitive, worktable to decide, in the moment, how they should respond to their students' contributions. Thus, there are vulnerabilities in the efforts of sharing teacher authority (Oyler & Becker, 1997). We think that this might be why many teachers avoid this kind of teaching—they think it might lead to chaos and lots of management difficulties—which, as part of the deficit perspective described in chapter 1, was thought to be more likely to occur in urban schools. Or, as the case with the teachers in our project, they had few personal experiences in seeing collaborative interactions and discourse in action. However, despite the difficulties that the teacher researchers had in their efforts to create ways of collaboration, the chapters clearly show how capable these urban students were when they were given opportunities to share their ideas and interpretations in the various literacy curriculum genres. In fact, the teachers frequently remarked that it was the children's exciting, interesting, and intelligent questions and comments that kept these teachers resolved to overcome the problems that emerged in their inquiries.

THE POLITICAL SIGNIFICANCE OF COLLABORATIVE DISCOURSE

In developing collaborative interactions and discourse, there is more going on than teachers merely finding the right "methods" to improve the literacy learning of students who have been historically oppressed (Bartolome, 1994). In forging collaborative arrangements with their students, the teacher researchers challenged the deficit view that many urban personnel—and many in the society at large—still have regarding low-SES and ethnic-minority children (Pappas, 1999). Instead of seeing their students as "at risk," which is the usual term for such urban children, these teachers viewed them as "at promise" (Oyler, 1996a; Swadener & Lubeck, 1995). Bartolome (1994) called these efforts a pursuit of a *humanizing pedagogy* that respects and uses the history and perspectives of students of color as an integral part of educational practice. They actively worked to structure classroom curriculum genres so as to allow and encourage the students' rich, cultural funds of knowledge from homes and communities (Moll, 1990, 1992) into the classroom discourse. They developed what Gutierrez (Gutierrez, Baquedano-Lopez, & Turner, 1997; Gutierrez, et al., 1995) called the *radical middle, third space* where both teacher and student scripts intersect, giving potential for authentic interaction and learning to occur. As the various chapters show, given the opportunities to do so, these students demonstrated convincingly that they had ample linguistic, cultural, and intellectual resources to form the bases of their schooling.

Thus, sharing power with students in collaborative classroom interactions and discourse not only provides better literacy instruction—because it has higher expectations for students, it engages students more fully, and it enables teachers to meet students' current understandings—but it also has a broader political significance. The teacher researchers purposefully examined how they might alter the power relationships between teachers and students. As Geertz (1973) argued, "to rework the pattern of social relationships is to rearrange the coordinates of the experiences world" (p. 28). Thus, when teachers assign new roles for urban students as valued informants and thinkers, these children live new experiences. Power relations are learned and become a part of children's identities as they participate in the particular social practices of the world. Classrooms can provide the conditions for interaction that expand students' expressions and possibilities to learn new identities (Pappas, 1999). Consequently, the teacher researchers' decision to rework the pattern of social relationships was an ethical choice—and a *political* one.

The interactions between students and teachers may reflect the relations of culture and power in the society, "but they also *constitute* these relations and, as such, embody a transformative potential" (Cummins, 1994, p. 299). Therefore, to use Cummins' terminology, the "collaborative microinteractions," between the teachers and the students in the various curriculum genres described in the chapters, are extremely significant in that they illustrate how to resist and challenge the historically entrenched "coercive macrointeractions" in the broader society. When teacher-dominated IRE, monologic-discourse patterns are radically altered to create interactions that allow for joint participation and strategic assistance, multiple literacies develop. These new power arrangements, invoked at the local school site, "begin to rupture the transcendent script in the culture at large" (Gutierrez et al., 1995, p. 469).

This book, then, describes the journeys of urban teacher researchers as they attempted to find ways to take seriously their students' ideas and points of view. They found ways to let their students know that what they think counted. They fashioned collaborative classroom discourse to accommodate these goals of inclusion. These were important pedagogical acts, but they stand for much more—the collaborative discourse that realized these teaching practices represents critical discourse for social change (Fairclough, 1992).

REFERENCES

Almasi, J. F., McKeown, M. G., & Beck, I. L. (1996). The nature of engaged reading in classroom discussions of literature. *Journal of Literacy Research, 28,* 107–146.

Bakhtin, M. M. (1981). *The dialogic imagination: Four essays by M. M. Bakhtin.* M. Holquist (Ed.) & M. Holquist & C. Emerson (Trans.). Austin: University of Texas Press.

Bakhtin, M. M. (1986). *Speech genres and other late essays.* C. Emerson & M. Holquist (Eds.), & V. W. McGee (Trans.). Austin: Austin University Press.

Barnes, D. (1992). *From communication to curriculum* (2nd ed.). Portsmouth, NH: Boynton/Cook.

Barnes, D. (1993). Supporting exploratory talk for learning. In K. M. Pierce & C. J. Gilles (Eds.), *Cycles of meaning: Exploring the potential of talk in learning communities* (pp. 17–34). Portsmouth, NH: Heinemann.

Barnes, D., & Todd, F. (1995). *Communication and learning revisited: Making meaning through talk.* Portsmouth, NH: Boynton/Cook.

Bartolome, L. I. (1994). Beyond the methods fetish: Toward a humanizing pedagogy. *Harvard Educational Review, 64,* 173–194.

Bloome, D., & Bailey, F. (1992). Studying language and literacy through events, particularity, and intertextuality. In R. Beach, J. L. Green, M. L. Kamil, & T. Shanahan (Eds.), *Multidisciplinary perspectives on literacy research* (pp. 181–210). Urbana, IL: National Conference on Research in English.

Bloome, D., & Egan-Robertson, A. (1993). The social construction of intertextuality in classroom reading and writing lessons. *Reading Research Quarterly, 28,* 305–333.

Cazden, C. B. (1988). *Classroom discourse: The language of teaching and learning.* Portsmouth, NH: Heinemann.

Cummins, J. (1994). From coercive to collaborative relations of power in the teaching of literacy. In B. M. Ferdman, R.-M. Weber, & A. G. Ramierz (Eds.), *Literacy across languages and cultures* (pp. 295–331). Albany: State University of New York Press.

Edwards, D., & Mercer, N. (1987). *Common knowledge: The development of understanding in the classroom.* London: Routledge.

Fairclough, N. (1992). *Discourse and social change.* Cambridge, England: Polity Press.

Freedman, L. (1993). Teacher talk: The role of the teacher in literature discussion groups. In K. M. Pierce & C. J. Gilles (Eds.), *Cycles of meaning: Exploring the po-*

tential of talk in learning communities (pp. 219–235). Portsmouth, NH: Heinemann.

Geertz, C. (1973). *The interpretations of cultures: Selected essays.* New York: Basic Books.

Gutierrez, K., Baquedano-Lopez, P., & Turner, M. G. (1997). Putting language back into language arts: When the radical middle meets the third space. *Language Arts, 74,* 368–378

Gutierrez, K., Rymes, B., & Larson, J. (1995). Script, counterscript, and underlife in the classroom: James Brown versus *Brown v. Board of Education. Harvard Educational Review, 65,* 445–471.

Lemke, J. L. (1990). *Talking science: Language, learning, and values.* Norwood, NJ: Ablex.

Lindfors, J. W. (1999). *Children's inquiry: Using language to make sense of the world.* New York: Teachers College Press.

Lotman, Y. M. (1988). Text within text. *Soviet Psychology, 26,* 32–51.

Manke, M. (1997). *Classroom power relations: Understanding student-teacher interaction.* Mahwah, NJ: Lawrence Erlbaum Associates.

Mehan, H. (1979). Learning lessons. Cambridge, MA: Harvard University Press.

Moll, L. C. (Ed.). (1990). *Vygotsky and education: Instructional implications and applications of sociohistorical psychology.* Cambridge, England: Cambridge University Press.

Moll, L. C. (1992). Literacy research in community and classrooms: A sociocultural approach. In R. Beach, J. L. Green, M. L. Kamil, & T. Shanahan (Eds.), *Multidisciplinary perspectives on literacy research* (pp. 211–244). Urbana, IL: National Conference on Research in English.

Nystrand. M. (1997). *Opening dialogue: Understanding the dynamics of language and learning in the English classroom.* New York: Teachers College Press.

O'Connor, M. C. & Michaels, S. (1993). Aligning academic task and participation status through revoicing: Analysis of a classroom discourse strategy. *Anthropology and Education Quarterly, 24,* 318–335.

Oyler, C. (1996a). *Making room for students in an urban first grade: Sharing teacher authority in room 104.* New York: Teachers College Press.

Oyler, C. (1996b). Sharing authority: Student initiations during teacher-led read-alouds of information books. *Teaching and Teacher Education, 12,* 149–160.

Oyler, C., & Becker, J. (1997). Teaching beyond the progressive-traditional dichotomy: Sharing authority and sharing vulnerability. *Curriculum Inquiry, 27,* 453–467.

Pappas, C. C. (1999). Becoming literate in the borderlands. In A Goncu (Ed.), *Children's engagement in the world: Sociocultural perspectives* (pp. 228–260). Cambridge, England: Cambridge University Press.

Pappas, C. C., & Barry, A. (1997). Scaffolding urban students' initiations: Transactions in reading information books in the reading-aloud curriculum genre. In N. J. Karolides (Ed.), *Reader response in the elementary classroom: Quest and discovery* (pp. 215–236). Mahwah, NJ: Lawrence Erlbaum Associates.

Ramirez, A. (1988). Analyzing speech acts. In J. L. Green & J. O. Harker (Eds.), *Multiple perspective analyses of classroom discourse* (pp. 135–163). Norwood, NJ: Ablex.

Shuy, R. (1988). Identifying dimensions of classroom language. In J. L. Green & J. O. Harker (Eds.), *Multiple perspective analyses of classroom discourse* (pp. 115–134). Norwood, NJ: Ablex.

Swadener, B. B., & Lubeck, S. (Eds.). (1995). *Children and families "at promise": Deconstructing the discourse of risk.* Albany: State University of New York Press.

Wells, G. (1990). Talk about text: Where literacy is learned and taught. *Curriculum Inquiry, 20,* 369–405.

Wells, G. (1993). Reevaluating the IRF sequence: A proposal for the articulation of theories of activity and discourse for the analysis of teaching and learning in the classroom. *Linguistics and Education, 5,* 1–37.

Wells, G. (1994). The complimentary contributions of Halliday and Vygotsky to a "language-based theory of learning." *Linguistics and Education, 6,* 41–90.

Wells, G. (1998). Some questions about direct instruction: Why? To whom? How? And when? *Language Arts, 76,* 27–35.

Wells, G., & Chang-Wells, G. L. (1992). *Constructing knowledge together: Classrooms as centers of inquiry and literacy.* Portsmouth, NH: Heinemann.

Willinsky, J. (1990). *The New Literacy: Redefining reading and writing in the schools.* New York: Routledge.

Young, R. (1992). *Critical theory and classroom talk.* Clevedon, England: Multilingual Matters.

About the Authors

Teacher Researchers

Anne Barry received her master's degree in curriculum and instruction from National-Louis University, and received an English as a second language endorsement from the state of Illinois. She has been teaching for 20 years and currently teaches first grade at Jungman Elementary School. She continues to her interest in teacher research, especially in collaborating with the University of Illinois at Chicago.

Bernadine Braun received her master's degrees from several Chicago institutions. She has taught, or as she likes to say, "her pupils taught" her, at Andersen Elementary School for the past 36 years. She enjoys learning new things and learning how to do old-time things. She enjoys creating things, crafts, cooking, knitting, poems, decorating cakes, decorating, woodworking, weaving, and new ways to teach subjects to her students.

Sarah Cohen has taught in the Chicago public school system for many years. She left to teach in a private, bilingual school in Cuernavea, Mexico for 1 year. Her teaching career began in Vermont when she studied in the teacher education program at Prospect School and Center for Higher Education. This was a unique program that combined a year-long internship in the Prospect School (a progressive school with multiage, activity-based curriculum) with intensive site-based course work in the history and philosophy of education and in methodologies. She taught at Jungman during her inquiry. She currently teaches first grade at Inter American Magnet School, a dual language (Spanish and English) program where she has been fortunate to be able to combine her interest in children and teaching with her love of languages. She is also the parent of Abraham, a preschooler, who relishes books, language play, and stories as much as she does.

Demetrya Collier completed her undergraduate degree at Chicago State University and received her bachelor's degree in June 1972. Ultimately deciding to teach in the city, rather than the suburban districts around Chicago, she began teaching at Andersen Elementary School in the fall of 1972 where she has remained since. Several years later, she returned to school and earned a master's degree in urban teacher education at Governor's State University, with an emphasis in early childhood education. Andersen has been the only school in which she has taught and considers it to have been both a challenging and rewarding experience.

Paul Fowler taught sixth grade for 3 years and then taught seventh and eighth grade social studies for 2 years at Andersen. He plans to travel to Thailand to explore life elsewhere. In his own words, "My walking shoes are worn, my backpack is light, and I can whistle a mean 'Oh, Susanna.'"

Susan Jacobson graduated from Western Illinois University in 1990. Her first teaching job was as a substitute teacher in the Chicago public schools, and eventually joined the faculty of Jungman Elementary School. For the first year she taught sixth grade, and added teaching an English as a second language pull-out program during her second year. From then on, she has taught fourth grade. She plans to return to school to pursue a master's degree in reading at the University of Illinois at Chicago. In her free time, she enjoys reading, aerobics, and spending time with her family.

Hawa Jones is originally from Liberia, in western Africa, and comes from a family of teachers. She enjoys living in the United States because of the freedom she has here. She has four sisters and is married with one child. She enjoys sewing, reading, and "shopping" and has always wanted to be a teacher. She teaches at Jungman Elementary School.

Renuka L. Mehra was born in the United States of Indian parents, and is the second of 4 girls. Her parents returned to India shortly after her birth, so her elementary and secondary school education was completed there. She returned to the United States when she was 20 years old, and completed her undergraduate degree in education at the University of Illinois, Chicago. She has recently completed her master's degree at Northeastern Illinois University. Her teaching career has always been at Andersen Elementary School and she is currently the Reading Coordinator at Andersen.

Dorothy A. O'Malley had always wanted to be a teacher. After receiving her bachelor's degree in elementary education form the College of St. Teresa in 1956. She taught third grade the following year, but left on maternity leave at the end of the year. She spent the next 16 years raising her 9 children, and in 1985 received her master's degree from the University of Illinois at Chicago. She taught at Jungman during her inquiry. She is now retired after 20 years of teaching. She misses teaching, but she says she has taken with her all the wonderful lessons and experiences she learned from her students, but most especially, the third graders who participated in this teacher research. She currently enjoys taking trips with her husband and family, reading, the theater, and playing golf and bridge. She continues to be involved in community, church, and education organizations.

Sonia Torres Pasewark completed her master's degree in education at the University of Illinois at Chicago, with an emphasis on bilingual education. Her first teaching job was at Jungman, which she says was very challenging and introduced her to the many difficulties that bilingual education presents. After a year of teaching at Jungman Elementary School, she taught at another Chicago public school in a bilingual setting. She recently became a very happy, stay-at-home mom raising her 2 daughters.

Michael Rassel had been teaching at Andersen Elementary School for more than 12 years. He completed his undergraduate work at DePaul University in the Goodman School of Drama in 1984. In 1997 he received his master's degree in education from Loyola University. In addition to his work as a teacher, he has performed in and directed several plays in the Chicago area. For Michael, the classroom and the theater are one and the same–a place to grow, collaborate, and above all, to learn. He is presently an assistant principal at Foreman High School.

Sonia White Soltero As the youngest of 4, Sonia was born and raised in Argentina. She has also lived in Uruguay, Brazil, and Costa Rica and has visited Africa several times while her parents resided there. She calls herself the product of Latin American bilingual education. She has a bachelor's degree in elementary education and a master's in bilingual education. She has recently received her PhD in bilingual education from the University of Arizona. She has been a bilingual teacher for more than 15 years, 7 of which were spent at a Native American reservation. During the past several years, she has been teaching at Andersen Elementary School in Chicago.

Pamela Wolfer received her bachelor's degree in education from the University of Illinois at Chicago in June 1989, and completed her student training sessions in 3 Chicago public schools. She found great hope and desire to make a difference in the urban communities among the many staff members and decided to join in their efforts. She began teaching at Hans Christian Andersen and remained there for many years. She feels that her teaching experience has been very rewarding and challenging. She is now retired to raise her family. She plans on making her future involvement in education as a parent and community member, and hopes that her past experience in teaching will give her and understanding and productive insight into her community's scholastic needs.

University Researchers

Diane Escobar completed a master's degree in Applied Linguistics at the University of Illinois at Chicago, and more recently received a master's of education from the same institution. In Chicago, she taught English as a second language (ESL) in various and multicultural settings. For 5 of these years, she worked at a 2-year bilingual college where she held various faculty and administrative positions. She has also taught French, Spanish, and English to high school students. On the project, Diane, with university–researcher, Shannon Hart, collaborated with teacher–researchers, Anne Barry, Susan C. Jacobson, Hawa Jones, and Dorothy A. O'Malley, at Jungman Elementary School. Currently she is using what she has learned from these elementary teachers to support the emergent literacy of her young daughter, Sophia.

Shannon Hart, with university–researcher Diane Escobar, collaborated with teacher–researchers Anne Barry, Susan C. Jacobson, Hawa Jones, and Dorothy A. O'Malley, at Jungman Elementary School. She is currently working with teachers at Northeastern Illinois University in Career Planning and Placement. She lives with her partner, 2 dogs, and 3 cats. They are anticipating the adoption of their first child in early 2000.

Jane Liao received a master's of education from the university of Illinois at Chicago. On the project, she, with university–researcher Dian Rubin, collaborated with teacher–researchers Bernadine Braun, Demetrya Collier, Renuka L. Mehra, Michael Rassel, and Pamela Wolfer at Andersen Elementary School. She currently teaches first grade at a Chicago public school.

Linda Montes was responsible for organizing the project office and transcribing endless hours of audio- and video-tapes of exciting teacher–student dialogues in 2 languages. She loved every minute of it and learned so much. She received a master's of education from the University of Illinois at Chicago. She currently teaches second grade at a Chicago public school. She is the mother of a 4-year-old wonder boy who doesn't like school. Go figure! Her present aspirations include to continue her higher education by completing a PhD program.

Caitlyn Nichols, with university–researcher Liliana Barro Zecker, collaborated with teacher–researcher, Sarah Cohen, Sonia White Soltero, and Sonia Torres Pasewark, at both Andersen and Jungman Elementary Schools. She received a master's degree in early childhood education from the University of Illinois at Chicago. She is currently taking a break from teaching to raise her 2 children, Alyssa and Zachary.

Christine Pappas was the director of the project and worked with all of the university– and teacher–researchers. She is a professor in the College of Education at the University of Illinois at Chicago, where she teaches courses on language, classroom discourse, and literacy. Her current interests involve the research and teaching–learning of genre and teacher inquiry.

Dian Rubin, with university–researcher Jane Liao, collaborated with teacher–researchers Bernadine Braun, Demetrya Collier, Renuka L. Mehra, Michael Rassel, and Pamela Wolfer at Andersen Elementary School. She received a master's degree at the University of Illinois at Chicago. Her teaching includes 3 years of high school in a special education setting, and over 6 years of post-secondary experience teaching adults. She currently works with adults and some youths, ages 16–22, at United Cerebral Palsy Association of Chicago. Dian has a special interest in children's literature and especially enjoys adolescent fiction.

Henry Tabak, Jr., with university–researchers Jane Liao and Dian Ruben, collaborated mostly with teacher–researcher, Paul Fowler, but also teacher–researchers at Andersen Elementary School. Hank has acted, worked on set design and lighting, and written plays, before, during, and after his educational training in communication and theater at the University of Illinois at Chicago, where he obtained his BA in 1984 and MA in 1989. He has taught English as a second language (ESL) for the City Colleges of Chicago; speech and writing for Roosevelt University; and special remedial classes to high school dropouts, recovering alcohol and substance abusers, and ex-offenders. Since 1998, he has worked in the Writing Across the Curriculum Center at Harry S. Truman College in Chicago. He is currently writing his PhD dissertation at UIC.

Liliana Barro Zecker collaborated with all of the teacher– and university–researchers in this project as a postdoctoral fellow at the University of Illinois at Chicago. With university–researcher Caitlyn Nichols, she focused especially on the bilingual classroom inquiries of teacher–researchers Sarah Cohen, Sonia White Soltero, and Sonia Torres Pasewark. She received a doctoral degree in psychology and education at the University of Michigan. She is currently an assistant professor in the School of Education at DePaul University where she continues to explore with her students, pre- and inservice teachers, young children's development, and learning of language and literacy.

Author Index

Subject Index

A

ABC books, 103–126,
Aesthetic stance, 192–193, 197, 288, 292–294
Apprenticeship in learning, 62, 158, 227, 280, 288
Author's chair, *see* Sharetime

B

Bilingual classrooms, teacher research done in, 61–77, 157–181, 225–250
Book language, 274

C

Code switching, 158, 160, 161–168, 178
Collaborative classroom discourse, 6–9, 10–11, 16, 76, 114, 129–130,134, 141–152, 153–154, 205, 207, 226, 227, 244, 248, 280, 288, 325, 327–331
political significance of, 325, 327–331

Collaborative classroom interactions, *see* Collaborative classroom discourse
Collaborative school–university action research, 1, 13
Conferences, 44–51, 64–65, 82, 86–94, 289–295
Critical points/incidents, 17, 19
Cross discussion, 114, 134, 144, 328
Cueing systems, 104
Culturally and linguistically responsive pedagogy, 1, 11
Curriculum genres,
definition of, 9–11
sites of teacher research,
drama, 183–184, 185–202, 203–221
language richness, 223, 225–250
literature discussion groups, 224, 307–324
novel study, 224, 279–306
pretend reading, 223–224, 251–277
reading-aloud, 101–102, 103–126, 127–156, 157–181, 205–208, 281–289
writing, 33–34, 35–59, 61–77, 79–99
transforming, 11, 102, 130, 229, 244, 248, 249, 325, 326–327